BEFORE THE EUROPEAN CHALLENGE

Before the European Challenge

Challenge

The Great Civilizations of Asia and the Middle East

Jaroslav Krejčí

Assisted by Anna Krejčová

State University of New York Press

First published in U.S.A. by
STATE UNIVERSITY OF NEW YORK PRESS
Albany

For information, address State University of New
York Press, State University Plaza, Albany, N.Y. 12246

Printed in Hong Kong
Library of Congress Cataloging-in-Publication Data
Krejčí, Jaroslav, 1916—
Before the European challenge.
Bibliography: p.
Includes indexes.
1. Asia—Civilization.   2. Middle East—Civilization
3. Civilization, Oriental.   I. Krejčová, Anna.
II. Title.
DS12.K74   1990   950   89–11594
ISBN 0–7914–0168–5 (hardcover)
ISBN 0–7914–0169–3 (paperback)

To the memory of my parents

Contents

x   *Contents*

Preface and Acknowledgements

This book has a long history. My interest in the topic was prompted by the great changes in the world which occurred as a result of World War II. At that time I also realized that my law studies, together with a range of related subjects, and my professional specialization in macroeconomics were not a sufficient basis for understanding what was going on around me.

The idea to write crystallized during the late 1950s in a labour camp, over a wheel grinding glass for chandeliers. Intellectual inspiration came from different quarters. The historical materialism dominant in my country at that time was challenged by Sorokin's super-rhythm of various mental orientations and by Toynbee's quest for global entities and their dynamics. Yet at my grinding wheel I started to develop my own ideas on the ups and downs in the course of history and decided to learn more about its various paths over the globe.

After my release from the labour camp in May 1960 (a result of the first amnesty for political prisoners in Czechoslovakia) I was allowed to take up only a menial job in a cooperative workshop, which fortunately did not absorb all my working energy; so I was able to pursue my intellectual interests vigorously. In Prague there was a well-equipped Oriental Institute whose chief librarian Mr Manoušek supplied me (and I acknowledge herewith my gratitude for his preferential treatment of my needs) with first-class reading matter on the countries and epochs which are the subject of this book. Professor Jaroslav Heyrovský and his family also provided me with valuable books. In order to organize the vast amount of information, I conceived, as a working hypothesis, my own concept of civilization and of its rhythm of crystallization, flourishing and waning. I received invaluable help from my wife, who not only did not divorce me as she had been asked to do by her police interrogator during my trial, but supported me in all my undertakings. Thus within seven years we were able to produce a typescript of over 2000 pages with chronological tables and graphs, which we managed to take with us when we left Czechoslovakia in August 1968.

Before that, a short-lived Prague Spring had brought for me a partial return to economics; for some months I had even served as an expert for the government. After we left Czechoslovakia we spent a four-month sojourn in Vienna, which I am happy to say was generously covered by academic grants (the Graduate Institute for Advanced Studies even enabled us to carry our research a stage further). From the beginning of 1969 we settled in England for good. The then Vice-Chancellor of the University of Lancaster, (now Sir) Charles Carter, was favourably inclined towards our programme, and as a temporary arrangement created for us a research unit, proudly labelled the Czechoslovak Research Unit on Macrosociology; but in the long run we had to offer something more practical. My wife, a psychologist with a long educational and clinical practice and with a PhD from Charles University in Prague (for a few years before we left Czechoslovakia she had been a Lecturer at its Pedagogical Faculty), obtained tenure earlier than me as a Senior Lecturer and then as Principal Lecturer in Psychology at Preston (now Lancashire) Polytechnic.

I put on offer what I had in stock. Apart from my expertise in national product accounts, for which the Russian and East European Centre at St Antony's College, Oxford, found an intermittent use, the University of Lancaster gave me the opportunity to work in various departments. Apart from teaching, researching and publishing on various aspects of modern Europe (Czechoslovakia, Germany and ethnic problems in general were the main topics), I was invited by Professor Ninian Smart to lecture in his broad-based Department of Religious Studies at Lancaster University. His appreciation of my approach was a great encouragement to me. My Czech text now proved particularly useful. My course, 'The Role of Religion in Social Structure and Development', covering Asia and the Middle East (which I gave for ten years before retirement), became popular amongst students: the external examiners were happy with the results, and it afforded me a great deal of job satisfaction. The work with the postgraduates was especially stimulating and led to further research in the field. My seven years of seemingly esoteric studies in the wilderness had not been in vain.

Before my wife and I retired we were able to complete yet another common project already conceived in Prague: the book on *Great*

Revolutions Compared: The Search for a Theory (published in 1983 and reprinted in 1987). Then the idea from the grinding wheel returned to me in a new form. The result is the present book.

Dr Karel Werner of Durham University kindly read the chapters on India and Iran; Dr David Waines and Paul Morris of Lancaster University read the chapters on Islam and Judaism respectively. I am indebted to them for their most useful comments. Needless to say, however, responsibility for anything I have written is exclusively mine. In particular I have to extend my gratitude to Dr Graham Bartram, who carefully read and edited the whole text; and above all to my wife, the most involved and busy co-worker on this project.

Furthermore I am pleased to acknowledge the continuing support of the University of Lancaster (under its successive Vice-Chancellors Philip Reynolds and Harry Hanham), which after my retirement provided me with emerital research facilities. I would also like to express my appreciation for the award of the Leverhulme Emeritus Fellowship which for two years contributed towards my secretarial assistance.

Last but not least I have to remember with gratitude my many friends, especially those who were co-inmates in the labour camp, who by showing keen interest in my work encouraged me to carry on even in times which appeared hopeless.

JAROSLAV KREJČÍ

A Note on Spelling and Dates

Spelling

The Chinese names are spelt according to the new Pinyin system of Romanization, with the exception of names taken from a quotation or a book title, and further names which, combined with English endings, have become already familiar in the earlier spelling such as Taoism, in contrast to Dao Jia in Pinyin.

The author is indebted to Mr Luo Gang of Baotou in the People's Republic of China for advice in this matter.

In the case of Arabic names, only those diacritic marks are used which express specific phonemes that cannot be Romanized by a particular letter of the Latin alphabet, i.e. 'ain and hamza. Nuances of hard or soft pronunciation are omitted.

Dates

All dates are given according to the modern Christian calendar unless other dating is specifically indicated.

1 Introduction

The Europeans came into direct contact with the great nations of Asia and became acquainted with their cultures at a particular turning point in world history. It happened at the time when the Europeans began their great leap forward whilst the other civilized peoples were tending to rest on their oars. This contrast was manifested by the fact that it was the Europeans who discovered the East (and also the Far West) and not the other way round. The Chinese maritime exploration of the beginning of the fifteenth century ended at the eastern shores of Africa, whilst the somewhat later European overseas expansion eventually reached every nook and cranny of the globe. By the beginning of the twentieth century virtually the whole world was in one way or another in the process of Europeanization; individual nations were either European colonies or modelled their political and economic systems on the European example.

Though for about two centuries or so from the first circumnavigation of the globe the Europeans spent a lot of their energy sorting out problems arising from their great cultural transformation, and much of their energy was wasted in internecine warfare, the unprecedented advance of science and technology gave them an incontestable superiority over the rest of the world. Later it was again the new spiritual ventures of a fast-changing Europe which began to radiate into other civilizations. The inflammatory concepts of personal liberty and of greater equality between men set in motion a process which not only changed the face of Europe but began to appeal to other nations as well.

The unequal distribution of the benefits of the new values of freedom and equality between on the one hand the victorious Europeans and on the other hand the native subjects in the colonies or indirectly dependent countries created an additional motive for the emancipation of those who were discriminated against–a motive whose legitimacy the Europeans themselves eventually recognized. After the Europeans had weakened themselves in two devastating

1

world wars and had become divided into two antagonistic blocs, the hour of retreat arrived. A political metaphor saw the globe divided into three worlds: the Euro-American north-west, with democracy and capitalism as the main characteristics of its social system; the Euro-Asian north-east, with dictatorship and state socialism as its all-embracing features; and, broadly speaking, the South, or the Third World, which still had to shape its profile.

At first sight it seemed that what was going on in the Third World was merely a process of political emancipation, the creation of many more sovereign nation states which would follow either the one or the other pattern of social arrangements established in the north of the globe. If that had been the case, the polarity of the north would have been extended to the world as a whole. But soon a new element appeared. Both variants of 'modernity', to borrow the term fashionable among social scientists, were found wanting. Neither of them proved to be suited to the mentality and attitudes of many Asian and Middle-Eastern peoples.

Having tried various kinds of adaptation, many Third World nations began to look to their own pasts and their traditional views and values for inspiration. Naturally, it is not one Third World which has begun to emerge, but several different blends in which elements of the two 'northern' variants are mingled with widely varying elements of the domestic tradition.

The whole process is still at a very early stage and its future contours can only be guessed at. At the time of writing its most salient feature is the revival of Islam. Both its principal versions, the Sunnite and the Shi'ite, are becoming powerful agents of the political and social changes to which the products of a hundred years of Europeanization are now being subjected.

The other religious traditions of Asia operate in a less conspicuous, but no less persistent, way. The Hindus, the Sikhs and the Buddhists are trying to preserve their respective communal identities and, up to a point, to place their particular stamp on the political regimes of their countries. Last but not least the Confucian virtues which reflect a pragmatic and secular rather than a deeply religious attitude survive as the strongest motivational base for both private life and work morale in the Fast East.

Thus everything that is now going on in Asia and the Middle East can be described with reference to a single common denominator: it is a revival of the domestic tradition as a response to a prolonged foreign challenge. In places it takes the form of a more or less selective kind of reception; elsewhere it becomes an outright rejection of foreign influences. These various responses have manifested themselves with differing degrees of intensity.

In the last quarter of the twentieth century Asia and the Middle East are alive with a new endeavour; this time the aim of their peoples is not simply to emulate Europe or America and to catch up with their material standards, but, while adopting from the West anything deemed to be useful, to reassert their own cultural identity.

From the overall point of view, it is the countries in the orbit of the former Chinese influence in the Far East that appear to be the most dynamic. Their success is particularly conspicuous in the area of economic growth. Frugality and an enterprising spirit, diligence, the endeavour to acquire new skills and the rising level of education are at the root of the rapid advance of that part of the world.

It is not only Japan, which mastered all the skills and niceties of the Euro-American civilization and outdid her teachers in technical performance and economic achievement, that has been making spectacular headway, but also minor countries less keen to adopt the political aspects of Europeanism, such as South Korea, Taiwan and Singapore, or ones like Hong Kong that are in the last days of the colonial era.

The giant of the area, China, having survived the disasters of a century of civil wars and the short sharp shock of the Maoist social engineering, seems to have embarked on a great historical venture: the building up of a new civilization in which all she has learnt from abroad is to be integrated into her time-honoured socio-psychological framework.

Looking at the Middle East we find an area with a dynamism of a different kind. The energy of its peoples is to a large extent absorbed by in-fighting. Furthermore the windfall profits from the oil trade allowed some of the Middle Eastern countries to acquire unprecedented riches which have only partly been used for the advancement of their peoples. The restitution of the state of Israel in the heart of the Middle East, after two thousand years of its non-existence, has been a particular source of stress in the area. It seemed for some time that, if not all Muslims, then at least all Arabs would unite against what in their view could only be an intrusion.

Yet the Islamic revival, which is to a large extent a response to the permissive ethos of the Euro-American civilization, also brought with it traditional divisions and conflicts. Combined with and complicated by an exacerbated ethnic consciousness (a response to an earlier European challenge), the divisions within Islam have led in one particular spot to a war, in which the ethnic issue, pitting Arabs against Iranians, has been intertwined with the religious conflict between the Sunnites and the Shi'ites. And this is not the only 'hot' divide amongst the Muslims. Under these circumstances, a 'take-off' along Far Eastern lines does not seem to be imminent. But the potential for it must not be underestimated.

Southern Asia with its Indo-Aryan, Indo-Dravidian, Malayan, Tibeto-Burmese and other minor groups of nationalities offers, at the time of writing, a variegated picture. The most populous political unit in the area, India, has scored quite a few points in her effort to build up a multi-ethnic, federal, lay state with parliamentary democracy and equality before the law as its political guidelines. Unfortunately these principles do not yet seem to have established firm roots in the Indian body social. The caste prejudice and a communal consciousness based primarily on religious affiliation survive in strength. Though India's economic and cultural achievements cannot be underestimated, her growth is mainly taking place in the demographic rather than the economic or political dimension.

The very high birthrate is a feature common to the whole of southern Asia. For the rest, most countries in the area attempt to build their nationhood upon various factors of cohesion such as ethnicity, religion or a colonial past which created particular political units with artificial boundaries. In this endeavour, traditional ethno-religious strife, such as in Sri Lanka, or geopolitical constants such as the southward expansion of Vietnam, bear witness to the astounding tenacity of ancient tendencies.

All these recent developments in Asia and in the Middle East are by no means merely fortuitous ventures; they have historical roots which in several instances reach far back into the past. Thus an understanding of what is now going on in these increasingly important areas of the world demands a look backwards, a look at the origins and the development of forces which, at the time of writing, are re-emerging to prominence in the societies in question.

This book aims to contribute to this kind of historical perspective. It gives a general comparative account of what can be described as the great civilizations of Asia and the Middle East. It reviews, in a nutshell, the basic world-views and value patterns which gave individual societies in those areas their specific cultural profile, and juxtaposes these world-views with the social arrangements in those societies. The reader will realize that there was not always a direct link between the two. Individual, basically religious, world-views and values may have functioned as ideational backbones of the cultures in question and may have provided the normative guidelines for generally accepted behaviour; but apart from a few key factors of a religious nature, such as the belief in a revealed law, in the Heavenly Mandate, in reincarnation, etc., social life was moulded to a greater or lesser extent by secular, pragmatic considerations.

In order to avoid the danger of perceiving the civilizations in that part of the world as more or less static entities, the account takes the form of a historical narrative, focused on what are deemed to be the most relevant events and features in the process of continuous change. Culture, in the sense of artistic creation, has already been explored by an abundant literature, and is therefore touched on only marginally in this context.

Most chapters of the book deal with civilizations which at the time of writing are still alive, i.e. whose views and values are still shared by the population in the countries concerned. This is the case with Islam, Hinduism, Sikhism, Buddhism, Confucianism and, up to a point, with Judaism and Shintoism.

Two chapters of the book, however, are devoted to civilizations which do not have any obvious direct links with the present. One of them deals with Ancient Mesopotamia and Egypt, the other with Zoroastrian Iran. There are good reasons for including these 'dead' civilizations in our framework. Though people in those lands may no longer believe in the ancient deities or share the archaic values, and though the Zoroastrian communities in Iran and India may within our perspective be negligible quantities, they are not entirely without echoes in modern history.

The unfortunate Shah of Iran who wanted to modernize his country as fast as possible, while safeguarding its cultural identity, looked for inspiration to the pre-Islamic grandeur of Persia; though this might have been merely a royal whim, it was, on balance, less shattering than the subsequent venture of the ayatollahs, who have drawn their inspiration from a less distant past. The modern Egyptian leaders have been more cautious. They refer to the grandeur of Pharaonic Egypt merely for the purposes of advertisement abroad, while trying not to offend the feelings of the domestic revivalists of Islam.

There is however one weightier reason for paying attention to the pre-Islamic, pre-Christian civilizations of the Middle East. Abraham was not the only father of the monotheistic tradition and of its Judaeo-Christian branch. Moses came after Akhenaten, and probably not too long before Zarathushtra. The mediated universal monotheism of the former and the dualistic eschatology of the latter are reflected in Christianity with a particular emphasis. The moral teachings put down in writing in Pharaonic Egypt and in Cuneiscript Mesopotamia foreshadow in several respects the Sermon on the Mount. Why should they not be given the full credit that is their due?

2 The Rise of the Levant: The Cuneiscript and Pharaonic Civilizations

2.1 THE GENERAL SETTING

According to the present state of historical knowledge, the first civilized societies emerged towards the end of the fourth millennium BC in the lower valley of the Euphrates and Tigris and in the Delta and lower valley of the Nile.

In our context it is not important to know precisely when this happened, i.e. to decide between the so-called shorter and the longer chronology suggested by different specialists in the field. Nor shall we be bothered by the question of primogeniture. Though the present state of archaeological knowledge tends to point to what is nowadays lower Iraq as the birthplace of the first civilization, and though there are reasons for inferring that the development of Egyptian civilization was speeded by a foreign stimulus which could not ultimately have come from any source other than Mesopotamia, the socio-cultural and economico-political profiles for the ancient civilizations in Mesopotamia and Egypt are so clearly different from each other that no contrary evidence of mutual give-and-take can do much to alter this. Clearly, at the dawn of history, the emerging species' civilization appeared with two distinct understandings of the human predicament, and two distinct styles of life and of artistic expression. It is easy to tell at first sight whether a given artefact belongs to the ancient Egyptian or to the ancient Mesopotamian culture.

Looking at ancient Mesopotamian and ancient Egyptian history as two alternative paths taken by the development of civilization, we can discover outstanding common features, but also striking contrasts.

The most conspicuous common feature is their mythopoeic thought, which is far from being peculiar to these two civilizations alone. For the modern mind, mythopoeic thought is difficult to follow. Lacking any logic, as we understand it, knowing no definite demarcation between fantasy and real experience, it confronts us with a world which we can make at best tentative efforts to comprehend. Nevertheless even with this mythopoeic world-view, these people were able to invent useful tools, harness natural resources and build up a functioning societal organization on a large scale. Although compulsion, too, had an important subsidiary role to play, the common belief in the myths underlying the rationale of the state, so to speak, was the main spontaneous source of social cohesion.

With respect to the organization of those societies issues emerged which were only to a small extent peculiar to the two civilizations. More often than not these issues were of a general nature; we shall meet them, in variations great and small, in other societies which we shall discuss on our journey along the paths of civilization. If we give them more space in this chapter than we shall give to similar issues in other civilizations, it is because, to our knowledge, they appear here for the first time in world history. We want to show the ubiquitous nature of these issues, and thus provide the reader with material from which he or she can draw their own conclusions.

Another feature the two civilizations had in common was the type of agricultural production, which in both instances was based on an elaborate irrigation system in an otherwise arid alluvial plain of river valleys. The fact that the first civilizations in history, not only in Mesopotamia and Egypt but also in the Indus and Yellow River valleys, depended on irrigation rather than rainfall is well-know; and the explanation–that such a type of agriculture required more co-operation and the organization of larger communities than elsewhere–is also widely accepted. We need not go beyond this point and get involved in Wittfogel's generalizations about 'hydraulic agriculture' giving rise to 'agrohydraulic despotism'.[1] At best we can accept the term 'agrohydraulic' as denoting a certain technique, without any further implications concerning the political or cultural framework.[2] Further discussion may help to explain and substantiate our reservations on this point.

The striking contrast between ancient Mesopotamia and ancient

Egypt lies in the psychological dimension. On the one hand we have the artistically-endowed Egyptian, confident in his ability to cope with his (in principle orderly) human and natural environment; on the other hand there is the more technically talented inhabitant of Mesopotamia who had to develop a wider range of capabilities in order to cope with the unpredictable world around him. In a turbulent political history, marked by waves of large-scale immigration and by conquests, the people of Mesopotamia were more innovative in terms of practical discoveries and technology, whilst the more sheltered Egyptians, who only occasionally experienced ethnic turmoil, showed greater achievements in art and in religious speculation.

It is clear that the agrohydraulic mode of production was not enough by itself to shape identical or even similar cultures. There were other, more fundamental, ecological circumstances, which contributed to the shaping of human dispositions; various dispositions framed different courses of action, which in their turn reinforced – by the accumulation of differences – the environmental impetus. We shall discuss this environmental factor in more detail in section 2.4.

But let us first look at the two different psyches more closely and try to give a brief account of the predicaments of people in the two distinct cultures. We shall start with Egypt because her history and culture constitute a more self-contained and therefore more easily demarcated entity.

2.2 THE SPIRIT OF EGYPT

From the very beginning of their scholarly efforts the Egyptologists were puzzled by the immense complexity of the various approaches and often contradictory views of the ancient Egyptian thinkers. As the unearthing, deciphering and analysis of written and archaeological documents went on, however, a more clear-cut and progressively more coherent image started to emerge from beneath the cover of extremely variegated forms of expression.

For an ancient Egyptian everything revolved around a fantastic world of spiritual forces, which was not separated by any clear boundary from the realm of terrestrial creatures, be they men or animals. The interpenetration of myth and reality, of sacred and profane, was amazing. Sometimes, mythopoeic thought generated notions which, even in its own terms, are patently absurd. An example of this can be read in the funeral song of King Unis, the last monarch of the Fifth Dynasty: the king, having ascended to heaven, starts hunting gods, and his butchers and cooks prepare them for his meal.[3]

Another amazing feature of the ancient Egyptian culture was, to borrow H. Frankfort's term, 'multiplicity of approaches', an abrupt juxtaposition of views which we should consider mutually exclusive.[4] This kind of pluralism may reflect the artistic mind of the ancient Egyptians: an artistic creation does not aim at the truth but at beauty, and this is more decisively a subjective phenomenon.

Thus there is no one, single, Egyptian genesis; there are several myths of creation, each developed and upheld in a certain place or rather temple, but all of them, it seems, respected and accepted everywhere. The paradox of the creation itself – that it was the only dynamic act of supreme importance in what from then on was a rather static universe – was apparently a hard nut for the ancient Egyptians to crack.

It is not our concern to discuss the subtleties of ancient Egyptian theology. One point only has to be stressed, namely that amongst the whole pantheon, consisting mainly of zoomorphic gods immanent in nature, there was one exception: Ptah, originally an earth-god, was supposed to be the primary source of existence; he was believed to have created the world by the utterance of his thought, a prototype of the creative 'logos', a theory which was later to play such an important role in Christian theology.

Yet within the religious pluralism there were nevertheless some common underlying principles. Thus there was no dividing line between the world of nature and the people of Egypt. The natural and the social order were intricately interwoven. The same rules permeated everything. This was the divine order, the *maat*, which men and gods alike had to follow. There was no sense in opposing it; the highest virtue which man could achieve was to live in harmony with this order, whose earthly and also heavenly representative, or rather link, was the ruler of Egypt, a god-incarnate – the Pharaoh.

The idea of harmony implied a rather static order of the universe. If there was any movement in nature, it was seen as recurrent and regular. Both the fauna and the flora experienced change only with respect to individual specimens, which however always behaved in the same way, so that the species could be considered as static. A similar situation was supposed to be ideal for people as well.

This kind of mentality found its reflection in Egyptian art, especially in visual art and literature. Their main concern was to help the onlooker, reader or listener to maintain his positive orientation towards harmony and thus to behave in accordance with what was deemed to be right. Painting and narrative were accordingly characterized by an elevated, stylized beauty rather than by tension or excitement.

One element in the cosmic order of the ancient Egyptians, however, was the ever-present experience of death, which in the absence of any metaphysical explanation, was perforce a gravely disturbing factor; it was a significant event of change in the framework of general harmony. In the case of non-human creatures death could be more or less ignored; the individual animal was viewed as an element, perhaps we may add an occasional element, of its eternal species. Such a comfortable submerging of the individual fate in the perpetual, non-changing existence of the species could not easily be transferred to human beings. Here the Egyptian mind was not prepared to be satisfied with the survival of the species. Thus the disturbing factor of death had to be charmed away. The answer was the belief in eternal life for one's spiritual substance, which was conveniently deemed to be of a very complicated nature.[5] The belief alone, however, was not enough; men had to take concrete steps and apply various elaborate means to ensure that their souls would have a reasonable post-mortem existence.

What to a superficial observer seems to be an excessive obsession with burials and funerals in ancient Egyptian culture, is in fact a logical consequence of a particular world-view. The disturbance resulting from an individual death had to be made good at all costs. That this happened in different ways is the consequence of the Egyptians' basic tendency to allow and even – to be on the safe side – to require, a number of alternative approaches.

All in all, the ancient Egyptians developed a fairly optimistic view of the human situation. Although their preoccupation with death and the arrangements to be made in connection with it seems to point to a rather dark outlook, the very nature of these arrangements bears witness to the conviction that man does possess the means to influence his fate in the nether world. To put it bluntly, he was, in principle, master of his fate. He was not like his Sumerian counterpart who – as we shall see later – was at the mercy of gods' whims; the Egyptian knew what to do and how to behave in order to have a reasonably good post-mortem existence.

Yet even within this well-publicized and reassuring framework, people were afraid of possible snags and pitfalls. The common people could not see the after-life other than in terms of their earthly lives; thus they imagined the way to the nether world to be beset with various kinds of obstacle, especially the extortion of tribute by malevolent individuals – be they janitor, ferryman or even judge. For that reason one had to be cautious and there was good cause to use protective magic.

As we said, the arrangements available in the case of death in ancient Egypt were far from uniform. They differed according to historical time, geographical space, and social stratum, ranging from purely material devices differentiated according to the status of those concerned (pyramids, sarcophagi, stored food, armaments, clothing, and different sorts of amulets), to the generally valid standards of moral behaviour.

How men had to behave was amply described in collections of teachings drawn up by high officials of the kingdom. The most ancient is known by the name of its author, Ptah-hotep – a name which makes manifest the relationship of the person with the god Ptah, and means 'Ptah is satisfied'. In one way or another the principles contained in the moral teachings permeated most of ancient Egyptian literature.

As time went on, there seems to have been a trend towards a deeper ethical and religious motivation in this 'normative' literature. To appreciate the wide range of motive, adduced for good behaviour, we need only to sample a few extracts, beginning with the writings of the vizier Ptah-hotep (*c*. twenty-fifth century BC). These reveal a thoroughly practical concern, with only a few statements on a higher ethical level, such as: 'Wrongdoing has never brought its undertaking into port. (It may be that) it is fraud that gains riches, (but) the strength of justice is that it lasts. . . '

There then come quite a few recommendations which reflect shrewdness rather than a moral stance:

> If thou art a poor fellow, following a man of distinction, one of good standing with the god, know thou not his former insignificance.
> If thou desirest to make friendship last in a home to which thou hast access . . .beware of approaching the women.
> Bow thy back to thy superior, thy overseer from the palace.

Opposition to a superior is a painful thing, (for) one lives as
long as he is mild . . .[6]

The teaching of Amen–em–opet (sometime between the tenth and
the sixth century BC) is attuned to a higher level of morality:

> Guard thyself against robbing the oppressed and against overbear-
> ing the disabled. Stretch not forth thy hand against the approach
> of an old man, nor steal away the speech of the aged.
> Do not strain to seek an excess, when thy needs are safe for thee.
> Do not confuse a man with a pen upon papyrus – the
> abomination of the god. Do not bear witness with false
> words . . ., and so on.

But above all Amen–em–opet puts forward ideas which may sound
familiar to our ears. We have a foreshadowing of the Book of
Proverbs, (25; 21–22):

> He who does evil, the (very) river-bank abandons him, and his
> floodwaters carry him off . . . .So steer that we may bring the
> wicked man across, for we shall not act like him – lift him up,
> give him thy hand; fill his belly with bread of thine, so that he
> may be sated and may be ashamed.

And a premonition of the Sermon on the Mount:

> Do not spend the night fearful of the morrow. At daybreak what
> is the morrow like? Man knows not what the morrow is like. God
> is (always) in his success, whereas man is in his failure; . . .[7]

Thus, in ancient Egyptian civilization religion already reveals its
widest possible range of levels and approaches: from primitive
witchcraft serving base interests to the sublime moral heights.

For Egyptian thinkers wrong-doing was a matter of error, not of
sin; the individual could learn correct behaviour and should be
taught it. As the teachings put it: 'There is no child that of itself
has understanding.'[8]

In principle, man's destiny in the nether world depended on the
balance of good and bad works. A declaration of innocence, a
negative confession, stating that all sorts of wrong-doing had not
been committed by the person concerned, was to be delivered by
the soul of the deceased before a tribunal presided over by the ruler
of the nether world – Osiris. Oddly enough, the objective truth was
not necessarily sought; a well-recited formula was supposed to
convince the assizes. And in the case of anything going wrong,

witchcraft could be called upon for help: a small statuette provided with an appropriate charm and placed in the grave would perform all the heavy or dirty work which the deceased might be required to do.

However, in spite of all the tricks and flaws in the basically ethical concept of salvation, the fundamental idea that man can take his fate into his own hands is discernible behind the various sorts of recipe against adverse influences. As has been said already, the whole universe behaved according to certain rules, which affected not only people's natural environment, but also people themselves. It lay in the power of the individual to learn these rules and to behave accordingly.

2.3 THE SPIRIT OF SUMER

Unlike the Egyptians, the Mesopotamians were not one nation. The ancient Cuneiscript civilization in Mesopotamia was the continuous work of several successive nations; yet the first one, the Sumerians, can be credited with having laid the foundations of that civilization.

The Sumerians, like the Egyptians, were not concerned about possible inconsistences in their thought. They too developed various stories of the creation, but there was a strong tendency to unify them into one particular myth. Whether this happened as early as the Sumerian phase of Cuneiscript civilization, or later, is not certain, but from the rise of Babylon the unified version of the creation prevailed. In it the creation of the world and mankind resulted from 'a cosmic battle, the fundamental and eternal struggle between those two aspects of nature: Good and Evil, Order and Chaos'.[9] Once, however, the order was established, men had to follow meticulously the divine ordinances that upheld it.

The Egyptian concept of cosmic and moral order – maat – also had a Sumerian parallel in what may be described as the rules governing cosmic bodies, nature and men alike – in the Sumerian language *me*. And, as in Egypt, so too in Sumer the idea of the creative power of the divine word was one of the basic tenets, most intimately connected with the god Enki (who in that capacity corresponded to the Egyptian god Ptah). But *me* was a kind of code decreed by the assembly of gods and might also have contained the precepts of individual gods; it was not a corollary of the act of creation.

The Sumerian gods resembled human beings, both in appearance and in behaviour, but were immortal and more powerful than men. Their commands were credited with creative power, a power which however was not equally distributed among them. Of the altogether about two and a half thousand known deities, only seven who were deemed to 'decree the fates', and fifty other 'great gods', wielded the greatest creative power. Nothing in the universe and in society escaped the gods' surveillance; everything, natural phenomena and human activities, was thought to follow the gods' regulations; however, what these regulations were, could be seen *ex post* rather than beforehand. Apart from gods in charge of natural or social phenomena there were gods who acted as guardians or intercessors for individual people (rather like angels) and some deities were also in direct command of individual city states.

The Sumerian view of the human situation was much less sanguine than the ancient Egyptian view. Let us cite the authority in the field, S. N. Kramer:

> The Sumerian thinkers . . .were firmly convinced that man was fashioned of clay and created for one purpose only: to serve the gods by supplying them with food, drink, and shelter, so that they might have full leisure for their divine activities. Man's life was beset with uncertainty and haunted by insecurity, since he did not know beforehand the destiny decreed him by the unpredictable gods. When he died, his emasculated spirit descended to the dark, dreary nether world where life was but a dismal and wretched reflection of its earthly counterpart, . . .the Sumerians accepted their dependent status just as they accepted the divine decision that death was man's lot and that only the gods were immortal.[10]

The story found in Egyptian literature of the deceased king hunting gods is unimaginable in Sumer. On the other hand both Egyptians and Sumerians alike were required to make provision for the material well-being of their gods. Providing the gods with adequate food was one of the features of the ancient pre-prophetic religion.

As far as moral conduct is concerned, the Sumerian gods blew hot and cold. Although they were supposed to cherish truth, justice and mercy, they also made arrangements in their *me* for all kinds of vicious behaviour such as falsehood, violence, oppression, etc. The Sumerians do not seem to have been unduly worried about this ethical inconsistency. Their mythopoeic thought spared them the frustration which followers of prophetic religions were to experience when they wanted to resolve the problem of theodicy, i.e. divine justice combined with the contrast between god's perfection and the imperfection of his creation. Instead the Sumerian view was epitomized in the saga of a righteous man (a prototype of the biblical Job) who without any obvious reason, and therefore undeservedly, was beset by a prolonged series of misfortunes and disasters, from which he was eventually delivered only beause of his unwavering obedience and his entreaties to his god.[11]

Unlike Egypt, where no punishment could be inflicted without previous wrong-doing, and, as we saw, wrong-doing was a kind of error that could be avoided by means of proper education, in Sumer there seems to have been a belief in something like hereditary sin, of which anybody could be called to bear the consequences. Otherwise, a Sumerian thinker could not have written a sentence such as: 'Never has a sinless child been born to his mother'.[12] An Egyptian would hardly have understood such a stance.

At first sight it might seem that attributing to the human situation such an uncertain, even shaky basis, could have led to some kind of fatalism. This, however, did not happen. It seems that, as with Calvinist predestination, the Sumerians tried to behave in such a way that they could recognize whether the grace of the gods was with them or not. Like the Calvinist entrepreneur, the Sumerian citizen devoted his energies to concerted activity, both economic and occasionally also inventive. But unlike a faithful Calvinist, for whom success in fostering the puritan virtues of self-restraint and hard work provided living testimony of his predestination, the Sumerian thinkers resolved the dilemma (and their Akkadian and Chaldaean pupils followed suit) in a less sophisticated way: they accepted the whimsical rule of their gods without too much ado and, while trying to placate them by all the means provided by their customary ritual, turned their attention to that side of their lives in which the gods seemed not to be directly involved.

As the Sumerians had nothing good to look forward to after their souls had departed their bodies, and as their gods did not always provide them with good examples of moral behaviour, they focused their interest and energy on practical knowledge and technology, in which they made spectacular breakthroughs. Almost all the inventions of the river valley civilizations first cropped up in Sumer: the plough and the wheel, bronze metallurgy and stone and brick architecture, the calendar and the measurement of time (the clock), implying some rudiments of mathematics and astronomy, and last but not least, writing; all these epoch-making innovations are believed to have been first achieved by the Sumerians. Furthermore, the Sumerian cuneiform script became accessible to a much broader section of the population than did the hieroglyphs invented somewhat later in Egypt.[13]

The epic of Gilgamesh epitomizes the range of the Sumerian spiritual drama: leading from indulgence in the voluptuous life, through a defiant quest for immortality, a quest which aimed at bypassing the will of the gods and thus had to fail, and ending with the humble acceptance of their verdict and a concentration on the service of one's own city state, the appropriate field for man's self-realisation.

As H. Frankfort said: 'Mesopotamia achieved her triumphs in an atmosphere of deep disquiet. The spirit pervading her most important writings is one of disbelief in man's ability to achieve lasting happiness. Salvation might be experienced emotionally in the annual festivals of gods, but was not a postulate of theology.'[14]

Nevertheless, despite all the differences in their views of the human predicament, the Sumerians and those who took over their heritage developed the same sense of correct human behaviour as the Egyptians, with a similar gap between a down-to-earth pragmatism and a loftier morality. To illustrate this point let us quote from a tablet of Akkadian wisdom:

> As a wise man, let your understanding shine modestly, let your mouth be restrained, guarded your speech. Like a man's wealth, let your lips be precious. Let affront, hostility, be an abomination unto you. Speak nothing impertinent, (give no) unreliable advice. Whoever does something ugly – his head is despised. Hasten not to stand in a public assembly, seek not the place of quarrel; for in a quarrel you must give a decision, and you will be forced to be their witness. They will fetch you to testify in a lawsuit that does not concern you. When you see a quarrel, go away without noticing it. But if it is really your own quarrel, extinguish the flame . . .Unto your opponent do no evil; your evildoer recompense with good; unto your enemy let justice (be done).[15]

It seems that whilst the Sumerian and Egyptian views of the human predicament diverged, their understanding of what a human being has to do in order to avoid difficulties was not that much different. Apparently metaphysical thought can permit itself a greater variety than is allowed to pragmatic considerations. This appears to be true even if the divergence on the metaphysical level is due in part to tangible environmental reasons, as will be shown in the next section.

2.4 GEOGRAPHY AND POLITY

The striking difference in the mental orientation of the two most ancient civilizations can hardly be explained by their mode of production, which in both cases was based on irrigation agriculture. It was, rather, the wider ecological setting which determined the different shaping of mental attitudes and fostered the different understandings of the human predicament.

The Egyptian concept of an orderly universe with cognizable rules of conduct for every creature can be related to the mainly regular environment of the Nile valley. The orderly course of the river and the fairly regular floods facilitated a comparatively simple irrigation system without long distance canals and additional work during the summer heat. The Nile also provided the main transport artery, that could be comfortably navigated in both directions: the gently downstream current was matched by regular northerly breezes which could be used to sail upstream.

In addition, the clear-cut demarcation of vegetation from desert, which on both sides of the valley provided a natural barrier and a horizon for an established civilization, could not fail to shape the mentality of the people and impress upon it a sense of order, regularity and balance.

In contrast to the situation on the shores of the Nile, conditions in the Tigris-Euphrates valley were uncertain and rather difficult. The rise and fall in the water-level of the two rivers tended to be irregular, heavy floods could result in landslides, and neither of the two rivers was by nature particularly suitable for water transport. The cultivable area was not so neatly demarcated from its inhospitable surroundings as in the Nile valley; the particular type of desert and high mountains both offered suitable launching points for a foreign invasion.

These ecological differences between Egypt and Mesopotamia go a long way towards providing us with the key to their divergent frames of mind and world-views. The experience of a stable natural environment, and the relative infrequency of foreign intrusions, nurtured the idea that the universe as a whole was similarly well-ordered; harmony with such a universe was then the best course for man to follow.

In Mesopotamia, on the other hand, the natural environment and also the vulnerability to foreign invasions produced a general feeling of irregularity and insecurity. Unlike in Egypt, the civilization in Mesopotamia could hardly build on the supposition of an orderly, predictable universe. Although such a supposition might have been felt to be desirable – as is suggested by the myth of creation, whose crucial plot is the defeat of chaos and the establishment of divine rule – their primary life experience clearly contradicted such an image.

Irregularity and uncertainty implied arbitrariness in the cosmic paradigm, an arbitrariness which their myth-loving thought embodied in the form of a contest or bargaining between gods whose own characters reflected all the possible virtues and vices of their human subjects. Under these circumstances nothing could be taken for granted, not even the regular sequence of the seasons: a special ritual involving all the religious and secular dignitaries, a ritual attaining huge proportions and mass participation in the Babylonian period of the Mesopotamian civilization, was believed to be instrumental in ensuring the timely spring resurrection of nature from its winter sleep.[16]

Surveying the first two civilized societies from the perspective of the three millennia of their history, we discover several basic issues, or dilemmas, whose continuous presence during that long era gave the history of the two civilizations its special character. But at the same time the very occurrence of these issues points to a more general, ubiquitous and yet multifaceted human activity, which can be described in a shorthand form as the struggle for wealth, power and prestige or dignity.

Unfortunately we cannot follow this development backwards, to the prehistorical era. What happened then is purely a matter of conjecture, based on archaeological evidence, the interpretation of myths, or on the retrospective extrapolation of events and tendencies from the historical epoch.

The fact that at the dawn of history Egypt appears on the scene as a politically united country, under one sovereign ruler, whereas Sumer is divided into a host of city states in which the sovereignty itself seems to have been divided, is significant; even if we cannot exclude the possibility that before unification Egypt, too, at least as far as the Nile Delta is concerned, experienced a period of rudimentary city states.[17]

Occasionally Egypt, too, relapsed into disunity either by its own fault or as a result of foreign invasion; but these were exceptions which, as far as literary evidence allows us to judge, were resented as something abnormal, and on each occasion Egyptian society was able, comparatively quickly, to mobilize the resources needed to abolish such an anomaly.

A more serious challenge to the principle of changeless harmony emerged from the ideological ferment generated by the cultural elites who, in the long run, could not be constrained by the straitjacket of one static world-view.

In Mesopotamia, on the other hand, where the need for harmony had not been elevated to a cosmic principle, the struggle was due mainly to inter-state rivalries: at first between the Sumerian city states, later between the nation states within the wider orbit of the Cuneiscript civilization, and between these nations and the invading tribes.

The pluralism of Mesopotamia was not primarily religious and conceptual, as in Egypt, but a political and ethnic reality. The history of the Cuneiscript civilization cannot be properly understood without taking into account on the one hand the ramified network of its constituent units and, on the other hand, the comparative ease with which it radiated and expanded outwards, while conversely being subject to constant infiltrations and periodic invasions.

The difference can be clearly seen if we compare the extent of the political expansion and cultural radiation of the two civilizations.

The Pharaonic civilization of Egypt assimilated only one non-Egyptian country, viz. Nubia in the upper Nile valley. Eventually, when the decay of the Pharaonic civilization in Egypt was well under way, Nubia experienced a period of the blossoming of what may be described as a para-Pharaonic civilization. The Egyptian political presence in Syria had, as will be shown later, only a limited cultural impact.

In contrast to the Pharaonic civilization of Egypt, the Cuneiscript civilization of Mesopotamia was the work of several nations which successively assimilated, further elaborated and passed on the Sumerian heritage.

Broadly speaking, the successive nations of Mesopotamia and its neighbourhood can be grouped under three headings. Firstly, the mainstream nations, so to speak: the heirs of the Sumerians in direct lineage, such as the Akkadians, the Amorites (the Old Babylonians), the Chaldaeans (the New Babylonians) and the Assyrians; in succession, they all contributed to the building of the Cuneiscript civilization. With some qualifications, the Kassites and the Aramaeans can be added to this list. Secondly, the collateral nations, whose Cuneiscript civilization was a kind of variant or adaptation of the mainstream civilization; to their group belong the people of Elam in the east, the people of Mari, Ebla, Ugarit, etc., in the west, and the people of Urartu in the north. Thirdly, the outlying nations whose particular civilizations absorbed and assimilated only some elements of the Cuneiscript civilization, such as the Subareans and the Hurrians in Upper Mesopotamia and above all the Hittites in Asia Minor.

The appearance of these three groups of nations within the wider orbit of the Cuneiscript civilization is illustrated in Figure 2.1 overleaf, in which historical time and geographical space are the two dimensions.

2.5 EGYPT: THE STRUGGLE FOR HARMONY

Despite the image of harmony implying a static ideal of no essential change in the cosmic and human order, society in Pharaonic Egypt was subject to a series of significant changes – thus proving that no myth or theory can confine human action to a prescribed path. As it is, the long time which elapsed before these significant changes occurred perhaps bears witness to the strength of the mental attitudes underlying the world-view of the Pharaonic civilization.

The world-view of the ancient Egyptians, in the form in which it has become known to us, most probably developed only after Egypt's political unification, perhaps as an *ex post* rationalization and/or justification of that achievement.

Unfortunately the Egyptologists have not yet been able to find out how and precisely when the political unification of Egypt occurred. It seems that it was a gradual and lengthy process, hampered by frequent reversals, and extending over several centuries. For sometime two separate kingdoms, Upper and Lower Egypt, vied for supremacy; even after the king of Upper Egypt subdued the king of Lower Egypt and crowned himself in his stead, there elapsed a long period before this event was fully accepted and adequate institutional measures were taken to implement the unification of the crowns.[18]

22

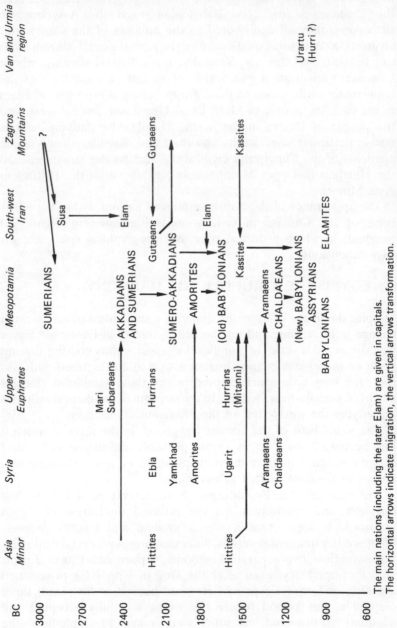

Figure 2.1 The ethnic scheme of the Cuneiscript civilization in space and time.

The main nations (including the later Elam) are given in capitals.
The horizontal arrows indicate migration, the vertical arrows transformation.

We may perhaps get nearer to an understanding of this process by invoking a comparison with the birth of the United Kingdom of Great Britain. There too the unification of the English and Scottish crowns preceded by about one hundred years the unification of legislation and various other institutions, which in turn did not fully obliterate the separate political and cultural identities of England and Scotland. Also, the fact that an anti-unionist insurrection of the Scots had to be quelled may have more than one parallel in ancient Egyptian history. The union of treasuries, granaries and of water control, and also the co-ordination of the religious cults of Upper and Lower Egypt, seem to have occurred several centuries after the supposed unification of the crowns; however, unlike the United Kingdom of Great Britain, the United Kingdom of Egypt was eventually given a capital city – situated on the border between the two kingdoms. According to tradition, the city of Mennofer (in Greek, Memphis) developed around the fortress erected by King Menes, the unifier of Egypt.

It may well have taken the duration of the First and Second dynasties (from *c*. 3100 to 2700 BC) before Egypt became effectively united. The changes in the religious nomenclature of the Pharaohs between the First and Second dynasty point to some political changes as well. It seems that the principle of harmony had still to be worked out.

Apparently this ideal had to be bolstered by extolling the ruler of the united Egypt to an unprecedented degree. Not only was the Pharaoh, as a god incarnate, as an earthly representative of the world order, *maat*, to be an absolute ruler, but his earthly presence had to be preserved for ever. The pyramids built for the Pharaohs of the Third and the Fourth dynasty (*c*. 2700 – 2500) were the most conspicuous manifestation of that idea.

In the present context we cannot go into the intricacies of the ancient Egyptian understanding of immortality, intricacies resulting from the plurality of concepts, such as *ka*, and *ba*, and *akh*; these can be translated, though not quite adequately, as 'vital spirit', 'soul' and 'transfigured spirit', respectively. For our purpose we may be satisfied with the simplifying assumption that the spiritual transfiguration after death required some material and ritual help such as a proper grave, a mummy, some sort of worship, magic etc. For a Pharaoh, who, although god-incarnate, also needed some help in his spiritual transformation, something exceptional and durable had to be invented. Thus around 2600 the pyramids became the inaccessible graves of kings who were to be buried within a huge mass of stones designed to withstand the corrosive effects of time. This solution, seemingly guaranteeing the king's immortality, appears to have been a challenge to those who aspired to a similar, even if less conspicuous, salvation. The response was the proposition of an alternative form of post-mortem transfiguration, leading gradually to an equalization, or rather, approximate equalization, of human beings' chances of achieving it.[19]

More modest buildings, which the upper strata could well afford, and still more modest means such as prayers and magic, accessible to everybody, began to be available to the Pharaoh's subjects. The Ossirian myth, being the focus of a popular cult, opened the door to less material considerations in the quest for a better after-life. Although the moral impact of the idea of the last judgement, in which every deceased person would be examined with respect to their good or bad behaviour, was blunted by the deep-rooted practice of magic, the significance of the emergence of this basically ethical idea must not be underestimated. Although the admonitions of that epoch were, in principle, sets of practical, often opportunistic pieces of advice on how to deal with various awkward situations, the underlying tenor was that people had to learn how to behave properly in order that society could live in a civilized manner. As one of the founding fathers of Egyptology, Flinders Petrie, put it, the ancient Egyptians aimed ideally to be 'easy, good natured, quiet gentlemen, who made life as agreeable as they could all round'.[20]

It has been assumed that the Pharaoh's loss of his exlusive claim to salvation also symbolized a decline in his worldly power. E. Meyer even suggested that the Pharaoh had to acknowledge his duties towards his people.[21] The curbing of Pharaonic absolutism seems to have set in motion a process which in due course led to a political upheaval of immense consequences. At issue was the growing tension between the central and the local government.

This tension resulted in a sort of pendulum swing, also observable in other societies, from a centralized rule of an absolutist type towards a decentralized, more or less feudal kind of hierarchy, and back again. In contrast to other societies, such as China, Iran and Asia Minor, which experienced a similar seesaw development, in Egypt these shifts occurred on a diminishing scale. There was virtually only one period in the history of Pharaonic Egypt when the central administration ceased to operate. This apparently happened in the last two centuries of the third millennium BC. The nadir of this development was marked by the complete collapse of the central Pharaonic power *vis-à-vis* foreign infiltrations, invasions and social upheavals.

The main document which is widely believed to describe the events of this period, the so-called Ipuwer papyrus, is unfortunately preserved only in fragments, and furthermore in a form which makes it also possibly applicable to the invasion of the Hyksos, more than three hundred years later.[22] Some scholars interpret the fragments of the Ipuwer papyrus as the description of a social revolution.[23] This might be the case; but, more probably, we are dealing with a coincidence of various developments, such as invasions, usurpations and revolts, whose cumulative effect was an unprecedented social mobility which, in some areas, turned the social pyramid upside down.

The consolidation was a tedious process, in which for some time two dynasties (one based on Lower, the other on Upper Egypt) vied for power. Eventually that of Upper Egypt, known as the Eleventh dynasty, gained the upper hand in the whole country. Under the Twelfth dynasty (*c.* 1990–1790), Egypt experienced considerable economic growth and an upsurge of cultural creativity. It seems that during those two centuries, which embrace the greater part of the epoch of the Middle Kingdom, Egypt found its internal balance and thus perhaps came closest to its ideal of harmony.

Harmony, however, is an elusive ideal. It is something that people can achieve in their art, in music, poetry, painting, sculpture, architecture, pottery, etc., rather than in their living together.

As far as harmony in art is concerned the ancient Egyptians definitely achieved their ideal. Even if we do not know their music, and even if – because of the omission of vowels from their written language – their poetry cannot be fully appreciated, what remained and is accessible to us gives us a clear image of harmony as the supreme value.

With respect to the society as a whole, the Middle Kingdom can be positively, if tentatively, summed up as the era in which the Pharaoh was a real boss again. However, his role was defined as that of a good shepherd rather than merely the traditional god-incarnate.[24] The royal bureaucracy, the literate and numerate scribes with technical expertise in accounting, the calendar and weather forecasting, could carry on their work as their knowledge and conscience dictated. The local dignitaries preserved for some time their hereditary offices but kept them, to borrow J. Hawkes's words, as faithful lieges of the Pharaoh.[25]

2.6 EGYPT AS A GREAT POWER: BETWEEN MACHIOCRACY AND HIEROCRACY

At the beginning of the nineteenth century BC the internal balance of the Middle Kingdom was upset once more. A process not dissimilar to that of three to four hundred years earlier set in; the elements of this one, however, can be more readily reconstructed from literary and archaeological evidence: the intra-dynastic quarrels, the weakening of the central authority, the growing proportion of foreigners amongst the officials of the realm, and eventually the emergence of secessionist states, one in the western part of the Delta, and the other in its eastern part, the latter founded by foreign invaders, known under their hellenized name as the Hyksos. The traditional, legitimate kingdom was gradually pushed to the south and forced to acknowledge the sovereignty of the invaders, whose military superiority was bolstered by the use of horses, previously unknown in Egypt. Meanwhile Nubia seized the opportunity and became independent.

Although there is some evidence that the Hyksos were quite keen to assimilate the Egyptian culture, they were not readily accepted by the Egyptians. Whether they were too tainted by the vestiges of the Cuneiscript civilization acquired during their sojourn in Syria, as Arnold Toynbee suggests,[26] or whether it was simply because they were not prepared to accept a second-class position within Egyptian society, as for instance the less culturally committed Libyans and Nubians did, the Hyksos after some one hundred years of domination in Egypt were expelled by their vassal king of Upper Egypt.

With this achievement the vigorous New Kingdom emerged; it answered to the powerful foreign challenge with an equally powerful response. The Egyptians learned a new military technique: the combination of the composite bow and the chariot, whose construction they managed further to improve.[27] In order to forestall any further attack from Syria, the New Kingdom not only kept a standing army, but embarked on a large-scale expansionist policy. Syria, with its host of small principalities and city states, was made a dependent bridgehead or glacis and Nubia was reconquered.

Successful conquests brought home booty and tribute in the form of bullion, wares and slaves. This increased both the prestige and the material equipment of the army. As the victories were deemed to be due to the special favours of the gods, for which the priests claimed responsibility, temples participated abundantly in the spoils. Thus, gradually, the traditional bureaucracy of the scribes was joined by two other professional elites: the machiocracy and the hierocracy.

Thus within the social pyramid with the Pharaoh at its summit, a more complex structure of elites developed. This situation could not but create a breeding ground for interprofessional rivalry. Towards the end of the fifteenth century, the Egyptian priesthood appeared on the scene as a unified organization (a trade union, so to speak) headed by the high priest of the god Amon, with his seat in the capital city Veset (Thebes). With the position of the high priest of Amon there emerged the first dangerous seeds of govermental dualism, seeds which were to grow and flourish during the next two hundred years.

While the elites ramified and proliferated, religion continued to develop its theological dimension, which implied various attempts at systematization. Together with the sophistication of religious concepts and beliefs there was a distinct move towards a kind of henotheism, i.e. a situation where, at the top level, the whole pantheon is represented by one particular god, the other deities being specialized emanations or derivations from him. In Egypt, however, the straightforward henotheism was elaborated into the concept of a trinity, composed of Amon, the god of the capital city, the sun-god Re, and the god Ptah (originally an earth-god, but long since transformed into a god of creative thought). Thus a tripartite elite found its counterpart in a godly trinity presiding over the pantheon.

While this process was going on, a vigorous attempt was made to reorientate the Pharaonic civilization to other goals, an attempt which however failed and in so doing only accentuated the previous development. Amenhotep IV (1377–1357) decided to proclaim a new religion and introduce a new style of government. He chose one god – the sun – but not in the traditional form of Re, but in the new form of a sun-disc, Aten. Amenhotep (meaning 'Amon is satisfied') appropriately changed his own name into Akhenaten ('the spirit of Aten').

Aten was deemed to be an exclusive and universal god, who after several years of competitive coexistence became a jealous god, so that all other cults had to be abandoned. As a corollary to the universalistic message peace had to prevail; consequently the imperial interests abroad, especially in Syria, were not adequately protected. This did not please the machiocracy, which otherwise was not under direct threat of reform as was the priesthood. The new search for truth going beyond the traditional forms found its most conspicuous reflection in visual art, which in contrast to the stylized fashion of the previous epoch, looked for a realistic reflection of its subject-matter. Harmony had to be sought in religion rather than in art.

However, this far-reaching reform, implemented by force and therefore all the more resented, did not survive its instigator. As we shall see on other occasions in this study, prophecy cannot be successfully carried out from the throne. A prophet needs dedicated followers, ready to bring all sorts of sacrifice and even suffer martyrdom, and not merely the obedient servants or sycophants which a crowned would-be prophet has at his disposal. Thus, in the absence of a flock of genuine believers, the backlash could not but succeed. All the work of the 'great heretic' was destroyed and in due course forgotten. Only the reinvigorated cult of the sun-god Re can perhaps be considered as a lasting effect of Akhenaten's abortive reformation.

The evaluation of Akhenaten's religious reform is a controversial issue amongst historians. Was Atenism a prototype of 'modern theistic thought' which 'flashed for a moment like a brilliant comet against the black night of Egyptian anthropomorphic religion', as F.G. Bratton put it? Or was it, as many suppose, merely the extreme position reached by the development of Egyptian theology, which in Akhenaten's thought crossed the ill-defined boundary of henotheism and attempted to enthrone the monotheistic creed as the official religion in Egypt? Or was Atenism not an outright monotheism but, as J.A. Wilson suggests, a two-tier theism, in which Akhenaten and his family worshipped Aten, and everybody else worshipped the Pharaoh Akhenaten as a god, a physical son of Aten.[2]

Another bone of contention is whether Atenism was an intellectual religion lacking in real ethical value, or whether, on the contrary, it was in Atenism that the time-honoured key concept of Egyptian religious thought, *maat*, attained its full, undiluted assertion.

Last but not least, the idea that Atenism might be a culmination of the domestic tradition has to be viewed in the context of the many foreign influences operating at the royal court at the time of Akhenaten and his father, who on the other hand might have already begun taking cultic countermoves against the growing power of the traditional priesthood.[28]

Be that as it may, one conclusion can in my opinion be drawn with some confidence; namely, that Akhenaten's religious reform was a serious attempt to forestall the spiritual crisis which began to build up as a result of the growing power and riches of the caste-like priesthood. This view is corroborated by what happened after the reform had failed.

For some time it seemed that under the able and energetic military commander Horemheb (Pharaoh 1347–1319) Egypt would recapture her previous vigour, but this turned out not to be the case. Horemheb's followers, the Ramassids, seem to have been concerned more with the display of their glory than with the real strength of their country: reported instances of peasants fleeing the land bear witness to excessive taxation and other public or private burdens. The last great achievement of the Ramassids was the repulsion of the mass attack of the so-called Sea Peoples on the shores of Egypt towards the end of the thirteenth century.

From then on, Egyptian society was set on a downhill path. The priests tried by all kinds of means to assert their dominance over the population. Magic permeated an unprecedented number of activities. The practice of ordeals was introduced into the judiciary; the cult of animals – as the true representatives of the unchanging cosmic order in contrast to the volatile nature of man – attained its apogee. It is no wonder that the practice of religion in the temples often became discredited; the spread of various types of personal piety, and the scepticism amongst the educated strata towards religious beliefs in general, testified to a serious crisis of the established religion.

In this social climate, the hierocracy took the final step in their struggle for power. In 1085 BC the Theban high priest (Hrihor) arrogated to himself the powers of the Pharaoh, a status subsequently claimed by some of his priestly successors. Unfortunately the moral decadence of the wealthy and powerful hierocracy served to undermine the integrative forces in the society. The way was open to regional secessions. In the Delta these tendencies were prompted by the rise of prosperous cities; elsewhere they were fostered by local dynasties and by the reappearance of quasi-feudal elements in the social structure.

A decline in the martial virtues led to an increase in the engagement of mercenaries. Their leaders gradually assumed power and from 950 Egypt was ruled by dynasties from their ranks: first Libyan, then Nubian.[29] The Nubian dynasty with its main base in the deep south was, however, not strong enough to protect Egypt from a new invasion from the north-east, this time not by semi-nomadic semi-barbarians, but by the great military power of Assyria, the most expansionist representative of the Cuneiscript civilization in Mesopotamia. Although the Assyrian occupation of Lower Egypt was only a brief episode (671–655), it heralded the advent of an era of foreign domination. The national recovery which followed the humiliating Assyrian occupation in the Delta and Lower Egypt was marked by a further spread of foreign influences. The dynasty, which from its capital Sais in the Delta became the symbol of a cultural renaissance, tried to adapt Egypt to the circumstances of the wider modern world. Yet its efforts foundered on the prevailing conservatism and the rivalry between the dominant machiocracy, mostly of foreign, Libyan or (later) Greek origin, the growing timocracy of the cities, and the xenophobic, narrow-minded priest-hood.

Thus when the first universal empire in the Levant – the Persian empire – entered upon the historical scene, Egypt could not withstand its military strength, and became a Persian province for a hundred and twenty years (525–404). After a final period of independence (404–343), a rather subdued recovery, Egypt was again conquered by the Persians, but in 332, their rule gave way to conquest and long-term domination by the Greeks and Hellenized peoples.

A gradual transformation of the Pharaonic civilization set in. After about five centuries during which a Hellenistic dynasty was succeeded by Roman rule, Egypt became the Coptic branch of the nascent pan-Christian civilization.

The Pharaonic civilization survived only as a kind of replica outside its original orbit. Nubia, which from the sixteenth century on was under strong Egyptian influence, had by the beginning of the last millennium BC turned into another Egypt, though it was not completely impervious to other external influences as well. The type of culture and political organization which from about 850 spread up the River Nile further to the south – the Napatan and Merovitic cultures – has been already described as the para–Pharaonic civilization. Severed from its mother culture to the north, it lingered on in its peripheral position until, in the fourth century AD, the Ethiopian Aksumites dealt it the *coup de grâce*.

2.7 SUMER AND AKKAD; FROM THE CITY STATES TO THE EMPIRE

Although the nature and the development of the ancient Mesopotamian institutions are still matters of conjecture rather than of established knowledge, some elements can nevertheless be taken from granted. The main pattern of their long-term evolution can also be traced with a reasonable degree of confidence. Because this course of development foreshadowed what was to happen later in many other societies in various parts of the world, we shall attempt to outline its main contours.

As has been said already, Sumerian society was articulated into several city states, each of which was, in theory, the property of a particular deity, who apart from that capacity might also have a specific function within the pantheon. Such were the heaven-god An, the air-god Enlil, the water-god Enki, and the great mother goddess Ninhursag, to name only the most important deities out of the fifty 'great gods' and hundreds of lesser deities worshipped in Sumer.

The power constellation in these city states seems to have been pluralistic. There were apparently two supreme dignitaries: the *lugal* and the *ensi*. The former was in charge of the military functions of the government, the latter was head of the main temple, which involved not only religious but also economic and technological expertise. The mutual relationship between the lugal and the ensi varied with the circumstances. As some literary evidence suggests, there was also scope for a counsel of elders and for a general warriors assembly to consider issues of peace and war.[30]

In Sumer there was no theocracy, no god-incarnate of the Egyptian type. The power elite seems to have been composed of rudiments of the military aristocracy, together with the priesthood, scribes and also perhaps some wealthy commoners. The unity of the Sumerian culture was symbolized by the general recognition of the city of Nippur with the temple of the supreme god Enlil as a religious capital, which was supposed to stand aloof from all internal strife.

Political unification on a wider geographical scale was achieved, as in the Graeco-Roman world, by one city state imposing its hegemony upon the others. In the history of Sumer this happened towards the end of the exclusive Sumerian presence in the area, in the twenty fourth century BC, when the ruler of the city Umma, Lugalzagessi, subdued all the other Sumerian city states, thus creating the first pan-Sumerian polity.

The political unification of a society accustomed to living within the pluralistic framework of the city states was not a matter of military strength alone. It required the adaptation of internal social and political structures and the appropriate religious confirmation and justification. Within Sumerian society itself, the preconditions necessary for such a complex change did not apparently exist at that time. As Dyakonov suggests, Lugalzagessi was satisfied with a more or less confederative arrangement. He preserved the local ensi in their dignity while entrusting them with the responsibility for local self-government, and had himself confirmed as lugal of the conquered cities by the local warriors assemblies.[31]

A more resolute move towards unification had to come – as in the case of the Hellenic civilization – from the periphery. A role similar to that which Macedonia played with respect to Greece, was in Mesopotamia performed by Akkad. The Akkadians represent the first known major wave of Semitic immigration into civilized Mesopotamia. From the twenty seventh century they began to settle to the north of the Sumerian settlements and infiltrate the Sumerian area itself. Around, or after, 2300, the Akkadian King Sharrukin (Sargon I) defeated the Sumerian Lugalzegessi and incorporated his 'confederation' into his own wider empire.

The building of the Sargonid empire necessitated some political and structural changes in the Sumero-Akkadian society. They can be summerized as follows:

(a) A new capital (Agade) was built, where the king could rule as a sovereign without interference from the traditional local elites.

(b) A standing army endowed by land allocation was created (a prototype of many similar arrangements in different countries and epochs, the best known being the Russian Cossacks).

(c) The administration of the subdued cities was entrusted to the scions of the royal family and to people from the royal retinue, the beginnings of a court aristocracy.[32]

(d) Under royal protection and a united administration the irrigation schemes could be better coordinated, new roads built, measures and weights unified; merchants from Sumer and Akkad could extend their trade to most neighbouring countries, in particular to north Syria and beyond the Taurus mountains into Asia Minor (timber, ores and stone being the main materials in which Sumer and Akkad were lacking); last, but not least, the dangerous foe of the Sumerian cities, Elam, was annexed to the Sargonid empire.

Difficulties came mainly from the local dynasties that had been subdued and the aristocracy connected with them. They were prepared to exploit any opportunity to emancipate themselves. The priests of the temples of former city states were also dissatisfied because of the loss of their autonomy.

Sargon's third successor Naram Sin, in an effort to strengthen his position, arrogated to himself honours appropriate to a god. Lavish subsidies to the temples were intended to pacify the priestly opposition. This, however, went against the very roots of the Sumerian world-view; the priesthood of the religious capital Nippur, pronounced in the name of eight deities a curse on the king, who retaliated by destroying the Nippur temple.

Then, however, came a caesura in the pattern of development. With the fifth generation the vigour of the dynasty was exhausted and the empire began to disintegrate. The neighbouring nations such as the Elamites, the Lullubi, the Hurrians and above all the Gutians intensified their pressure on the Sargonid empire. The Gutians eventually became the rulers of the Akkadian territories while the Sumerian south experienced a period of cultural upsurge, known as the Sumerian renaissance.

The struggle against the Gutians was started by the ruler of the Sumerian city of Uruk, and was completed by Ur Namu, ruler of the Sumerian city of Ur. As a result the whole of Sumer and Akkad were reunited under what is known as the Third Dynasty of Ur. In recreating a unified monarchical empire the Sumerians followed the Akkadian tradition rather than their own. Under Ur Namu the Cuneiscript civilization experienced its most intensive political and to some extent also economic centralization.

The remnants of the Sumero-Akkadian military nobility were largely wiped out together with the Gutian invaders. The new 'court' aristocracy gradually became intertwined with the loyal priesthood. Although the temple economy was still of paramount importance (according to Dyakonov's estimate temples owned about 60 per cent of the cultivated land)[33] and the officials were rewarded with a kind of benefice *(ilkum)*, neither kind of possession constituted a form of freely disposable property. There are sufficient documents attesting the tight central supervision of the whole of the economy.

Also in the religious sphere, centralization found its corollary in the renewed desire of the ruler for a more exalted form of veneration. It seems, however, that in theory this type of honour evoked the idea of a king by the grace of god rather than of a god-incarnate in the Egyptian manner. At least under Ur Namu, there was no dramatic confrontation with the Enlil's priesthood in Nippur (where the temple had meanwhile been rebuilt) as had occurred under Naram Sin.

At that time the Sumero-Akkadian integration became complete. The Sumerian language continued to be used for liturgical purposes, while Akkadian became the language generally spoken in the whole Sumero-Akkadian orbit, and in addition widely used by the neighbouring nations as a *lingua franca*.

2.8 THE MULTI-ETHNIC CUNEISCRIPT CIVILIZATION

With the Sumero-Akkadian synthesis the Cuneiscript civilization acquired a particularly strong capacity to assimilate newcomers and influence its neighbours. Most of the latter took over the Sumero–Akkadian cuneiform script intact; some were inspired to a new cuneiform syllabary. Yet not only the script, but also the ideas began to travel, east, north and west, far more than they had done previously.

Around 2000, the Semitic Amorites, who had already for some time been raiding and infiltrating Mesopotamia, started to come in great numbers, settling down and assimilating with the Sumero-Akkadian culture and style of life. Within two centuries, most local rulers in the Sumero-Akkadian orbit were of Amorite origin. The previously insignificant Akkadian city of Babylon was destined, under its most prominent ruler of the Amorite dynasty, Hammurabi (*c*.1792–1750) to become the centre of a new Mesopotamian integration.

That there was a deliberate policy to this effect can be seen from the most famous document of his rule, known as Hammurabi's code. This was in fact a collection of casuistic legal provisions preceded and followed by hymnic eulogies, and as such not the first of its kind in Mesopotamia but valid for a larger area than its predecessors. Although in principle the contents follow the Sumero-Akkadian tradition, the penalties and punishments reveal a more severe treatment of law-breakers.

Another, perhaps more remarkable, synthesis was achieved by the Babylonian priesthood. Inspired by ancient Sumerian sources, they conceived of a new, integrated, myth of creation, known (like a papal encyclical) by its opening words as *Enuma elish*, meaning 'when on high'. According to this myth, the supreme god was the Babylonian city-god Marduk, who – to keep the link with the Sumerian tradition – was supposed to be the son of the Sumerian heaven-god An. Significantly, the myth saw genesis as a tedious process; formidable forces of chaos had first to be defeated, and only from their debris (actually the corpses of deities representing them) could the world as we know it be created.

The glorious period of the Amorite dynasty (the so-called Old Babylonian Empire) was also marked by a new blossoming of the arts and by progress in mathematics. In the realm of *belles-lettres* there was a particular achievement that was symbolic for the Cuneiscript civilization as a whole: various Sumerian legends of Gilgamesh were woven into one coherent epic written in the classical Akkadian. Its underlying philosophy, discernible behind the fantastic stories and adventures, was outlined at the end of Section 2.3. Here we can only add that the Gilgamesh epic became so popular that it was translated into almost all the other languages in the wider Mesopotamian orbit, including the Hurrian and Hittite tongues.[34]

As regards his attempt to unify Mesopotamia under his rule, however, Hammurabi was successful only towards the end of his reign and, several years after his death, a gradual process of disintegration, prompted by foreign pressures, set in. The Kassites attacked from the east, the Hurrians from the north; the whole period, known as the 'Dark Ages', culminated in 1595 with the Hittites sacking the city of Babylon. When after that disastrous event the historical scene again brightened up, Mesopotamia found herself being ruled by a Kassite dynasty, which remained in power until the middle of the twelfth century, and thus proved to be the most long-lived dynasty in the history of Cuneiscript Mesopotamia.

The Kassite period in Babylonia, though seemingly uneventful, nevertheless left a significant imprint on the subsequent development of the Cuneiscript civilization.

The Kassites and the Hurrians brought with them the skill of horsemanship, important mainly in war but later also useful for other kinds of activity. The Kassite warlords who took over the reins of power from the Babylonian aristocracy also became landlords of vast stretches of cultivated land. This, it seems, implied a kind of authority over the local population similar to the feudal lordship – including the collection of various levies and taxes, the corvée upon the waterworks, etc.[35]

In contrast to earlier periods the benefices largely became hereditary and their holders often exercised some kind of lordship not only over the peasants but also over the craftsmen. As many cities succeeded in strengthening their position *vis-à-vis* the central government, the latter was quite keen to support their commercial activities. Thus the centralizing trend which started with the Sargonid dynasty of Akkad and culminated with the Third dynasty of Ur was reversed.

One other invention, the most important in the long run, was not the work of the Kassites. It was introduced to Mesopotamia by the Hittites. This was iron metallurgy.

At first sight it might seem that such an epoch-making discovery must have made a deep impact on the socio-economic structure of the civilized societies. Or to put it in terms of a well-known theory: the immense increase in the productive forces which was made possible by iron tools must have led to a new mode of production, ushered in by some sort of revolution.

This however was not the case; iron metallurgy did not primarily affect the fabric of existing civilizations; its main impact was felt beyond their geographical orbits. The iron plough made possible the agricultural cultivation of heavy soil outside the alluvial plains; thus its use enormously increased the geographical area in which civilization could be developed. Furthermore, in Mesopotamia and Egypt it took a long time before the real iron age set in.

The Hittites exploited their knowledge of iron metallurgy in two ways. Firstly they were able to build their civilization on new territory, where bronze age tools could not have supplied them with adequate sustenance. Secondly they used iron weapons in expanding their political power, although this did not make such a spectacular impact as might have been expected.

At any rate the new iron technology was by no means a sufficient basis for a new type of civilization. The Hittite culture was largely syncretic. There were some original features in the organization of the state, such as the power-sharing between the military aristocracy and the royalty; there was a well-developed sense of law, of individualism, and, above all, of historical truth, which favourably distinguishes the Hittite documents from those of ancient Egypt and Mesopotamia;[36] also their occasionally used hieroglyphic writing seems to have been the invention of their next of kin – the Luvites. In many other respects the Hittites were disciples of the aborigines, most of whose religious beliefs they took over, and of the Sumero–Akkadians, from whom they learnt the cuneiform script (which then became their standard script), and many other artefacts.[37]

In Mesopotamia proper subsequent notable developments were due not so much to the advance of the productive forces as to the interplay of the three main nations within the Cuneiscript civilization: the Babylonians in the south, the Assyrians in the north, and the Elamites, emancipated from the Akkadian influences, to the east.

From about 1500 to 600, Mesopotamia was the battleground for the conflicting aspirations of the three above-mentioned nations; occasionally (for one or two centuries) the scene was varied by the addition of other competitors: the Hurrian state of Mitanni (*c.* 1500–1350), the so-called New Hittite Empire (*c.* 1380–1250), and the newly developed state of Urartu (*c.* 830–730).[38]

Beneath this interplay of what one might term the official nations, with their diplomatic games, dynastic marriages, intrigues and wars, yet another process of ethnic transformation was taking place. From about the eleventh century a mighty new wave of Semitic immigrants – Aramaeans and Chaldaeans – began to settle: the former in Assyria, the latter in what had previously been Sumer and Akkad, but had been known from the time of the Amorites as Babylonia. At the start both were resented as intruders, and the Assyrians made vigorous attempts to bar further infiltration by them. Yet later, when Assyria was in the middle of her empire-building and her human resources were over-extended, the Assyrian rulers embarked on forcible transfers of population from the conquered countries. Thus further Aramaean tribes were settled in Assyria.

The three-cornered contest amongst the main Mesopotamian nations, in which the Assyrians won the upper hand, proved to be fatal for the Cuneiscript civilization. Babylonia, though militarily the weakest, was to a considerable extent protected by her prestige as the cradle of the common civilization. This however was more respected by the Assyrians than by the Elamites, whose imperialistic aspirations were hampered by internal dissensions rather than by concern for cultural affinities.

Whilst the Assyrian policy towards Babylonia vacillated between a soft and hard approach, many Babylonians looked to Assyria for protection against the Chaldaean encroachment. The strongholds of the pro-Assyrian party in Babylonia were the cities, which from the

Kassite period re-established a good deal of their autonomy, and Assyrian rulers were ready to respect this autonomy as a *quid pro quo* for their collaboration. On the other hand, the priesthood of the leading temples, and the immigrant Chaldaean tribes, were staunchly anti-Assyrian.

The Assyrian role within the Cuneiscript civilization can be characterized as an example of a chance lost through over-ambition. Situated in a border area of what constituted the heartland of that civilization, the Assyrians were destined to play the role of marchmen. Unlike the Babylonians they possessed fertile crop-plains in the rain-belt but like the Babylonians they lacked metal ores, large timber and horses. They demanded tribute in these commodities amongst the hill tribes along their border, and combined economic and political interests in repeatedly sending military expeditions to those turbulent areas from which they could have been menaced at any time. The Assyrian military virtues were their response to the challenge of their human environment. Many times overrun, they survived in a dependent position (especially under the Mitanni rule in the fifteenth century); their power elites apparently harboured a strong will for self-assertion which eventually brought them to strike back. And this they did with unprecedented determination and cruelty.

Towards the end of the eighth century BC, the Assyrians ruled the whole of Mesopotamia and Syria. Around the middle of the seventh century they extended their rule over Egypt. But towards the end of that century they collapsed in the war with the Iranian Medes supported by the Babylonians, whose alienation from the Assyrians became complete at that time. Soon after the final defeat, the Assyrian nation disappeared from the earth's surface.

The Assyrian rulers apparently over-extended the human and economic resources of their people. Unlike the Sumerians and the Akkadians, the Assyrians also lacked the ability to assimilate other people: the foreigners who settled in Assyria remained ethnically alien elements speaking their own tongue, generally one Aramaean dialect or another; when the Assyrian polity collapsed, the remnants of the Assyrians, reduced in numbers by constant military campaigns, dissolved amongst the Aramaean population which they themselves had helped to make more numerous in their own country.[39] Furthermore, the previous Assyrian campaigns against Elam and Urartu were counter-productive; they helped the Medes and related tribes to establish their supremacy in Iran and, eventually, to become the rulers of Mesopotamia itself.

The Neo-Babylonian empire which emerged after the fall of Assyria did not enjoy its triumph for long. After less than a century, it was incorporated into the Persian empire, which thus became the master of all the territory where the multi-ethnic Cuneiscript civilization had flourished.

Under the new masters the Cuneiscript culture still had a lot to offer. The Persians learnt its script via the Elamites and adopted some of its forms of government. The Babylonians' scientific knowledge, especially mathematical and astronomical, was unrivalled and was much appreciated by the new rulers, but as a going concern the ancient civilization of Mesopotamia was on the wane and its once irresistible spell had gone.

Under the corrosive impact of the Hellenic culture, which especially gathered momentum after the Macedonians defeated the Persians and conquered Babylon (331), the Cuneiscript civilization was virtually dissolved by the beginning of the Christian era.

2.9 THE SOCIAL STRUCTURE OF ANCIENT MESOPOTAMIA AND EGYPT

Having reviewed the ups and downs, the rhythm of integration and disintegration of the two most ancient civilizations, let us stop for a while to ponder the nature of their respective social structures.

A Marxist would readily categorize them either as slave-holding or as oriental despotic formations. The former position would be taken by those who accept the Soviet historians' verdict in this matter, the latter by those who tend to consult Marx himself rather than the scholars following the line decreed by Stalin.

Yet it will be clear from what has already been said that either of these conclusions would be preposterous. There were not all that many slaves in those societies, and despotism appeared only occasionally or did not affect all the subjects of the realm. In fact, it is extremely difficult to ascertain the real situation of the working people and the nature of ownership and often also of government.

If we examine the key elements of the power structure we find that social power was highly concentrated at the top and extensive in coverage only during particular periods: in Egypt in the age of the pyramids (i.e. under the Third and Fourth dynasty), in

Mesopotamia during the reign of Naram Sin of the Sargonid dynasty, and then during the Third dynasty of Ur.

In Egypt, as in Mesopotamia, power was legitimized by tradition which was in essence religious; yet the power elites were not uniform throughout: in Egypt the bureaucracy, the machiocracy and the hierocracy all enjoyed a prestigious status and occasionally vied with each other for the leading position. In Mesopotamia the aristocracy, either military or administrative, the priesthood, and in the earliest period, the council of elders and the assembly of warriors, all exercised some sort of power.

Even greater difficulties confront us when we come to assess the status of the working population, the type of ownership, and the means by which economic resources were allocated. Let us start this time with Mesopotamia.

From the clay tablets in the Sumerian language it has been deduced that the population was in principle divided into four basic categories. The Sumerian terms for these can be roughly translated as nobles and priests; commoners; clients; and slaves. The clients were either dependents of the temple (i.e. of the priesthood), or of the nobility.[40] The type of ownership is more difficult to categorize. It seems that temples, like nobility and commoners enjoyed some kind of private property, but neither the clients nor the slaves were completely without property rights. The free market seems to have had a wide scope, but the final allocation of economic resources was to a considerable extent influenced by the power relaltionships within the community (city state) as a whole.

The complaints which for instance Urukagina, the usurper king of Lagash (*c.* 24th century), claimed to have dealt with concerned the appropriation of the best lands and cattle by the temple officials, and the extortion of exorbitant tax in kind, work (corvée) and fees (for funerals and divorce) from the commoners and clients; these were clearly cases of extra-economic compulsion.

The quantitative proportions of the individual social strata and types of ownership can not be assessed, though some partial guesses have occasionally been made. As had already been mentioned, I.M. Dyakonov estimated that under the Third dynasty of Ur, 60 per cent of the cultivated land was owned by the temple. One conclusion however can be drawn with a reasonable degree of certainty, namely that the slaves were not the main category of the labouring population. The Soviet commentators on the first volume of the *History of Mankind*, published under the auspices of UNESCO, made a cautious and carefully balanced statement on this point, in which they said:

the early 'urban civilization' . . . is characterized by the growth of private property, by the division of society into classes, by the creation of the state which enables a part of the population to live on the produce of the other part, i.e. it is characterized by the exploitation of one individual by another. The exploiters tend to make the most of the labour of the exploited; and thus the complete proprietorship of the slave-holder over the workman who is turned into a slave becomes now the optimal form of exploitation enabling the owner to acquire not only all the surplus product of the slave but also part of the product necessary to the latter's maintenance. Other types of exploitation exist side by side with slave-owning. We usually term this stage of history 'slave-holding society'. A great part or even the majority of the population remain in this period personally free and retain their organization in the form of different, more or less self-ruling, communities – rural or urban.[41]

The Soviet scholars seem to know best that the Marxian categories are, to say the least, debatable.

Hammurabi's Code does not reveal much more on the structure of Cuneiscript societies than could be deduced from the more ancient Sumerian codes. The Code itself, like some other documents of the epoch, points to three categories: *awelu*, *mushkenu* and *wardu*, usually translated as free men, clients (or plebeians or villeins) and slaves. The second category of *mushkenu* seems to have constituted the bulk of the population; the slaves, as in most ancient civilizations, were recruited either from prisoners of war and their descendents or from impoverished free men who sold themselves or their children to their creditors. Occasionally enslavement was imposed as a punishment.

Later documents from post-Amorite Babylonia and above all from Assyria reveal a picture which reminds us somewhat of the West European Middle Ages. There are the unruly and ambitious aristocracy, the privileged autonomous cities, royal boroughs so to speak, ruled by a kind of patriciate, the craftsmen and shopkeepers organized in guilds, and the peasants bound to their respective village communes. Some allotments of land were also granted in exchange for military service.

Although the king was undisputed sovereign in political and also in priestly matters (he was king and high priest in one person), his position was not entirely that of a despot. Even when imperial expansion was at its height, in the second half of the eighth century the Assyrian kings had to cope with strong elements of a pluralistic constellation of power. Tiglath-Pileser III (744–727) succeeded only in curbing and not in suppressing the independent power of the nobility and of the priesthood. His successor Shalmaneser V (727–722) decided to go further and abolish the immunities granted to the nobility and to privileged cities (the immunities mainly concerned taxes and compulsory work), but was overthrown by a palace *coup d'état*. Sharrukin (Sargon) II wanted to have a free hand for his military ventures and therefore not only restored the privileges of the upper estates, but also granted privileges to some other Babylonian cities[42] which he wanted to lure away from their support for the Chaldaean pretender to the Babylonian throne. As the privileges meant less taxation, less compulsory work, and in the case of the cities, fewer soldiers, somebody else had to compensate for the loss to the treasury. As always in this kind of situation, the peasant had to pay the bill in the form of increased prestations of all sorts.[43] To alleviate that burden and also to make good their losses of their own people arising from the continual military campaigns, the Assyrian kings organized large-scale transfers of population from the conquered lands to Assyria. By law, i.e. the will of the king, the transferees became Assyrians, obliged to perform all the duties of an Assyrian including military service.

Thus instead of examples of slave-holding formations or oriental despotic formations within the Cuneiscript civilization, we come across various elements of social structure and power constellation which we shall meet time and again on our journey along the paths of civilization. In Mesopotamia we encounter the city states with their dual leadership, one part representing what may be roughly described as the military power, and the other the priestly power, but both enjoying a commanding position in the economy as well; and the kingdoms, where kings had to cope with the recalcitrant aristocracy, the ambitious priesthood, and sometimes even with the staunch patriciate in the autonomous cities. Within the aristocracy itself we meet the *noblesse d'epée* and the *noblesse de robe*; within the cities, the patriciate and the guilds; in the countryside, the village communes and elements of bondage; and everywhere, slaves, and above all people with an intermediate status which can scarcely be adequately defined but for which the Roman term 'client' appears to be acceptable. If we add the mosaic of the types of property, extending from the property of the court and of the temple, through the property owned by the communes and families, to individual private property, which to some extent could also be enjoyed by the slaves, we discover that the task of describing the social formation of these areas in familiar terms is virtually impossible.

Nor in the case of Pharaonic Egypt do we get a more clear-cut picture of the social structure. The Pharaoh was the supreme owner of all lands. Other people could enjoy ownership, or rather possession rights, only as the result of a gift, which, in theory at least, was always revocable. The actual situation changed with time and circumstances. The most frequent beneficiaries were the temples (on behalf of their gods), and servants of the gods, whether nobles or commoners. Anybody could make large endowments to the funerary cults.

The working population was, as a rule, free, but the peasant did not have a great deal of scope to utilize this freedom. The main – albeit narrow – channel of upward social mobility was military service (especially from the era of the Middle Kingdom); but under exceptionally favourable circumstances education too opened the door to the prestigious profession of the scribe. The craftsmen and skilled workers seem to have been in a better position than the peasants. There are even references to workers' associations with some kind of self-rule.[44] However, the field workers employed on the royal, temple, or other large estates were virtually bondsmen. Slaves worked in different capacities, but their proportion seems to have grown up to the time of the New Kingdom. A census from that epoch distinguished 'soldiers, priests, king's servants and all the craftsmen'.[45] The category of the king's servants apparently was a residual item; but to the total, nobility at the top and slaves at the bottom should be added.

In Section 2.6 we mentioned the proliferation and differentiation of the power elites from the time of the Middle Kingdom; the main pillars of the Pharaoh's power then were the scribes, the soldiers and the priests. We also mentioned those periods when the centralized power gave way to local rulers, a kind of hereditary, quasi-feudal, aristocracy.

An imaginative, but unfortunately not adequately documented, attempt to characterize the changes in what may be called the social formation of ancient Egypt was undertaken by Jacques Pirenne. In his opinion, ancient Egypt experienced three cycles of legal relationships and social institutions. Periods marked by individualism, private ownership, contractual freedom, more equal rights for women and comparatively small differences of legal status among the population, alternated in Pirenne's view with periods of feudal or tribal collectivism of the patriarchal type, with limited contractual freedom, limited rights for women, ownership based on the tenure of public office, and peasants as bondsmen under the feudal hierarchy of landlords.[46]

In view of the large gaps in his documentation, Pirenne's theory can be taken merely as a speculative proposition to the effect that some elements of social structure display a cyclic rather than a unilinear development. We shall investigate this propostion when discussing other civilizations in this study.

As far as the two most ancient civilizations are concerned, only the changing prevalence of integrative or disintegrative tendencies can be safely deduced from the historiographical and archaeological material. Although the rhythm of this alteration is not quite regular, its individual phases, i.e. the periods during which one of the two tendencies prevailed, can be measured in terms of a number of centuries.

3 The Contrasts of Syria: Peoples of the Script and People of the Book

3.1 FROM SHEBA TO CARTHAGE: THE WEST SEMITIC CIVILIZATION

3.1.1 The Phoenician Venture

The shortest distance between the Nile and the Euphrates is about 600 miles. It is inconceivable that the space in between (today occupied by the states of Syria, Lebanon, Jordan and Israel) could have remained uninfluenced by the civilizations which emerged in Egypt and Mesopotamia. As the evidence discovered so far shows, the Mesopotamian influences appeared earlier and also proved to be the stronger. Yet in the second millennium BC the impact of the Pharaonic Egypt gathered momentum, and a third foreign culture, that of Crete and the Aegean, reached the Syro-Palestinian shore.

Thus the coastal strip between what is now Turkish Iskanderun at one end and Rafah on the Israeli–Egyptian border at the other, became, together with its hinterland, a mixing zone of civilizations, the first known case of that sort of historical development. Through the combination of cultural cross-breeding and native genius, the peoples of the area developed a cultural life of unusual creativity.

But amongst all the various ethnic groups of the Canaanites and other Semites such as Amorites and Aramaeans, and other nations such as the Hyksos, the Hurrians, the Hittites and the Philistines, who lived in that area for greater or lesser periods of time,[1] there were in particular two nations which made a special contribution to the further development of civilzation as a species; the Phoenician branch of the Canaanites on the one hand, and the Jews or Hebrews on the other. To epitomize briefly the character of their respective achievements we may say that the Phoenicians invented the phonetic script and the Jews the sacred book; and we have to add that the main dimension of their success was, respectively, geographical space in the case of the Phoenicians and historical time in the case of the Jews.

Phoenician phonetic writing, the culmination of a development whose early beginnings can be variously traced in the Sinai Peninsula, in Byblos and in Ugarit, became the model for the many types of script used by nations in almost all parts of the old world, from the South of Spain to the Gobi Desert.

The Phoenicians themselves, never united in one polity let alone empire, spread their settlements to most of the shores of the Western Mediterranean, and were the first to undertake wide-ranging littoral navigation along the coasts of Africa. Commerce, rather than military ventures, was the main means of their expansion. In that respect their successes were paralleled by those of their ethnic cousins in the Syrian hinterland (Aramaeans, etc.) and in south western Arabia (Minaeans, Sabaeans, etc.); these peoples opened up the caravan routes to the south and east, and from their Yemenite strongholds the Sabaean ships traded with countries around the Indian Ocean.

In wealth and geographical impact the Hebrews were the poor relations of the Phoenicians. Their advance was not external. They focused on the internal life of their community, which they tried to keep within the commandments of their exclusive God, aloof from foreign influences. As their political aspirations failed and the voice of their prophets became muted, they embodied their cultural endeavour, the gist of their *raison d'être*, in a Book and in the observation of a ritual. Together, these enabled them, despite being expelled from their homelands, dispersed all over the world and forced everywhere to live as a minority, to survive until the present. Their Holy Writ not only became a model for the Holy Writs of the worldwide monotheistic religions of the Christians and the Muslims, but was also to a large extent incorporated into them.

Leaving aside the question of whether or to what extent the Phoenicians and the Jews were prompted to their outstanding achievements by foreign challenges, we shall focus our attention on the specific development of the two civilizations themselves.

Like the Cuneiscript civilization at its Sumerian stage, the Phoenician civilization was also split into a host of city states; but unlike the case of Mesopotamia, there was no real imperial period in Phoenician history. Neither Tyre, the most powerful of the city states in Phoenicia proper, nor Tyre's daughter, Carthage, the dominant city on the African shore and in the Western Mediterranean, developed their hegemony into any form of unified polity. Although the Carthaginian hegemony over the Phoenician settlements in the Western Mediterranean in some ways resembled an empire, in fact the role of the city of Carthage was merely that of a leader and protector of the other Phoenician city states which enjoyed an extensive autonomy. In her own territory Carthage was largely in the position of a tenant; she continued paying rent to the native chieftains from whom she had acquired the land even after she was powerful enough to repudiate any such obligation. Apparently there was some important give-and-take in that arrangement: to keep her position as protector of the other Phoenician settlements, Carthage needed more soldiers than her own people could supply, and these were hired as mercenaries from the native African population. The only area where the Carthaginians enjoyed full sovereignty was in their possessions in southern Spain, which they acquired after their first war with Rome, as a result of which they lost the hegemony over the Phoenician settlements in Sardinia and Sicily.

If Carthage – confronted with the expansion of the Greek colonies and later with the growing power of Rome – could not establish a more commanding position, her mother city Tyre, for a long time a leading city state in Phoenicia proper, was even less able to do so. This country fell under the hegemony of a succession of large continental powers – Egypt, Assyria, Persia and eventually Macedonia. When the Hellenistic state of the Seleucids established itself as heir to the Persian empire, Phoenician cities had already succumbed to the spell of Hellenization. In contrast to the Phoenician mother country, Carthage was not absorbed, but destroyed by Rome; evidently she was too powerful to be dealt with in any other way.

There was yet another point in which the Phoenician civilization resembled Sumerian Mesopotamia, namely the pluralistic constellation of power in the city states themselves. Although the patchy documentary evidence of the earliest period (around 1000 BC) points to some kind of kingship, this institution did not develop into rule by great kings or Pharaohs as was the case in Mesopotamia and Egypt. The development in Phoenician cities more closely paralleled that of the Graeco-Roman civilization, where the kings gave way to magistrates elected from what may be described as a patriciate, i.e. a combination of a timocratic and an aristocratic oligarchy. Furthermore the consultative assemblies of elders or possibly men-at-arms, seem to have become more properly institutionalized than in Sumeria.

Deficient though it is, the best information on the organization of the Phoenician city state is that relating to Carthage. According to Aristotle, there were two elected chief magistrates (*suffetes*), analogous to the Roman consuls, a senate of 300 members, and the general assembly of the whole free male population. Apart from that there was a judiciary body of 104 members (naturally composed of the patriciate), whose task was to protect the interests of the community (as understood by its wealthy strata) against the encroachments of powerful individuals. Military commanders, if successful, were likely to acquire immense riches and thus influence and possibly manipulate the theoretically pluralistic institutions. Both their wealth and their profession could be inherited, and this in fact placed some families in the continuous possession of what was deemed to be excessive power. What precisely the power of the *suffetes* was and for how long they were elected, is not known. But it seems that the period of their magistracy was limited to one or two years, but with a possibility of reinstatement; they 'neither could declare wars, nor control the state treasury, nor lay down regulations for moral conduct'.[2]

Unlike their Sumerian counterparts, the Phoenician city states remained oligarchic republics until their destruction or incorporation into Hellenistic empires. Another contrast can be seen in the more free market orientation and the greater reliance on slave labour of the Phoenician world. It can perhaps be suggested that in Tyre and Carthage the slaves became the main factor of production. The social system of these states, together with some of the Greek communities and the later Roman republic and empire, constitute the only truly slave-holding formations in the Ancient world.

And what about Phoenician culture in general and religion in particular? It seems that their commercial genius and pragmatic mentality did not particularly favour the development of the arts. Although Sumero-Akkadian, Egyptian and even Minoan influences can be felt in the Phoenician motherland, the response to them was rather poor. What has been preserved both of their visual art and of their literature corroborates this value-judgement. One cannot avoid the impression that the Phoenicians appreciated their own perfected script more as a means of practical, commercial and administrative communication than as a way to convey ideas.

Our knowledge of the Phoenician religion has come down to us primarily through their Judaic adversaries rather than through less prejudiced sources. However, the Old Testament provides telling testimony of how such a primitive and uncouth religion as that of the Phoenician Baals and Els attracted the ancient Hebrews. Their prophets had to wage a constant war against the foreign gods whose worship was repugnant to them. Sacred prostitution, and the habit of providing the gods with food and drink and human sacrifices, seem to have been the main causes of resentment on top of the main issue: the challenge to the one, exclusive God of Israel, posed by the many male and female deities of their neighbours.

But even in the Phoenician pantheon one god emerged in a supreme position. As in Cuneiscript Mesopotamia it was the god of the most powerful city – i.e. Tyre in the mother country, and Carthage amongst the colonies. As Carthage had been founded as Tyre's colony, the same deity – Melquart – became the chief god throughout the Phoenician civilization. The religious link was apparently much stronger than the political one: Carthage and other colonies of Tyre for many years sent annual homage and tithes to Melquart's shrine at Tyre.[3] However when the power of Tyre declined, it was Eshmun the god of Sidon, who gained pre-eminence in Carthage.

On the whole, however, all the Phoenician deities had, like their Sumerian counterparts, a double role: they were patrons of their cities and, at the same time, had a functional portfolio, so to speak, within the pantheon. Only the long-standing practice of human sacrifice (especially of children from prominent families), intended to avert the wrath of the gods, gives the Phoenician civilization a particular twist.

It remains an unresolved question whether the Phoenicians had an integrated priestly cosmogony of the type that the Babylonians had. There are some indications that they might have. According to the Hellenistic and early Christian authors, a certain Sanchuniathon, priest of Berytus, wrote a comprehensive work on the creation of the world, on the gods and their characters, on their changing positions in the divine hierarchy, and on their inventive activities to the benefit of mankind.[4] However this Phoenician story did not really take hold. It remained to their Jewish cousins to write a story whose impact on the spiritual development went far beyond the confines of its original conception.

3.1.2 The Broader Context

According to the ancient chronicles the Phoenician drive to the West started in the twelfth century. Although archaeological evidence dating from such an early period is scant, the general setting seems to corroborate the dating.

Whether the Phoenician maritime expansion started as a response to the post-Minoan *Völkerwanderung* which *inter alia* saw the sack of Troy and Ugarit and brought the Philistines to the shores of Syria, as Arnold Toynbee suggests,[5] or whether the Phoenician decision to take to the sea was merely a substitution of the sea for the desert, the natural environment of their ancestors, as Olmstead sees it,[6] one thing seems to be established beyond much doubt: namely that a power vacuum which emerged in the north-eastern Mediterranean following the destruction of the Minoan state in Crete, based on Knossos, opened the Mediterranean for all kinds of venture.

Be that as it may, we can observe the first manifestation of a seesaw movement which was to characterize the pattern of political and cultural development in the Mediterranean to our day. Its first impulse came from Europe. Though Egypt repulsed the invasion, the Asian shores of the eastern Mediterranean were strongly affected.

This attack was almost immediately followed by the Phoenician counterstroke: they moved to Cyprus, to the Aegean and further to north Africa (Utica) and southern Spain (Gades). Everywhere they founded merchant colonies, but only in the western Mediterranean were they able to establish some sort of political domination.

By the mid-eighth century Europe was on the march again. The Greeks began their overseas expansion and soon after clashed in the western Mediterranean with the Phoenicians. After a period of shifting alliances amongst individual city states on both sides of the main ethnic divide, the Greek position was taken over by the Romans.

In this context we may also ask the question why in the great contest in the Mediterranean the Phoenicians eventually succumbed to the Greeks in the East and to the Romans in the West. Without pretending to give a full answer we can point to just two circumstances: the Phoenicians commanded fewer human resources than their adversaries and on top of that they lacked an adequate rural, peasant, element in their population, an element which, with only a few notable exceptions, has been at the basis of any military strength up to the present day. This was especially conspicuous in the western, Punic, part of their orbit, where the Phoenicians had to rely on the co-operation of African or Hispanic peoples for the supply of soldiers and also to a large extent of civilian labour, both free men and slaves.

Phoenicia, though the most conspicuous, was, however, only one branch of the Semitic civilization which emerged in the area between the Cuneiscript and Pharaonic civilizations. There were two more related Semitic branches, one in the Syrian hinterland and the other on the territory of modern Yemen in south west Arabia.

The traditional bias of our historiography – the preoccupation with what is directly related to our development – leads to the neglect of civilizational development in the outlying areas. To redress this lopsided view, we have to say a few words about the other two members of the West Semitic 'pagan' triplet.

From about the middle of the second millennium BC the Syrian hinterland was settled by the Aramaeans, a Semitic people closely related to the Canaanites. From them the Aramaeans learned the phonetic script and passed it on to other Levantine nations. Being uninterested in empire building, but also being a tough people, they succeeded in sustaining their city states and principalities (foremost among them Damascus) in comparative freedom under the various intermittent hegemonies of greater powers. They not only populated the vast stretches of land between Phoenicia and Mesopotamia but also absorbed smaller ethnic groups in that area. In the Persian empire, educated Aramaeans became the main source of recruitment for the civil service. The Aramaean language became, alongside the Persian and the Elamite, the third official tongue of the Persian empire, and the Aramaean script became a model for the Persian phonetic alphabet, after the Persians decided to abandon the Cuneiscript learnt from the Elamites. For many centuries to come, the Aramaean language was to play the role of the Levantine lingua franca. Even the Jews who stayed in their homelands substituted Aramaean for their Hebrew in the post-exilic era. A great language without an empire is surely a remarkable cultural achievement.

The southern branch of the West Semitic civilization developed more along the same kind of lines as Phoenicia. At the time when the Phoenicians were starting to colonize west Africa and southern Spain, in the south west corner of Arabia (what is now Yemen) there emerged several polities, which gradually developed into several kingdoms: the Minaean, the Sabaean (the biblical Sheba), the Kataban and the Hadramaut.[7] Their peoples believed in and worshipped similar gods and used a similar type of script as the Canaanites, Phoencians and Aramaeans did. Large-scale irrigation schemes and cisterns provided water for a thriving agriculture, and the availability of long-distance caravan and sea transport facilitated a widely-ramified international trade not only with Syria, Mesopotamia and Egypt but also with India and the eastern coast of Africa. The Minaean and Sabaean harbours provided a landing stage between the Indian Ocean and the Mediterranean. In contrast to other parts of the Arabian peninsula this was particularly prosperous and cultivated area; no wonder that the Romans called it *Arabia Felix*.

To judge by the literary documents discovered so far, the literate strata were primarily concerned with the gods and with business – rather as in the case of Phoenicia. In the organization of their states, there was a strong tribal element with definite religious overtones. In the history of the Minaean and Sabaean kingdoms, there seems to have been a shift from priestly rule (hierocracy) to a rule by the landed and/or military aristocracy. From about the beginning of the Christian era to the fourth century AD Sheba dominated the whole area; but then she became increasingly tossed about by internal dissensions between those who embraced Christianity and those who preferred to convert to Judaism. This gave the foreign powers the opportunity to interfere: the Ethopians on behalf of the Christians (after several earlier attacks they occupied what was then the Himyarite kingdom of Yemen in 525 AD), and the Persians in support of Judaic interests (they took Yemen in 575). Meanwhile the commercial activity was dying out and the collapse of the main dyke devastated much of the irrigated land; a large number of the inhabitants were forced to emigrate.[8] The spirit of the civilization disappeared and with it *Arabia Felix*. Nevertheless, its prosperous millennium or so has to be recorded with appreciation, but also as a memento that regress in development may assume abysmal proportions.

To sum up and complete the highlights of this story: apart from the phonetic script which the Canaanites started and which their offshoot, the Phoenicians, perfected, the ancient West Semitic civilization of Canaan, Phoenicia, Syria, north Africa and 'Arabia Felix' contributed several technical innovations to the general cultural fund of mankind: the domestication of the camel,[9] the lining of storage cisterns with impermeable lime-plaster, and improvements in navigation (the trireme) can be regarded as the most significant. The phonetic script and the improvements in transport facilitated various kinds of conveyance; people, commodities, information and ideas could be more easily transferred over a long distance. Through the efforts of these Semitic peoples human communication took a major step forward.

3.2 SECLUSION OF THE JEWS; FROM THE JUDGES TO THE PROPHETS

It is difficult to coin a single, all-embracing, name to identify the spiritual profile of the extended and ramified Western Semitic civilization described in the previous Section. It perhaps makes more sense to characterize this civilization by pointing to its main achievements.

It was an open civilization striving for exchange and communication. In doing so it was particularly successful in overcoming the natural constraints of seas and deserts; it eased written communication by devising a simplified and more flexible script. Needless to say, the openness of this civilization encouraged the accommodation of foreign influences. Syncretism was accepted as something natural and was not considered a sin. This civilization could assume many shades and acculture various foreign elements.

Amidst this, so to speak, extrovert civilization, right in the middle of its three main branches, emerged a racially related but spiritually quite distinct civilization – introvert in nature, and seeking to preserve its religious identity at any cost. Here we are not at a loss as to which epithet to use: 'Judaic' is the obvious choice.

But can we call it a civilization? Did the Hebrews really succeed in creating a community which could be compared with the other societies described, in the context of this study, as civilizations?

Actually the Judaic case is unique in history. Understandably, the Jews wanted to have a community of their own, with their specific and exclusive God and his commandments, a God with whom they believed they lived in a sort of covenant. But they were not particularly successful in their efforts to integrate the population of a certain area which they saw as their fatherland, and which they, with reference to their covenant with their God, considered to be their Promised Land.

In my understanding of Jewish history as a drive for a particular civilization I come close to the position taken by Mordecai Kaplan in his *Judaism as a Civilisation*. But I have to stress a significant qualification. Writing in a multi-ethnic, multi-religious but in principle monolingual United States of America in the first third of the twentieth century, Kaplan stresses different constituent elements of civilization from those which in my opinion are more adequate to the world at large. For Kaplan it is a particular land and language, particular laws and folk customs, folk sanctions, and folk arts, and a particular social structure, which make a people into a civilization.[10] Surprisingly, Kaplan does not explicitly mention religion, but lets it in under the heading 'mores and law', i.e. as religion in its practice rather than in its principles.

With the possible exception of these two (mores and law) Kaplan's criteria need not necessarily constitute a civilization, but merely a nation. As has been shown in the previous Section, the Assyrians differed from the Sumerians on most of Kaplan's criteria, but nevertheless they can be rightly considered as belonging to one and the same civilization. History abounds with instances of that kind. We shall have ample opportunity to refer to them further in this book. In this context I only wish to emphasize that in my opinion it is not so much the land, language and mores, but rather a particular world-view and the ethical code based on it, which are the key factors in the content of a civilization. The acceptance of a world-view by a given people, and their conduct of their lives under the law framed according to that world-view, go to make up the sociologically relevant expression of this content. Kaplan seems to be hesitant with respect to the comparative importance of the content and of its form (mode of expression), but eventually he too has to say: 'it is chiefly through its content that a civilization comes to possess individual character.'[11]

The syncretic spirit of the Jews' neighbours was infectious. On top of that the Promised Land was situated at the crossroads of the military campaigns and imperial expansion of various, much larger and more powerful nations. Thus the struggle for identity and its preservation against heavy odds absorbed most of the energy of the Hebrew nation. And whilst with a few short-term exceptions, they failed to assert themselves fully on their own territory, they succeeded

– to an extent that went beyond mere compensation – in surviving after the destruction of their polity, when they were dispersed all over the world. In the diaspora, the Judaic community outlived all the other civilizations which were its contemporaries in the Levant and in Europe. What was in one way an abysmal failure provided the impetus for a tremendous success in the other direction.

Our standard knowledge of Jewish history is largely filtered through the prism of our acquaintance with the rise of Christianity. Although a lot has come down to us by this route, nevertheless there are important issues and developments which only the specialists in Jewish history bring to our attention.[12] In order to right the balance, we consider it expedient to give here a brief account of the main events and confrontations which mark the Jewish quest for separate identity and survival.

For our account it is not essential to know when the Jews or Israelites, or to put it in ethno-linguistic terms, the Hebrews, settled in the country to the west of the River Jordan and the Dead Sea. Of greater relevance is the historical moment when some of the Hebrews later left that or the nearby area and moved to Egypt, where they spent some time before returning to what they considered their Promised Land.

The Egyptian experience, of which the main hero was Joseph, and which was brought to an end by Moses, may explain why the sons of Israel embarked on a religious path which differed so greatly from that of the peoples of Canaan. If the timing suggested by Rowley[13] is correct, namely that the Jews came to Egypt around 1360 BC, then the Pharaoh whom Joseph served would be the religious reformer Akhenaten. Without attempting to answer the question whether the monotheistic conception which is so characteristic of Judaism originated in Akhenaten's (or perhaps his father's) mind or whether it was brought to Egypt with Joseph, we can take it for granted that there was some give and take and that the Egyptian experience contributed to the strengthening of the monotheistic bent in Judaism. The Egyptian influence can also be seen in some other texts of the Old Testament such as Proverbs, etc., but this may be a result of later Judaeo-Egyptian contacts.

Like the Holy Writs of other religions which set down the teaching of their founders, the five books of the Old Testament connected with the name of Moses (the Pentateuch) were written long after the period when the historical Moses lived, and therefore reflect the conditions of a different epoch. Nevertheless, there is no reason to doubt the gist of the story, namely that a strong leader with definite religious ideas led the Jews from their temporary abode in Egypt, and that when after a long and eventful wandering they eventually arrived in Canaan (it is widely accepted that this happened towards the end of the thirteenth century BC)[14] they had different religious views from those Hebrews who had not experienced that migration. Two versions of Genesis bear witness to this difference: one calling the God of Israel Yahwe and – within the Israelite community – uncompromisingly monotheistic, and the other using the term Elohim, which being a plural, admits to some hesitation on this issue.

Furthermore, the tendency towards polytheism amongst the Israelites is amply attested by other books of the Old Testament. The meaning of the whole history of the Israelites lies in the defensive struggle against these tendencies. Within one context of this struggle, however, the religious message developed and issues other than monotheism versus polytheism gave rise to variations. The original tribal ethics, according to which Yahwe required the merciless destruction of the enemies of his people together with their flocks, and punished those who did not obey this command,[15] gave way to more rational and in many instances also more gentle attitudes.[16]

For some time the main danger for the Jewish community came from the Philistines who settled on the shores of southern Syria, shortly after the Jews coming from Egypt settled in Canaan. The technical superiority of the Philistines, who kept the process of iron metallurgy secret, seemed to give them every chance of prevailing as the dominant nation. Yet the Jews, having been the underdogs for a century and a half, got to know the military craft of their adversaries and, sustained by their indomitable spirit, nurtured by their merciless tribal God Yahwe, they turned the tide and established their independent polity throughout the Promised Land. The phase of 'Judges', analogous to the Phoenician *suffetes*, passed into the phase of Kings, David and Solomon; Israel became for a while a sovereign polity – not, however, like the Phoenicians and also the Philistines, organized in several independent city states, but becoming one national kingdom with one temple as the centre of national worship. Yet an independent and, given the circumstances, adequately strong state was no safeguard against foreign cultural influences. Many, Solomon amongst them, took religious purity lightheartedly and indulged in cults other than that of Yahwe.

After Solomon's death, the unity of the Jewish kingdom broke down (*c*. 935 BC), and the Jews were divided into two monarchies, Israel and Judaea, neither of which was in a better position to withstand cultural influences from abroad. Divided, the Jews were also more exposed to political pressures.

In the first half of the ninth century the more populous and economically developed Israel, whose king was married to a Phoenician princess, was almost absorbed by the Phoenician civilization. In Judaea the situation was not much better. The danger of a loss of cultural identity was averted by military coups; they were instigated by the exhortations of prophets, excited fortune tellers and worshippers of Yahwe, such as Elija, Elisha and others, but performed by military commanders – in Israel by a certain Jehu (in 841) and in Judaea with the help of foreign mercenaries (in 836).

According to the 2nd Book of Kings, 10:30, Yahwe was most pleased with the massacres performed in order to uphold the monopoly enjoyed by his cult amongst the Jews. 'And the Lord said to Jehu, "Because you have done well in carrying out what is right in my eyes, and have done to the house of Ahab according to all that was in my heart, your sons of the fourth generation shall sit on the throne of Israel."'[17]

Thus by a resolute and merciless military action, the supporters of Yahwe succeeded in stemming the absorption of both the Jewish kingdoms within the surrounding West Semitic civilization. This however did not mean the end of syncretic tendencies amongst the Jews. It was especially the veneration of images and statues that attracted the Jewish masses. Even Jehu, the purifier, relapsed into the sin of syncretism (2 Kings, 10: 31).

The middle of the eighth century brought a new issue to the attention of the prophets: economic progress and increased social differentiation. This was an opportunity for the prophets, who were the voice of the national conscience, to speak not only on behalf of the one and only God but also for the God of Justice and sometimes, even, for a God who required love from his flock.

Amos and Hosea were the main voices of this new tendency in Israel: 'Hate evil, and love good, and establish justice in the gate' demands Amos (5: 15), and Hosea puts the idea still more explicitly: 'For I desire steadfast love and not sacrifice, the knowledge of God, rather than burnt offerings' (Hosea, 6: 6). And in Judaea, Isaiah and Micah struck a similar note: 'Woe to those who call evil good and good evil. . . who acquit the guilty for a bribe, and deprive the innocent of his right,' exlaimed Isaiah (5: 20 and 23), seconded by Micah: 'He has showed you, O man, what is good; and what does the Lord require of you: but to do justice, and to love kindness, and to walk humbly with your God' (Micah, 6: 8)

Unfortunately this gentler tendency which, by the way, echoes some points already made by the Egyptian and even the Akkadian sages, did not become the main stream in the development of Judaic thought. The spiritual upsurge initiated by the four great prophet-moralists was marred by a combination of internal and external forces: common human weakness and a new wave of Assyrian invasions, which was facilitated by dissensions and jealousies between the two Jewish kingdoms. Israel was conquered and ceased to exist as an independent kingdom; about 7 per cent of the population was deported and settled in north western Iran, then inhabited by the Medes.[18] As Yahwe was deemed to have failed to protect his people, many turned to Assyrian gods. Only after the decline of Assyrian power could an attempt at religious purification be got under way again.

But, apparently, the well-tried forcible method was no longer deemed to be adequate to the task. The commandments of Yahwe had to be fixed in writing and the Holy Book had to be legitimized by recourse to the tradition. This duly happened when in 621 BC the high priest Hilkiah found in the Jerusalem Temple a text of the Law (supposedly Deuteronomy) which the prophetess Huldah declared to be the genuine text of the Covenant. King Josiah proclaimed it as binding and carried out its precepts: 'And Josiah took away all the abominations from all the territory that belonged to the people of Israel, and made all who were in Israel serve the Lord their God' (2 Chronicles 34: 33).

The worship of the Lord was to be centralized in the Jerusalem Temple so that the syncretic tendencies found widely at local shrines might be eliminated. But as Olmstead observed: 'By the new mode, (the peasant) could be religious only in Jerusalem and there only at the three yearly feasts . . . the intimate relation between official religion and the home life was broken . . . . the peasant became a 'pagan', one of the 'people of the land' as they were stigmatised by the officially 'Pious'. All opportunity for influence by the advanced people was lost.'[19] Only much later, at the time of the Maccabees, was this gap in religious integration filled by the institution of the synagogues, which took on the pastoral work among Jews living beyond the reach of the Temple.

Though the tightening of religious discipline and ritual found a favourable response amongst the prophets, the greatest of them at that time, Jeremiah, soon realized that greater ritual rigidity might endanger the genuine religious feelings reflected in people's consciences, kept alive with the help of the voices of the prophets. Against the strict, 'You shall not add to the word which I command you nor take from it' of Deuteronomy 4: 2, Jeremiah responds: 'How can you say "We are wise, and the law of the Lord is with us? But, behold, the false pen of the scribes had made it into a lie" (Jeremiah 8: 8). Thus to the contrast of the righteousness versus ritual a new contrast was added: the living prophecy against the written Book, ever developing prophecy against the fixed doctrine. We shall meet both these contrasts repeatedly on the paths of various religions, Western and Eastern.

Yet external events did not allow the Jews to work out these contrasts among themselves. A respite won during the death agony of the Assyrian empire did not last for long. The great power contest for the Syrian territories broke out between Egypt and Babylonia; in it the sympathies of the Jews were divided. The upper strata sided with the more sophisticated and less intrusive Pharaos, whereas the common folk were more at ease with Babylonia, where the Chaldaean population were closer to them both in language and in style of life. After the first conquest of Jerusalem in 597 BC, the Babylonian king Nabukadnezar II took some hostages from the pro-Egyptian strata but allowed Judaea to be ruled by the house of David under Babylonian hegemony. When however soon after that Judaea entered the anti-Babylonian coalition with some Syrian principalities, Nabukadnezar took Jerusalem for the second time, destroyed its walls and the Temple, and deported more of the elite to Babylonia; the third wave of deportees followed in 581, after an attempt to gain more autonomy for Judaea had failed.

Although the total number of deportees comprised 20–25 per cent of the whole Judaean population, it was this fraction – apparently the elite – which turned out to be decisive for the further development of the Judaic community.

3.3 FROM THE PROPHETS TO THE LAW; THE CONSTITUTION OF JUDAISM

The trauma of exile, even if its material and other conditions were favourable, brought to a head the old issue: what is the way to preserve our identity? The observance of rites and customs, or the path of gentle righteousness? In a mixed multi-cultural society symbols and behaviour matter more than thoughts and sentiments; thus in the Jewish case the choice was evidently for the visible, ostentatious forms of religious life. The easy conditions of assimilation which the ethnically related Chaldaean Babylonians offered, and for which many Jews also decided to opt, made a visible demarcation still more imperative.

Like the sojourn in Egypt, the Babylonian captivity made a deep impact on the further development of the Judaic religion. Although some time-honoured Sumerian motifs, especially the stories of Job and the Flood, may have been incorporated at that time into the Judaic scripts, and perhaps even some Zoroastrian ideas, such as the happy end of history with a Messiah, may have been picked up, the need to preserve a communal identity did not allow the Jews to indulge in anything more than the assimilation of some foreign ideas to their own world view and values.

At that time also the ethical aspects of the prophecy were carried a step further. Ezekiel, who may be considered the spiritual leader of the exiles, spoke up against the traditional idea of inherited responsibility: 'The son shall not suffer for the iniquity of the father, nor the father suffer for iniquity of the son; the righteousness of the righteous shall be upon himself, and the wickedness of the wicked shall be upon himself' (Ezekiel, 18: 20).

And later the Tritto-Isaiah (i.e. what according to biblical scholarship is the third layer in the canonized version of Isaiah) brought the religious message to the verge of becoming a personal and universal ethic:

> Thus says the Lord: heaven is my throne and the earth is my footstool; what is the house which you would build for me, and what is the place of my rest? All these things my hand has made, and so all these things are mine, says the Lord. But this is the man to whom I will look, he that is humble and contrite in spirit, and trembles at my word (Isaiah, 66: 1–2).

Yet these prophets did not represent the main thrust of what was to happen when Babylon fell and the Persian victor allowed the Jewish exiles return home. At that moment the enormous success of assimilation became apparent. The Jews returned rather reluctantly, in trickles, and their return was not always welcomed by the local population. In the predominantly rural conditions of Judaea there were few opportunities for urbanized people (merchants, craftsmen, teachers, etc.). Some goods were soon in short supply and inflation became rampant. On top of that the returnees had in many respects different views on religious matters.

Only with the help of the Persian authorities (and this is significant for that phase of Judaic development) was it possible to rebuild the Temple. Then, much later, probably in the fifth century BC under the auspices of the Jewish dignitaries, Ezra and Nehemiah, released by the Persian court, the orthodoxy based on the five books of Moses (the Pentateuch) was imposed by force on the recalcitrant nonexilic population of Judaea. The Jews became the people of the Book; the voice of the living prophets became silent. But the Book and its commandments were only for those who were born into the Judaic community. As a precaution against foreign influences Ezra ordered all mixed marriages to be dissolved.

Here an interesting paradox emerged with respect to Jewish identity. Whereas at home the Jews preserved until about the fifth century BC their own language and customs, but were inclined to the reception of foreign religious ideas and cults, abroad – in exile and in the diaspora – it was the other way round. There they tended to stick to the purity of their religion, while adopting the language and external habits of the host country. At home it was nationalism, abroad religion which prevailed. As however the orthodoxy required precedence to be given to religion, Jewish identity was, paradoxically, better safeguarded in the diaspora.

The principle of ethnic purity introduced by Ezra went so far that the inhabitants of Samaria, capital of the former kingdom of Israel, were not allowed, because of their non-Jewish origin, to take part in rebuilding the Temple of Jerusalem. As a result the Samaritans organized themselves into an autonomous religious community with its centre at Mount Garizim. Thus Ezra's ministry not only petrified the doctrine but also – against the noble vision of Zechariah (2: 11; 8: 20–3) – closed the door to proselytizing and brought about a schism in the Jewish community.

For the sake of fairness it also has to be stressed that the ethnocentric policy pursued by Ezra met with fierce opposition. Its echo penetrated even into the canonized version of the Old Testament. The stories, told in the books of Ruth and Esther, of mixed marriages receiving divine benediction, are examples of that mood.

Ezra apparently did not possess enough power to enforce his

measures and had to rely on the help of the Persian authorities:

> And I Artaxerxes the king make a decree to all the treasurers in
> the province Beyond the River: Whatever Ezra the priest, the
> scribe of the law of the God of heaven, requires of you, be it
> done with all diligence,'. . . and so on, until: 'Whoever will not
> obey the law of your God and the law of the king, let judgement
> be strictly executed upon him, whether for death or for banishment
> or for confiscation of his goods or for imprisonment (Ezra, 7:
> 21–6).

This paradoxical situation, in which orthodoxy had to be enforced
by a heterodox ruler, was not unique in history; political expediency
was its main reason. However in this particular case there might
have been something else behind it that can only be surmised. Persia
was in those days under the spell of Zoroastrian teaching. The
worshippers of Ahura Mazda might not have found the worship of
Yahwe as strange as other religious cults. In the Iranian milieu there
might also have been some memory of the Israelites deported there
by the Assyrians. On the other hand the Jews themselves seem not
to have been totally closed to Zoroastrian influences; at least there
was some affinity in their respective eschatologies and in the
expectation of a Messiah. Thus there might have been additional
grounds for an understanding between the Jews beleaguered by
their polytheistic Semitic rivals and the Persians with their tendency
to monotheism. But this explanation is only a conjecture. The
Persian king Cyrus and his successors might merely have been
'enlightened' monarchs more interested in their political aspirations
than in any ideological integration of their empire.

When however the Persian empire fell and from Alexander's
short-lived empire the Ptolemaic monarchy based on Egypt emerged
as the sovereign power over the Jews, the honeymoon between the
secular power and the Jewish theocracy began to run into difficulties.

With the Hellenic or Hellenized rulers came the Hellenic culture
and its corrosive influence. The Jewish community was not sufficiently
welded together to withstand the lure of an open and sophisticated
culture. The Jewish leadership lacked the magnanimity and imagination to prevent their more open-minded and curious fellow-believers
from looking elsewhere for inspiration.

The Hellenistic epoch, witnessing the foundation of many new
cities, and the related occurrence of migratory movements, gave
the Jews ample opportunity to emigrate under quite favourable

conditions; although they did not share the privileges of the Hellenic population, they enjoyed legal protection and enough freedom to pursue their businesses and also perform their particular cult.

The link with the homeland consisted in paying a tribute to the Temple at Jerusalem, and visiting it at least once during the individual's lifetime. Except for religious practices, the Jews became widely assimilated with their environment. Thus, towards the end of the third century BC it became necessary to translate the Judaic Holy Writ into the Greek language.

The linguistic assimilation eased the access to Greek literature and thus opened the door to the influence of Greek philosophy. The Jews in the diaspora were largely under the spell of philosophical abstraction, with the help of which they tried to interpret the simple biblical stories.

Ecclesiastes, one of the books which was incorporated comparatively late into the canonized version of the Judaic Writ, reflects with its melancholic prudence and resignation the mood of that epoch. One may wonder how a piece of work like this could have been included in the Judaic canon. Perhaps the last verse of the last chapter (Ecclesiastes, 12: 13), which might have been added *ex post*, a verse exhorting the reader to fear God and keep his commandments, 'for this is the whole duty of man', saved it in the eyes of those who selected the texts for canonization.

In 198, Palestine, which until then had been a part of the Ptolemaic kingdom, came under the rule of the Seleucids, who had meanwhile lost a good deal of their possessions in Iran and shifted their centre of gravity from Mesopotamia to Syria.

At the beginning there was no change in the position of the Jews. They were recognized as one of the four autonomous ethnic groups (foreshadowing the Ottoman *millets*). At their head was a high priest who took responsibility for collecting taxes and military levies, and, as a *quid pro quo*, the Seleucid monarchy respected and sanctioned the Jewish cult and its requirements. The import of ritually unclean animals to Jerusalem was forbidden, non-Jews were not allowed to enter the Temple, and the Sabbath had to be observed.

One Seleucid king, Antiochus IV (Epiphanes, 175–164), however, upset the balance. In his endeavour to speed up the synthesis between the Hellenic and the Levantine population and culture, a synthesis whose spontaneous pace seemed to him to be too slow, he decided to exert pressure on the Jews. Against the established customs Antiochus began to appoint the high priests from the ranks of the philhellenic Jewry, authorized the building of a Hellenic cultural and gymnastic centre in Jerusalem and increased the fiscal claims upon the Jewish community. When riots broke out, Antiochus sacked and plundered Jerusalem and built a fortress near the Temple for his army. In order to put a definite end to Jewish particularism, Antiochus decided to syncretize the cult of Yahwe with that of Zeus, both in Jerusalem and in Garizim.

Many Jews welcomed the move as a good opportunity to abolish Jewish particularism, which produced many inconveniences for them: 'Many even from Israel gladly adopted his religion; they sacrificed to idols and profaned the Sabbath' (1 Maccabees 1: 43). Yet this was an abomination of desolation to the faithful Jews. The attempt to endorce a religious and cultural amalgamation provoked a bitter insurrection led successively by three brothers – Judas, Jonathan and Simon of the Hasmonean family.

Although the Seleucid monarchy had at their disposal more human and material resources than the insurgents, the international situation, especially the interference of Rome, did not allow the Seleucids to benefit from their superiority. Thus it came about that, after twenty five years of devastating war, the Jewish theocracy, or to be more precise, hierocracy, regained its *de facto* independence.

It may be of interest to refer in this context to Rostovtzeff's views on the nature of the Maccabaean revolution. After acknowledging that Antiochus Epiphanes, policy had found approval among the higher classes of Judaea and that 'Judas and his followers were ready to die for the old tradition and for their monotheistic seclusion', Rostovtzeff says:

> In fact Judas represented the ideals and the dreams of the large masses of the natives, a class neglected by the government and exploited by the city bourgeoisie. The revolt of Judas was directed more against the ruling classes than against the central government. We may assume similar aspirations in other parts of the territories of Epiphanes, especially where the Greek settlers were few and the ancient tribal organisation was still alive and vigorous.[20]

This might have been true at the beginning of the Maccabaean wars but subsequent developments, to which we shall turn shortly, indicate that despite all the social overtones, it was the ethno-religious issue which determined the sides in this confrontation.

In essence, it was the continuation of what Mircea Eliade describes as the conflict between on the one hand religion which is cosmic in structure and as such abounds with 'joy in life', and on the other hand fidelity to one God, creator of the world and master of history.[21]

3.4 THE DILEMMA OF JUDAISM; WHAT KIND OF IDENTITY?

The emancipation from the Seleucid empire was the last opportunity for the Jews to establish their own Judaic state. For some time the Jewish community was ruled and administered by a high priest, an office which became hereditary in the Hasmonean family. Towards the end of the second century BC however, the high priest began to assume the royal title. As the Seleucid kingdom, hard pressed by the Iranian Arsacids from the East and by the Romans from the West, began to disintegrate, the Hasmoneans exploited the situation in order to enlarge their realm: Samaria, Galilee and Transjordania were annexed and the restrictive ethnic policy introduced by Ezra was abandoned. The population of the annexed territories was given the choice either of embracing Judaism, which was manifested by circumcision, or of emigrating. Thus the principle *Cuius regio, eius religio* appeared for the first time on the stage of history.

Yet as had happened many times in the past, the political successes of the Jewish kings were not matched by a sustained religious fervour on their part. This contrast led to a clash of forces under Alexander Jannaeus (103–76 BC), who – as his name indicates – openly favoured Hellenization; also he relied more on foreign mercenaries than on his own people. Thus the age-old dilemma between the observation of God's commandments and the pursuit of a vigorous secular policy again became an issue. The opposition to the king was exacerbated by increases in taxation and nurtured by the Pharisees, orthodox teachers who through the network of synagogues looked after general religious education. The ensuing armed resistance was suppressed with the utmost cruelty after a prolonged civil war. Thus the sovereign Jewish state became a disappointment to the orthodox believers.

Anyhow the successors of the hellenizing Alexander Jannaeus had little time to bring about the reconciliation of the dynasty with the Pharisees. Just as the reconstitution of the independent Jewish state was due to the international situation, so also was its end. The

Roman expansion to the Levant helped the Jews to get rid of their Seleucid masters, but when the time was ripe the Romans came and took everything that remained of the Seleucid empire (65–63). The Jewish state again became, as under the Seleucids, an autonomous hierocracy, but in 40 BC a non-Jew (Herod) was appointed king of Judaea. The Romans, being accustomed to cultural pluralism, were ready to respect other religions, but expected others to show a similarly conciliatory and outgoing attitude. Under these conditions, Hellenism supported by the Roman order and Roman military power continued to radiate its cultural influence amongst the Levantine nations.

As with any encounter of two civilizations, of which one is more prestigious, more open and consequently more attractive, whilst the other has to rely on restrictive measures to protect its identity, the continuous impact of the Graeco-Roman civilization on the Judaic community produced a wide spectrum of responses. The basic positions ranged from those who chose assimilation with the open and more prestigious culture, through those who wanted to work out an honourable accommodation with it, to those who favoured outright rejection of it. Within this range of responses, typical for such a situation, there were various schools of thought and types of policy.

The rejectors moved between two poles: the re-establishment of the Jewish kingdom (the Zealots) on the one hand, and the passive expectation of an apocalyptic end to the sinful world on the other. The accommodators (pragmatists) were represented by the two main schools, the Pharisees and the Sadducees, both expert in law and ritual; whilst, however, the Pharisees saw the minute observation of ritual as constituting the meaning of life, the Sadducees stuck strictly to the Holy Writ alone and considered the tradition as less binding. The more liberal or even lax attitude of the rather aristocratic Sadducees was more than matched by the Pharisees' populism, by their ability to link popular customs with the written law, which they were particularly assiduous in interpreting; their educational and pastoral work made the synagogues the main foci of Judaic ethno-religious integration.

Finally there were also those for whom neither ritual nor wealth and glory could bring satisfaction, and who preferred to withdraw into seclusion, living an exemplary life and observing not so much the letter as the spirit of the law. The representatives of this stream within Judaism were the Essenes. However greatly they might have been respected by their neighbours they seem to have constituted only a small fraction of the Jews.

The outcome of a civilizational encounter in which differentiation takes place along the above-mentioned lines, depends on the relative strengths of the communities involved. A weaker partner can hope at best for an honourable accommodation. In such circumstances, the radicals usually bring disaster down upon their cause. That is what happened in this case.

By their head-on collision with the Roman power, a collision which, after occasional local riots and mutual massacres, culminated in a series of extremely ferocious wars, the Zealots and their daggermen (*sicarii*) brought about the destruction of the remnants of the Jewish community in Judaea.[22] After the war in Judaea (66–70 AD), the insurrection in Cyrene, Egypt and Cyprus (115–17) and again in Judaea (132–5), the Jewish community in the fatherland was virtually annihilated. Judaea was renamed Syria Palaestina and the Jews were forbidden – under penalty of death – to enter Jerusalem,[23] which was converted into the Graeco-Roman city of Aelia Capitolina.

But before this happened, the Jews – Zealots, Pharisees and Sadducees alike – cast out from their midst their own prophet, who brought to a culmination a particular tradition with Judaism, a tradition marked by its gentle, ethical and more universalistic, or ecumenical, nature; the tradition of Amos and Hosea, of Isaiah and Micah, of Ezekiel, the Third Isaiah, and perhaps also of others whose names have not been preserved for us.

But Jesus of Nazareth, crucified as a false Messiah of the Jews, returned as a living Messiah of the Gentiles. Refused by the Jews, he passed the best of their religious genius on to the Greeks and the Romans, those very nations who by their mere existence posed a deadly threat to the Jews' ethno-religious identity. In turn the Greeks and the Romans, and then other nations in their orbit and even beyond it, based their own religious communities and civilizations on Jesus' message. Thus occurred one of the greatest paradoxes of history, a paradox to which we shall pay particular attention in another book.

Meanwhile another paradoxical development took place within the Judaic community itself. During the ferocious and devastating war between the Zealots and the Roman power in Judaea, in 70 AD, the Romans allowed the loyal Johanan ben Zakkai to organize a centre of Judaic teaching in Jamnia, in West Judaea.[24] There, after twenty years or so of assiduous work, a selection was made of those Judaic religious writings which were to be considered as authoritatively accepted and generally binding. Thus under the protection of those who destroyed the Jewish ethno-religious state, the scriptural basis of the Judaic religion was created, a basis well suited to be further elaborated in the diaspora. As Arnold Toynbee observed, the Pharisees who dissociated themselves from the Zealots when the latter took to arms, saved not only themselves but the Judaic religion into the bargain.[25]

The survival of the Jews in the diaspora is *mutatis mutandis* a continuation of their history before their annihilation in, and dispersal from, their homeland. Assimilation, accommodation or seclusion – these three alternatives confronted any Jewish family, any individual Jew, during the almost nineteen centuries following the destruction of their Temple in Jerusalem. Until the terrible holocaust of the mid-twentieth century, which was visited upon the Jews by a European nation to whose culture they had made a most sincere effort to accommodate or even assimilate themselves, and which by its consequences brought about a fourth option: the recreation of the state of Israel in Syria Palaestina. For the third time the Jews had the option of returning home.

In this context, one cannot ignore the words of Amos:

> For lo, I will command, and shake the house of Israel among all the nations as one shakes with a sieve, but no pebble shall fall upon the earth. All the sinners of my people shall die by the sword, who say, 'Evil shall not overtake or meet us.' In that day I will raise up the booth of David that is fallen and repair its breaches, and raise up its ruins, and rebuild it as in the days of old;. . . .I will restore the fortunes of my people Israel, and they shall rebuild the ruined cities and inhabit them; they shall plant vineyards and drink their wine, and they shall make gardens and eat their fruit. I will plant them upon their land, and they shall never again be plucked up out of the land which I have given them,' says the Lord your God (Amos 9: 9–11 and 14–15).

However nothing can be brought back in its original form. And perhaps even from the Jewish point of view this would not be desirable. The Jewish state has been re-established under substantially altered conditions. Jews in the diaspora, after centuries of harsh treatment by the Latin and Orthodox Christians, eventually accommodated themselves happily with the modern Euro-American civilization with its endeavour to guarantee human rights and personal liberties, and with its record of continuous technological and economic growth. The impact of this civilization on Jewish culture was more pervasive than any other. The new Israel has virtually been created as one more nation state, i.e. one more unit of its ethno-political structure, or geographical articulation. It is a triumph both for the Maccabees and for Antiochus Epiphanes.

The most powerful state of the modern civilization of the West, the United States of America, became the main sponsor and protector of the Israeli state. The parallel with the role of the Persian empire after the Babylonian captivity is striking. But there is yet another, more striking parallel. As at the beginning of the crystallization of the Judaic civilization, so also now the Jewish state is surrounded by several Semitic states whose peoples do not share the world view and values of that civilization with which the modern Israelis are associated. This time the neighbours are Arabic speakers and adhere to the Islamic religion, which at present is experiencing a remarkable revival. And as at the time of the unfortunate collision with Rome, so also now most Jews live in the diaspora, but in a much better position than then to give help to the new Israel.

In their own land, the Israelis live with their age-old divisions: the orthodox, sometimes even zealous, minority face-to-face with a majority more or less accommodated to the Euro-American, more or less secular, civilization. And on top of that, the geographical area has again resumed a position at a crossroads of civilizations, this time on a worldwide scale – the liberal civilization of the north west versus the communist civilization of the north east. Though not the only one, nor perhaps the most important, it is definitely a very sensitive crossroads.

Will the Jewish nation-state with its resuscitated Hebrew language be given a better chance than its Davidian or Hasmonean predecessors? Or will the worldwide confrontation, conditioned and accentuated by contradictory world views and values, put a definite end to the Jewish endeavour to assert their identity in its three separate but overlapping forms of collective existence: as a religion, as a nation and as a state?

4 The Great Iranian Ventures: The Peripeties of Ahura Mazdah

4.1 THE GENERAL SETTING

In the previous chapters we touched upon a polity which intervened in the development of all the civilizations discussed so far. During the sixth century BC, Mesopotamia, Syria and Egypt became provinces of the Persian empire, the first truly universal empire of the Levant. By this act the Cuneiscript, the Pharaonic and the West Semitic civilizations were pushed a bit further on the way to dissolution, whilst the Judaic civilization received a revitalizing stimulus. Yet not only the civilizations of the Levant were affected. On three sides the Persian power expanded beyond the geographic orbit of the Levant: into Central Asia, into the Indus Valley and into the Balkan peninsula. In the last instance the Persian expansion issued in a fatal confrontation with the Graeco-Roman civilization, a confrontation which for many centuries to come was to remain the key issue of the area: it eventually took the form of a Levanto-European contest, in which from the fourth to the seventh century AD each side stood for a particular religious orientation. What made the impact of both ancient and also medieval Persia on the outside world possible, an impact impressive not only in its longevity but also in its depth and variety?

As always with such plots of history it would be preposterous to look for one sole cause. But within the plural and also changing structure of causation, there may be some more relevant or constant factors which helped to turn an accident into a protracted, long-term issue. Looking into the successes and failures of the 'great

70

nations' we may suggest four factors as the most relevant for their changes of fortune: numbers, resources, skills and motivation. Not all these variables need to be simultaneously present: a strong motivation combined with superior craftsmanship may make good the lack of the other two factors. On the whole it very much depends on the strength or intensity of individual factors. In a protracted war, when knowledge picked up from the other side removes initial disparities in the level of military technique, and the motivation amongst the rank-and-file loses momentum, it is the size of the armies and of the economic resources which matters.

Amongst these four factors, motivation seems to me to be the crucial one. Where there is motivation, the necessary skills can be acquired more easily than in a mood of apathy; then the economic resources can be magnified beyond what is offered by nature. And, in fact, numbers can also be increased by motivation, by the desire to have children and to inculcate in them the qualities of endurance and commitment. Such a structure and hierarchy of causation is, in my opinion, applicable to any kind of competition, not only to a military confrontation.

Bearing in mind this proposition, we can look more closely into the origin and the course of the great Iranian ventures which for more than one thousand years stamped its mark on the history of the Levant. As standard European historiography tends to treat this topic as merely an outside catalyst of European developments, we feel we have to give it more space, in order to expound the main issues of Iranian history in their own right.

The Iranians were the Western branch of the great southward move of the Aryan peoples coming from somewhere between the modern Ukraine, the Caucasus, the Urals, and the Altai. Probably in the sixteenth century BC their Eastern wing penetrated into the Indus Valley, where they overwhelmed the local population with their highly developed urban civilization, and began to build on its debris their own Indo-Vedic civilization.

The western wing of the Aryans settled, probably by the second half of the second millennium BC, in the country which from then on was called Aryana, i.e. contemporary Iran. The Iranians were divided into many tribes, of which three made a particular impact on history: the Medes (in the north-west), the Persians (in the south) and the Parthians (in the north-east).

The Medes were the first to appear on the scene of written history, i.e. in the Assyrian and Babylonian annals of the ninth century BC. In the second half of the eighth century the Assyrians tried to extend their empire into the territory of the Medes; the Medes organized themselves against this in what seems to have been a tribal confederation. Subsequent developments were complicated by the attacks of the Scythian nomads, but in the second half of the seventh century the Assyrian *hubris*, which devastated Elam and estranged Babylonia, gave the Medes a good opportunity; in alliance with the Babylonians they knocked Assyria off the stage of history and took over vast stretches of her territory.

Meanwhile the Persians, who had formerly been under Elamite domination, emancipated themselves, and after a short-lived acceptance of Median hegemony became, at the turn of the sixth century BC, the leading power amongst the Iranian tribes. Apparently not only their numbers and the martial virtues of their leadership, but also the capacity to learn various skills from their foes, contributed to their success. But what, in my opinion, was a particularly important element in the structure of causation, was their particular religion, which, as time went on, became their national creed.

Here we can almost detect a parallel with Judaism, but at the same time we can discern the basic differences which were at the root of the very different paths and achievements of the two religions. First of all, the Iranians were more numerous than the Jews and were settled in a larger area, which was a harder nut for foreign invaders to crack. Further they were not afraid of syncretic tendencies, but allowed the teaching of their Prophet – Zarathushtra – to be infiltrated by foreign ideas, and for a long time their priesthood tolerated other cults. Consequently their kings had a freer hand to pursue their imperial policy. And when the hour of trial came and the Iranians had to withstand the overwhelming challenge of Hellenism, their priesthood did not incite their people to a wanton zealotry; in their quiet seclusion, more like the Pharisees in Jamnia, they put down in writing what they understood to be the message of Zarathushtra.

Armed with a Holy Book and a well-organized priesthood, the Iranians managed to bring about a renaissance of both their religion and their empire. Thus Iran was not denied the achievement of the 'sociological trinity', i.e. the three dimensions of communal identity: a great nation got its great religion and its great empire into the bargain.

As a great nation-empire endowed with a particular, basically prophetic, religion, Iran became for more than one millennium the bulwark of the West Asian cultural identity. In the first instance, under the Achaemenids (*c*. 550–330 BC), it stood up against the nomadic pressure from the north-east and against the corrosive influence of the Hellenic culture from the west. Then came two centuries of Hellenic political and cultural ascendancy. From the end of this period until the beginning of the seventh century AD, Iran under the Arsacids and Sassanids had to withstand simultaneous pressures on the one hand from the hybrid empires of the Kushans and Ephtalites straddled on the slopes of the Hindukush and stretching to Central Asia and the Punjab; and on the other hand from the Roman empire with its changing faces: first pagan, then united Christian, and eventually with its Eastern, Byzantine, lore.

For the last four hundred years of its sovereign existence, Zoroastrian Iran stood firm not only against the military ventures on its territorial borders but also against the influence of the neighbouring cultures, the Christian in the West, and the Buddhist in the East – cultures whose absorptive strength many other societies found irresistible.

But it was perhaps this very success which was also the main cause of its eventual undoing. After passing through several stages during which different interpretations of the Zoroastrian message were tested and various types of political structure were experienced, the antiforces of exhaustion began to operate. Neither syncretism nor orthodoxy, neither reform nor revolution, neither sophistication nor vulgarization could stop this fatal development. Eventually in the life and death struggle with the Byzantines the Iranians exhausted themselves to such an extent that they became an easy prey to a new ethno-religious polity, which – under the banner of Muhammad – took over their lands and people and incorporated them into the new civilization of the Levant. Only a tiny minority has survived to this day, and a small community of Parsees – a Zoroastrian diaspora – found refuge and survived in India. A pale parallel to what was to be the Jewish predicament.

But the Iranian nation did not dissolve within the new civilization. Although it surrendered its particular religion and for its own language adopted the Arabic script, it brought the development of its own secular culture to unprecedented heights. Furthermore, it asserted itself as a formidable political force and as the source of a new religious inspiration within what at the beginning appeared to be an exclusively Arabic undertaking.

After a devastating onslaught by the Mongolian nomads on the

Islamic world, an onslaught of which Iran had to bear the brunt, the Iranians succeeded in absorbing the invaders and bestowing upon them their Muslim creed. At what we Europeans consider to be the beginning of the modern era, the Iranians went through a revolution which made them embrace that version of Islam which amongst the Arabs became the affair of a small minority. Thus in making the Shi'a their national religion, the Iranians demarcated once more their identity in the three basic sociological dimensions: ethnic, political and religious. And as the experience of the most recent Iranian revolution indicates, not even the all-encompassing wave of Europeanization promoted by the native rulers could alter that position.

4.2 FROM ZARATHUSHTRA TO MAZDAISM

Having stressed the role of religion in the Iranian venture we have to say a word about its tenets and message. However here we meet with more difficulties than with any other religion whose remnants are still with us. We do not know when Zarathushtra lived and what his teaching really was. The Zoroastrian Holy Writ, the *Avesta*, is, like the Old and New Testaments, a work of many authors living in different epochs; furthermore, unlike in the case of the Judaic and Christian Bible, the chronological layers of individual contributions are less identifiable.

To judge by the language in which individual parts of the Avesta are written, the oldest layer, supposedly conceived during Zarathushtra's life, is the so-called *Gathas* (the sung verses). A somewhat later layer, written in prose, is known as the *Gathas of Seven Chapters*. Both these compositions form the so-called *Yasna* (book of liturgy). Only this part of the Avesta is believed to have been composed before the Hellenic interlude; it alone may therefore be considered as relevant for the first epoch of the Iranian venture, the Persian empire under the Achaemenid dynasty.

Like any other great religion, the teaching of Zarathushtra stems from an opposition to the current religious practices; it seeks to reconstruct them on a higher spiritual and ethical level. Though we do not know the state of Iranian religion before Zarathushtra, it can be inferred from his allusions and polemics that it abounded in ritual, which in addition was burdened with costly and harmful sacrifices. The protection of cattle against sacrificial slaughter is a frequent topic in the Gathas. It is difficult to evaluate to what extent this attitude was influenced by practical considerations, or whether it reflects a similar development which took place in Hinduism, where the cow became the symbol of man's brotherhood with other creatures. However, the later development of Zoroastrianism drew a clear link between good and evil creatures, and thus moved in a different direction from religions based on the concept of metempsychosis (reincarnation), such as Hinduism and Buddhism. It is also difficult to imagine what the intoxicating effects of the sacrificial drink were that were produced from the plant *haoma* which Zarathushtra forbade.

One thing however seems to be clear: Zarathushtra was very much aware of the unavoidable reality of everyday life, of the irreconcilable contradiction between good and evil, between truth and lie; the awareness of this contradiction was at the heart of his teaching. As in Zarathushtra's view man has a free will, he is able to recognize and distinguish between good and evil, and it is his responsibility to make the right choice. But men have not only to take the right choice but also the right action. 'He who by word or thought or with his hands works evil to the follower of the Lie or converts his comrade to the good, such a man does the will of Ahura Mazdah and pleases him well' (Yasna, 33: 2).[1] Thus we find embedded in the Holy Writ itself the principle that the end justifies the means, a dangerous proposition with imaginable consequences for the time when Zoroastrianism was to mature and assume the position of an exclusive orthodoxy.

The struggle between good and evil permeates the whole universe. In Mary Boyce's view Zarathushtra's hymns suggest 'that he must then have witnessed acts of violence, with war-bands, worshippers of the Daevas, descending on peaceful communities to pillage, slaughter and carry off cattle. Conscious himself of being powerless physically, he became filled with a deep longing for justice, for the moral law of the Ahuras to be established for strong and weak alike, so that order and tranquillity could prevail, and all be able to pursue the good life in peace.'[2] There are not only good and evil men but also good and evil deities, the good *Ahuras* and the evil *Daevas* (Hindu mythology developed just the opposite evaluation of what had been common Aryan categories) and even good and evil animals.

Amongst the Ahuras Zarathushtra extolled one whom he called Ahura Mazdah, the Wise Lord, and heaped him with virtuous attributes, seven in number, which eventually developed into separate entities. As these virtues or holinesses (Iranologists translate the respective term of the Gathas – *amesha spentas* – as Holy, or Bounteous, Immortals)[3] have some parallels in other religions such as Buddhism and Christianity, it may be worthwhile to list them here in full. In Zaehner's translation they are: the Holy Spirit, the Good Mind, Truth or Righteousness, Right-Mindedness, the Kingdom, Wholeness and Immortality. Whilst the Holy Spirit is an exclusive attribute of Ahura Mazdah, the other six virtues are his gifts to mankind, though the Kingdom may be temporarily usurped by the forces of evil headed by the Evil Spirit (Angra Mainyu). Wholeness (in the language of the Avesta *Haurvatat*) also means prosperity, and is meant both in a material and in a spiritual sense. In Zaehner's words 'Zarathushtra is the Prophet of life and of life ever more abounding.'[4] Apart from the seven Holy Immortals there is yet another virtue, that of hearkening to the voice of God, a virtue possessed by Zarathushtra. He saw Ahura Mazdah and heard his voice. Zoroastrianism is a revealed religion.

This, with more than a pinch of salt, seems to have been the gist of what Zarathushtra spoke. But when was it that he spoke like that? Here the Iranologists disagree enormously. The time range varies from 1600 to 600 BC.[5] But whichever estimate is correct, one thing seems to be certain, namely that soon after Zarathushtra's death, his teaching became subject to considerable alterations. As any religion has to make concessions to the needs and understanding of the less sophisticated, there is always a danger that the lofty concepts and ideals will become debased. Also any new religion which wants to take hold of the masses has to compromise with traditional beliefs and practices. This happened with Zoroastrianism more than with any other religion.

Ahura Mazdah, who for Zarathushtra was a pure spirit, creator of light and darkness, acquired a corporeal form – the sun – and with it also the female deities, '*ahuranis*', as consorts. On top of that the worship of the traditional Iranian gods – such as Mithra and Anahita – was admitted to the Zoroastrian cult, and other deities whom Zarathushtra wanted to degrade to the position of evil deities (daevas) were also rehabilitated, together with the rites using intoxicating liquor. And all this was permeated by fanciful myths and rites, sustained by the traditional hereditary priesthood – the *magi* – who also took care of the interpretation of the new religion.

Thus Zarathushtra's heritage turned into a complex, syncretic and priestly religion called the Good Religion of the Worshippers of Mazdah (*Daena Mazdayasni*), which can also be translated simply as Mazdaism. Its basic article of faith formulated in Yasna, 1: 1 reads: 'I confess myself a Worshipper of Mazdah, a Zoroastrian, a renouncer of the daevas, an upholder of the Ahuras (or Ahura).'6

This was quite the opposite to what happened in Jewish history. If the prophets had not intervened, the Jewish worshippers of Baals and Els might have produced a similar blend of beliefs and Yahwe might have got his consorts and companions. And who knows whether at a crossroads of civilizations as Judaea and Israel were, Judaism might have experienced the same kind of renaissance as Mazdaism did.

4.3 THE PERSIAN LEVANTINE EMPIRE AND THE HELLENIC COUNTERSTROKE

The rise and fall of the Persian empire belongs to the well-known epics of world history. We need not relate it in this context. What however we cannot omit is a brief account of the structural and ideological aspects of the Persian polity.

First of all we have to bear in mind that the Achaemenid dynasty originated in a comparatively less developed Iranian tribe, in the mountainous part of Iran known as the province Fars, and that the rule of this tribe was superimposed not only on the other Iranian tribes but also on quite foreign nations, such as the Babylonians, the Lydians, the Aramaeans, etc., nations on a different level of cultural and socio-economic development and thus also with a different social structure. The administration and policing of such an extensive and variegated empire required a good deal of flexibility, imagination and understanding of human relations.

The Persians were the ruling nation. They did not pay taxes but were bound to serve as soldiers and civil servants all over the empire. The administrative division of the empire respected historical conditions and social differences. The civil and the military rule functioned separately. As everywhere else, the top social strata were the aristocracy, not necessarily of Persian origin, and the priesthood (the magi), who were in principle worshippers of Ahura Mazdah but were also ready to perform services on behalf of other deities. The king, who ruled by virtue of the decision of Ahura Mazdah, was deemed to be the supreme owner of all cultivated land, and of manufacturing workshops whose labour consisted of prisoners of war turned into slaves. Most peasants were bound to their, to some extent autonomous, commune and obliged to perform public work (corvée).

But the situation varied from country to country. In Babylonia the peasants were more like serfs, whilst in the less developed provinces of the mountains the peasantry enjoyed a freer status. According to Herodotus the non-Iranian provinces paid much higher taxes than the Iranian ones. In provinces with a long-standing tradition such as Babylonia and Syria (including Phoenicia), some cities and temples enjoyed communal autonomy.

Within such a complex and variegated structure the Phoenician ports were thriving, and Babylonian astronomy attained a perfection unsurpassed until the modern era. The government took care of irrigation, the construction of canals and highways, and the organization of ports and maritime transport; it also tried to regulate prices and wages, but it is not known with what success. It seems that as time went on the market played an increasing role as the economic regulator.[7]

It seems that the Achaemenids were already from the beginning of their rule favourably disposed toward the worship of Ahura Mazdah. This may have especially been the case with Darius. However the more official zorastrianization of Persia seems to have taken place only after the Persian expansion to Europe had suffered a double setback: at Marathon (490 BC) and Salamis (480). Decrees against the worshipping of daevas (under Xerxes) and then the acceptance of the Zoroastrian calendar (under Artaxerxes) point in that direction.

However the confrontation with the Hellenic world had fatal results for Achaemenid Persia. Although the leading Greek city states were for a long while not able to exploit their spectacular victories, and exhausted their own strength in a fratricidal war by the second third of the fourth century BC, on the periphery of the Hellenic civilization a vigorous tribe, the Macedonians, led by a talented and ambitious king, managed to impose their peace on the Greek heartland; his son, supported by valuable resources from there, launched a counter-attack on Persia. The story is too well-known to be repeated here. Within eight years the whole Achaemenid empire was conquered by the extremely efficient army led by Alexander the Macedonian. The great epoch of Hellenism in the Levant set in.

Although, from the point of view of the Levant, it was only an interlude, it nevertheless left long-lived vestiges in the whole Levantine orbit, not only in the areas which had already for some time been under the Hellenic cultural influence, such as Asia Minor (whose coasts were largely settled by the Greeks), Phoenicia and the Nile Delta. The most amazing Hellenization took place in Bactria (now Afghanistan and adjacent territories), where the Greeks came in contact with Indian culture in general and Buddhism in particular.

Alexander did not enjoy for long the fruits of his sensational success, and his personal empire fell apart along lines which corresponded more with the established traditions; but each new polity continued to be ruled by a Hellenized dynasty.

Though there had been many wars before the demarcation of individual domains took place, the first century of the Hellenistic epoch in the Levant was a period of general upsurge. Greek settlers poured in and new cities were founded by the hundred. The Hellenic type of urban autonomy found a fertile ground amongst the remnants of the self-governing traditions, especially in the Syrian and Mesopotamian cities. New great centres of syncretic culture emerged in Egyptian Alexandria, Syrian Antiochia and Mesopotamian Seleucia, and in Pergamon in Asia Minor.

As is well known, the concept of absolute monarchy entered the Hellenic mind and the successive dynasties tried to make the most of it for their own benefit, but to the great dissatisfaction of those who cherished the tradition of an independent polis.

The economic upsurge seems to have been helped by a combination of political and monetary circumstances. The Greeks got possession of the immense Achaemenid treasury. In the struggle amongst Alexander's successors, the *diadochi*, most of the gold and silver of this treasure was disbursed and thus effective demand was stimulated.[8] The courts of individual successor dynasties became not only particular spenders but also promoters of cultivated life in their capitals. The Hellenic schools and gymnastic institutions propagated a new hedonistic style of life. The Greek language was largely substituted for the Aramaeic as the lingua franca.

We might imagine a social climate not dissimilar to that of the twentieth century AD. The spread of Hellenism was a phenomenon similar to the spread of the West European and North American way of life throughout most countries of the world in the nineteenth and twentieth centuries AD. This parallel may also be helpful in understanding the reactions which took place in both instances. We do not know yet what outcome the contemporary response of the 'Third World' to the Euro-American and Euro-Asian (Soviet) challenge will have, but we do know how the Levant of the six centuries from c.300 BC to c.300 AD reacted to the Hellenic challenge.

When discussing the case of the Jews we mentioned several types of response; all of them emerged simultaneously. In Iran a similar range of responses developed successively. In the first instance, it was assimilation which prevailed, at least as far as the upper strata were concerned. Then gradually, a tendency towards an honourable accommodation, allowing for the co-existence of two types of civilization on the same soil, gathered momentum. And eventually, when Zoroastrianism became firmly established, the zealots took command of Iranian society. The whole process can be rightly described as a renaissance; a renaissance which, however, like any other phenomenon of that type, gave birth to a different creature from the one which was to be reborn.

The first political impetus which by its chain-effects paved the way for the Mazdaic renaissance came from the North-Eastern part of the Levant. It was carried by the nomadic Parni, who around 248 BC took possession of the Seleucid province of Parthia and soon accepted its dialect and the Graeco-Iranian culture of its elite. The Parnian king Arsak founded a dynasty which for 472 years ruled, first in parts, and later throughout the whole of Iran, which thus became known as the Parthian empire. The Arsacids were neither over-ambitious nor ideologically committed, so that under their rule the religious (Zoroastrian) and national (Iranian) renaissance could take its spontaneous course.

4.4   THE RENAISSANCE OF ZOROASTRIANISM

In the syncretic social climate and religious tolerance of the Parthian polity, various interpretations of Zarathushtra's teaching emerged. Although our information on this development is extremely scarce, we may nevertheless assume that it ran broadly as follows.

According to the oldest layer of the Avesta, the Gathas, there were originally two twin-spirits, one by its thoughts, words and works good, the other evil. Ahura Mazdah was supposed to be their parent. The Gathas of Seven Chapters however identified the Holy

Spirit (Spenta Mainyu) with Ahura Mazdah; thus liberating, as it were, Angra Mainyu from Ahura Mazdah's parenthood and making him independent. The Ahura Mazdah, identified with light, was assigned to heaven (on high), and Angra Mainyu to endless darkness. This was the basis of the Zoroastrian dualism which was later to become the orthodox position.

However, as – to borrow Zaehner's words – 'to the religious consciousness a limited God can never be wholly satisfying',[9] a solution had to be found which would bring both conflicting deities under a supreme overarching principle. This came about with the help of the concept of 'Infinite Time' (*Zurvan*), a concept bearing some affinity to the Greek religious-philosophical thought of those days. Thus in contrast to the original conception of Ahura Mazdah as the only God (if the syncretic additions of Anahita, Mithra, etc. are not taken into account), Zoroastrianism was beset by two contradictory versions: on one hand the dualistic version with Ahura Mazdah (in the later Persian language Ohrmazd) as the good Spirit of truth and light and Angra Mainyu (in later Persian: Ahriman) as the evil Spirit of untruth and darkness; on the other hand the monotheistic form with Zurvan as the supreme God, parent to both those spirits and presiding over their cosmic struggle until the consummation of time, when Ohrmazd would establish his final supremacy. This happy-end eschatology seems to have become the common ground of both versions of Zoroastrianism. In the end the forces of darkness would be defeated and all mankind would be rehabilitated; the mythical son of Zarathushtra, Saoshyans, would assist at that event. There was no eternal hell but only purgatory in the Zoroastrian religion. Wishful thinking gained the upper hand over all the theological and exuberantly mythical speculations.

The re-emergence of Zoroastrianism from the nether world of Iranian society was a gradual process; it progressed hand in hand with the cultural and linguistic emancipation of the Iranian elite. Its pace can be seen from the changes of the royal names and from the written texts on the coins. As an outward symbol of that change, at some point in the first century BC the Zoroastrian calendar was reintroduced in the Parthian kingdom.

This was also the time when the Seleucid kingdom disappeared from the historical scene and, on their western border, the Parthians were confronted with a much more formidable foe – the Roman republic.

The Zoroastrian renaissance seems to have been facilitated by two factors to do with the intruding Hellenic civilization. In the religious sphere Hellenism could offer nothing more than a merely mechanistic syncretism that identified foreign deities with the Olympic ones, together with an allegorical interpretation of the resultant hybrids for the sophisticated.

On the practical plane, the appearance of Rome in Syria and Asia Minor confronted Parthian Iran with a dynamic foe, who either by direct aggression or indirect interference posed a dangerous challenge to the Arsacid empire. The Arsacids had a good reason to look for support to spiritual forces able to bolster the national spirit and cultural identity of their people.

According to tradition the first royal promoter of the Mazdaic renaissance was the Arsacid King Valakhsh, in Greek transliteration Vologeses (*c*.51–77 AD). Under his auspices an extensive quest for Zoroastrian texts was organized. The interest in the ancestral religion went hand in hand with the return to a native language for literary purposes. At that time the medieval Iranian language – the Pahlavi – was substituted for Greek in official use, and a body of literature, both religious and secular, also gradually developed in that language.[10].

The ancient texts were written in a different script and language which, being another Iranian dialect from many centuries earlier, was not fully understandable to the collectors who also had the ungrateful task of verifying the authenticity of the texts. The editors of the new text of the Yasna had to rely widely on the oral tradition and even with this help they were not able to produce a wholly comprehensible text. Thus a commentary – the Zand – was added to what was supposed to be the message of Zarathushtra. After further additions to the most ancient layer of the sacred texts (Yasna) the tripartite Avesta-Zand eventually became the Holy Writ of the Zoroastrians.

This process however was not completed under the Arsacids. It apparently required more effort and resources than they were able to devote to that task. The Parthian empire lacked a strong, centralized government. It was a conglomerate of semi-independent kingdoms and satrapies whose mutual relationships were involved in a process of continuous change. As time went on, a development took place which may be described as progressive feudalization. After 87 BC, when the direct line of Arshak died out, a council of nobles began to interfere with the royal succession. A powerful nobility was a menace not only to the king, but also to the rest of the population, especially the peasants. The cost of the knights' internecine wars and the chivalresque culture had to be paid by an increased burden imposed upon the common people. Also the continuous border warfare against the Romans in the West and against the nomadic invasions in the North and East, contributed to the political instability. Not only individual kinglets or satraps occasionally revolted, but also the Mesopotamian city of Seleucia on the Tigris took to arms against the government. Its defiance lasted seven years before it was put down.[11]

By the end of the second century AD, the Arsacid rule became increasingly shaky. In 224 AD the seat of power shifted back to the long-established province of Fars (Persia), whose kings had been vassals of the Arsacids from 140 BC. With King Ardashir I the Sassanid dynasty claimed a direct lineage from the Achaemenids and ascended the throne of the Iranian king of kings (*shahan shah*).

With that event, the process of feudalization was reversed and a strong central government was substituted for the loose structure of the Parthian polity. Ardashir was particularly successful in his border warfare both against the Romans in the West and against the Kushans in the East. At the same time Ardashir devoted himself more vigorously to the task of collecting and editing the Zoroastrian tradition. The selection was entrusted to a priest by the name of Tansar, whose claim to be the bearer of the authoritative interpretation of the tradition was apparently recognized by Ardashir. Thus the first canonized version of the Avesta-Zand was produced.[12]

It may be worth while to quote the respective passage from a later Zoroastrian document (the Denkart) which gives the story of the restoration of the 'Good Religion' after its long eclipse. The passage is taken from the full reproduction of that story in Zaehner:

> His Majesty, the king of kings, Ardashir, son of Papak, following Tansar as his religious authority, commanded all those scattered teachings to be brought to the Court. Tansar set about his business, selected one (version) and left the rest out of the canon: and he issued this decree: The interpretation of all the teachings from the Religion of the worshippers of Mazdah is our responsibility; for now there is no lack of certain knowledge concerning them.[13]

After a long period during which they had been preoccupied with ritual and other outward manifestations of religion, the most conspicuous being the substitution of sacred fires for statues and images,[14] the magi assumed with Tansar the role of authorized interpreters of the Avesta. The role of Ardashir and Tansar in the development of the Mazdaic religion can be compared with that of Josiah and Hilkiah in the development of Judaism. In Judaism, however, prophecy was still alive at the time, and the Holy Writ could be nurtured from further creation, whereas in Zoroastrianism it had to draw inspiration from other sources.

Anyhow, the real meaning of what was put down in the Gathas in the old Avestan language was not properly understood and translated into the Pahlavi of the Zand. In contrast to the commentators of the Rig-Vedic tradition in India, says Zaehner, 'The Pahlavi commentators on the Gathas understood nothing at all and did not hesitate to set down a meaningless concatenation of words which was supposed to render the thoughts of their Prophet.'[15]

4.5 THE HERESIES AND THE ORTHODOXY

No wonder that under the circumstances described in the previous chapter, the authoritative interpretation by the high priest was the only way to provide the Zoroastrian Holy Writ with a definite meaning. The more so as the 'Good Religion', the Daena Mazday-asni, became exposed to competition from two directions. From the West, where Ardashir pushed back the Roman power, came the Christian message born in the bosom of the Judaic community but gradually becoming, after appropriate adaptations, a message of the Mediterranean counter-culture. From the East, where Ardashir subdued the Kushans, spread the teaching of Buddhism; it was in the Kushan empire that Indian Buddhism shed the predominantly philosophical garb of its Hinayana version (Lesser Vehicle) and having developed into a fully-fledged religion of the Mahayana (Greater Vehicle) acquired a strong missionary appeal. Christianity and Buddhism only got as far as knocking at the gates of the Sassanian empire, but their impact touched the spirit of those for whom religion was not merely ritual and the recital of dead letter.

The Christian and Buddhist challenge gave pause to the new Iranian prophet – Mani – and made him attempt a thorough-going reorientation of the Zoroastrian message. After all the materialistic interpretations of the cosmic struggle between Good and Evil, interpretations which the generations of magi had turned into a lifeless ritual, Mani could not accept that the dividing line between the two forces symbolized by Light on the one hand and by Darkness on the other, could cut both across the sphere of spirit and across the sphere of matter. For Mani only spirit could be good, matter would always be evil.

Such a concept was an outright attack on a basic tenet of the Zoroastrian tradition. But there were many more. A classical representative of gnosis, with its characteristic blend of metaphysics, mythology and mysteries, Mani saw himself as God's messenger and in that capacity successor to Zarathushtra, to Buddha, to a certain Aurentes, and above all to Jesus. He maintained that the link between Jesus and himself was mediated by a certain Parakletos, the spirit of Truth, whom Jesus had promised to send to the world and who revealed to Mani a hidden mystery.[16]

Unfortunately, Mani's teaching is known more from the literature of his enemies than from his own writings. Nevertheless some documents in Coptic, Sogdian, Ujghur and other languages allow an approximate reconstruction of what he stood for. It was a kind of mystical gnosis, aiming at a direct, intuitive perception of the hidden substance of life without any rational, conceptual mediation. In accordance with the belief that only a dematerialization leads to salvation a strict asceticism was required from the elect. To make this negation of the Zoroastrian position palatable, Mani tried to dress his ideas up in Zoroastrian mythical terms, for which purpose his own prolific demonology and angelology was well suited.

But despite all its oddities Mani's teaching contained a germ which seems to have been politically attractive to the Iranian ruler. Ardashir's son and successor Shapur I (240–70 AD) was impressed by the unifying possibilities of a religion which claimed to be the fulfilment not only of Zoroastrianism, but also of Christianity and Buddhism, and furthermore was not a simple syncretism of the type cultivated by the Hellenistic and Roman rulers. It was a genuine religion, which by virtue of its three-fold inspiration well suited Shapur's quest for a broader ideological basis than that offerd by the Avestan orthodoxy.

Mani's ideas however became utterly unacceptable to the Zoroastrian high priest Karter and other magi. Shapur, therefore, in his effort to enlarge the ideological basis of the Iranian community, preferred to move in a less contentious direction. He decided to leaven Zoroastrian thought with already established, but less shocking, elements from other cultures. On this the already mentioned Denkart has the following to say:

He (i.e. Shapur) collected those writings from the Religion which were dispersed throughout India, the Byzantine Empire, and other lands and which treated of medicine, astronomy, movement, time, space, substance, creation, becoming, passing away, qualitative change, logic, and other arts and sciences. These he added to the Avesta . . . and he examined the possibility of basing every form of academic discipline on the Religion of the worshippers of Mazdah.[17]

This opening seems to have been successful. The reflection of Hellenic and Indian ideas is clearly visible in Pahlavi literature of that epoch. After Shapur's death, however, the internal contradictions issued in open conflict. Weak rulers, attacked by Rome in the West and by the revolting Kushans in the East, were not in a position to withstand the pressure of the priests who aimed at exclusive domination for their own interpretation of the Zoroastrian religion (Daena Mazdayasni). To give the word to the authority in the field:

The death of Shapur left the religious field open to his fanatical high priest Karter . . . Zoroastrianism appears for the first time as a fanatical and persecuting religion. The list of the sects persecuted, however, shows how justified the early Sassanian kings were in seeking a unifying force that would weld their Empire together, for not only do we find Jews, Christians, Manichees, and Mandaeans (*Nasoraye*) mentioned, but also Buddhists and Brahmans . . . . Every effort was made too to extirpate all non-Zoroastrian religions, including the 'Zandiks' who were probably Zurvanite materialists, and, what is more, strict uniformity was to be the rule within the Zoroastrian Church itself.[18]

The victory of Karter's orthodoxy may remind us of the triumph of the Roman Church under Innocent III (Pope from 1198 to 1216). In both instances the church gained the upper hand over the secular power; though in Zoroastrian Iran this primacy was not an institutional matter to the same extent as in Catholic Europe. The royal power ('the kingdom') of the Iranian rulers was one of the seven beatitudes – *amesha spentas*, a religious sanctification in which the high priests – *mobadan mobad* – were lacking; the practical effects, however, were very similar.

The public disputation between Karter and Mani at a council of the magi held in the presence of the king concluded with the condemnation of the teachings of Mani. This was followed by his imprisonment and death (probably in 276 AD), and a fierce persecution of the Manichees. Almost a thousand years later, in 1209, Innocent III succeeded in organizing a crusade against the Cathars of Southern France, who were supposed to have strong Manichaean connections. In both instances, the inquisition and persecution of heretics heralded the shattering of the spiritual power of the respective church.

Political considerations however did not cease to play a role even in ecclesiastical policy. The fact that in the Roman empire Christianity was until the beginning of the fourth century AD an officially discouraged, occasionally persecuted, religion could not remain unnoticed by the Sassanids, who for that specific reason decided to be tolerant towards that particular religion. When, however, in 325, Christianity became the official creed of the Roman empire, its fortunes in the Iranian empire changed dramatically. From 340 Christianity became a forbidden religion in Iran.

Nor was the official Zoroastrian church always given a free hand. Against the orthodoxy maintaining the dualist position of Ohrmazd (the Pahlavi version of the old Iranian Ahura Mazdah) against Ahriman (Angra Mainyu), a more monotheistic position, with Zurvan (Infinite Time or Space) at the top was able to gain some ground, with the support of several Sassanid rulers.

Zurvanism however could not offer a united front against the well-organized orthodoxy. Within its fold there was a wide spectrum of versions, ranging from a naively mythical one which described the birth of Ohrmazd and Ahriman in Zurvan's womb in the form of a fairy tale, to a philosophico-astrological one, which used astral movements to explain worldly phenomena, thus denying the basic Zoroastrian principle of free will.

The discussion between the fatalists and the believers in free will found its expression in the writings of the high priest Aturpat, writings which are in the Zoroastrian tradition that is considered to be the quintessence of orthodoxy. Aturpat did not deny the role of fate but limited its effects. While reading the relevant passage from the Denkart (attributed to Aturpat) we might imagine a discussion similar to that of today, which tries to sort out to what extent nature and to what extent nurture determines our attitudes and our behaviour. Aturpat tried hard to be fair to both sides. He divided the things of this world into twenty-five parts: we have again to consult the Denkart, to show how he managed:

> five (he assigned) to fate, five to (human) action, five to nature, five to character, and five to heredity. Life, wife, children, sovereignty, and property are chiefly through fate. Salvation and damnation, and the qualities that make a (good) priest, warrior, or husbandman are chiefly through action. Eating, walking, going in to one's wife, sleeping, and satisfying the needs of nature are chiefly through nature. Worthiness, friendship, goodness, generosity, and rectitude are chiefly through character. Intelligence, understanding, body, stature, and appearance are chiefly through heredity.[19]

In no case could fate cheat men of their salvation; misfortune was supposed to be the test of men's character.

Yet even with Aturpat's scholastic ingenuity the issue could not be resolved satisfactorily. The Pahlavi texts reveal a concept which points to a kind of predestination rather than to the traditional concept of free will. This is the term *khwarr*, translated by Zaehner as 'the final cause of each man: it is what God intends him to be and it pre-exists his physical birth, . . . almost exactly what is meant by the "talents" of Christ's parable.'[20]

Thus the predestination aspect of the *khwarr* is subject to qualification. It should be understood as a disposition, a capacity which has to be fully developed and brought to completion. Furthermore, the concept of *khwarr* is projected on to the whole history of mankind. There will be a final victory of Ohrmazd, Evil will be destroyed and all mankind will be made excellent (*frashkart*).

But there is yet another point where the parallel with Jesus' teaching is striking. After glimpsing the staggering superstitions,[21] the formalized ritualism, and the practices bordering on various sorts of magic, we cannot but be stunned when we read in the Denkart:

> Do not regard this world as a (permanent) principle, for it has not long existed. Leave (all care for) the things of this world to God, and concern yourself (rather) with God's business, nothing doubting. (Then only) will the world be presented to you in a way that both your body and your soul will be perfected. Take to yourself personally the things of the spirit; for if you reject these, you will lose all wordly good. Make God a guest within your body; for if you make him a guest within your body, then

you make him a guest within the whole material world.[22]

Both on the dogmatic and on the ethical plane religions display the widest possible range of levels and attitudes. Any living religion, in which, so to speak, the Word became Flesh, is a communion of saints and sinners, a scale of angelic and devilish attitudes, each of which has a chance to flourish more than the others, given the appropriate circumstances. Catholic ecclesiology describes the role of the church in society in terms of three categories: a suffering, a militant and a victorious church. One of the lessons of world history is that a suffering church gives the best chance to the saints; in the militant church the angelic and the devilish types have an equal chance; whilst in a victorious church, the saints tend to be amongst the heretics.

4.6 REVOLUTION AND REFORM

In this section we would like to complete our story of the struggle over the cultural orientation of Iranian society with an account of the mounting social tensions in that society. Although the first Sassanids succeeded in imposing a centralized rule on what had earlier been a conglomerate of principalities, and a structure of four clearly defined estates was substituted for a looser feudal hierarchy, there was ample scope for friction. As in many other societies, the three upper estates, the nobility, the priesthood (the magi) and the bureaucracy (the scribes) competed for privileges at the expense of the fourth estate, comprizing all of the free (i.e. not enslaved) working population.

At this point, it may be useful to summarize briefly the image of social structure which was preserved for posterity by Pahlavi and Arabic writings. Each of the four estates was divided into sub-estates or classes. Thus the nobility, whose main task was service in arms, was divided into several classes whose demarcation is clear only in the upper echelons. They were: members of the royal household; members of the six supreme aristocratic families; other higher nobility; lower nobility, knights and gentry. The clerical estate comprised two priestly categories (*mobads* and *herbads*), judges, supervisors and educators. The bureaucratic estate also included astrologers, doctors, poets and musicians. The core of the fourth estate consisted of the peasants, hence its name – *vastrioshan*. However the craftsmen and merchants were sometimes classified separately. Each estate had its hereditary chairman who was a kind of government official.

How far this scheme functioned in practice it is difficult to say. One thing however seems to be certain, namely that with this neat categorization there disappeared the time-honoured autonomy of the cities, which the Arsacids continued to respect but which was abolished by the Sassanids. Otherwise the lot of the peasantry probably remained unchanged. They were bound to their village community by the fact that this community was liable for its members' duties (taxes and corvées). The ownership of the land was, as elsewhere, divided, but it seems that the upper owner left a considerable dispositional right to the effective possessors who tilled the land. The market economy was limited to the towns, of which only some were engaged in what could be described as foreign trade. Rights and duties were divided extremely unequally. As in most societies in history, the peasantry knew only duties; taxes, whether in money or in kind, public works and military service did not leave them much time for themselves.

Under these circumstances, where the ruler wanted to have a strong army, he had to take some protective measures on behalf of his potential recruits i.e. in the first instance the peasantry. In Sassanian Iran this kind of enlightened policy is linked with the name of Jazdagird I (399–420), who in addition also showed a remarkable religious tolerance. Another attempt to ease social tensions was, according to some sources, undertaken by King Peroz (459–84), who had to face a severe food shortage as a result of several very bad harvests.[23] However Peroz perished in the war with the nomadic newcomers – the so-called White Huns or Ephtalites – who then started to impose tribute to Iran and interfere in its internal matters. This shake-up apparently helped to free those forces in Iran that were working for social change.

The motivation for such an undertaking was present in the very essence of the Zoroastrian religion. As it was man's duty to fight against evil and as the Zoroastrian eschatology was not one-sidedly spiritual in nature, one can well conceive that people might have got the idea of pushing the course of history in the right direction by social action.

This, so to speak, Marxian idea, seems to have been at the basis of what may be described as the Mazdakite social revolution, a prelude to the last rally of the Zoroastrian civilization. As this social revolution, whose goal was a more equitable distribution of property and wives in Iranian society, was the first of its kind in which we have some, albeit far from adequate, historiographic information, it may be worthwhile to give it rather more detailed coverage. Although enough attention has been devoted to the sociological and ideological roots of the Mazdakite movement, there are a few dark corners which allow for alternative interpretations.[24]

Concerning the social structure of Iran during that epoch, there is a rare consensus between Western and Marxist Iranologists; both agree that the socio-economic formation of Iran at that time was more or less feudal. Unlike the feudalism of the Parthian epoch, the Iranian feudalism of the late fifth centry AD was, after the vigorous attempts of the first Sassanids to curb it, of a comparatively tough nature. As Christensen discovered, the landlords wielded not only economic power but also fiscal and military power over the peasant population, who were in fact in the position of bondsmen. On top of that there was a tedious military duty – service in the infantry – which was not rewarded, and peasants as privates had to live off the country.[25]

The Mazdakite movement, however, was not initiated by bondsmen. According to the Persian tradition, Mazdak belonged to the priestly estate, the magi. Nor is it clear to what extent the lowest estate took part in it. Although these people might also have been its beneficiaries, the sources contain only a few general statements on the participation of the common folk in the movement. The Soviet Iranologist, Pigulevskaya, accepts their participation as a matter of fact because according to her Marxist conviction a social revolution cannot be carried out without conscious action by the exploited masses.[26] The Czech Iranologist, Otakar Klíma, is more cautious when he says: 'The recent Soviet resumés claim that Mazdak's supporters were mainly from the class of small peasants. This opinion seems to be fully justified, although we may conceive it only on the basis of a deduction. I had already arrived at this conclusion myself, although I have not found anything in the texts to substantiate it.'[27] Nor is the participation of the urban population mentioned in the sources. Klíma, however, justifies this conjecture by analogy with the social movements and revolts of the later, Islamic, period.[28]

The need was not only for adequate food but also for wives. The polygamy enjoyed by the upper strata, and the harems of the higher nobility, deprived the less fortunate men of the opportunity to find suitable wives. Although the strict estate barriers prevented a nobleman from taking a woman of a lower estate as his first wife, the possibility of having concubines and female servants in the house also made a considerable drain on the numbers of pretty young girls from the lower estates.

Although similar conditions (an unsatisfied need for goods and women) also existed in other societies, they did not lead to the same kind of unrest as Iran witnessed at that time. The reason for this particular reaction in Iran lay in the conjuncture of the political and the religious crises. As has been amply demonstrated by scholars from de Tocqueville to Barrington Moore, oppression or any other cause for dissatisfaction per se is not by itself a sufficient condition for revolt. If the oppressed accept their position as just or if they have no time because they have to spend it all keeping body and soul together, they merely carry on with their dreary lot. The would-be revolutionaries have to be convinced that they have got a case. The Zoroastrian teaching might have been interpreted in a way that would furnish such a case.

As has been said already, the Zoroastrian religion was not an ascetic one. One of its virtues was prosperity, both in a spiritual and in a material sense; all the followers of Ahura Mazdah were entitled to enjoy this virtue. To borrow Zaehner's words, 'The Good Religion, indeed, gives its authoritative approval to the furtherance and refinement of legitimate prosperity . . . and (worldly) pleasure.'[29]

We may find a reflection of this principle in legal practice in the provision that a husband might cede one of his wives, even the privileged one, to another man who fell in need of a wife through no fault of his own; the consent of the respective wife was not necessary.[30]

The Mazdakite revolutionary action was in fact an extension of these potentialities inherent in the religious law. Mazdak apparently tried to make this practice more general, partly by inducing the king to take more resolute measures in that direction, partly by encouraging the direct, forcible redistribution of property and the dissolution of harems.

Arabic and other sources often refer to Mazdak as a Manichaean. This, however, squares oddly with the content of the Mazdakite reform. Although Mazdak's religious views might have been strongly influenced by Mani, especially as far as the mythical elements and the stress on sobriety and vegetarianism are concerned, Mazdak's stress on the equal distribution of land and wives, or as some sources claim, on their common usage, indicates that Mazdak adhered more faithfully to the Zoroastrian tenets than Mani. Mani, having identified the principle of light and truth with the spirit and the principle of darkness and untruth with matter, could hardly have provided the basis for Mazdak's programme. Whatever Mazdak's mythical and cabbalistic views might have been, his actions were in line with the Zoroastrian concept of human prosperity (*haurvatat*).[31]

The beginning of Mazdak's actions is generally located in the year 494 AD. At that time, according to the Arabic historian al-Tabari, King Kavad, son of Peroz, became a supporter of Mazdak's teaching. Probably it all started, as Klíma sees it, with mass demonstrations demanding the redistribution of corn and other food accumulated in royal and private granaries. The king seems to have given his consent; private property was taken by force.[32] The king's connivance with what in the owners' view must have been robbery could not be accepted without some opposition from those adversely affected. The position of the royalty must have been very weak at that time. The king could not effectively contain either the Mazdakites or the nobility. So it came about that in 496 the nobles captured him, locked him up in a remote castle and elevated his brother Jamasp (or Zamashna) to the throne. Kavad, however, escaped and with the help of the Ephtalites regained the throne in 499 or 500. More than ever before he was determined to curb the power of the higher nobility. Even if he did not fully sympathize with Mazdak, he must have seen in him a welcome ally for his policy.

The following twenty-five years of Kavad's rule were marked by a precarious tripartite balance: between the king in the middle, the Mazdakites on the one hand and the high aristocracy and clergy on the other. Kavad seems to have been able to play both sides off against each other without allowing either of them to attain the dominant position. On top of that the situation was complicated by almost continuous warfare – with the Byzantines in the west, the Ephtalites in the east, and Caucasian tribes in the north – warfare that was accompanied by a forcible large-scale transfer of defeated tribes and people from the conquered provinces to the Iranian homelands.[33]

The internal tensions produced by Kavad's balancing policy could not, however, last for long; nor could the unofficial interpretation of the Zoroastrian tradition.

The counter-attack of the Mazdaic church and the high aristocracy came with the help of the successor to the throne, Prince Khusraw. Khusraw persuaded his father to put an end to Mazdak's interference in government matters. And Mazdak's case was resolved like that of Mani: in 528 or 529 a council of magi, at which not only Mazdak and his entourage but also a Christian bishop were present, discussed and condemned Mazdak's teaching.[34] On Khusraw's demand Mazdak was extradited to him and executed together with all his followers present at that council.

The massacre of the Mazdakites deprived the movement of its leadership. Some of the Mazdakites escaped, mainly to Central Asia; according to some sources Mazdak's wife was among them and became a recognized leader of what subsequently appeared to become a religious sect. Actually the Mazdakites always described themselves as followers of one common religion. Several later uprisings in Central Asia are generally linked with the Mazdakite tradition.

In Iran itself, the wide-ranging reforms already begun under the rule of Kavad were carried out more energetically by his son, Khusraw (531–79 AD). The question whether these reforms were undertaken as a response to the Mazdakite challenge, or whether the Mazdakite movements functioned merely as a catalyst, has to be left unanswered.

Concerning the content of the changes, the sources are in principle unanimous. The reform seems to have had one main objective, namely to strengthen the power of the shah, both internally and externally. To that end the power of seven big aristocratic families and also of the high priest had to be trimmed. Young aristocrats were invited to the capital to assume government functions and perform services at the royal court. So a considerable section of the first estate was made into the court aristocracy, a kind of change which we have already encountered in the empire-building epoch of cuneiscript Mesopotamia and which we shall come across again on other occasions in this book. The command of the army, which until then had been in the hands of one nobleman, was divided into four regional sections, and the role of the gentry and yeomanry in the army was strengthened by royal subsidies for those not wealthy enough to take a fully-equipped part in war.

The treatment of the peasant became more considerate, with respect both to his work duty and to his tax-paying capacity. One of the earliest measures in this direction was the abolition of the ancient custom that tax had to be assessed according to the crop in the field (before harvest). Not only did this practice often result in an unduly high tax, but also the waiting for the assessor often produced delays which led to the decay of the crop. The reform introduced taxes more specifically differentiated according to the fertility of the land, the state of irrigation and other conditions affecting prosperity. Henceforth an allowance had to be made in the case of drought or other emergency. On the other hand, estate barriers were made more impregnable and the already very narrow channels of vertical mobility became virtually non-existent. According to the Arabic historian, at Taalibi, Khusraw even forbade the education of children from the lowest estate, on the grounds that, if educated, they could demand better jobs and thus affront the nobles.[35]

Property and family relationships were to be reconstituted, yet this could be carried through only to a limited extent. Not all the land appropriated by the lower gentry could be taken from them, and families could not easily be reunited. With regard to the harems, hardly anybody was interested in their more elderly denizens, yet with respect to the polygamous family as such, minutely detailed instructions were issued regulating the treatment of children whose fathers could not be traced; they had to be adopted by the families with whom they happened to be at that time.

In sum, the outcome of all this was a reinforcement of royal power and of estate barriers, a weakening of feudal relationships, a strengthening of the bureaucracy and an improvement in the position of the gentry (*dekhanan*) and yeomanry (*azatan*). These two classes were virtually the main beneficiaries of the whole upheaval. They became not only the backbone of the military power of the empire but also the main bearers of medieval Persian culture; literature and the arts found in them keen and stimulating consumers. The peasantry, which always bore the brunt of wars and disasters, benefited from a more equitable and orderly taxation system. This gain, however, was put in jeopardy by the recurrent wars.

And what about ideology? As has been said already, royalty had a sacred function in Iranian society. Ardashir declared the interpretation of the Mazdaic religion to be his own responsibility. Shapur I used this prerogative to try to introduce some new, foreign, elements into the *corpus canonicum* of the Mazdaic religion. Khusraw I attempted to put a final seal on the quest for orthodoxy. He was the first to understand royalty as a bond between god and man.[36]

Thanks to the Mazdakite movement, Khusraw's father, Kavad, had already enjoyed a considerable degree of independence from the priestly power. He himself appointed his successor to the throne, whereas the previous custom considered the decision on the succession to be a prerogative of the three highest dignitaries, namely the high priest, the chancellor and the commander-in-chief. Kavad also made charity a religious obligation. Wealthy Zoroastrians had to distribute a certain part of their revenue amongst the poorer of their fellow-believers.[37]

Although it is impossible to assess how far this law was implemented in practice – as in the case of Kavad's earlier law on the 'charitable' transfer of wives – the proclamation of the principle together with the new economic and fiscal policy of Khusraw nevertheless characterizes the social climate of the post-Mazdakite era.

4.7   RALLY, COLLAPSE AND TRANSFIGURATION

Khusraw's reform, which wound up the Mazdakite revolution, had contradictory effects on the further development of Iranian society. In the first instance the position of the common man improved most probably, but the already narrow channels of upward mobility were completely frozen. The prerogatives of tightly-knit estates were substituted for the ambitions of the great aristocratic families, whose role in the society declined considerably. As Frye put it, the empire began to be ruled by 'generals and top religious and bureaucratic officials' rather than by the kings themselves.[38]

Such was the situation when the Sassanian empire entered the final round of its permanent struggle with the West. But the bastion of the latter, the Byzantine empire, was no better equipped for that occasion. Each empire intervened in the affairs of the other: unsuccessful pretenders to the throne found refuge at the other empire's court, and this provided the opportunity for military adventures. Thus from what at the beginning appeared to be only occasional interventions in the dynastic squabbles of the other side, there developed a devastating war which lasted a full quarter of a century.

Khusraw II, the hero of this epic, almost re-established the Achaemenid empire; he conquered Syria and Asia Minor and stood on the Asian shore before Constantinople. But Heraclius I, the hero of the nascent Byzantine empire and civilization, outflanked him by a sea route and penetrated through Armenia to his capital Ctesiphon. Khusraw was assassinated by his own military commanders and his successor concluded a humiliating peace. The complete exhaustion of both powers was soon to be revealed.

Up to then both the Iranians and the Byzantines had looked upon the Arabs as poor neighbours who could afford only semi-independent polities, such as the vassal kingdoms of the Lakhmids (dependent on Iran) and the Ghassanids (dependent on Byzantium). Towards the end of the sixth century AD the Arabs were no match for the Persian power. Bahrein and vast stretches of the Eastern coast of Arabia were under Sassanid sovereignty and in 575 AD a Persian expedition took possession of Yemen, which until then had been under Ethiopian rule.

In the thirties of the seventh century AD the balance of forces was quite the opposite. The Arabs, united and inspired by the new and immense spiritual and social force of Muhammad's religion, within twenty years wiped out the whole Sassanian empire and chased the Byzantines out of Syria and Egypt. The story is too well-known to be retold at length in these pages.

Our concern in this context is what happened to the Iranians and to the Zoroastrian civilization. Deprived of royal protection the Mazdaic church lost a good deal of its appeal; the new rulers who, on the whole, proceeded cautiously without introducing any abrupt changes, found amongst the Iranians sufficient readiness to co-operate. For conversion to Islam there were good political and economic incentives; power was reserved for Muslims, and non-Muslims paid an extra tax. But mass conversions were also due to the declining popularity of the Mazdaic religion. As T.W. Arnold said:

> But the Muslim creed was almost eagerly welcomed by the townsfolk, the industrial classes and the artisans, whose occupations made them impure according to the Zoroastrian creed, because in the pursuance of their trade or occupations they defiled fire, earth or water, and who thus, outcasts in the eyes of the law and treated with scant consideration in consequence, embraced with eagerness a creed that made them at once free men, and equal in a brotherhood of faith.[39]

Furthermore, in many points concerning beliefs and ritual, striking similarities could be found between the teaching of Zarathushtra on the one hand and that of Muhammad on the other. To borrow again Arnold's words:

For the Persian could find in the Qur'an many of the fundamental doctrines of his old faith, though in a rather different form: he would meet again Ahura Mazda and Ahriman under the names of Allah and Iblis: the creation of the world in six periods; the angels and the demons; the story of the primitive innocence of man; the resurrection of the body and the doctrine of heaven and hell. Even in the details of daily worship there were similarities to be found and the followers of Zoroaster when they adopted Islam were enjoined by their new faith to pray five times a day just as they had been by the Avesta.[40]

Muslim rulers soon acquired a comparatively good understanding of the differences within Zoroastrianism. On the whole Zoroastrians were also a People of the Book and many streams within their religion, such as the non-materialistic Zurvanites and those who believed in Ohrmazd's superior position vis-à-vis Ahriman, could be considered as monotheists. Thus only the outright dualists were required to abandon their creed.

Under these circumstances the Zoroastrian civilization took about four centuries to die out, more or less peacefully, by a kind of process of dissolution.[41] But before this happened its theologians and philosophers managed to put down in writing the last version of the Zoroastrian world view and tradition. Most of our sources on Zoroastrian religion date from that epoch.

Iranians who converted to Islam had in the first instance to accept the status of mere clients of those Arabic families whose proximity to the Prophet made them the elite of the new polity. Only later, after having engaged themselves, in the mid-eighth century AD, in the struggle for the change of dynasty, did they become Muslims in their own right; as such, they taught their former masters how to effectively run a multinational empire. The Abbasid caliphate was no longer a purely Arabic institution; it drew extensively on Persian administrative experience.

But all this belongs to the next chapter of our journey. In this context we would only like to stress that the Iranians made Islam their own religion and contributed to its master institutions, which successively played the key role in the process of civilizational integration: the caliph, the law (*Shari'a*) and the mystic orders (*sufi tariqas*).

While doing so, the Iranians developed to the full their particular artistic bent, which flourished especially in poetry, in the epic and in visual art, a bent which was by no means constrained by the limitations imposed by the iconoclastic and puritanical tendencies of the original Islam. For the full assertion of these latter attitudes the Iranians had to wait until the Shi'a assumed the dominant position in their country.

5 The Ways of Islam: Integration and Disintegration

5.1 THE GENERAL SETTING

Islam, literally meaning submission, i.e. to the will of the One God, was not a new idea in the Levant. In all the civilizations discussed so far, personified gods were supreme beings, though with different emphases on the scope of their supremacy. In Pharaonic Egypt, God's supremacy was blurred by the idea of cosmic order, and by man's power to learn what had to be done and thus to force a way to salvation. In Judaism a certain qualification of God's exclusive supremacy lay in the idea of the covenant, and in Zoroastrianism the devil (Ahriman) assumed a position unknown in other religions. Only in the Sumerian view, which was then inherited by other nations of the Cuneiscript civilization, was the supremacy of the gods so absolute that petitional prayer and sacrifices alone could mollify them. More often than not these gods were immanent in nature. The idea of God's undisputed transcendence appeared in Zoroastrianism, matured in Judaism and from there was inherited by the Christians and Muslims.

But Christianity was born into a society whose brain and backbone lay outside the Levant. In order to win its heart, Christianity had to adapt itself. The Judaic idea of an exclusive God-Creator had to compromise with the spirit of Greek philosophy and with the Roman sense of organization. We intend to say more on this topic in another context. Suffice here only to note that Christianity eventually ramified its concept of one God into a highly metaphysical concept of Trinity, within which the Son of God, God incarnate, saviour and founder of the Church, became the key factor.

In this way Christianity was in a position to appeal to people of various traditions, including those in which the dividing line between the world of the gods and the world of men was not absolutely clear cut.

The Church's synthesis however became suspect to the strict, unyielding monotheists for whom the idea of incarnation was wholly unacceptable. And this was the spiritual and emotional breach into which Muhammad's Islam stepped. Starting as a message for the Arabs beyond the pale of Christian and Zoroastrian communities, Islam eventually became a religion of the whole of the Levant. In it the Sumerian and Semitic tradition of the Levant developed into an uncompromisingly monotheistic and transcendental religion; this religion then provided the ideational basis for the cultural, and for a long time also political, unification of the Semitic peoples, and on top of that the spiritual basis for the absorption of the Iranian, Hamitic and Turkic ethnies plus fragments of other nations into the Islamic civilization.

Within fifty years of Muhammad's death almost the whole of the Levant came under the domination of the Islamic community. The remnants of earlier civilizations survived as local residues which only slowly and gradually dissolved within the mighty tide of the new Islamic civilization. Meanwhile, however, the internal dissensions between various Islamic denominations brought about tensions which more than eight hundred years later issued in an open schism with far-reaching consequences.

The history of the multi-ethnic Islamic civilization is marked by a constant duel between centrifugal and centripetal forces. Although the term 'dialectical unity' has been so often used and misused that it has almost lost any cognitive meaning, in the case of Islam it furnishes an apposite characterization of the tenor of its history. The trend towards political disintegration was always matched by the integrative forces within its cultural and social infrastructure. And even when a breach in the latter was brought to the surface, the integrative elements were so firmly established that they preserved the basic common framework until the time when the Islamic civilization, like other civilizations of the Old World, was exposed in all walks of life to the corrosive challenge of modern Europe.

In the following pages we shall give an account of the birth and life of the Islamic civilization with its dramatic routs and rallies, its moves towards disintegration and reintegration, up to the days of its confrontation with the modern civilization of the Euro-American West. Bearing in mind that at the time of writing Islam, with its time-honoured divisions, plays an increasingly important role in the world, we shall give the origins and development of these divisions particular attention.

5.2   FROM MUHAMMAD TO THE UMMA

Although the word Islam means submission, Islam as a religion and as a historical phenomenon means much more. All the three basic dimensions of the world view, the cognitive, the normative and the transcendental, are covered by its content.

'Thus have We sent to you a messenger
from amongst yourselves to recite to you Our revelation,
to purify you and to instruct you in the "book" and
the wisdom and to teach you what you do not know'

says the Koran in 2:151.

At the time when Muhammad began to develop his message, the west and the centre of the Arabian peninsula was, so to speak, an island of tribal paganism engulfed by, and partly also intermingled with, elements of the prophetic, more or less monotheistic religions. The Arabic principalities on the Syrian and Iraqi borders professed one or the other version of Levantine Christianity (Monophysite or Nestorian); Yemen was the scene of a Judaeo-Christian contest, which eventually gave foreign powers, Ethiopia and Persia, the pretext to intervene. The eastern shores of Arabia were under the domination of the Zoroastrian Sassanids and in the city of Medina (then known as Yathrib) there was a strong Judaic community.

But the engulfed Arabs were not without a deeper religious intuition. There was a kind of monotheistic tradition, represented by people known as *hanifs*. It is difficult to gues how strong this monotheism – the *Hanifiya* – might have been. Muhammad attached this term to Abraham who in his view was 'neither Jew nor Christian'.[1] But in the Islamic terminology the period immediately preceding Islam is described as the *Jahiliya*, i.e. Age of Ignorance, a term which does not seem to give much weight to the Abrahamic tradition at that particular time.

Nevertheless, the challenges of Judaism and Christianity to life in Arabia must have been strong enough. The reflections of their Holy

Writs and traditions, together with Muhammad's reproach that the Jews and Christians spoilt the purity of the monotheistic tradition, amply demonstrate the point.

Yet the genealogy of Muhammad's message is not our concern. For the Muslims it came as God's revelation and for us the main point is that on Muhammad's message a world view was built which, in due course, the whole of the Levant and even other parts of the world were to make their own. Whilst the politically-inspired bids for a pan-Levantine empire (the Assyrian, the Persian and the Graeco-Macedonian empires) failed, the religious message carried by people who did not bear the marks of a time-honoured civilization met with an unprecedented success.

The rise and spread of Islam is one of the outstanding examples of the role of ideation in history. W.M. Watt tried hard to uncover the economic and social roots of Islam in Mecca, Medina and elsewhere; but he also had to admit that 'economic and traditional factors do not completely determine the social response, since variations are possible through differences in intellectual and imaginative capacity'.[2]

But, having said that, W.M. Watt nevertheless wanted to establish the primacy of social over religious thought: 'Muhammad's bid to remedy the social evils of his time could not have succeeded unless he had brought other men to follow him and this was impossible unless what he proclaimed was (or involved) an ideational system. From this we conclude that the function – or at least a function – of ideation is to make it possible for a large number of men to co-operate consciously.'[3]

But ideation is not only a matter of the rationalization of human wishes. It is a complex phenomenon in which sentiments, interests, passions and, last but not least, deeply ingrained habits, the genius loci, play decisive roles. And these many sources and features of any great ideation are also at the root of its internal differentiation with its multi-faceted cross cuttings and nuances.

To understand Islam and its historical development, to understand the nature and the course of Islamic civilization we have to try to sort out this complexity paying due regard both to its spatial and to its temporal dimension. Fortunately, Islam and its history has for many years now been the subject of painstaking and excellent studies. With the help of their analyses and insights we shall attempt in this chapter to give an account of the ways of Islam during the first thousand years of its existence.

As has been said already, Islam was born in a society which had only been touched to a moderate extent by the earlier civilizations of the Levant. Furthermore Muhammad addressed his message to people whose minds were not totally hostile to religious innovation. Only the vested interests of the ruling families in Mecca and the Judaic tribes in the city of Medina (Yathrib) opposed Muhammad's message and policy.

In a tribal society divided into an urban and a pastoral sector and lacking a common and effective political superstructure, Muhammad had to solve not only religious but also political issues. In this sense his position resembled that of Moses rather than that of Jesus. Understandably, Muhammad also had to adapt his stance as the situation developed. He had to exert a sensible balance between firmness in principles and flexibility in practical arrangements and policy. His example in this respect helped his community to survive in times of crisis after his death.

In founding a new religion, Muhammad gave the Arabian peoples, divided into independent tribes, two important assets: a common organization and a sense of historical mission. Both the transcendental roots of this mission and an organized community were essential. The energy which the Arab tribes, on the one hand pastoral and nomadic and on the other hand urban, invested in mutual raids and petty wars, was diverted outwards: within less than one century the Islamic community, the *umma*, was to rule a vast empire. Hitti rightly described Muhammad as a triple initiator: of religion, of nation and of state.[4]

The tremendous success of Islam was at the same time a formidable challenge. Internal issues emerging from the life of the Islamic community and from its religion mingled with external issues resulting from the rule over peoples of other religions. A particularly grave problem arose from the increasing numbers of non-Arab converts to Islam, converts who brought with them attitudes and approaches different from those of tribal Arab society.

The basic principles of Islam are comparatively simple. A strict monotheism, and a sense of duty towards God and one's fellow men, are manifested in the so-called five pillars: the confession of faith in the exclusive God Creator and his messenger Muhammad; the prayer (later fixed at five daily); alms-giving (later developed into a tax on property); fasting (one month in a year, and whenever appropriate as a penance); and the pilgrimage to Mecca (at least once in a lifetime, health and money permitting). Also associated with the belief in one exclusive God is the belief in angels and especially in the Last Judgment.

In particular circumstances, the able-bodied men may be required to serve in the Holy War (*Jihad*) against the pagans until the latter are converted, or against peoples of other monotheistic or scriptural religions (peoples of the Book) until they accept the domination of Muslim rulers and pay them taxes. Under these conditions the conquered people became protected people, the *dhimmis*.

Whether or not a religion was tolerated, however, was not only a matter of its principles but often also a matter of political expediency. The peoples of the Book *par excellence* were those who followed the Bible: the Jews, the Christians and the Sabians (also known as Mandeans or Nasoreans, i.e. followers of St John the Baptist). The Zoroastrians, as long as they could be considered monotheists, and to some extent also the Manichees, obtained this status later.[5] In the more remote areas, where Muslims were a tiny minority, the criteria were even more lenient. Thus there were areas where even the (for the Muslims) openly idolatrous Hindus or occasionally the Buddhists were tolerated. On the other hand, all non-Muslims were expelled from Hijaz.

Territories which were dominated by Muslims were described as *Dar al-Islam*, i.e. the sphere of Islam, whilst all the rest of the world was dubbed *Dar al-Harb*, i.e. the sphere of war. As will be shown later on, however, war remained endemic also within the sphere of Islam, and these wars were almost always fought between the Muslims themselves.

The ethical requirements are formulated on several occasions in the Koran. The most coherent is the following commandment in Sura, 17: 23–37:

Thy Lord has decreed that ye shall not serve ought but him; and to parents kindness . . . . And give the kinsman his due, and the poor and the wayfarer. But do not lavish wastefully. Do not keep thy hand fettered to they neck, nor yet spread it to full width. . . . And slay not your children in fear of poverty. We will provide for them. Beware: to slay them is great sin. And approach not to fornication; it has always been vileness and evil as a practice. And slay not the soul that God has made inviolable, save for just cause . . . . And approach not the possessions of the orphan, except for what may be better, until he reach his full strength. And fulfil your compact. Verily your compact shall be required. And give full measure when you measure and weigh with just balance . . . . And make no accusations of foul deeds where thou hast no knowledge: verily hearing, sight and mind, all these shall be questioned about it. And walk not on the earth with self-conceit: thou wilt neither split the earth nor touch the mountains in height.[6]

Thus it was possible to introduce some substantial innovations. As Allah is repeatedly presented in the Koran as the compassionate, the merciful, a serious effort was made to substitute other penalties for the blood revenge and to introduce a sense of social responsibility ('next to piety or fear of God come equity and just dealing', 5:9).[7] Enslavement of a fellow-Muslim was forbidden.

Some improvements were achieved especially with respect to the position of women. Polygamy was limited to four wives and even this was qualified with the provision that they had to be treated equally by their husband. The conditions of female inheritance were also improved. But the most effective edict was the Koran's ban on the killing of girl babies – apparently a widespread custom in the Age of Ignorance, *Jahiliya* (before God revealed his will in the Koran).[8]

The straightforward commandments, the simplicity of the ritual and, last but not least, the deeper meaning it gave to one's life – these apparently were the most appealing features of the Islamic religion.

On top of that, it was particularly significant for the Arabs and for Arabic-speaking people that the Koran was an outstanding masterpiece of the Arabic language. As Gibb put it, 'No man in fifteen hundred years has ever played on that deep-toned instrument with such power, such boldness, and such range of emotional effect as Mohammed did.'[9]

But this was not enough to keep together even a simple community, to say nothing of a multi-ethnic and, for about half a millennium, multi-religious empire, over which the Islamic community, the *umma*, presided as its supreme, commanding layer. There was a need for apposite integrative institutions; in the Islamic civilization these emerged gradually, often in an improvisatory fashion, and only as time went on did they become formalized and rationalized. Simultaneously attempts were made to achieve integration by alternative means, attempts which occasionally succeeded in welding together smaller 'splinter' groups within the Islamic body social.

5.3   THE UMMA AND THE CALIPHS AND IMAMS

The first master institution of the nascent Islamic civilization was the caliphate. As Muhammad did not claim to be anything more than God's messenger (*rasul Allah*), and was believed to be the last such, 'the seal of the prophets', his successor could not claim to be more than the Caliph (*khalifa*), i.e. successor or deputy, of the messenger of Allah.[10]

The foundations of the caliphate were laid within the thirty years after Muhammad's death; during that period four Caliphs of patriarchal stature, Abu Bakr, 'Umar, 'Uthman and 'Ali, all considered righteous by the Sunni tradition, successively commanded the faithful. All of them were in some way related to Muhammad, the first three through his wives, and 'Ali both by virtue of being his cousin and by marriage to his daughter Fatima. This constituted their claims to leadership, but they needed a further qualification: the consent of, or rather negotiations with, some elders within the broad family and companions of the Prophet. Two of the first four Caliphs, 'Umar and 'Uthman, were murdered by their foes, 'Ali, by his former supporters, who accused him of softness in defending his claims and seceded from his camp (the Kharijites). The fifth Caliph, Muawiyah, closely related to 'Uthman, won power after a prolonged struggle against 'Ali – a victory won by politicking rather than fighting – and founded the first caliphal dynasty, the Umayyad dynasty. 'Ali's older son resigned his claims for financial compensation, while his younger son, Husayn, together with his four sons and other relatives, was killed in an abortive bid for power at Kerbela (in 680 AD). This event has to be borne in mind because at the time of writing it still plays a significant role in one basic internal quarrel within Islam.

Meanwhile steps were taken in order to demarcate clearly the new religious community and to establish its power apparatus. On the religious plane two events in particular have to be mentioned. Seventeen years after Muhammad's death, under 'Umar, the Islamic lunar calendar (in which a year is eleven days shorter than the Gregorian year) was initiated: its starting date was the *hijra*, Friday, the day after the Prophet's flight on 15 July 622 AD from Mecca to Medina where he began his career not only as a religious but also as a political leader. Nineteen years after Muhammad's death, under 'Uthman, the canonized version of the Koran was collated. In contrast to other religions (such as the Jewish and the Zoroastrian) where the faithful had to wait centuries or even a thousand years for the canonized version of their Holy Writ, the Muslims had their Holy Book within two decades.

On the political plane a skilful combination of strength and diplomacy *vis-à-vis* the conquered peoples was of paramount importance. In the first instance local administration was left in the hands of the locals who accepted the Muslim domination. It took about forty years for the administration of the conquered lands to become adequately manned by the Arabs. In effect, the Islamic community, the umma, headed by the caliph, became the backbone of the polity, which was superimposed upon civil societies of other religions while leaving them a reasonable amount of communal autonomy. A similar pattern, involving the superimposition of the polity of the conquerors on the conquered societies, had long been familiar. But the substitution of ideological, i.e. religious, criteria for the blood relationsihp was what made the position of Islam different. The caliph thus appeared in three guises: to the Muslims as their spiritual and secular ruler in one person, and to the dhimmis (protected non-Muslims) as a merely secular ruler. Thus emerged a complex situation marked by overlapping and changing loyalties and scales of stratification.

Significantly the most grave problems which the caliphate had to face originated within the Islamic community. The rule over the infidels created comparatively fewer difficulties; the Monophysite and Nestorian Christians, who under Byzantine rule had been under heavy pressure to conform to their rulers' orthodoxy, relaxed under the more tolerant caliphs. The Zoroastrians, whose apparently more monotheistic wing was also tolerated, were in no mood to resist the new masters. Only occasional strongly discriminatory or repressive measures, such as the imposition of increased taxation upon the dhimmis, led to disturbances; the most serious of these were several uprisings of the Copts in Egypt, that took place under the first Abbasids. However peasant revolts, apparently sparked by similar causes, also cropped up elsewhere irrespective of religious affiliation.

Within the Islamic community, the umma, there were several types of division; some of them were determined by blood relationships – and on many occasions tribal rivalries still exploded in bitter confrontations; others were caused by the adherence to a particular shade of religious opinion or a political party, which often made the conflicts still fiercer.

Islamic society itself was stratified according to the proximity of individual families and tribes to Muhammad and according to the honours won in the wars of conquest considered to be holy wars. This was a meritocracy which *via* inheritance turned into a type of aristocracy. At the beginning these people were rewarded merely by higher stipends from the government, but income from land tenure later played a more important role.

Political and religous divisions run across the stratification outlined above. Here the main dividing line was later to become that between the Sunnites on the one hand and the Shi'ites on the other. *Sunna*, to borrow W.M. Watt's term, means the 'example of Muhammad as enshrined in tradition',[11] which has been accepted as a source of guidance supplementary to the Koran. The Sunnite theologians and lawyers gradually developed a flexible method of interpretation, including analogical reasoning, the consensus of experts and, up to a point, where none of these was available, an independent judgment (*ijtihad*). Thus except for the basic principles of faith, Sunnite orthodoxy was a matter not so much of dogma as of method of interpretation.

The *Shi'a* means simply the party, i.e. 'Ali's Party; 'Ali, Muhammad's son-in-law (husband of Fatima), was believed to be, right from the death of the Prophet, his legitimate successor. 'Ali's descendents were, in the Shi'ites view, cheated of their right to succession by the Umayyads. Thus, the Shi'ites developed their alternative succession of legitimate leaders, the so-called *imams*, who by virtue of their lineage going back to 'Ali possessed a charisma deemed to be superior not only to the Caliphs, but also to the orthodoxy of the Sunnites. Thus, one of the contrasts endemic in almost all scriptural religions also developed in Islam – namely that between those for whom the main authority is the Book and the supporting tradition, and those for whom the supreme authority is a personal charisma. To the basic article of faith, that there is no other god than God and Muhammad is his Prophet, the Shi'ites later added that "Ali, the Prince of the faithfuls, is associate to God' (*wali Allah*).

But this was a long way from being the end of the divisions. The fissiparous tendencies were alive in both camps, and additional cross-cutting schisms cropped up. Tribal rivalries and theological differences were the main lines of division. One school of thought, the Kharijites, was not satisfied with a charismatic leadership but stood for a charismatic community as a whole. In their view the sinners could not be lawful members of the Islamic community; the most radical thought amongst the Kharijites – known as the Azraqites – stood for the physical liquidation of sinners.

Yet by the mid-eighth century AD the main bodies of the Kharijites and the Shi'ites had the opportunity of being involved in more constructive ventures. They were not alone in opposing the Umayyads; it was not only the latters' legitimacy which was contested, but also their policy *vis-à-vis* the non-Arab converts to Islam.

From the time of their conversion, the non-Arab Muslims were fitted into what was still basically a tribal organization, as clients (*mawali*) of various Arabic tribes. This ethnic inequality within the Islamic community (umma) understandably aroused resentment. It was in particular the Persians (Iranians) who could not swallow the privileged position of the Arabs, and became staunch supporters of those Arab factions who showed more sympathy for the desire for greater equality. The Persian drive for more self-assertion within the Islamic community also articulated itself in a literary movement known as the *shu'ubiya*.

The co-operation of various dissenting groups helped 'Abbas, a distant relative of Muhammad, to launch a successful revolt against the Umayyads (who ruled as caliphs from 661 to 750 AD). The new Abbasid dynasty (*de iure* 750–1258, *de facto* 750–945) introduced a series of far-reaching innovations which with respect to the structure of Islamic society may be considered as revolutionary. The capital was transferred from the largely non-Muslim Damascus to the newly-founded Dar as-Salam (i.e. Abode of Peace), which became better known under the name of the previous Persian village at that place – Baghdad (i.e. the Gift of God). The non-Arab Muslims, amongst whom the Persians were the most numerous, enjoyed equal status with the Muslim Arabs; many of them were recruited to the caliphal service which, organized according to the Persian tradition, developed into a kind of imperial court. Thus, as bureaucracy proliferated, the Caliph gradually lost touch with his people. The main problem for the Abbasids then was to keep a balance between the Arab and the Persian elements in their service.

But neither the enlarged power base nor the elaborate adminis-tration could stop the centrifugal forces which began to operate on the periphery of the Islamic empire. The only surviving descendent of the Umayyad family managed to escape to Spain where, after fierce fighting, he established an independent amirate. In other outlying provinces there emerged independent dynasties which only nominally, if at all, recognized the Caliph in Baghdad as their spiritual head.

The first to take the opportunity were the Kharijite Berbers in the Islamic Far West – the Maghreb. Their opposition to Arab rule started soon after the conquest of their territories. Partly they took to arms, partly they tried to adapt Islam to their own image. One of their leaders, Salih, flouting the explicit ban on any such undertaking, translated the Koran into a Berber dialect and laid down a modified moral code and ritual.[12]

But it was only after the Abbasid takeover of the caliphate that two independent Kharijite states emerged in Maghreb. One was founded in about 757 in the southern oases by what may be considered the Kharijite 'centre' stream – the Sufrites; the other was founded a few years later in the mountains of Algeria by Ibn Rustum, the Iranian born leader of the Kharijite 'right-wing' – the Ibadites.

The Rustumid, Ibadite state, whose history is better known than that of the Sufrite polity, and which is also of particular sociological interest, preserved its independence until the beginning of the tenth century AD. It was governed by a charismatic religious man, the *imam* who was by no means a despot. The religious elders and the chief justice, the *qadi*, exercized control over the actions of the imams and supervised public morality.[13] It seems that neither a religious orthodoxy nor a heavy tax or work burden were imposed upon the community, whose members enjoyed a civic status and a degree of personal freedom that were unusual for that epoch. Polemics between Muslims of different schools of thought and occasionally even with the Christians are abundantly recorded in the Ibadite state. In Julien's words: 'Every Ibadite . . . was potentially a rebel. Often the imam kept his place only by means of adroit political manipulation. If a conflict broke out coalitions promptly formed and took up arms.'[14]

The main body of the Shi'ites was affected by a major split which occurred over the succession of the sixth imam – Ja'far, who died in 765 in Medina. His oldest son, Isma'il, was found guilty of drinking wine and was therefore rejected by the majority stream of the Shi'ites; they recognized as the rightful imam Isma'il's younger brother Musa, and after him his five successive descendents until the twelfth imam, Muhammad al-Muntazar, who in 878 mysteriously disappeared, becoming the 'hidden' imam, but whose reappearance is 'expected' (this is the meaning of the word *muntazar*). 'In due time he will appear as the Mahdi ('divinely guided one') to restore true Islam, conquer the whole world and usher in a short millennium before the end of all things.'[15]

Some Shi'ites however did not recognize Musa, and regarded Isma'il as the legitimate, the seventh, imam, who is also supposed to have disappeared into hiding (around 760), and is expected to come to rule as Mahdi. Thus though the principle of charismatic succession from 'Ali is the same, the number of recognized imams (together with other doctrinal issues) constitutes the difference between what are known as the Seveners or the Isma'ilis, and the Twelvers (*ithna 'ashariya*) or simply the Imamis, within the Shi'a.

To complete the picture we have still to mention the third and most moderate stream of Shi'a: the Zaydis. They do not believe in a hidden imam, and they recognize as their founder 'Ali's great-grandson Zayd. In 788 their follower, Idris, founded an independent principality in what is nowadays Morocco, which survived until 974. But the main power base of the Zaydis became Yemen.

Later the Isma'ilis became a hotbed for several extremist and even terrorist movements. On the spiritual level, the extremism lay mainly in various shades of esoteric teaching, full of gnostic and neoplatonic ideas and numerical symbols. Some Isma'ilis even embraced as a legitimate protective measure against persecution, a particular doctrine of dissimulation, which required them to hide the true essence of their teaching from outsiders.

Yet in the period under discussion the greatest impact was made by the followers of Hamdan Qarmat, who around 900 established a separate polity on the Arabian shores of the Persian Gulf. Most of what is known about this Qarmatian state comes from the pen of their enemies: the picture that emerges is of a community that was strongly egalitarian, with regard not only to property but also to the position of women. Some sources describe the Qarmatians as sharing wives and wealth, but this cannot be taken for granted. What can be more readily accepted is that the Qarmatian economy largely depended on raids and that the Qarmatians were renowned for the many atrocities they committed. At any rate, the Qarmatians managed to survive as an independent community for more than one and a half centuries.

5.4   FROM THE CALIPHS TO THE SHARI'A

Of the fourteen Umayyad Caliphs, who between them ruled for 89 years, three or four can be classified as statesmen of high standing. Others had reputations as voluptuous *fainéants*; one was famed for his outstanding piety; the rest were rather mediocre figures. Almost all of them had to devote greater or lesser effort to fighting the fissiparous tendencies resulting from ideological, tribal or personal rivalries. Yet once the caliphal machinery was created and the charisma of the successor to the Prophet was routinized, the caliphate became a going concern; only a radical change of the whole social setting could seriously upset its operation.

This actually came about after a lapse of yet another one hundred and fifty years, after the Umayyads' successors, the Abbasids had inflated and promoted the caliphal apparatus without in the end being able to contain its Parkinsonian effect and hold its proliferating provincial branches together.

The gradual decomposition of the caliphate started soon after the Abbasid takeover, when governors of the outlying provinces began to act as sovereigns. After one hundred years or so of Abbasid rule, commanders of the military guards recruited from the slaves began to interfere in issues of caliphal succession and policy. This development came to a head in 945, when the Buwayhids took the office of the *amir al-umara* (a kind of majordomo), thus becoming secular rulers of what remained of the Abbasid caliphate.

Fortunately, during the first century of Abbasid rule, the Sunni scholars were able to create a differentiated system of Islamic law, the Shari'a, and thus to forge a new bond of integration; this then saved the unity of Islamic civilization at the time when the caliphate was no longer in a position to fulfil its integrative function.

There were altogether four schools of the Shari'a, all accepted by scholarly consensus. The first school, the so-called *Hanafiya*, named after Abu Hanifa (d. 767), excelled by virtue of a highly developed sense of tolerance and equity. Its method was in principle casuistic, making extensive use of analogy and free reflection. It was well suited to the relaxed atmosphere of the epoch.

However Abu Hanifa went too far for the conservatives centred in Medina and led by Malik Ibn Anas (d.795). His school, the *Malikiya*, was reluctant to use analogy and free opinion, and in cases where the tradition was not unambiguous, it gave preference to local practice.

The third school, the *Shafi'iya*, founded by Ibn Idris al-Shafi'i (d. 820), attempted a synthesis and followed the middle road between the two earlier schools. The Shafi'iya contributed most to the consolidation of the tradition (Sunna) by elaborating the method for verifying the *hadiths*, i.e. the statements on what Muhammad said or did in particular circumstances.

Here however we have to digress and explain what had meanwhile happened on the theological front. The quest for the correct interpretation of the tradition had for some time already been paralleled by the debate as to whether salvation depended more on faith and God's grace or on good works. Those who favoured faith and grace, the so-called Murji'ites (*murji'a* meaning the 'postponement' of judgement), were accused of laxity by the already mentioned Kharijites (the secessionists, i.e. from 'Ali's camp), who maintained that sinners cease to be Muslims.

Confronted with such a dilemma, a more rational school of thought emerged, the Mu'tazilites, who wanted to resolve the problem of theodicy (the vindication of the justice of an omnipotent God who created a world in which evil exists) by stressing man's free will and thus his full responsibility for his works. There were many more issues involved in the controversy, but the main bone of contention was the question whether the Koran was the eternal word of God, as the orthodoxy believed, or whether it had been created at the time of revelation, as was maintained by Mu'tazilites.

Had this issue remained an academic one, not much would have happened. But the Mu'tazilites overplayed their hand when they persuaded the caliph of the day, the enlightened al-Ma'mun, to make their stance official in the judiciary and the administration. The caliph required the respective dignitaries in Baghdad and in the capitals of the provinces to declare publicly the belief that the Koran was created; otherwise they were dismissed. Thus, as Hitti observed, 'by a strange irony of fate did the movement which had a party standing for free thought become a deadly instrument for suppressing thought'.[16] And another irony is that it happened under a caliph renowned for his open-minded support of the arts and sciences.

Although the government interference in theological matters (*mihnah*) was abolished within sixteen years, it produced a strong backlash reaction. One of the judges affected by it, Ahmad Ibn Hanbal (d. 885), founded the fourth school of Islamic law, which marked a full swing back to rigid orthodoxy. In contrast to the earlier schools of the Shari'a, who granted each other mutual recognition, the Hanbaliya often became intolerant. It was then largely agreed that the epoch of independent judgments (ijtihad) in law and theology was over; as the appropriate formula put it, 'the gate of the ijtihad was closed'.

Though further creativity was barred within the field of religious law, all the four schools remained available for individual rulers to choose judges from their ranks. In contrast to the canonic law of the Christians, the Muslims enjoyed a certain scope for differentiation.

Although the gate of the ijtihad was closed, the problem of theodicy, which the Mu'tazilites had tackled by positing free will and the rationality of divine action, remained open. The solution was left to a Sunnite theologian al-Ash'ari (d. 936), who broke away from his Mu'tazilite teacher and attempted a new synthesis. In his view, all acts originate with God; but they attach themselves to the will of men who thus 'acquire' them. This may look to us like a piece of sophistry; but a quotation from al'Ash'ari's work may illustrate his dilemma:

> Let us imagine a child and a grown-up person in Heaven who both died in the True Faith. The grown-up one, however, has a higher place in Heaven than the child. The child shall ask God: 'Why did you give that man a higher place?' 'He has done many good works', God shall reply. Then the child shall say, 'Why did you let me die so soon so that I was prevented from doing good?' God will answer, 'I knew that you would grow up into a sinner; therefore, it was better that you should die a child'. Thereupon a cry shall rise from those condemned to the depths of Hell, 'Why, O Lord! did You not let us die before we became sinners?'[17]

But however unpleasant the consequences of the doctrine of acquisition (i.e. of God's decision) might be for individuals, the absolute power and grace of God were vindicated.

Concerning the politically most sensitive issue, whether the Koran was created or eternal, al-Ash'ari took up a more straightforward position; he maintained that like all God's attributes, God's speech was eternal. But, he asserted, the Koran as we know it, i.e. a definite text of a certain length, etc., is only an expression, albeit a supreme expression, of the eternal speech of God which in itself is a 'mental word'.[18]

The closing of the ranks of the orthodoxy has to be understood against the background of the political disintegration of the Islamic polity. In 909, a Shiʻite of the Ismaʻili persuasion, claiming descent from Muhammad's daughter Fatima, succeeded in gaining power in Tunis, where he proclaimed himself the caliph. In 929 the Sunnite amir of Spain took a similar step, and the third, the Cordovan, Caliphate was born. In 969 the Fatimids conquered Egypt and in 972 transferred the caliphal seat to the newly-founded city of Cairo. Meanwhile in 935 a Shiʻite dynasty of the Buwayhids (Shiʻites of the most moderate, Zaydi persuasion) assumed power in Western Iran; in 945 they took Baghdad, forcing the caliph to acknowledge them as the chief commanders (*amir al-umara*). From then on the caliphs were merely figureheads, their names remembered in the Friday prayer and on the coins, but otherwise at the mercy of their amirs. Thus that unity of the secular and the spiritual power that had characterized the first three centuries of the Islamic era disintegrated even in the centre of the Islamic empire.

In that situation the Islamic law, and the establishments of higher education (*madrasas*) which began to be founded in the cultural centres of Dar al-Islam, became the main integrative institutions of the Islamic civilization. In outlying provinces, however, customary law also played a significant role.

At that time a marked advance was also made by the so-called non-Arab or ancient, i.e. mainly Greek, doctrines learnt in the previous century through the mediation of the Syrians. Surprisingly, the main centres of cultural activity shifted from Baghdad to the periphery, to eastern Iran, Central Asia and Spain. In the tenth century, Muslim Spain belonged to the economically most developed countries of the world, and Cordova was renowned as the most cultured and hygienic city in the Mediterranean orbit. Its liberal atmosphere was without parallel.

But at the turn of that century ominous portents appeared in many regions of the Islamic civilization. There were sporadic eruptions of religious fanaticism (in Egypt and even in Spain), but the most significant developments were the gradual ethnic shifts and invasions which affected first the periphery and then almost the whole of Dar al-Islam.

These changes were to upset the ethno-religious balance which had established itself during the three centuries of Muslim rule. The main aspects of this balance can be succinctly summarized as follows. The vast majority of Iranians abandoned Zoroastrianism and embraced Islam, but kept their language which even began to experience a new literary revival. Most Syrians, and also Egyptians and Andalusians, preserved their Christianity, but in their everyday life and for secular purposes, they began to use the Arabic language. The position of Jews was similar; they preserved their religious identity but otherwise became Arabicized. The Berbers of North Africa, after their several attempts to shake off Arab domination had failed eventually (following a new Arabian influx) became not only Muslims (having earlier been Christians or pagans), but largely also Arabic-speaking. Their individual tribes asserted themselves through sectarian and/or dynastic ventures. Only Hijaz, from where the non-Muslims had already been banned from the time of the second caliph, and with it a greater part of Arabia proper, was both ethnically and religiously homogeneous.

5.5 FROM THE SUNNA TO THE SUFIS

The fourth century of the Islamic era (roughly the eleventh century of our reckoning) was marked by great changes which affected the ethnic and social structure of the Levant. Islam itself underwent a spectacular reconstruction.

The ethnic shifts came both from without and from within, and both kinds were soon reflected in changes in social relationships. The Abbasid caliphs had begun to employ foreign mercenaries, mainly of Turkic origin. Their leaders, like the Libyan and Nubian mercenaries in ancient Egypt, gradually assumed *de facto* power in individual Muslim monarchies and eventually founded dynasties of their own. Understandably, the new masters raised new claims and there was a considerable redistribution of property; what at the beginning of the Islamic rule was considered to be the property of the treasury was gradually granted as benefice holdings (*iqta*) to the new military aristocracy. To begin with the position of the peasants as tenants did not change, but with the progression of what may be described as a kind of feudalization, substantial changes occurred in this respect as well.

The Turkic infiltrators or invaders became divided into various tribes and settled down in several waves. The size and density of their settlements varied, but, with the exception of the Islamic West, the Maghreb, which was the domain of Berberian militancy, the Turkic presence was felt everywhere.

The Iranians, who had so energetically supported the takeover of the caliphate by the Abbasids did not take much part in political developments during the epoch discussed in this section; they found their main self-realization in the sphere of culture. After having first mastered and enriched the Arabic language, in the eleventh century AD, they began to use their own language, the New Persian (*darik*), written in the Arabic script. The epic, together with lyrical and religious poetry, were the main genres in which the New Persian attained its artistic perfection. But their cultural activities were not confined to literature; in flagrant contrast to the spirit of Islam which, following the Judaic tradition, forbade any visual representation of living creatures, the Persians were of all the Muslims the most keen to make painting a legitimate branch of artistic creation.

All this was possible because a new spirit penetrated religious life. Intuitive and contemplative thought, the mysticism of the Sufis (the name is probably derived from *suf*, i.e. wool, pointing to the coarse garment worn by the ascetics) became the new popular way of Islam. It has been widely accepted that Sufi mysticism was a child of the non-Arab tradition within Islam; but as F. Rahman has shown, there is a genuine mystical element in those passages of the Koran which belong to the earliest, i.e. the Meccan, of Muhammad's messages. Muhammad's prophetic consciousness, which issued in his mission, was founded upon very definite, vivid and powerful mystic experiences briefly described or alluded to in the Koran (17:1; 53:1–18; 81:19–25).[19]

In that sense, Sufism can be understood as a turn away from the mature towards the young Muhammad, a turn of a kind which our contemporaries know so well from the development of Marxism outside the countries where it became established as a philosophy (ideology) of the state. This parallel may also be useful for our understanding of Sufism. The young Muhammad had mystical experiences which, however, did not find an echo in the Arab environment, in which merchants and pastoralists were the most active groups. When, however, Islam became the religion of other nations where some propensity to mysticism and gnosis happened to be endemic, it was just a matter of time before these mental attitudes made inroads into Muhammad's religion. And this happened at the time of the great ethnic and structural shifts of the fourth and fifth centuries of the Islamic era (*c*.1020–1220), when the established Islam of the theologians lost a good deal of its appeal.

In contrast to the Sunnites, the Sufis did not recognize the orthodox method of interpretation as a sufficient source of religious understanding, but cultivated also a direct, intuitive experience of God. Against orthodox knowledge (*'ilm*) and understanding (*fiqh*) they stressed intuition (*ma'rifa*). This implied a certain limitation of sensual perception for the sake of ecstatic experiences. The fear of the Last Judgment which played an important role in Muhammad's message lost its crucial position, and instead a motif of love became paramount. However, as Sufism spread, the love motif became conceived of in such broad terms that in Sufi poetry there was virtually no demarcation between religious, transcendental love and erotic love. This mood was especially fostered in the Iranian and the Indian environment.

Each new religious idea needs a corresponding institution. The Sufis found theirs in the associations of like-minded people which eventually developed into orders led by particularly experienced mystics, the *shaykhs*, and following a particular road (*tariqa*). The full members of these orders were wholly dedicated to contemplation and the ecstatic life, while others were, so to speak, part-time participants who otherwise followed their worldly professions.

The Sufi orders became a new master institution in Islam, the third after the caliphate and the Shari'a. W.M. Watt characterized the social function of the Sufi orders as follows:

> The establishment of such an order met a deep religious need of the masses, and may be said to mark the beginning of a new phase in the development of Islam . . . . Besides being a consequence of the cleavage between the scholar-jurists and the masses the formation of the sufi orders . . . produced in their shaykhs a new group of intellectuals who to a great extent wrested the leadership of the masses from the scholar-jurists. This was especially the case when the teaching of the order deviated from normal Sunnite teaching. Some of the orders were very successful among rural populations, where official Islam had roused little enthusiasm – doubtless because the Shari'ah, coming out of a background of Arab merchants and nomads, was often irrelevant to the life of an agricultural community or even detrimental to it.[20]

With the Sufi shaykhs there emerged a cult of personalities who were considered to be more worthy of affection than the historical or hidden imams of the Shi'ites. After his death an exemplary shaykh became a saint and his tomb became a centre of worship. Celibacy, until then alien to Islam, became a sign of sainthood, as did the renunciation of various worldly pleasures which, particularly amongst the ruling classes, had assumed quite repugnant proportions. Amongst the Sufis there was also a resentment against slavery, harems and the services of eunuchs, institutions which appeared to be unworthy of truly religious people.

The close contact with ordinary people and the living example of the mystics and their new emotional form of worship, including music and dancing (whirling), gave the Sufis a particular missionary appeal and integrative strength. It was largely owing to them that the invading nations became accultured in the Islamic civilization, which, however, by the same token, came to differ considerably from its original form.

But the old spirit of Islam was still alive. The Seljuk Turks, who in about 1040 pushed their way over Central Asia to Iran and established their rule over most Asian Muslim countries, supported the Sunnite orthodoxy. Under the auspices of the great Persian vizier Nizam al-Mulk, who served two successive Seljuq sultans, al-Ash'ari's theology was established, about 1065, as the orthodox doctrine of Sunni Islam.

But at the same time another great Sunnite theologian, al-Qushayri (d. 1074), deciphered the writing on the wall and advocated the reconciliation of Sufi methods with the orthodoxy. This call virtually amounted to a reopening of the gate of ijtihad (free judgment in religious matters); another great Sunnite scholar, al-Ghazali (1057–1111), completed what al-Qushayri had recommended.

Starting as an orthodox scholar of al-Ash'ari's school, al-Ghazali was soon attracted by Sufism, but then became a sceptic and, eventually, turned to Sufism again. His greatest achievement was, in H.A.R. Gibb's words, that he 'was able to reestablish theology on a basis of personal mystical experience . . . now, the "way" of the mystics, stamped with the approval of *ijma'* (consensus) and accepted as orthodox, opened a new stage in the history of Muslim religious development'.[21]

But as M.G.S. Hodgson pointed out, there was also a practical justification for this approval: the division of labour. The Sufis dealt with the inward side and the *'ulema* with the outward side of the same faith and truth.[22]

The new approach gained new converts for Islam everywhere, but especially in those countries which were only then being brought under Muslim rule: Asia Minor, northern India and Africa south of the Sahara.

One of the reasons for the spread of Sufism may also be seen in the endeavour to escape from the dire consequences of the disasters which in the thirteenth century affected considerable areas of Dar al-Islam. We shall have more to say on these events in the next section. Here we should mention two outstanding Sufis of that epoch, who, by their writings and by the orders they founded, made the most powerful impact on the shape of Islam: Ibn al-'Arabi of Murcia, with his pantheistic monism and esoteric interpretation of the Koran; and Jalal ad-din ar-Rumi (pen-name Maulavi), whose extensive mystical poetry became a cornerstone of Sufism and in the Turko-Iranian environment acquired even more popularity than the Koran.

The Sufi orders cropped up in great numbers and in various guises. One basic point of difference amongst them was whether they were urban, with a more educated following, or rustic orders, more prone to superstition. In the north-west and in Black Africa, some militant orders also emerged. By their stress on esotericism and the cult of the shaykhs, the Sufi orders competed with radical Shi'ites who as a result lost many supporters.[23] It is no wonder that they eventually turned against Sufism, as will be shown in section 5.10.

In this section we have yet to mention another substantial change which resulted from the ethnic shifts and which complicated the traditional process of societal integration: Shari'a lost its exclusive or at least dominant position as the regulator of interpersonal and social relationships. New rulers, or their viziers, began to pass new laws and establish new courts competent for what may be described as the public law. Thus two parallel kinds of jurisdiction emerged: the traditional, religious Shari'a, applicable mainly to family matters, to matters of inheritance and worship, and adjudicated by the time-honoured qadis; and the new, as it were secular, or state law (often called *siyasa*), which up to a point linked up with the traditional customary law (*'urf* or *'ada*), but which from the middle of the thirteenth century onwards became entrusted to special courts and judges (*hajib* etc.). Under these circumstances Shari'a could not keep its role as the master institution of the Islamic civilization.

On the whole it may be said that Islam, as it emerged from the great ethnic shifts and repercussions of the twelfth and thirteenth centuries AD, had an outlook which was very different from that of the preceding epoch. The fact that Islam could absorb all the ethnic shifts, survive, and even gain new ground, was due to two crucial factors: religious reconstruction through Sufism, and a new military and administrative organization – the Mamluk-Janissari system, to which we shall turn in the next section.

5.6 ISLAM UNDER A TWOFOLD ATTACK

The reconstruction of Islamic society which took place from the fifth to the seventh century of the *hijra* (i.e. *c*.1050–1350 AD) was far-reaching and complex. Most conspicuously it affected religious life, the ethnic composition of Dar al-Islam and its geographical extent: the loss of Spain was more than compensated for by the gains in Africa, and above all in Asia, where Muslims conquered most of India, and Indonesia became a rewarding target for their missionary activities. Last but not least there emerged in Asia Minor a new powerful Muslim state, the Ottoman Empire, which in the following two centuries incorporated the whole of the Byzantine part of Orthodox Christendom into the Islamic political orbit. The Russian part of Orthodox Christendom also experienced a period of domination by the new, Turkic, converts to Islam.

But there were also significant changes in the political and socio-economic structure of the Islamic civilization. As war played the dominant role both with respect to the extent of Dar al-Islam, and in deciding who ruled in its individual parts, the political regime and also the socio-economic arrangements responded to the demands of military efficiency.

These demands emerged not only from the never ceasing internecine warfare but above all from the foreign infiltrations and invasions from abroad, the Dar al-Harb. For Muslims accustomed to the reverse situation (i.e. Muslims attacking the outside world), this must have been a traumatic experience.

The infiltrations, taking the form of tribal migrations from beyond the frontiers, brought about a different type of social upheaval. New nomadic elements were added to the already variegated population, new types of property, possession, taxation, etc. had to be grafted upon the system which the caliphate and Shar'ia had established. The infiltrators were mainly of Turkic origin and pagan, but were keen to embrace Islam.

The attackers, i.e. the people who were as a matter of principle hostile to Islam, came from two corners: from Western Europe, and from Mongolia. In the mid-thirteenth century these attacks almost became a co-ordinated assault. In military terms Islam could withstand these attacks only by developing a military apparatus which was without parallel in any other civilization, and which we shall discuss shortly. Psychologically the decisive factor in Islam's survival was Sufism, with its inner and more emotional religiosity. The socio-economic changes were the least imaginative; they resulted from the new military structure in the Islamic states. We shall say more about these changes in section 5.7.

The creation of an appropriate military apparatus began as early as the eighth century, when the original striking power of the predominantly Bedouin armies was on the wane. The caliphs began to employ professional soldiers. But developments did not follow the pattern established by Pharaonic Egypt or Carthage, where ample use was made of the mercenary armies. The Muslim rulers preferred a tighter hold over their guards. They acquired them as slaves, most often bought as boys, who were then properly trained and educated and, of course, converted to Islam. Under the strict discipline they were encouraged, by the prospects of promotion to the ranks of military nobility, to show their martial, and possibly also managerial, prowess. These guardsmen, called Mamluks (i.e. purchased white slaves), were wholly dependent on their masters; they enjoyed their status only for one generation, and their sons could not become Mamluks by inheritance. Thus the Mamlukdom could not succumb to that intergenerational decay which the Tunis-born Arab historian, jurist and statesman, Ibn Khaldun (1332–1406) discovered to be the iron law of development to which elites in his world were subject.[24]

Thus the new system of the Mamlukdom offered its masters not only a high degree of efficiency but also, as long as supplies of a good stock were available, and the principles upheld, a protection against inter-family feuds.[25]

In the Muslim West (Maghreb) there were warriors of yet another kind in operation: the military religious orders or rather militant sects of Almoravides and Almohades, closely related to their respective tribal backgrounds. The first of them, the Almoravides (*al-Murabitun*, i.e. inhabitants of a ribat, a kind of monastery),[26] were based on the tribes of the Western Sahara and adhered to the conservative, Maliki, school of Islamic law. Towards the middle of the eleventh century the Almoravides became masters of the whole of Maghreb (North Africa). After the collapse of the Cordovan caliphate in a protracted civil war (1009–31) they were able to stop the advance of the Christians against the Muslim domains in Spain, which had fallen into anarchy.

However an excess of power and of family and tribal rivalries, combined with the softening effect of the cultivated and prosperous urban surroundings of Andalus, weakened the moral and military strength of the Almoravides. Their grip on their empire relaxed and the Spanish Christians were able to renew their attacks.

Meanwhile, in Maghreb, there emerged a new prophet and leader, Ibn Tumart, who founded another conservative and puritanical sect. Initially a follower of al-Ash'ari's orthodoxy, Ibn Tumart eventually assumed the position of an *imam*. After protracted fighting, his followers, the Almohades (*al-Muwahidun*, believers in the absolute unity of God), recruited mainly from the Berbers, defeated the Almoravides and took over their possessions, including those in Spain.

The Almohades, however, were able to hold the Islamic half of Spain only for about two more generations. Between 1212 and 1248 the Muslim domain in Spain was reduced to the small emirate of Granada between the Sierra Nevada and the Mediterranean coast.

Under the Almohades, Muslim Spain, the Andalus, experienced its last cultural blossoming. In the highly cultivated climate it was in particular science and philosophy which made spectacular advances. Even the Sufi movement found a significant resonance there. However, the social climate in Maghreb and Andalus did not favour a reconstruction on the lines of that which took place in the Islamic East. On top of that the military organization was not in a position to escape the intergenerational decay which affected equally the Arab and the Berber elites.[27]

As is well known, Spain was not the only Muslim territory under Christian attack. Another assault was directed against the Syro-Palestinian coast of Dar al-Islam.

From the viewpoint of the Islamic civilization the Crusades were an unprovoked aggression. They might have made more sense in the Islamic terms of the Holy War, the Jihad, than in terms of anything related to the Gospels. But even if we think of Christianity in political terms, and consider the strengthening of Christianity in the Levant as a goal, the Crusades were counter-productive.

Until then, Syria and Egypt were still inhabited by many Christians. In Egypt the Copts, and in Syria the Jacobites, the Greek Orthodox, the Maronites and also the Armenian Gregorians formed a substantial part of the population. With the exception of the Armenians, who also possessed their own kingdom in the neighbourhood (the so-called Lesser Armenia on what is now the Turkish Mediterranean coast around Adana), the Levantine Christians remained cool *vis-à-vis* the Latin Christians, whose record of tolerance was far from impressive. They saw them as unwelcome intruders rather than as liberators.

Furthermore, the aggressiveness of the 'Franks', as the Crusaders were called by the Muslims, could not remain without some response in kind by the Muslims: a more determined drive to convert the Levantine Christians to Islam. However this drive was perhaps due more to the other, more dangerous attack on Islam, which came from the depths of Asia.

The eruption of the Mongols and their conquest of the great part of the Eurasian Continent from the South China Sea and Korea in the East to the Mediterranean Sea and the Carpathian mountains in the West is a unique phenomenon in the history of the nomadic peoples, a phenomenon unprecedented in its scope and design. All the civilizations of the Old World of that time were affected by it. Yet the main brunt was borne by the Islamic and Chinese civilizations. The assault on the Islamic civilization was the most devastating.

Like many other invasions, the Mongolian invasion of the Levant was caused by circumstances on both sides; population pressure at home and lack of political stability in the invaded countries. The great Seljuk empire was in a state of decomposition, which allowed the Caliph in Baghdad to recuperate some of his pristine power. Transoxania and a great part of Iran were ruled by the Shah of Khwarizim. His power, however, was no match for that of Genghis Khan, who skilfully exploited the diplomatic blunders and lack of determination of his adversary. Within a couple of years the Kwarizmian empire was destroyed. In 1258 Baghdad was sacked, the Caliph slain and Iraq devastated.

At the time of the conquest the nomadic Mongols showed no appreciation of the urban civilization and field agriculture. They tended to turn the cultivated countryside into pastures for their flocks. The immediate effect was the devastation and depopulation of wide areas, especially in Central Asia, Iran and Iraq. These countries never fully recovered from that blow.

Only two Muslim states were able to stop that avalanche: Egypt, ruled from 1250 by the Mamluks; and the Delhi Sultanate in India

(1206–1526), with a similar military organization. Only the new master institution proved to be a match for the Mongolian war machine. However, as will be shown later, the Mamluk system, by its very nature, led to socio-economic changes similar to those brought by Mongolian rule.

As masters of Central Asia, Iran and Iraq, the Mongolians had to resolve two cardinal problems. One concerned their future socio-cultural orientation, the other the socio-economic structure of the subjugated peoples.

At the time of their great conquest, the Mongolians professed what may be described as pagan shamanism, but they were interested in deriving benefits from any other religion they came across. Their superstitious pragmatism, a mental disposition similar to that of the Chinese, advised them to be on good terms with the representatives of any religion. And their political instincts advised them to embrace eventually the religion of their subjects. This made even more sense when, after the death of Genghis Khan's grandson Möngke in 1259, the Mongol empire broke up into four domains (*ulus*, i.e. a kind of patrimony).

But the problem was that the subjects of the Mongolian rulers often professed more than one religion. In the Dar al-Islam of those days there were many Christians, especially of Nestorian persuasion and their Church undertook wide-ranging missionary work throughout the Mongolian domains. Some Turkic nations, such as the Uighurs, had professed that brand of Christianity before they turned Muslim. Quite a few Mongol dignitaries had Christian wives, and Christian scribes served in Mongolian chancelleries. The other side of the coin was that the Levantine Christians, whether Nestorian, Monophysite or Armenian, were, in contrast to the Muslims, keen to collaborate with the Mongols; they even turned to them for help in resolving their mutual feuds.[28] The contrast to the attitude of most Levantine Christians towards the Latin Christian invaders in Syria and Palestine is amazing.

The Latin Christian powers welcomed the *rapprochement* of their Levantine cousins with the Mongolian rulers. They saw in the latter potential allies in their own struggle against the Muslims – and indeed the Egyptian Mamluks had to fight against both of them as if they were in fact allies. There were even some hopes amongst the Christians that the Mongolian rulers would have themselves baptized. But they decided otherwise. Both the Il-khans who ruled Iran, Iraq and a good deal of Asia Minor, and the Chagatais who ruled Central Asia, preferred to embrace Islam.

This decision also bore upon their endeavour to get the problem of socio-economic reconstruction resolved. Both the Il-khans and the Chagatais had to make their *Herrenvolk* understand that it was to their advantage to exploit their subjects economically and not to treat them as a hunting ground. This apparently was not an easy task, and required a top-level political decision and top-level enforcement. In the empire of Il-khans this shift occurred under Ghazan Khan (1295–1304) and in the Chagatai ulus under Kebek Khan. (1318–26). In both instances Islamization was accompanied by the integration of the Mongolian code, *Yasa*, into the Islamic institutions. What this really meant will be outlined in the next section.

In this context only one more feature of the development has to be stressed. Namely, that the effect of both foreign attacks on Dar al-Islam, that of the Crusaders and that of the Mongols, spelt the decline and in some quarters even the end of Levantine Christianity. As a response to the Latin Christian challenge and in revenge for the collaboration of the domestic Christians with the hated Mongols, the Muslims abandoned much of their former tolerance *vis-à-vis* their Christian minorities. In a short time the Christian communities in Central Asia, Iran, Iraq and in the interior of Asia Minor virtually disappeared. In Lebanon, Syria and Egypt the decline was less conspicuous; a number of Copts, Maronites and other Christians have survived as ethno-religious minorities until the time of writing. But Nubia (the present Sudan), which until the eleventh century preserved its independence and Coptic Christianity, became thoroughly Islamized in the fourteenth century.

It was only from then on, i.e. from the eighth century of the hijra, that the greater part of Dar al-Islam became a purely Muslim land. The complex reconstruction of 1050–1350 happened to be a decisive step towards a more thorough integration of the Levant in the Islamic civilization. Until then the Muslim community was in many parts of the Levant only the upper layer superimposed on communities which did not share the Islamic world-view and values and which were allowed to keep, within certain limits, their own integrative institutions. Although in the period under discussion this principle was not abandoned, its practical impact was considerably reduced. In most parts of Dar al-Islam, Islam became the religion of the entire population.

Furthermore, in this epoch two stepping-stones were prepared for a new Islamic expansion: one in northern India and the other in the north-western corner of Asia Minor. These new ventures will be discussed in sections 5.9 and 6.5.1.

5.7   THE SOCIAL STRUCTURE OF THE ISLAMIC CIVILIZATION

Although Islam is a religion with a particularly strong interest in social issues and the organization of society, and the Islamic law did its best to bring this interest to practical implementation in a more systematic way, actual developments often took other paths. Gradually a complex system emerged which can hardly be described in conventional categories.

The difficulty with a clear-cut categorization lies in the fact that the main changes arose from the superimposition of the newcomers' societies on the resident societies or, to put it more precisely, of the victorious elites on the defeated elites. The position of the subject population largely depended on the way these elites had sorted out their mutual relationship.

The original Arab conquest, especially of the lands which had been under Sassanian and Byzantine rule, does not seem to have worsened the position of the peasants and other working people. On the contrary it may have brought about some improvements, but it is extremely difficult to assess their extent.

The village communities, or as some would prefer to say, the village communes, remained the main form of peasant organization; these communities guaranteed their members a comparative stability and security, but allowed for little mobility. Whether by law or by pressure of circumstances, the peasants were almost everywhere attached to the soil and obliged to perform labour services and often also to serve as foot soldiers. In Iran the villages were headed by the gentry, the *dihqans*, who kept their position by conversion to Islam; as the village usually followed suit, both village and gentry were rid of the claims of the Zoroastrian priesthood (the magi) in the area. But the magi might have their own possessions, and above all the great nobility owned large stretches of land.

The basic position was that the Muslims were the conquerors and were entitled to some form of booty. According to the Koran one-fifth had to be set aside for the Prophet (and after his death for the central treasury), and the remainder was to be divided among those who had done the fighting. This principle was implemented having regard to the local circumstances; the lawyers tried to bring some system into the practice, though in many matters their opinions differed. What is best known is the theoretical position of individual schools of the Shari'a, rather than the actual situation. From scattered evidence, however, it can be inferred that all the conquered lands became, directly or indirectly, the property of the Islamic community which then, according to the circumstances, transferred a part of these rights to other users.

As in most societies, ownership and possession were two different things, with a range of possible gradations between these two categories. A special category of the Islamic law was constituted by the pious foundations, the *waqf*; exempt from taxation, they were destined for the upkeep of mosques, *madrasas* (schools), Sufi dwellings, shrines, and charitable institutions such as infirmaries, shelters for old people and for widows, etc. There might also have been family waqf destined for particular people of religious merit.

In theory, the Islamic law required everybody to pay some kind of tax to the treasury. In a nutshell the position was as follows: those who held lands had, if they were Muslims, to pay the tithe (*'ushr*); if they were not Muslims, the higher land tax (*kharaj*) was exacted. From other possessions the Muslims paid obligatory alms (*zakat*) and the non-Muslims the apparently higher poll tax (*jizya*). This differentiation provided a powerful incentive for conversions but sometimes made the Islamic authorities reluctant to accept them. But as more and more people became Muslims, and the treasury did not want to lose revenue, various measures were taken to make the converts pay the same dues as before their conversion. On the occasion of the one hundredth anniversary of the hijra, an ingenious decision was promulgated, namely that as the taxable land was the common property of the umma, which could not be deprived of any of its revenue, the land could not be sold to a Muslim, but if its cultivator became a Muslim and did not want to move, he had to pay a rent for it to the commune, and the latter would pay the tax to the treasury.[29]

There were many different ways to bypass the rules of the Shari'a. Thus, for instance, where the local leaders capitulated by treaty, they might do so with a provision that they would pay a fixed sum annually; individual taxpayers would then continue to pay the old taxes or whatever their leaders required from them.[30] Later, when the practice of tax farming expanded, the common man could do little about the amount of tax which was required or extorted from him.

But as long as the caliphs and the Shari'a exercised their authority, some rules were usually observed which contained safeguards against the worst abuses. The situation began to deteriorate with the emergence of the Turkic immigrants, who often entered into the military service of local rulers and had to be compensated for their services. Only exceptionally were they paid a salary; according to Nizam al-Mulk (cf. p. 120) this was the practice of the Samanid and Ghaznavid dynasties (the former ruled north-east Iran and parts of Central Asia, the latter succeeded them and ruled what is now Afghanistan and the Punjab).

Otherwise with the new masters and their Mamluks, a new type of possession, analogous to the European benefice, was introduced. The beneficiaries, the *muqta'*, military or civil, obtained either an assignment of land, or an assignment of its revenue. In practice there was little difference between these two; both were described as *iqta'*, the assignment of land as *iqta' at-tamlik* and the assignment of revenue as *iqta' al-istighlal*; however, the former was regarded as a heritable title and was at first scarcely distinguishable from private property (*mulk*).[31]

With each wave of Turkic immigrants or invaders, the iqta' system expanded and with it also the contents of the claims arising from it. This development may be summarized as follows: the first sporadic iqta' were offered as early as the second half of the seventh century. From the middle of the tenth century under the Buwayhid dynasty in Iraq and West Iran, iqta' became hereditary.[32] From the middle of the eleventh century the Seljuks attempted to systematize this type of possession and developed their hierarchical structure. The position of the tax collectors (tax farmers) became, in fact, a part of this structure. One of the consequences of this development was that peasants became dependent on individual landlords rather than on the authorities of the state.

But this was not the only path that led towards the personal dependence of the peasants on their landlords. Peasants and even small gentry, hardpressed by the increasing taxation, looked for protection to the powerful muqta', and the muqta' who wanted to be powerful looked for additional land and people. Thus, whether of their own accord or because they were coerced, small farmers commended themselves with their land to the authority of great landlords. Commendation (*iltija*) appeared sporadically as early as the tenth century, but became more frequent with the ethnic shifts from the eleventh century onwards.

The social relationships which emerged from the spread of iqta' and iltija can be described, without hesitation, as feudal. This however does not mean that there was in history one ubiquitous social formation which can be simply called feudalism. As will be shown further in the course of this study, feudalism is a multifaceted, multidimensional phenomenon. In any given instance, its individual aspects may be shaped in a number of different ways. Thus we may conceive of a wide range of feudalisms.

Without prejudice to further investigation, I would like to pick out two types of relationship relevant for our categorization: first, the relationship between those individuals who in some way share the upper, dispositional and revenue bearing, ownership, i.e. between the sovereign as the supreme owner of all the lands on the one hand, and on the other hand, those who enjoy, possibly in a further hierarchical differentiation, some power and a share of income from individual parts of those lands; second, the relationship of those who till the land and take care of the flocks to those in immediate authority over them (whether landlords or officials of the realm).

In both instances there are a number of significant variables. In the upper tier the issues of primary importance are three. Firstly, whether there is any reciprocity of rights and duties, i.e. whether the relationship between the ruler (sovereign) and his feudatories (vassals) is based on some kind of contract or whether the authority of the ruler is not limited by such considerations.

The second crucial issue in the upper tier is the extent to which the ruler (sovereign) abandons to his feudatories (vassals) the command over his subjects in the lower tier, i.e. whether he transfers to the vassals only economic rights, such as collecting taxes, or other prerogatives of the sovereign as well, such as recruiting levies and administering justice. The third issue that may be present is the possible extension of the feudal relationship into the urban sector.

In the lower tier the following issues are of primary importance:

(a) the extent of the sovereign rights handed over to the landlords;
(b) the extent of prestations, i.e. taxes and work load (*corvée*); and
(c) the scope of possible mobility (the right to abandon one's place of work).

In my view, the failure to distinguish between the two tiers of social relationship is at the basis of our difficulties with the term feudalism. In using this term, Western scholars usually have primarily in mind the relationships in the upper tier, whilst Marxists focus their attention on the lower. The outcome is, that in the Marxist interpretation feudalism is basically a socio-economic category, whereas in the view of Western scholars it is fundamentally a political one. As however in real life the political aspects can hardly be properly dissociated from the socio-economic ones, we have to look at the totality of the power structure and social status at various levels of social stratification. Here we may discover a striking contrast. In the upper tier people may be surprisingly free and powerful; they may operate within a kind of pluralistic power constellation, under a sovereign whose power over them is very limited. When we focus on the lower tier, however, we see that the people of the upper one may be in possession of a power at once highly concentrated and extensive (a virtually totalitarian constellation) over these working subjects, who as a rule constitute the vast majority of the population. The more rights the sovereign cedes to his vassals, the heavier the duties of the subjects tend to be, and the more their mobility is limited; such a situation can be described as a 'tight' type of feudalism, in contrast to a loose type where the subjects are less dependent on their landlords.

Between the eleventh and the fourteenth century AD Islamic society underwent an evolution from the mere vestiges of feudalism, via a loose, towards a very tight kind of feudalism. In contrast to West European feudalism, in the Islamic society there was little scope, if any, for contractual relationships in the upper tier;[33] also there were no autonomous towns, but only occasional autonomous city quarters, which had to be inhabited and administered by one particular guild of craftsmen or shopkeepers.

The dual process of the extension of upper tier feudalism and the tightening of lower tier feudalism started, as has been said already, with the Turkic immigration, and attained its apogee after the Mongolian conquest, when in the Islamic lands the Mongols became Islamized and their code Yasa became an integral part of the Islamic law.

According to the Yasa, a codification of customary law, each Mongol was assigned to his military contingent, composed in a hierarchical order of tens, hundreds and thousands of soldiers. This assignment constituted a kind of personal bondage.[34] Once the

Mongols realized that living from regular revenues was better than living from plunder, which in an occupied country was bound to bring diminishing returns, they became interested in extending their concept of bondage to the sedentary population.[35] Thus what had earlier been a *de facto* bondage to one's commune, a bondage dictated by circumstances but not enforceable by punitive measures, became a bondage *de jure*, a complete serfdom. It seems that in this respect it made no difference whether the Mongolian lord (*tarhan*) enjoyed a hereditary tenure of his apanage, the so-called *soyurghal*, or only a temporary tenure, the *tuyul*. On top of that the serfs became subject to the administrative and judiciary power of their lords, who thus became, with the exception of religious matters, their total masters.

Surprisingly, the tightening of the lower tier feudalism did not only affect those Islamic countries which had been conquered by the Mongols. Egypt and Syria experienced a similar development under the rule of the Mamluks. Here, however, the influence of the Crusaders also played a role.[36] But according to H. Rabie the main reason for this adaptation was the influx of Mongol refugees and exiles into Egypt. Although they were not acquired as slaves, the Mamluk sultans conferred the iqta' on them in return for military service, which because of their military prowess[37] was highly appreciated.

Thus the Egyptian peasants, the *fallahin*, also came to be treated like serfs (*qinn*). In principle the fief holders (muqta') had also to perform some non-military functions, such as seeing to the irrigation and cultivation of their holdings (iqta'); but as the muqta' more often than not did not reside in their holdings, these economic tasks were entrusted to special agents (*wakil*) who, being men on the spot, knew how to squeeze the maximum from the fallahin and safeguard a fat share for themselves.[38]

However, as F. Tauer pointed out, there were two circumstances which, up to a point, relieved the pressure of the fiscal apparatus on the peasantry. One was the high revenue derived by the Mamluk treasury from the increased overseas trade, which as a result of the Mongolian invasion and disruption shifted from the Iranian and Anatolian ports to the Egyptian and Syrian harbours. The other was the brisk turnover of military and administrative dignitaries, which prevented them from taking a firmer hold on their benefices.[39]

Absenteeism of the feudatories was also the usual practice in Iran and Iraq; many tarhans (Mongolian warlords) continued their nomadic style of life. There was no *demesne*, no land directly managed by the landlord as in Western Europe; but peasants hardly benefited from its absence. The working duty, the *bekar* (*corvée*) on the construction and upkeep of roads, canals, government and tarhans' buildings was extensive, and an additional tedious obligation was the billeting (*nuzl*) of all sorts of government officials, feudatories, soldiers and their personnel.[40] However, some kinds of work were usually done by slaves. They worked in households, in orchards, in river and sea transport and occasionally also in construction. This may to some extent have reduced the claims on the working time of the peasant bondsmen, who constituted the vast majority of the working population.

The peasant's living standard depended largely on the extent of his possession of the means of production other than land. Under the crop sharing system (*muzari'a*) which prevailed in Iran, the output was divided into five, or possibly six, not necessarily equal parts: one was due to the owner of the land, one to the owner of water, one to the supplier of the seeds, one to the owner of the beasts of draught, one to the owner of the work tools and one to the supplier of the labour force. Peasants who worked with their own beasts, tools and seeds enjoyed membership of the village commune which provided them with a not inconsiderable degree of help and protection. Less fortunate peasants not only had a lower share of the fruits of their work but were completely at the mercy of their landlords.[41]

The grafting of the Mongolian institutions onto the Islamic ones revived the old problem of the differentiation of taxes according to religious affiliation. The Mongols introduced quite a few new taxes, direct and indirect (turnover tax), to be paid by everybody, Muslim and non-Muslim alike. Expeditions to collect these taxes often resembled predatory raids during which those affected tried to hide themselves.[42] A serious attempt to bring some order into the chaotic situation was made by the already mentioned Ghazan Khan, who ruled from 1295 to 1306. He also took positive measures to bolster agricultural production by encouraging increases in the area under cultivation, by making land tenure more secure and by suppressing illicit extortions; but his reforms do not seem to have survived his rule.

On the whole, we may conclude that as a result of the Mongol conquest the tax system and the government administration became more complicated and burdensome than under the rule of the

Shari'a; the licence of those in power knew virtually no bounds. The numerically reduced working population had to work harder and enjoyed less of the fruits of their work than before.

It is small wonder that, under these circumstances, religion in its emotional, mystical form became the main outlet for human distress, a compensation for the mounting difficulties of everyday life. The Sufi brotherhoods led by their shayks sometimes became foci of political unrest, riots, and even attempts at creating their own local polities with a greater degree of latitude for common men. This seems especially to have been the case with the East Iranian town of Sabzawar, ruled from *c*.1336 to 1381 by a strange condominium of local gentry and a popular Sufi order. Constant in-fighting between the two wings of what is known as the Sarbadar community prevented the Sarbadars from making a wider impact on Iranian society. The community survived only as long as the central authority in Iran was weak. Timur easily wiped it from the political landscape.[43]

5.8 THE CONTRASTS IN THE SPIRIT OF ISLAM

5.8.1 General Comment

Like all the other civilizations which we have discussed so far, the Islamic civilization presents us with a wide range of tunes which do not always sound like a symphony. A certain degree of cacophony has always been present within great cultures.

In Pharaonic Egypt it appeared in the staggering contrast between the Memphite theology and its Ikhnatonian offshoot on the one hand, and the sorcery and animal cultures of the popular religion on the other. In Cuneiscript Mesopotamia the contrast was between the rudimentary scientific quest and the exuberant mythology of the national festivals. With respect to the Phoenicians we can contrast the pragmatic mind of merchant people with the superstitious ritual requiring human sacrifices in order to avert the gods' disfavour.

Amongst the Zoroastrian Iranians there was a tremendous gap between those who were able to understand Zarathushtra's message as philosophical speculation with acute ethical consequences, and those who saw it merely as a flag, a code name for irrational and often abominable practices masquerading as worship. Rarely did a revealed religion cover such a vast range of contradictory mental attitudes as in the Zoroastrian religion.

The Jews seem in this respect to be something of a special case. They managed by a concerted effort to keep the extremes out of their world-view. Syncretism, which had the potential to drag their minds down to the utmost depths of superstition, was combated, though not always with success, and the corrosive influence of Hellenic philosophical speculation, which contained more than a germ of scientific curiosity, was warded off. Those who wanted to syncretize on either level had to do so outside the Judaic community. The success, however, was only partial. It merely helped to keep the range of contrasts a bit narrower than was the case with other religions. The gap in later Judaism between, on the one hand, thinkers such as Maimonides and, on the other, the Kabbalah and similar practices, is vast enough to leave us in no doubt that in Judaism the situation was only quantitatively different from that which obtained elsewhere.

Islam in a way inherited something from all the civilizations whose soil it had touched. But the most significant feature appears to be the Muslims' awareness of the breadth of the various tunes, and the effort which they devoted to making these different tunes into a symphony. Nowhere else, save perhaps in India, did the religious men and philosophers try so hard to overcome and synthesize contrasts as they did in Islam.

In the first instance this took the form of admitting without too much fuss that there were two legitimate fields for the exercise of the human intellect: on the one hand the Arabic sciences (*Ulum al-Arab*) which concerned theology, law, philology, linguistics, etc., and on the other the non-Arabic (*Ulum al-Ajam*) or ancient sciences (*Ulum al-Awail*) concerning everything else. The latter could be studied provided that the pillars of the Islamic faith were not overtly called into doubt. And as these latter were comparatively narrowly circumscribed and the interpretation of the teaching involved the use of an elaborate but flexible method, the gate was wide open for the absorption of all the available ancient, i.e. mainly Greek and Indian, knowledge.

The transmission of Greek knowledge to the Arabs and other Muslims was due mainly to the Syrian Christians, both Jacobites and Nestorians, who saw to the translation of most of the ancient Greek writings into their respective variants of the Syrian language; from there the translation into Arabic was easier. Though the Syrian Christians did not develop a particularly original culture of their own, their contribution to the development of culture on a more general, as it were supra-civilizational level, must not go unappreciated.

Individual civilizations, with their particular world-views, moral codes and institutions, always have limits beyond which they cannot extend their intellectual and moral horizons. To use another metaphor: they cannot step over their shadow. There are rare occasions when people manage to grasp and combine values from various civilizations. Furthermore, there are people who are able to pick up time-honoured ideas, rethink them and test their validity against new experiences.

As is also well known, cultural achievements can be accumulated. But, and this is a strange thing, to that end they have to travel from one civilization to another. Here I have in mind mainly the sphere of knowledge. The value of art is too subjective and varies with the changes in fashion. We can to a certain degree compare levels of cultural creativity within one and the same civilization; then, following A. Kroeber, we can say whether one period was more creative than the other. But we would run into great difficulties if we wanted to decide a ranking order between different civilizations and cultures. Each has its own artistic style, which in a given period attains its apogee; the value judgement on their respective charms is merely a matter of personal preference.

From the global point of view we may pick out the salient contributions of individual civilizations and collect them into a special category which can be described as the cultural fund of mankind. But as historians know only too well, this cumulative process is not a unilinear one. It began, at the level of 'civilized' social life in four or five places in different parts of the globe, and took paths that were parallel though not synchronic. There was a lot of overlapping, intertwining and other sorts of give and take. It was like a relay race during which the baton was sometimes lost and even forgotten and then rediscovered, refurbished and carried further.

5.8.2 The Quest for Knowledge

In the transmission and extension of human knowledge the Islamic civilization played a particularly important role. Its main contribution to the ancient sciences lay in the areas of astronomy, chemistry, geography, mathematics, medicine and philosophy. Amongst the Arabic disciplines, apart from theology, the focus was on law, philosophy and linguistics. Historiography can be counted under both headings; it also embraced pre-Islamic, mainly Persian (i.e. Iranian) history.

With respect to science the most creative period was from the second to the seventh century of the Islamic era, i.e. from the middle of the eighth to the middle of the thirteenth century AD. Not only native Arabs, but also Arabicized scholars of other nations, especially the Persians and people of Central Asia, took part in that fascinating venture. Many of them were involved in more than one discipline, some of them were also interested in art; and in all these areas their contribution was outstanding.

The importance of the scientific achievement of Arab and Arabicized scholars for the development of science in Western Europe has been widely acknowledged. At this point, I would like to assess why it was the younger Islamic civilization, and not the older Christian one, that witnessed such a spectacular transmission of ancient scholarship and such a spectacular advance in scientific thought.

Although such an assessment can only be a tentative one, we can be sure that the different attitudes of the two post-Hellenic civilizations towards the development of science were due to a combination of factors; amongst these are the well-known psychological duo, nature and nurture, which will provide us with our basic framework.

On the side of nature we must mention first the freshness of the Arab mind, its youthful character, keen on novelty and venture; and secondly, the fact that there was wide-ranging crossbreeding, which was not confined to the Arab ethnie alone.

On the side of nurture it was the limited scope of religious dogma in Islam – limited in comparison with the Christianity of that epoch – which allowed the pragmatic and speculative thinkers, a group reminiscent of Mannheim's floating intellectuals, to develop their exploratory urge and capabilities; on top of that there was, in contrast to the Christian elite, quite a keen interest in the culture of the subject peoples, the tolerated *dhimmis*.

The factors of nature and nurture together were supported by the environment. The Islamic civilization was superimposed on a wide range of societies and cultures at different levels of development. Dar al-Islam comprised territories of several ancient or senior civilizations whose high culture could not but be a source of inspiration to the Islamic thinkers. One of these civilizations,

Levantine Christianity, was only *in statu nascendi*, and its Syrian branch was, as has been said already, the main transmitter of the ancient Hellenic culture to the Arabs.

But it was not only the Syrian crossroads of civilizations which proved to be inspiring. There was also Central Asia, the *Mawara al-nahr* of the Arabs, the Transoxania of the Europeans, where civilizations met and created an ideal ground for cross-fertilization. Up to now we have touched only cursorily on this area – as an outpost of the Zoroastrian civilization. Transoxania, however, was more than that. It participated in the main stages of the Iranian development: from the rise of Mazdaism, through the Hellenic interlude, to the Zoroastrian renaissance, the Manichean heresy and Nestorian Christianity; it came under cultural influences from India and China; and all this was punctuated by repeated invasions by nomadic peoples from the northern steppes.

Together with the Iranian provinces on the other shore of the Oxus, Transoxania almost became a melting pot. But individual ethnic groups and religious communities lived side by side, more or less peacefully (this was especially the case under the tolerant Turkic khans), not giving too much opportunity for religious syncretism beyond what was represented by the Manichees. In visual art, which attained its peak before the Muslim conquest in the mid-eighth century, the cultural syncretism was more visible. The late Hellenic types of Buddhist saint were charmingly combined with the representations of females in the Indian Gupta style, and males, especially knights, appeared in the traditional Iranian style. To borrow R. Grousset's terms, it was '*un monde charmant et raffiné, survivant attardé des races d'autrefois*'.[44]

Understandably, the conversion of this world to Islam could not happen overnight; even after the conversion, a lot of the ancient spirit survived. This may help to explain why the Islamized Transoxanians gave Arabic culture so many artists and scholars. Central Asia, together with the province of Sindh on the estuary of the Indus river (earlier taken by the Muslims), were two passages through which Indian ideas and values had come to the heart of the Islamic culture, before Islam established itself more firmly in the Indian subcontinent in the course of the eleventh and twelfth centuries AD.

Central Asia was also the place where the Muslims acquired from the Chinese the technique of making paper, which was to remain the most convenient writing material up to the present day. It happened at the time of the battle on the River Talass (751), where the Arabs defeated the Chinese, who had established – for the second time in history – their sovereignty in that area. But as often happens in these cases, the technique taken over from abroad was significantly improved; instead of the Chinese bamboo paper the Muslims introduced a stronger linen paper made of flax.[45]

Another crucial technical improvement, most valuable for the development of arithmetic, was acquired from India: the zero as a sign for powers of the numeral chosen as a base. As will be shown in the context of the Indian civilization, hardly anywhere else did there emerge a meaningful concept of nothingness, but it was owing to the Arab genius that it was brought to full practical fruition.

While talking of the inspiration from Greece, China and India, we must not forget the contribution of the Levantine milieu itself. The Iranian poetic genius matched that of the Arabs, and in visual art most conspicuously succeeded in overcoming the Islamic taboos. The Iranian tradition was also instrumental in the development of Islamic mysticism.

Of the sciences the most conspicuous was the Babylonian tradition of astronomy, which, unaffected by the collapse of the Assyrian power, survived in the formerly Assyrian city of Harran. After the Muslim conquest, Harran's population, in order to conform to the concept of the tolerated dhimmis, adopted the name of Sabians, a Judeo-Christian sect, known as followers of John the Baptist.

Astronomy, mathematics, chemistry, geography and ophthalmology were the subjects in which the Arabs and the Arabicized Iranians (mainly Persians) made the most conspicuous progress. Here the scope for experimentation and empirical studies was considerably extended. The top astronomers worked with the assumption that the earth was round and their calculation of the size and circumference of the earth was astonishingly accurate.[46]

There are many great names which would deserve to be mentioned in this context. Suffice here to mention only five: the three great polymaths who, besides their work in other disciplines, developed Greek philosophy further: the Iraqi Arab al-Kindi (d. *circa* 873), the Transoxanian Turk al-Farabi (d. *circa* 950), and the Transoxanian Persian Ibn Sina (d. 1037); fourth, the most original Muslim physician, the Persian ar-Razi (d. 925); and finally the East Iranian astronomer, mathematician and natural scientist al-Biruni (d. 1050).

Apart from Syria and Central Asia there was a third place in the Islamic orbit where, somewhat later, the intellectual activity substantially contributed to the accumulation, complementation and transmission of human knowledge: to wit, Spain, the Andalus of the Muslims. In contrast to Syria and Central Asia, where the soil was permeated with a rich heritage of several ancient cultures, some of them still living at the time of the Muslim conquest, in Spain the legacy of the past was less impressive. The Romanized Hispanics under the Visigothic warlords could not compete with the sources of inspiration which the victorious Arabs could acquire elsewhere. So it came about that the Arabic scholars in Spain fed on resources acquired mainly in Syria.

A series of polymaths culminated in Ibn Rushd (known in Europe as Averroes; d. 1198), whose commentary on Aristotle opened Western Europe's doors to this long forgotten philosophical giant of Greek antiquity. In a philosophical treatise defending rationalism against the attacks of the leading Sufi mystic and scholar al-Ghazali, Ibn Rushd developed arguments similar to those used by the Christian rationalists in their effort to reconcile faith and reason. Something similar was true of the work of the Arabicized Jewish physician, astronomer, theologian and philosopher Ibn Maymun (known in Europe as Maimonides; d. 1204 in Cairo), whose attempt to explain prophetic visions as psychic experiences went too far to be digested by any theologian.

Another peak of West Arabic culture was the work of Abd ar-Rahman Ibn Khaldun, historian and pioneer of social science. His theory of historical development with its ups and downs, taking into account the external factors of physical environment as well as the internal factors of mental and emotional attitude, is considered to be the first attempt at a complex sociological theory. After completing a colourful career as chief justice and diplomat, trusted with the most delicate missions, Ibn Khaldun died in Cairo in 1406.

Ibn Khaldun was the last Arabic scholar whose intellectual contribution survived his civilization. In the fifteenth century the questing spirit moved to Western Europe, where since that time science too has found a more inspiring abode.

5.8.3 The Twilight and the Shadows

After a short glimpse of the heights of the Islamic spirit, we have also to give a brief account of its less glorious side. It can be found wanting on two counts. First, the Islamic theologians seem not to have been particularly concerned with the harems, eunuchism and similar degrading practices, though castration itself was forbidden by Islam and this ban was, it seems, widely observed. Having said that, we have to add for the sake of fairness that the Christian theologians did not succeed in extirpating similar practices at the Byzantine imperial court either; further, that though the use of eunuchs in the Latin West was forbidden, this ban did not prevent the Christians from castrating males and selling them through the Jewish intermediaries to their Islamic customers, who because of the ban on castration could not produce them at home. A nice example of an inter-religious collusion of hypocrisies.

The worst feature of the Islamic community was, as in so many other civilizations, its elements of ideological extremism. On the whole it should be said that the official Islamic establishment did not have a bad record in this respect. The range of tolerated religions was quite extensive. Not only Jews, Christians and Sabians, as stated in the Koran, but also the bulk of the Zoroastrians, Manichees and Hindus were in principle allowed to follow their own religion.

Punitive measures, including execution, were taken mainly against the so-called Zindiqs; these were originally the Zurvanite materialists, but later this label covered all sorts of unacceptable brands of Zoroastrianism and Manicheeism and, perhaps, even Hinduism and Buddhism. Occasionally Muslim theologians who spread heretical ideas were also put to death; the concept of heresy however was not a stable one. Under the Umayyad Hisham (724–43) two heretics were executed, one for teaching that the Koran was created, the other for maintaining the doctrine of free will. The Abbasid Caliph Ma'mun turned the cards upside down and, as we saw earlier, introduced a kind of inquisition (*mihnah*) against those who did not agree with the Mu'tazilites that the Koran was created and that man had a free will. In contrast to the Roman Catholic Inquisition, however, the Islamic mihnah had a limited objective. It affected only government officials, and the outcome was merely dismissal and not execution. Furthermore it lasted only 16 years (833–49). Yet executions of heretics were carried out on numerous occasions.

A new cause for religious persecution was created by the spread of the doctrine of gnosis amongst the faithful. This idea, that the true knowledge of God could be attained only by ecstasy, was not however considered anything particularly heretical in Islam, until a certain al-Hallaj (a Persian) felt that he was so much in the possession of the knowledge of God that he proclaimed: 'I am the Truth'. In 922 he was tortured and executed; Sufism had its first martyr.

With the exception of these and other similar instances, religious or social intolerance originated in the marginal sects or occasionally in the primitive, tribal spirit rather than in the Islamic establishment.

We have already mentioned the Qarmatian community whose raids terrorized Lower Iraq and the Arabic Peninsula. Two Bedouin tribes of Central Arabia, Banu Hilal and Banu Sulaym, had a particularly bad record as regards this activity. The Fatimids in Egypt, who considered themselves to be the guardians of Shi'ism, tried at first to contain them, and assigned them a certain area in Upper Egypt. When however in the middle of the eleventh century the North African local rulers refused to recognize Fatimid sovereignty any more and instead acknowledged the supremacy of the Abbasid caliphs, the Fatimid Caliph al-Mustansir encouraged the two unruly Bedouin tribes to move further to the west; he gave them some territorial possessions in that area in the form of iqta'.

This move spelt disaster for the heart of the Islamic West (present-day Tunisia and eastern Algeria), an area which had already for other reasons been experiencing a deep crisis. The shift of allegiance from the Shi'ite Fatimids to the Sunnite Abbasids was accompanied by large-scale massacres of the Shi'ites and by the confiscation of their property. Continuous internecine warfare between individual amirates and tribes undermined the political and economic strength of the Muslim states in that area, so that it became an easy prey for attackers. In the middle of the eleventh century the assaults came both from inland and from the sea. The dynasty of Qairawan which, like Carthage 1500 years earlier, also ruled over Sicily, lost this island to the Normans, and in Africa the Qairawan state virtually disintegrated into small political units. According to Poncet's account, some of them were bourgeois republics, some aristocratic principalities, some were tribal fiefs and others were fiefs of a kind of condottiere.[47]

In spite of the vigorous attempts of the Almoravides (c. 1061–1147), and above all the Almohades (c. 1130–1269), whose empire extended to beyond Tripoli, it was not possible to build up a strong and lasting Islamic polity in the Maghreb. To borrow Julien's words 'the history of the Maghreb . . . until the middle of the 16th century is that of a vain attempt to revive the past, of a long stagnation and a slow decadence'.[48]

Unlike Islamic North Africa, Egypt for some time remained unaffected by foreign pressures. Under the tolerant rule of the Fatimid caliphs, it continued to be the main bastion of the Shi'a.

However, one disturbing episode has to be mentioned, because modern Lebanon still lives with its consequences. In 996, abu-'Ali Mansur al-Hakim, a capricious boy of 11, became the Caliph. First he unleashed his rage against his own viziers and against the non-believers, Christians and Jews.[49] But then he turned his attack on the very basis of the Islamic creed. He declared himself to be the incarnation of God; oddly enough, his missionary, al-Darazi, succeeded in converting some hill people in Lebanon, known from then on as the Druzes, who have survived until the time of writing as a specific ethno-religious community which in the 1980s, became particularly vociferous.

But worse was still to come. Around 1090 a certain al-Hasan ibn al-Sabbah founded a secret Ismailite order, which eventually became known as the Assassins. This may be a derivation from the Arabic word *hashishin*, i.e. hashish users. The intoxicant was apparently needed to condition the rank and file, the *fida'is*, for the self-sacrificing acts of terrorism commanded by the Grand Master of the order, whose seat was in the north Iranian mountain fortress of Alamut.

The Assassins started their career by assassinating the great vizier Nizam al-Mulk, whom they accused of having helped to re-establish Sunna dominance in the Seljuk realm. They then carried on killing and maiming representatives of the Islamic elite, right and left alike, for 164 years until, in 1256, the Mongolian khan Hulagu sacked and destroyed Alamut and all the other fortified seats of the Assassins in Iran. The Syrian branch of the Assassins was liquidated by the Mamluk sultan Baybars in 1272. But the order survived; having abandoned its terrorist mission, it underwent a process of ethical transformation from a militant into a peaceful religious sect known as Khojas or Mawlas, a process of which we may find other instances in the course of the world's history.

At present there are a host of other surviving Isma'ili sects, of which one deserves a particular mention: the Nusayris, known also as the Alawites, living mainly in Northern Syria. Having acknowledged 'Ali as the incarnation of God, they constituted themselves into a separate community at the end of the ninth century and later adopted some Christian habits and types of worship. At the time of writing they form the main recruiting ground for the police and elite army units in the Republic of Syria.

In conclusion it may be said that with respect to its heights and its depths the Islamic civilization displays a record of comparative moderation. By not demanding too much from its believers, Islam as a religious and ethical doctrine avoided creating exaggerated tension between what was desirable and what was possible. Evil resulted mainly from human nature; religion did not add particularly strong motives for oppression. It was, to borrow Bertrand Russell's term, 'naked power' rather than ideological selfrighteousness which was the driving force behind most atrocities. Only with the great schism in the Islamic civilization at the beginning of the sixteenth century, to which we shall turn in the next section, did religious persecution assume wider proportions.

5.9   THE THRUST INTO EUROPE

Not only was the Mongolian assault on the Islamic civilization contained and the Mongolian ethnic segment absorbed; the Mongols set in motion forces which, in due course, acquired new space for Dar al-Islam, and further nations were converted to the message of the Koran. The acquisition of Asia Minor and of the Balkans in the northwest and of India in the east was the direct result of the great ethnic shifts of the twelfth to thirteenth centuries; these acquisitions attained their widest extent in the course of the sixteenth century. Indonesia, together with the Sahel zone and the eastern shores of Africa were gained into the bargain during the same era.

Nevertheless, the Mongolian conquest of Iran delivered a mighty shock to the Iranian people. After two and a half centuries of Mongolian and Turkic rule, during which the Iranian spirit looked to religion and art for escape, Iran reasserted herself as a particular, and in many respects self-contained, branch of the Islamic civilization.

Islam, an overtly martial religion, was well suited to the belligerent Turkic tribes pushed by the Mongols towards the west. Most of them embraced the Sunna, but various Shi'ite denominations and Sufi orders also found enthusiastic converts among them.

Amongst the Turkic migrants one particular, smallish, tribe brought to the far north-west of Asia Minor – the Osmanlis – turned this fate into its good fortune. Within two hundred years they established themselves as an Islamic great power in the former domains of the Byzantine empire and united almost the whole of Dar al-Islam to the west of the Zagros Mountain.

This remarkable achievement can be compared with that of Alexander of Macedonia which took place one thousand years earlier, but in the opposite geographical direction. It seems that the Ottoman sultan Mehmed I, the conqueror of Constantinople, was aware of, and liked, this historical parallel.[50] In terms of time and space Alexander's conquest was more spectacular: a much wider area was taken within one short life span, whilst it took the Ottoman empire seven or eight generations to attain its maximum size. But their empire lasted for longer as one polity. On the other hand, in terms of cultural impact, the Graeco-Macedonian conquest of the Levant initiated a process which together with its Hellenistic, Roman and Byzantine stages, lasted, to the west of the Euphrates at least, for a whole millenium. The Ottoman Islamic domination of the Balkans lasted half that time, being of similar duration to the Muslim domination in Spain.

Comparing the two Islamic incursions into Europe, the Umayyad into Spain and the Ottoman into the Balkans, we have to say that the Spanish venture was eventually the more successful in cultural terms; yet after the Christian reconquest, Islam was completely extirpated from the Iberian peninsula. On the other hand, the culturally less exuberant Islam in the Balkans and in the Volga region has survived until the present day.

There are further interesting contrasts in the territorial development of the Islamic civilization. The rhythm of cultural and political vitality differed considerably in various parts of Dar al-Islam. In the thirteenth century, when the Ottomans were beginning to build up their strength on the Dardanelles and the Bosphorus, the Almohades were losing most of the Muslim Andalus; in the middle of the fifteenth century, whilst the Ottomans were rounding out their Balkan dominions, the Muslim dominion in the Ukraine and southern Russia was starting to crack, and the 'Golden Orda' of the Kipchaks was beginning to decompose; and in the middle of the sixteenth century, at the same time as the Ottoman empire was attaining its widest extent (in Europe and elsewhere), the Russians completed their conquest of the Muslim khanates on the middle and lower Volga. Only the Crimean Tatars, having accepted the Ottoman suzerainty, held on until the eighteenth century.

The Ottoman sultanate was in a way a replay of the Umayyad and Abbasid caliphates. It was superimposed upon peoples of various ethnic and religious affiliations. The attitude towards non-believers followed the good Islamic tradition. The Muslims under the Ottomans were part of the pan-Islamic umma (in Turkish *ümmet*). The Christians and the Jews were organized in autonomous *millets*.

After the death of the last Abbasid Caliph in exile in Egypt in 1543, the Ottoman Sultan assumed the title and symbolic role of the Caliph, thus becoming titular head of all Muslims; this measure however was effective only within the Ottoman empire where there was a personal union of the head of the community of believers and the head of the state. Despite this union the dualism of law, which emerged from the great ethnic shifts in the twelfth and thirteenth centuries, became even more conspicuous. From the middle of the fifteenth century, the Imperial will, promulgated after deliberation in the Council of ministers, was published as a kind of secular code (*Kanun nama*).[51]

Thus paradoxically, under the Ottoman Sultans-cum-Caliphs, the Islamic civilization moved a step towards what may be called the separation of church and state. The grand vizier represented the secular branch and the great mufti or *shaykh al-Islam* was the chief interpreter of the Shari'a. That part of the sovereign's power which was administered by the vizier was in fact more extensive than the scope of the Shari'a. It affected all subjects of the empire including the dhimmis (members of protected religious groups), who were not bound by the Shari'a but by their own religious law.

The individual millets were represented *vis-à-vis* the sultan by their religious leaders. Apart from their judicial power in family and property matters they also had to perform important administrative functions on behalf of the state, such as the collection of taxes from members of their communities.

According to the Shari'a the dhimmis were exempt from military service, nor could they be enslaved. In this respect however, the secular law (*'urf*) overruled the Shari'a in one particular, and for the Ottoman empire essential, point, namely the selective, compulsory drafting (*devshirme*) of young boys from the Christian population in the European provinces of the Ottoman empire for military and administrative service to the sultan. From the time when devshirme was codified by Murad I (1360–89) until about the end of the sixteenth century, these conscripts, converted to Islam, properly trained and educated, and known as Janissaries (*yeni ceri*, i.e. new troops), were the main source of the strength and the vitality of the Ottoman empire.

As a new master institution the Janissary system resembled that of the Mamluks in its prime. The main difference was that the

Mamluks were acquired by purchase in the slave market, i.e. not from among the dhimmis. For about two hundred years the Janissaries were a highly efficient meritocratic corps. Surprisingly they constituted a minority (of between eight and thirteen thousand) amongst the Ottoman armed forces. The descendants of the Janissaries were not allowed to inherit the status of their fathers; they obtained small allotments of land as benefices (*timars*), mainly in Asia Minor, and served in the cavalry as the *sipahis*, who were much more numerous than the Janissaries.

The feudal elements in the Ottoman empire, inherited both from the Seljuks and the Byzantines, survived the centralizing tendencies of the Ottoman sultans. Apart from the meritocratic elite recruited from the Islamic converts there was a native gentry whose numbers were gradually increased not only from amongst the sons of the Janissaries but also through various kinds of promotion. There was also a growing number of dignitaries who were allocated large estates in the conquered European provinces. These holdings – a kind of fief (*zeamet* or *has*) – tended to become hereditary.

The bulk of the working population seems to have been in a position where it would be difficult to make a distinction between tenancy and serfdom. Side by side with the settled population the nomadic tribes roamed the countryside. In that respect Ottoman society, especially in its Asian part, did not differ from other societies of the Levant. Also like them, it displayed a cyclic pattern moving from a fairly centralized supreme rule towards more feudal relationships and back again, making for a changeable overall situation. It may be assumed that as in the case of the Byzantine empire, periods of tougher central government tended to be more beneficial for the peasants, whilst the times when feudal relationships were more widespread brought about an additional burden, which may however, in some areas, have been offset by a more effective protection against the depredations of the tax-collectors.

The superiority of the Ottomans over their adversaries in Europe lasted approximately until the end of the sixteenth century. In the seventeenth century there was a certain degree of equilibrium between the two. From the beginning of the eighteenth century the European foes of the Ottomans became stronger, and the expulsion of the Turks from Europe began.

Leaving aside the circumstances on the European side, where the new dynamism was due to a wholesale and complex civilizational transformation, we may suggest the following reasons for the

Ottoman decline. The education of the elite, such as the Janissaries, did not keep up with the progressive technical innovations in the West. The elements of meritocracy in the Ottoman system had by the end of the sixteenth century been largely replaced by other conditions of promotion. From 1565 the status of the Janissaries could be inherited. Fiefs were allocated not only for military, diplomatic, or other merits but were often granted for money. Tax farming became the general practice.[52] Towards the end of the sixteenth century the Janissary service was open to all free Muslims except the Negroes. Their numbers swelled enormously. The growth of favouritism and the protection of vested interests adversely affected the discipline and efficiency of the Janissaries and other elites.

There were also religious stirrings in the Ottoman Levant. Amongst the Turkic immigrants there was a widespread tendency towards syncretism. Vestiges of shamanism, reflected in the popularity of religious leaders called *babas* (whence the name *baba'is* applied to their followers), vied with the influences of the Sufi orders, the Shi‘ite sects and Christian beliefs.[53] The order of the *Bektashis* eventually emerged as the most popular; its religious practices combined elements of babaism, shi‘ism and Christianity.

It may be worthwhile to quote a pertinent passage from Franz Babinger, a German authority on the subject:

The Orthodox religious leaders were often spiritually arid. Remote from the common people, they had no consolation to offer but irrelevant dogmas and legalistic quibbles (*hiyal*). The dervishes were glad to replace them as the intermediaries between this world and the next. The mystical character of their rites and customs, often reflecting vestiges of older beliefs, held a strong appeal for the common people, whom the rationalism of Orthodox Islam simply failed to satisfy. The cult of saints, which had always been frowned on by Orthodox Islam and often bitterly combated, was particularly favoured by certain orders of dervishes. It offered the little man far more than the complex, and to the layman largely unintelligible, edifice of the religious law. Finally, we must not forget the charitable work done by the dervishes in their monasteries. The substantially pantheistic character of the dervishes' beliefs enabled them to take a more liberal attitude toward non-Moslems and won them a certain affection even among the Christian subject population, so much so that Christians and

Moslems occasionally joined in the cults of identical saints.[54]

Oddly enough the rule of the Ottomans over the infidels produced fewer problems than their rule over the heterodoxies within Islam. Already in 1416, in the aftermath of the political crisis following the unfortunate confrontation with Timur (at Ankara in 1402), a serious uprising broke out, led by the popular scholar-jurist Bedreddin, and aimed at far-reaching socio-political reforms. But the main danger appeared about a hundred years later when the revival of militant Shi'ism in neighbouring Iran forced the Ottoman Sultan Selim I (1512–20) to turn his military power against the interior of Dar al-Islam.

The conflict started with the Shi'ite insurrection in Anatolia in 1511. It prompted a change of sultan in Istanbul. The Janissaries forced the pious and complacent Bayazid II to abdicate in favour of his energetic son Selim. The Shi'ite insurrection was defeated with great effort and cruelty. No mercy was shown to the 'fifth column' within the Ottoman domains: on Selim's command almost 40,000 Shi'ites were massacred throughout Eastern Anatolia, and thousands were transferred to the European provinces. To forestall the expansion of the fiercely Shi'ite Safavids into the Arab heartland of Islam, Selim I conquered and annexed Syria, Egypt, Hijaz and Yemen, and his successor Suleyman I took Iraq and Bahrain; in North Africa the Ottoman suzerainty was extended to the borders of Morocco.

The victory of the Imamis (Twelvers) Shi'a and its establishment as the official religion of Iran, led to a series of Turko-Persian wars which, together with the intervals of peace, lasted more than a century; in these wars the Ottomans stood as champions of the Sunnite version of Islam, whilst the Safavids built their power on the Shi'ite revival. Thus the trend towards the crystallization of ethno-religious communities, which in the Levant had already been in operation for a long time, received a new impetus.

5.10 THE REVIVAL OF THE SHI'A IN IRAN

As has already been said, the Iranians abandoned their traditional Zoroastrianism without great tribulation. In its stead they looked for a satisfactory means of self-assertion within the Islamic community. At the time of the Abbasids (whom they helped to power) and under the local Turko-Iranian dynasties, especially the Samanids, the Islamized Iranians did very well in the arts, in science and in administration. Using mainly the Arabic, but later (especially in novels and poetry) also the new Persian language (*darik*), they in many respects matched and even surpassed the achievements of their Arab co-religionists.

But then came the Mongolian assault; though eventually absorbed, it called a halt to the economic and also the political, but oddly enough not the artistic, achievements of the Iranians. It may seem strange that *inter arma* the Muses were not silent. Yet we have to bear in mind that the Mongols were not only formidable devastaters but also great builders. They shifted populations from one area to another, selecting skilled workers for the settlements destined for development. While many irrigated fertile lands were laid waste, commerce, especially long-distance throughout the vast Mongolian domains, was encouraged. After the collapse of the Ilkhanid dynasty, the seats of individual princes became the *foci* of a quest for prestige, which meant support for arts and economic activity.

After the collapse of Timur's short-lived empire (*c.* 1380–1405), an empire which approximately covered the territory of the erstwhile Sassanian domains, Iran fell into anarchy. Timurid princes competed with each other for domination in the east, and the Turkic dynasties of Akkoyunlu (White Sheep) and Karakoyunlu (Black Sheep) and their offshoots vied with each other for power in the west.

At that time a local Sufi order headed by hereditary shaykhs in the Safavi family (called *Safaviya*) and based on the south-western shore of the Caspian Sea, adopted the Imami (Twelvers) Shi'ite orientation and started wide-ranging proselytizing activities. The religious status of the Safavid leader, at first recognized as the representative of the Hidden Imam, but later believed to be the Hidden Imam himself, continued to grow. The process culminated in the apotheosis of Shaykh Junayd as a divine incarnation in the mid-fifteenth century.[55] Furthermore, under this same Junayd the shi'itized Sufi order became militarized. While the spiritual caretakers, the *sadrs*, continued their missionary work, the military branch, the *Kizilbash* (red cap), spread the Twelver Shi'a by the sword.

Thus an ideological formation, assuming a distinctive profile within Islam, became militarized; under the strict command of an autocrat with transcendental claims, the new force won many converts in what is today Iran, Iraq, eastern Turkey and Soviet Azerbaijan. The ensuing continuous warfare brought a premature death to

Junayd and also to his son Haydar, the Safavi leader, leaving a 12-year-old boy Ismail as head of the order.

Ismail, endowed with the aura of a Hidden Imam, claiming to be God incarnate and later also the legitimate heir of the Sassanids (by the daughter of Yazdagird III, whom 'Ali's younger son, Husayn, the martyr of Kerbela, had allegedly married), undertook an ambitious military campaign in 1499. In the course of it he avenged his father's death, defeated the Akkoyunlu and conquered Tabriz. There, in 1501, at the age of 14, Ismail had himself crowned as Shah. Though Turkic-speaking, he did not adopt the Turko-Mongolian title of khan, but the Iranian title of Shah, invoking a tradition which could make a stronger claim on his subjects' total loyalty, and which was thus appropriate to his exalted religious status. In that position Ismail declared the Twelver form of Shi'ism (the *Ithna'Ashari*) to be the official and uniform religion of his subjects. Within ten years the Safavid realm embraced the whole of Azerbaijan, Iran and Iraq, and the Sunnite majority in these lands were forced to accept the Shi'ite version of Islam. The Sunnite 'ulema who opposed conversion were put to death.

Meanwhile the last remnants of the Timurid principalities beyond the Oxus were taken by the nomadic, but Islamized, Uzbeqs. In 1511 Ismail Safavi decided to support the ousted Timurid prince Babur on condition that he embraced his version of the Shi'a. Babur complied, apparently for opportunistic reasons, but having done so, alienated the settled population of Transoxania who ceased to support his claims. Thus, though Ismail's campaign on behalf of Babur was successful, it did not produce the desired effect. After eight years of turmoil, Babur abandoned his claims on Transoxania and turned his attention to India, which eventually became his promised land. There he carved out for himself a new empire, without being forced to give up his Sunnite version of Islam.

Having failed in Transoxania, which thus became the uncontested domain of the Sunnite Uzbeqs, Ismail got involved in a fatal confrontation with the Ottoman power. As has already been mentioned, the signal was the Shi'ite pro-Safavi insurrection in Eastern Anatolia in 1511, which ended with a large-scale massacre and the deportation of the defeated Shi'ites. At that time Ismail was engaged in the Transoxanian venture and could not help his followers in Turkey. When he eventually freed his hand and decided to intervene, he found that his military power was no match for that of the Ottomans. Though the latter's army had to be moved over a distance of more than a thousand miles and had to proceed through a scorched land (Ismail did not hesitate to devastate his own subjects' territory in order to stop the enemy), in the decisive encounter the Janissaries defeated the Kizilbash. In technical terms it was a victory of the musketry and artillery over the cavalry. The Ottomans were the first Muslim rulers to use firearms, whilst Ismail I thought their use unmanly and cowardly.[56]

Fortunately for Ismail I, his Ottoman adversary, Selim I, was not able to exploit his victory to the full. Though Selim was still able to take Tabriz, his Janissaries refused to stay over winter in what for them was a foreign, inhospitable land. Thus the Ottoman-Safavid confrontation ended in a stalemate which the later repeated bouts of warfare could do nothing to alter. As a preventive measure against the spread of Shi'a, Selim I took whatever he could of the Arab lands and incorporated them into the Ottoman empire, the bulwark of the Sunna.

Ismail's Safavi venture has often been described as a revolution. In a way it was, but mainly in the ideological sense. The political and socio-economic changes in Iran were less conspicuous. Though the strengthened absolutism in religion affected the whole range of social and political life, institutional changes were marginal. In Lambton's words, 'the theory of the ruler as the sole landowner became more definite',[57] yet the usual difficulties connected with the financing of a standing army forced the Shah, after the first bout of centralized rule, to assign revenues from particular lands, and then the possession of such lands to individuals as benefices. Finally, to refer again to Ann Lambton, such land 'became, or tended to become, by usurpation, *de facto* private property'.[58]

According to H.A.R. Gibb's footnote to A.J. Toynbee's treatment of the subject, Shi'ism in Persia stood in close relation to the trade guilds and 'provisionally identified with the artisan classes, as an expression of "class consciousness", against the aristocracy, whether Arab or Iranian, or in later times Turkish'.[59] Yet this factor seems to have played only a subsidiary role in the revolution, although its contribution to the consolidation of the Safavid power should not be underestimated.

In principle, there were two kinds of provincial government. First there were the so-called state provinces (*mamalik*), which were allotted to the Kizilbash chiefs in the form of (in theory) non-hereditary benefices (*tiyul*); the Shah received only a small part of the revenue from these provinces. Secondly, there were the so-called crown provinces (*khassa*), from which taxes were collected by the Shah's officials, whose eagerness to please their master led them to extort the maximum from the taxpayers.[60] The frequent shifts of power among the military and civil officials prevented the creation of a landed aristocracy in the West European sense.[61]

The Safavids ruled Iran for over two hundred years (until 1722), a period during which the sense of Iranian identity was resuscitated and strengthened. However, the nature of this identity was more religious and territorial than ethnic. The sociological trinity – one state, one nation, one religion – that had existed under the Sassanids, was not fully re-established. Within the ruling elite there was considerable rivalry between the Turkic Kizilbash, mainly established in military occupations, and the Persians, called *Tajiks* by their rivals, who worked mainly in the administration. (In the Islamic tradition this kind of contrast used to be described as one between men of the sword and men of the pen.) Later, however, as a result of the campaigns (holy wars) in the Caucasus, Armenian, Georgian and Circassian prisoners were brought to Iran, converted to the version of Islam valid in that country, and employed as 'slaves of the royal household' in the civil and military administration. Thus a third ethnic category, generally described as *ghulams* (slaves), became a part of the power elite, in which promotion went on merit rather than anything else. Under the intelligent and energetic Abbas I (Shah from 1588 to 1629) this uniformly Shi'ite but ethnically tripartite elite functioned as an easily manipulable instrument of autocratic rule; but later it became a source of discord.

There were, however, some other changes which weakened the Safavid realm. As the revolution was won not only by the military prowess of the Kizilbash but also by the zeal of the religious propagandists, the *sadrs*, these people tried to keep their influence alive. However the consolidation of the Safavid state required less turbulent ideologists and thus the opportunity was given to the newly emerging caste of Shi'ite 'ulema (theologians – jurists), known as the *mujtahids*. As also happened in the development of Judaism, the prophets, as it were, gave way to the lawgivers.

The rivalry between the sadrs, with their mystical attitudes on the one hand, and the mujtahids, dreary scholastics on the other, ended with the complete victory of the scholastics, who then turned on the mystics with a vengeance. Although they still had a mighty rival in the person of the shah, whose status as Imam could not be denied, and also in his sometimes too influential harem (wives and especially eunuchs), the mujtahids managed, with the support of the commercial middle classes, the guilds of the bazaars, to deliver a deadly blow to Iranian Sufism. Thus the general law of revolution proved also to be valid in the case of Safavid Iran. The ideological cadres, who fermented the revolution and kept its vital spirit alive, were suppressed; the military cadres, the Kizilbash, had to share their wealth and power with the men of the pen (the Tajiks) and the foreign parvenus (the ghulams); and a new hierocracy took over the ideological reins, which became tighter than ever before in Dar al-Islam.

Lacking in numbers and also, it seems, in ideas, the *mujtahids* had to seek help amongst their Arab co-religionists beyond the Iranian border. With their help they codified the *Ithna'Ashari* (Twelver Shi'a) theology and thus obtained the doctrinal basis for the institution of inquisition, which until then had been, in the world of Islam, conspicuous by the relative rarity of its appearance.

Thus at the time when the West Europeans, in a sudden upsurge of curiosity and maritime venture, and as a prelude to a formidable civilizational transformation, started to roam the seas and oceans in their bid for more wealth and power, the Islamic civilization split down the middle. Shi'ite Iran, an island in the centre of Dar al-Islam, stood against the vast Sunnite sea around, a sea in which the Ottoman empire to the west and the Mughal empire to the east were to play the last glorious acts of Islamic history.

Fortunately for divided Islam the Europeans were also divided, and their rivalries prevented them from making more powerful inroads into Dar al-Islam. It was mainly the Islamic outposts in Europe and in India that were most affected by the European advance. We shall come back to the fate of the Islamic civilization in India and Indonesia in sections 6.5.1 and 6.5.4.

6 From Indus to Mekong: Between Brahma and Buddha

6.1 THE SPIRIT OF INDIA: AN INTRODUCTORY NOTE

Of all the areas of high civilization in the Old World, India is perhaps the least accessible to historical examination. It has been a unique feature of her people – peculiar and barely explicable *genius loci* – that the attention of her 'literati' has been directed not to the sequence of historical events and their causal relationships, but to other problems. The interest of Indian intellectuals focused mainly on ideas, on the secrets of human existence, on contacts with the supernatural, on the depths of the human psyche and its relationship with the cosmos. Instead of history as we understand it, Indian thinkers developed various theories of cosmic cycles with periods of hundreds of thousands or millions of years. At the same time, however, Indian intellectuals did not neglect the practical aspects of everyday life with its economic and organizational needs and with its quest for beauty. It was especially the aesthetic urge that the Indian spirit developed, imbuing it with an unprecedented buoyancy and passion. Religion, understood not as a ready-made revealed message, but as an experience, an unceasing personal quest, and art, which is not satisfied with the representation of external appearance but aims at giving form to an inner, spiritual reality, obliterating any border between description and imagination, are the strongest features of the Indian achievement. In religion and in art the Indian spirit found its unique and most telling expression.

These achievements however varied in intensity from period to period. Whilst there were epochs during which the Indians seem to have devoted all their creative energy to the introvert scrutiny of the human predicament, there were, on the other hand, periods when the practical attention to political and economic organization made itself felt more distinctly. Yet both these endowments were strong enough to make an irresistible impact on the neighbouring

156

nations, who often did not hesitate to take over Indian institutions and the Indian way of life as the manifestations of a higher culture and as a guideline for the development of their own civilization. Thus the Indian culture radiated far beyond the horizon of its origin.

The ability to harmonize contradictions asserted itself not only with respect to the practical bent on the one hand and the speculative endowment of the Indian mind on the other. The striving to harmonize is perhaps still more striking within the spiritual sphere itself. Indian spirituality abounded with such a wide variety of concepts, approaches and nuances, that even the most ardent individualist longing for self-assertion in his particular view could be satisfied without stepping outside the Indian cultural framework. The concept of a counter-elite is scarcely imaginable within the context of Indian spirituality.

The extreme individualism of Indian thought contrasts conspicuously with the deeply ingrained collectivism in the sphere of social relationships. In everyday life, each individual is firmly embedded within his broad family, his kith and kin, his commune and his caste. Without this framework, an individual can exist only as an ascetic or as a religious thinker. And in Indian religious thought the ideas can be so surprisingly variegated that an observer accustomed to logical and systematic thought cannot but look with astonishment at the maze of paradoxes, whose deeper sense can only be discovered after a prolonged and tedious scrutiny.

Until recently Europeans tended to regard Asian societies as more or less static. They got to know Asia at a time when her various civilizations were going through periods of stagnation and declining creativity. The Europeans did not realize that this situation was preceded by prolonged periods of growth in most areas of life.

With respect to India, however, the idea of recording this growth would have gone against the above-mentioned ahistorical bent of the Indians. For our knowledge of Indian history we have to be grateful mainly to foreigners – to Greeks, Chinese, Arabs, Iranians, Turkic Muslims and, most recently, Europeans. From Indian literature historical conclusions can be drawn only indirectly. The most useful in this respect are the Buddhist writings, which by virtue of this fact demonstrate the special position of Buddhism within the Indian cultural spectrum.

All this, together with the innumerable monuments and artefacts of the material culture has, during the last two centuries, become a fascinating subject for critical European and later also American scholarship. To this scholarship we owe the discovery of many

Indian secrets, and also the knowledge that from the late nineteenth century onwards the Indians themselves began to feel the need to study their past in a factographic and systematic way. Thus, the combined harvest of all the various studies has become so rich that we can build on them a plausible picture of the development of the Indian civilization.

But, with respect to the earliest periods of Indian history, even our global approach runs up against the difficulty of timing. This applies not only to the very earliest period, with respect to which only archaeological evidence is available (the so-called Indus Valley or Proto-Indian civilization), but also to the whole of Aryan history before the appearance of the Buddha. The main literary source for that period is furnished by the Vedas, the first coherent and understandable literary document to spring from Indian soil. Although the Vedas and their accessories were not conceived as historical records, they nevertheless reveal the development of Indian thought. Though the timing or periodization of this development is also subject to a wide margin of error, its main course between 1500 and 500 BC can be charted with a reasonable degree of probability.

In addition, the later religious literature, the national epics and drama, the myths, cultic and normative writings also provide invaluable insights into the development of the Indian mind. Our assumption that the path of civilization can be better followed by reference to its social-cultural rather than to its economico-political aspects, is most conspicuously vindicated in the case of India. Up to the Muslim conquest of the greater part of India in the thirteenth century, our knowledge of what was going on in the economico-political sphere is more or less conjectural. The Indian literature dealing with this topic was concerned more with what should be than with what really was. The most detailed documents of that period take a decidedly normative stance. Though from about the fourth century AD onwards the political development can generally be followed with greater accuracy, the researcher in the socio-economic field comes up against the usual, almost ubiquitous, scarcity of reliable data. For the Indian mind it was the ideas and not the facts which deserved most attention. And it is in this sense that, to borrow Werner's words, 'Man, not the world, is the starting point of philosphical inquiry and although the final solution is envisaged in transcendence, it is . . . the human mind which is the

only instrument capable of grasping the significance of this term
. . .'.[1]

The Indian stock of ideas, the Indian way of thinking, however,
is something extremely difficult for an uninitiated outside observer
to grasp, especially when he or she is accustomed to using his/her
brain in the scholarly way of the Western tradition. In Indian thought
the procedure is quite different from what we, traditionally, consider
to be logical reasoning. The empirical approach is also different.
Whereas we lay more stress on correct, objectively testable and
reportable observations, the Indians prefer direct, intuitive insight;
they do not rely overmuch on the possibility of passing their
experiences on to others by means of clear-cut words.

It seems that mythopoeic thinking never disappeared from Indian
culture and in Indian philosophy it was not the syllogism but the
paradox which became the most popular ploy. Thus traditional
teaching in India looks very different from the teaching methods
characteristic of our tradition.

In Indian religion and philosophy we rarely come across concepts
with precise contours, but are confronted with a mass of synonyms,
homonyms and terms with overlapping meanings. Consequently a
lot of Indian thought appears to be contradictory. Though such
contradictions may occasionally result from incorrect translation and
thus misrepresentation, as a rule the contradictions are meant as
such. They are intended to reflect the world of phenomena, including
our behaviour, which, as we have to admit, cannot always be
understood in logical terms.

We also have to bear in mind that many concepts and theories
underwent substantial alterations both with the passage of time and
also from one school of thought to another. Thus it is little wonder
that any account of the positions taken by Indian thinkers is subject
to a greater or lesser margin of inaccuracy. For instance we prefer
to describe phenomena, events and processes in positive terms,
whilst the Indian tradition preferred a negative demarcation. This
can be illustrated by the case of the key concept of Indian religion
– the personal *eschaton: moksha* or *nirvana*. A famous example of
teaching on these lines is the Buddhist treatise, the Milindapanha,
where the renowned monk Nagasena gives a briefing on the teachings
of Buddhism to the Graeco-Bactrian king, Menander (whose name
becomes Milinda in the Pali language).

Another essential point of difference between the Indian approach
and ours lies in the evaluation of individual states of human

existence. Whilst we rely most on our consciousness and consider it as the basic condition of our perception and cognition, in the Indian tradition, true cognition comes from beyond our consciousness. Everyday human consciousness (operating by sensual perception) is virtually the lowest stage of being, the dream being a higher stage and dreamless sleep a higher one still.[2]

At this juncture another particular feature of Indian thought intervenes, namely an element of voluntarism. There *must* be a further, higher stage of existence beyond waking, dreaming and dreamless sleep, which brings us to the realization of true reality. In contrast to phenomenal reality, which is subject to continuous change and is accompanied more often by pain and suffering than by pleasure and joy, the fourth stage of existence means a reality which is unchanging, undifferentiated and imperturbable. And this existence is considered to be ideal. It is a state of blessedness which, unlike the Christian heaven, has as its opposite not a hell but a continuous chain of rebirths in the world of the senses.

But let us not be mistaken. The image of heaven and hell, just like the idea of ghosts and supernatural beings, was not alien to the Indian mind. These concepts even gatecrashed the originally least fanciful of Indian religions – Buddhism. As we saw in previous chapters, any religion which was to become the creed of multitudes could not avoid a wide-ranging differentiation of its levels of sophistication and imagination. In the case of India the gap between the heights of abstraction and the depths of superstition appears to be a particularly wide one. The idea of the unity of all living creatures, which in many respects obliterated the border between humans and fauna, contributed a great deal to the specificity of the Indian mind.

There are many other striking contrasts between the Indian world-view and our own. We shall touch upon them in the further course of our narrative. In the present context we have only to add that the above-mentioned specifities of Indian thought did not appear at once, but developed gradually as the Aryans came to Indian soil and mixed there with the indigenous population.

Bearing in mind that the Aryans who settled in India were closely related to the Aryans who settled in Iran, we cannot but be astonished at the very different world-views and different civilizations which the two kindred peoples developed in their new homelands. The different *genius loci* represented by the earlier settlers in the respective areas, combined with the different interplay of impulses, must have been stronger than the common ethnic background of the two branches of the Aryan people.

6.2 FROM EXCAVATIONS TO THE BOOKS OF WISDOM

6.2.1 The Proto-Indian Civilization

The earliest known civilization on Indian soil reached an astonishingly high level of organization and technical development. Known only from excavations, the civilization of the Indus Valley, also called the Harappan, or better perhaps the Proto-Indian civilization (*c.* 2600–1500 BC), offers a fine example of a bronze age urban culture. With its main cities, Harappa, in what is nowadays Punjab, and Mohenjo-Daro, in the present-day Sindh, the culture of the Proto-Indians was far superior to what was later, and for a long time to come, to constitute urban life in India. Actually after the destruction of the Proto-Indian cities there was a caesura of about half a millennium before anything that could be described as genuine cities emerged in the Indian subcontinent.

As regards rural life, however, the pattern seems to have been a rather less agitated one. The Proto-Indian agriculture seems to have been highly productive, thanks to a higher rainfall in those times than nowadays and to a well-designed irrigation system. Yet the villagers seem to have lived in very primitive conditions. In D.H. Gordon's view 'the normal village community was a peasant farming one of semineolithic type'.[3] If this was the case, then the Aryan newcomers who started as semi-nomads and gradually turned to a fully settled life may possibly have introduced some progress to rural life in India, yet as we shall see later, Indian rural society remained rather static for more than two millennia.

The most striking feature of the Proto-Indian culture was the carefully planned layout of the cities; they were built with particular architectural skill and attention to hygiene. Broad streets, regular blocks of houses and a ramified sanitation system with public and private baths and good drainage: these were features which in that part of the world were not to reappear until the modern, industrial era. Some big buildings provided with air-ducts and loading platforms were probably public granaries. The absence of large meeting places supports the supposition, derived from what has already been said, that the Proto-Indian cities were governed in a strongly centralized and authoritarian way.

Unfortunately, the Proto-Indian pictographs have not yet been deciphered and thus the inscriptions on the many seals found so far cannot tell us anything more than what can be deduced from the reliefs, statuettes and other artefacts, and a few scattered allusions in the Vedas. From this sparse evidence it can be inferred that the object of worship had some affinity with the much later stages of the development of religion in India. Besides the symbols of the Mother Goddess and phallus, there were found statuettes reminiscent of the dancing Shiva and of various positions of Yoga. These and many other artefacts point to the pre-Aryan roots of some elements of the Indian religious tradition.[4]

As far as the social structure is concerned, we can assume there was a ramified division of labour; there were not only various crafts and professions but – judging from the statuettes of squatting men wearing what look like dog collars – also slaves. But we would not be wide of the mark if we were to assume the existence of at least two city states in the Indus Valley with administrations similar to that of the Tigris and Euphrates Valley during periods of more centralized rule, such as for instance during the Third dynasty of Ur (cf. section 2.7).

That there were frequent commercial contacts between the Proto-Indian society and its Mesopotamian counterpart is a well established fact. Proto-Indian pottery and other wares have been found in Mesopotamia, likewise Mesopotamian artefacts in the Indus Valley. Yet it is more difficult to judge whether there was anything more than that. Some scenes on the Proto-Indian tablets are reminiscent of Sumero-Akkadian mythology, some statuettes seem to reflect the Sumerian fashion. Yet here the parallel ends. If there was any give and take, it seems that it did not go beyond some measure of inspiration. Toynbee's suggestion that the civilization of the Indus Valley was affiliated to the Sumero-Akkadian civilization is not borne out by sufficient evidence.

Unless any new discovery indicates the contrary, we shall be on safer ground if we consider the civilization in India as a basically native creation, the prehistory of which is not known. Neither can we exclude the supposition that the Proto-Indian civilization was impelled to a creative response by a foreign challenge. In view of the fact that only about sixty years has elapsed since the first archaeological work was done in the Indus Valley and the search is still going on, we would be well advised to suspend further judgment on this exciting opening chapter of civilization in India until more is known on the subject.

6.2.2 The Sacred Books – the Vedas

With respect to the sources of information on the most ancient Indian civilizations there is an interesting contrast: whilst what we know of the Proto-Indians is based almost exclusively on archaeological evidence (the allusions in the Vedas being the only other source of information), our knowledge of the subsequent period, the Vedic (*c.* 1500–500 BC), derives almost entirely from literature. This literature, the Vedas and their accessories, is predominantly focused on religious questions, covering a broad span from sorcery and ritual through prayers and hymns, to meta-physical speculations on the supernatural. Information on social life is provided merely by occasional allusions to events and institutions, and also to the desired effect of rites and prayers.

The Aryans came to the Indus Valley in several successive waves between the eighteenth and sixteenth centuries BC, either as infiltrators or as conquerors. It has not yet been firmly established to what extent the newcomers took part in the destruction of the Proto-Indian civilization. The archaeological evidence, however, indicates that this civilization had already been in decline before the Aryans' arrival.[5]

The Vedas (meaning knowledge or wisdom) had been orally transmitted for many generations before they were put down in writing. Neither authorship nor time of origin is known. It was believed – and this is still one of the basic tenets of Hinduism – that the Vedas had existed from time immemorial in the world of abstract spirituality, as an eternal sound (*shabda*); as such they were intercepted, memorized and passed on by the especially receptive wise men – the *rishis* (seers).

The complete corpus of the Vedas consists of four collections. In probable chronological order they may be listed as follows: first, the *Rig-Veda*, a collection of hymns and prayers; second, the *Sama-Veda*, a book of songs accompanying the sacrifices – largely musical paraphrases of the hymns in the Rig-Veda; third, the *Yajur-Veda*, conceived in several versions, and containing descriptions of the sacrificial rites for individual sacerdotal functions; and finally, the *Atharva-Veda*, containing charms and incantations.

To individual Vedic texts were added prosaic commentaries, which are known as the *Brahmanas*; texts for solitary contemplation, the so-called *Aranyakas*; and spiritual treatises of secret learning, known as the *Upanishads*. As the Upanishads are held to have been conceived and written towards the close of the Vedic period they are also called *Vedanta*, i.e. the end of the Vedas.

In reviewing this whole complex of literature we are struck by the amazing cycle of ups and downs in its sophistication. After the lofty heights and spiritual insights of many Rig-Vedic hymns the subsequent Vedic collections appear to be rather formalistic and primitive. Apparently, the popularization of the Vedic message and its transmission to the natives required something pitched at a lower level. The Atharva-Veda was for some time considered a foreign element and was only belatedly recognized as a legitimate part of the Vedas, once intermingling with the original population had made substantial progress. In S. Radhakrishnan's view, 'The religion of the Atharva-Veda reflects the popular belief in numberless spirits and ghosts credited with functions connected in various ways with the processes of nature and the life of man. We see in it strong evidence of the vitality of the pre-Vedic animistic religion and its fusion with Vedic beliefs.'[6]

But then once again there came an intellectual upsurge which this time had been foreshadowed in some parts of the Atharva-Veda and which culminated in the Upanishads. The Upanishads represent the apogee of religious and philosophical thought in the pre-Buddhist period. In contrast to Greek philosophy, the Upanishads are intuitive and contemplative writings. To borrow S. Radhakrishnan's words, 'The Upanishads are vehicles more of spiritual illumination than of systematic reflection. They reveal to us a world of rich and varied spiritual experience rather than a world of abstract philosophical categories.'[7]

Whilst most of the Vedic literature is anonymous, some of the principal thoughts of the Upanishads have been ascribed to individual authors. In a way the Upanishads summarize the values of Vedic thought, but at the same time they open new perspectives for Indian thought and thus preserve the authority of the Vedas for later periods of civilization in India.

6.2.3 The Books of Instruction and the Cosmic Order

Besides the Vedas and their commentaries there are many more auxiliary writings called *Upa-Vedas* or *Vedangas*, which are concerned with technical subjects, such as healing, warfare, astronomy, grammar, correct pronunciation (important for sacrificial formulae), etymology, music, dancing and poetry.

A particular category of auxiliary writings is formed by the so-called *sutras* or *shastras*. As a rule, they contain instructions on proper behaviour, or how to achieve a particular aim. One category of these instructions, known as the *Grihya sutra*, provides detailed regulations for family life; another one, the *Shrauta sutra*, is concerned mainly with social life; and the so-called *Dharma-sutra* or *Dharma shastra* is an extensive treatise on the principles of correct behaviour. One special piece of normative literature was the so-called Laws (or Code) of Manu (*Manusmrti* or *Manava dharmashastra*).

Though these Upa-Vedas, Vedangas, sutras and shastras are not considered a part of revelation and therefore do not enjoy the religious authority of the Vedas and their commentaries, they are nevertheless respected as the expression of the extraordinary inspiration of the wise men or seers (the *rishis*). Their precepts are rooted in the notion of a cosmic and moral order, the *rita*, which stems from the Rig-Veda.

Here, surprisingly, we come across a striking similarity to the ancient Egyptian concept of *maat*. Just as the Pharaonic wise men revealed the principles of maat in their Admonitions to their countrymen, so too did the Indian rishis use their sutras, etc. to expound the tenets of the rita.[8]

To make orientation easier let us outline the following framework of normative Vedic thought, the principles of which have survived until modern times. The framework can be ordered into three groups of four. There are to begin with four legitimate aims in human life. The first and most ubiquitous is the law of correct conduct, the *dharma*. This is differentiated according to social status and age, which constitute the two other groups of four. The second legitimate aim is called *artha*, which means everything that is useful (pursuit of economic activities, political organization, technology, etc.). The third legitimate aim, known as *kama*, includes the pursuit of all artistic and also erotic activities, in short what may be considered nice and agreeable. The fourth, most difficult but also most noble, aim in human life is the attainment of the liberation of the human mind, the so-called *moksha*. The state of mind which is achieved by this kind of liberation was later called *nirvana*: literally 'a blowing out', but meaning simply the extinction of the impermanent features of existence.

In the concept of moksha we encounter the most characteristic features of the Indian world-view. In it there is no place for human freedom in our modern Western sense; freedom in the Indian tradition means liberation from the bondage of the senses, liberation from want and desire. All subsequent Indian schools of thought were anchored in this principle and the main differences between them lay in the extent to which they elaborated it and in some cases pushed it further.

Each of these four legitimate aims has its proper place in men's lives (women receive little consideration in this respect) according to social status and age. Social status is in principle defined by the four basic castes or, as the Sanskrit term puts it, by the four *varnas*: men of learning (the *brahmins*), men of power (the *kshatriyas*), men of qualified labour (the *vayshias*) and men of service (the *shudras*). From the religious point of view – and this mattered most – only the upper three castes were worthy, i.e. were allowed to read the Vedas and participate in their rites.   At the origin of these divisions there apparently lay two contrasting but complementary principles, on the one hand the need for a division of labour (a functional viewpoint), on the other hand a racial discrimination that assigned the lowest position in the social stratification to the conquered peoples. However neither of these criteria was fully respected in practice; the castes did not prevent the mixing of races and social categories. Later these proliferated into a huge tisssue of subcastes often hierarchically ordered and with minutely detailed rules for mutual contacts on various levels.[9] Yet the lowest stratum of population – the outcastes or untouchables – remained completely out of the caste system, with a virtually subhuman status. Purity of descent and purity of occupation both played an important role in this stratification.

Understandably, a different law of conduct (a different dharma) applied for each basic caste. But a similar differentiation was also applicable, at least in the highest castes, with respect to the individual *ashramas*, i.e. stages of life. The ashramas were likewise fourfold: first, the period of preparation or apprenticeship, the *brahmacharya;* second, the period of a *grihastha*, i.e. the stage reached by the father of a family and householder; third, the period of a *vanaprastha*, i.e. the age when the man of standing retired as a hermit into the forests for a contemplative life. The fourth stage of life, probably added to the scheme in a later development, was that of an ascetic fully devoted to meditation. Men who reached this stage were called *sannyasins*; they had the best opportunity of achieving the most noble aim in human life, liberation from the bondage of the senses.

As has been said already, the law differed according to the castes and stages of life (hence *varnashramadharma*). Nevertheless according to the Shatapatha Brahmana, there were four basic human duties imposed on everybody, namely duty to the gods, to the rishis, to one's ancestors and to one's contemporaries. In order to fulfil these duties one had (a) to perform sacrifices, (b) to study the Vedas, (c) to conceive a son, (d) to be hospitable. Thus, we may complete the normative framework of Indian thought by adding to its schematic outline a fourth group of four, a universal moral tetralog. Later these generally valid precepts, known as *sanatana dharma*, attracted more attention, but as will become clear from our account, ethics in India remained, in principle, a differentiated set of rules.

During the later Vedic period there occurred a conspicuous change in the ontological position of the philosophy underlying religious thought, a position which also had practical consequences. For the Vedic people it was quite natural to try to manipulate the outside world by means of sacrifices and magic. Actually it was believed that the whole world had been created and was also being preserved by means of sacrificial ritual. According to the Yajur-Veda and Atharva-Veda, what was most important was the correct performance of the sacrifice (*yajna*) and the correct pronunciation of the sacred formula (*mantra*). Apart from that people who lived according to their respective dharma were supposed to be compensated in Heaven after their death.

Yet within the very fold of Vedic thought, a quite new, more sophisticated, position emerged. It first cropped up as a secret teaching in one particular version of Yajur-Veda. The new teaching is known as the theory of karma, or karmanic law. The new ontology conceives the whole universe as a coherent whole and human existence as an integral part of it. In a simplified form, i.e. omitting the metaphysical intricacies and terminological inconsistencies and ambiguities, we may explain the theory of *karma* as follows:[10]

By entering into contact with the phenomenal world the individual soul separates itself from the cosmic soul and passes through a cycle of incarnations in psychophysical organisms. This cycle follows the laws of causality and retribution. Each individual reincarnation occurs according to the merits, i.e. observance of dharma, of the previous life. The aim is to live in such a way that everybody can be reincarnated into a higher, i.e. more blissful, position within the world of living creatures, stratified from the lowest insect at the bottom to the highest caste amongst humans – the brahmins. The highest bliss is to be liberated from the life cycle altogether and to be reunited with the cosmic soul which, according to most schools, is identical with the cosmic principle of the absolute.

The karmanic law involving metempsychosis became the spiritual backbone of the Indian social system for more than two millennia. On the one hand, it provided the justification for inequalities and hardships and, on the other, it offered hope for the future. For those who believed it, the world must have appeared perfect: a person's predicament was the direct result of his or her deeds in the previous life. Belief in the karmanic law was the most effective inducement to follow one's own dharma or law of conduct, irrespective of whatever social discrimination it meant submitting to. No wonder that in the mental climate generated by these principles there was no scope for social revolution in India. The two basic social functions of religion pointed out by Max Weber, the justificatory and the compensatory, were present in their utmost harshness.

6.2.4   Vedic Society

Our picture of Vedic society can be drawn only tentatively. To judge by the allusions in the Rig-Veda, there was a steady shift from a semi-nomadic to a settled way of life. The basic social and economic unit tended increasingly to be the self-supporting village community, an institution which has survived almost intact until modern times. The family structure and law of inheritance were, amongst the Aryans, patrilineal, whilst amongst some of the subjugated population (called the Dasyas by the Aryans) it was probably matrilineal. In order to overcome this contradiction the Aryans may have started to introduce the secluded living space for women (the woeful *purdah*). This at least is the suggestion made by J.H. Hutton.[11] On the other hand J. Nehru takes the view that this institution was only introduced later under Persian influence and attained its widest spread in the Mughal period.[12] For a long time the marital relationship remained variegated; some allusions in the Vedas point to polygamy, others to polyandry and a few others to the levirate.

The most ancient songs of the Rig-Veda refer only to a two-tier division of the population: the Aryan newcomers and the subjugated Dasyas. To begin with the terms brahmins and kshatriyas seem merely to indicate social function. They do not appear as hereditary caste-like vocations until the Brahmanas (according to some dating from c.1000 BC onwards). Non-Vedic people could be admitted to these castes by a special ritual.

At the outset the caste system seems to have been largely a theoretical device; it was beyond anybody's power to prevent mixing taking place across the caste barriers, though minutely detailed rules were drawn up to differentiate between the status of the male and of the female partner involved.

The brahmins and kshatriyas were apparently the less numerous groups, and, being the ruling castes (*varnas*), they were more cohesive. On the other hand it seems likely that a further differentiation soon began to take place within the *vaishyas* and *shudras* (the latter mainly of Dasya origin); it resulted from the division of labour. Professional groups crystallized into guild-like bodies (*shreni*), but there was a tendency to turn them into hereditary castes or subcastes with particular religious rites and observances.

Of the four castes only three, the brahmins, the kshatriyas and the vaishyas were, from the religious point of view, fully-fledged castes. Only their members could take part in the Vedic worship, which was the mark of spiritual nobility. Being initiated into this worship by a special ritual, they were considered to be twice born people. But the underprivileged shudras were not the only representatives of the common folk. Outside the castes there were primitive tribes who were gradually confined to 'unclean' professions (the outcastes), and the slaves recruited mainly from prisoners of war or insolvent debtors.

The political organization of the Vedic period can likewise be only tentatively delineated. The Indian preoccupation with ritual bequeathed to posterity minutely detailed procedural regulations; however, we have little information on the extent to which they were upheld in practice. These procedural rules apply partly to the royal advisory assemblies, partly to assemblies which point to the existence of what may be called tribal republics. Classifications of various forms of government contained in some later sutras and shastras seem to be of a normative nature rather than factual descriptions. Nevertheless they indicate the existence of a variety of political regimes. The main variables were, on the one hand, the breadth of representation in the ruling on advisory assemblies and, on the other hand, the scope of the supreme power; in some instances this might even have encompassed the exercise of a kind of genetic policy (involving for example decisions on the viability of newborn children).

Some further idea of the social arrangements and political issues in Vedic India can be deduced from the allusions in the great national epics Mahabharata and Ramayana, whose time of composition is itself a matter of conjecture (it is generally situated somewhere between 400BC and 400AD, although some legendary material incorporated in these epics is much older).

It seems that competition for social power took place mainly between ethnic groups and later between the two upper castes, the brahmins and the kshatriyas. Originally the kshatriyas appear to have been the more powerful, but later, with the assimilation of the subject population, the brahmins became more important. This shift of the leading role in due course brought about a kshatriyan backlash, in the form of their active involvement in learning and religious thought. The growth in prestige of the kshatriyas is often linked with the age of the Upanishads and the decline of the role of ritual and magic, which had been the domain of the brahmins.

6.3　THE SPELL OF NOVELTY

6.3.1　The New Opening: From the Upanishads to the Buddha

The Upanishads are not the only expression of the new spirit and new balance of forces in the Indian civilization. From the ninth century BC an old Vedic phenomenon became widespread: the wandering ascetics who did not accept that religious knowledge was a matter for one caste only. Their ideas were largely non-theistic. Often they organized themselves into groups or brotherhoods known by the generic name *vada* (i.e. discourse), reminiscent of our medieval sects. Their teachers, called the *vadins* (those who assert), were not dissimilar to the Greek sophists, but the content of their discourses was quite different from that of their Greek counterparts.

The vadins were in search of religious knowledge. Many of them were ascetics (*shramanas*), who according to A.K. Narain represented the non-Vedic tradition rooted in the Proto-Indian past.[13] One surprising phenomenon was the great number of former kshatriyas in their ranks. A plausible explanation for this is that there was widespread frustration amongst the kshatriyas, a frustration due, on the one hand, to the concentration of political power in fewer hands through the creation of a smaller number of larger polities or states, and on the other hand, to the dominant role of the brahmins in the government service, where sacrifices played a crucial role.

The teaching of the vadins spread by oral tradition but from about the fifth century onwards it received an extraordinary boost from the introduction of writing for literary purposes. The oldest Indian writing, the so-called brahmi, had apparently been known earlier, but appears to have been used for commercial, administrative and musical purposes only.[14]

The late appearance of writing for literary purposes is apparently due to the general dearth of interest in visual art of a static kind. The Vedic period is in fact conspicuously lacking in such art. The Indian spirit found its best expression in sound, whether in music or in words, and in visual movement such as dance or drama. The idea of impermanence, of continuous movement, was conducive neither to the petrification of images nor to the systemization of ideas.[15] It was the foreign influences, especially the Persian and Greek ones, which eventually opened up this artistic avenue to Indian creativity. Significantly, the first products of Indian visual art dealt with Buddhist topics.

With the sixth century BC India entered a new phase of her civilization. The creation of the Vedas and also of the Upanishads came to an end; all their ideas had been put down in writing. The epoch of revelation had gone and a new epoch, that of enlightenment achieved mainly by one's own effort, set in. The greatest influence was exerted by two schools of thought: Jainism and Buddhism.

Jainism was founded by a certain Vardhamana, also known as Mahavira (i.e. great hero), who lived in the sixth century BC (the conventional dates, the first of this sort in Indian history, are 599–527 BC), and adopted the name of Jina, i.e. victor. Vardhamana was a member of an earlier *vada*, or as we may perhaps translate it, sect, whose teaching he transformed into a sophisticated doctrine. Jainism is basically an atheistic philosophy. The existence of gods is not denied, but they are neither creators nor lords of the universe. They too are subject to metempsychosis and to the karmanic law as humans are. The world is eternal and composed of six constituent elements: souls, *dharma* (lawfulness), *adharma* (lawlessness), space, time, and material particles. Karma is an especially subtle particle of matter. It enters the individual souls and binds them to the earth. By blocking the access of karma the soul can be liberated. The most effective means to this end is ascesis. The state of blessedness can, however, be attained already during life, by adhering to correct views and correct behaviour. The latter consists in following the pentalog: (1) do not kill, (2) do not lie, (3) do not steal, (4) preserve chastity and (5) do not enjoy the external manifestations of life.

In Jainism there also appears for the first time the idea of non-hurting or non-violence – *ahimsa* – which subsequently was to become the basic principle of most reform movements. Unfortunately for Jainism, this principle was extended uncompromisingly to protect all living creatures, thus barring the faithful from quite a few walks of life, especially agriculture. Consequently, the Jainists' scope for proselytizing was very limited.

Significantly, the most successful teaching was not developed by the rather austere and rigid Vardhamana-Jina, but by another atheistic thinker of kshatriyan origin, by the name of Gautama of the family of Shakyas, best known as the Buddha, i.e. the Enlightened One,[16] whose teaching was also more susceptible to wide-ranging further elaboration.

According to the tradition Gautama lived from 563 to 483. Born in what is now the borderland of Nepal and the Indian state of Bihar, he abandoned, at the stage of *grihastha*, his family house and kshatriya status, and set out on a search for the liberation of his mind – moksha. First he looked for a teacher who might enlighten him, but in vain; then he tried various methods of ascesis and self-mortification but these too failed him. Thus he realized that neither a life of pleasure nor ascesis was the right path, and embarked on a middle way of meditation and contemplation. Eventually by his own effort he reached enlightenment, or, we might also say, ultimate wisdom, and became the Enlightened One – the Buddha.

The gist of Buddha's teaching can be divided into the cognitive and the normative part. The cognitive section consists of the 'Four Noble Truths': first, life is permeated with suffering or dissatisfaction; second, the origin of suffering lies in craving; third, the cessation of suffering is possible through the removal of craving; and fourth, the way to this cessation is eightfold – the 'Noble Eightfold Path'.

The normative part of Buddha's message is expressed primarily in the 'Noble Eightfold Path'; right views, right aspirations, right speech, right conduct, right livelihood, right effort, right mindfulness, and right contemplation. But for easier understanding the social moral code was summed up in the 'Five Precepts': first, do not kill (this also applied to killing animals but was not imposed so rigorously on everybody as it was with the Jainists); second, do not steal; third, do not commit adultery or give way to self-indulgence; fourth, do not lie or spread malicious gossip; fifth, refrain from drugs and intoxicants. As in Christianity, there is a stricter set of rules (such as poverty and celibacy) for the monks and nuns, who by observing them are more likely to liberate themselves from the physical world and attain nirvana.

In contrast to the Jainists, for Buddha karma was not a part of matter but a process conditioned by men's attitudes and desires.[17] According to Buddha's understanding, nothing is permanent except nirvana. Thus, there is also no eternal soul, 'no enduring psychic entity or substance but a karmic process, a patterned flow of change through time'. All mental and physical phenomena have to be understood in the light of dependent origination (i.e. causal relationship), a psycho-physical process which extends over a succession of lives.[18] But all this is a metaphysical elaboration which could hardly have been grasped by the multitudes. Broadly speaking, the aim of a Buddhist continued to be a kind of liberation, whether one called it moksha or nirvana, similar to that aimed for by other Indians.

6.3.2 Early Buddhism

An immense pile of ideas, varying in nature from the philosophico-contemplative to the mythological and phantastic, was heaped by posterity upon Buddha's message. Gradually the noble and quiet cultivation of meditative insights became overlaid by exuberant importations from the realm of myth; thus the fanciful genius of India recaptured the teaching whose original bent had taken it too far towards one particular extreme of the Indian spiritual disposition. Yet this reabsorption of Buddha by his own socio-cultural background was a slow and lengthy process. Within the framework of this study we can reproduce only its main contours.

The focus of the Buddhist religious life was the community of monks and nuns – the so-called *sangha;* as has been said already, higher requirements were imposed on them than on the common folk. To use modern terminology, the Buddhist sangha was an elitist organization, a vanguard on the path to nirvana. The education of the laity was rather neglected for many centuries. In this respect there was a striking contrast with the Jainists, who paid proper attention to the education of their much less numerous flock.

As a tolerant religion par excellence Buddhism did not interfere in social life outside the sangha. Nevertheless the Buddhist ethic appeared attractive to many, because of its social implications. Buddha's dharma (law) did not differentiate people according to their castes, stages of life and aims in life. People's minds were focused on another type of stratification, namely that separating the monastics (male and female) from the laity. Outside the radiating influence of the Buddhist, and also the Jainist, communities, however, life was going on in the spirit of the traditional sutras and shastras.

Meanwhile, India was experiencing new invasions of the Indus Valley. The first, towards the close of the sixth century BC, i.e. at the time when Buddha began his missionary work in the lower Ganges Valley, was the Persian invasion under King Darius. It resulted in an occupation, lasting about two hundred years, of what once had been the heartland of the Proto-Indian civilization. There seems to have been no attempt by the Persians to alter the world view and culture of their Indian subjects. Their influence was of a more indirect kind: the challenge of a great, militarily strong empire was met in the eastern part of the Indo-Aryan settlements by attempts at unification on an unprecedented scale.

But the tendency towards political concentration did not gather momentum until after the second great invasion from the West, this time by the armies of Alexander the Macedonian (327–326 BC). Though it was of a shorter duration than the Persian domination had been, the impact of the Graeco-Macedonian occupation of the Indus Valley was more substantial. On the one hand it prompted the rise of the first Indian empire under King Chandragupta, the founder of the Maurya dynasty. In 305 BC Chandragupta was able to push the Hellenistic kingdom of the Seleucid successors of Alexander beyond the river Indus.

Under the Mauryas the Indo-Aryan civilization, freed of many socio-religious prejudices, undertook its great push towards the south of the Indian peninsula. Up to then, the Indo-Aryan settlements did not extend beyond the range of hills called Vindhya, thus leaving the peninsula proper to the Dravidians, of whose culture at that time we at present know little. In the world-view of the brahmins, the geographical extent of the Indo-Aryan settlements had a special religious connotation. It was only within this area, known as Aryavarta or Bharatavarsa, that the Vedic sacrifices and ritual could be effectively performed. Owing to the influence of Buddhism, Jainism and other non-conformist trends, the sacred concept of Aryavarta lost its commanding role.

Thus for the duration of an epoch at least the new religious outlook liberated Indian society from two particular constraints on social mobility: from the caste regulations, which impeded vertical mobility, and from the ban on travelling beyond the sacred land, which limited horizontal mobility. Under these circumstances, the way was open not only for an expansion but also for a reconstruction of the Indian body social.[19]

Yet the Mauryan empire, by its very nature, attempted to impose a new form of restraint on its subjects, namely that of an autocratic rule. Though in practice the tradition of advisory and other collective bodies could not be totally broken, the tendency was to substitute a centralized, bureaucratic rule in place of the time-honoured pluralism, and replace the rules of the shastras and sutras by the legislative power of the ruler. The theory of the new political regime was expounded in writing by the Mauryan minister Chanakya, better known as Kautilya, whose role in Indian history has sometimes been compared to that of Machiavelli in the history of Europe.[20]

Nevertheless the autocratic rule was in some respects favourable to social change. An orderly administration, less constrained by the prerogatives of the two highest castes, opened up more opportunities for members of other castes, especially in the economic sphere. Apart from the third caste, the vaishyas, it was especially the people of the lowest caste, the shudras, who were in a position to advance themselves. As craftsmen and small merchants, they were organized in guilds with elected chairmen, which performed some government functions such as collecting taxes from their members, safeguarding public works, etc. The cities ceased to be merely administrative centres and became centres of craftsmanship and commerce which eventually brought riches to these settlements. Especially the capital Pataliputra (present-day Patna) became a city renowned not only for its wealth but also for its cultivated and elegant way of life. There also seems to have been a spread of literacy in the urban areas.

The idea of the emperor's legislative power seems to have been particularly appreciated by the Buddhists, who began to see in a powerful and benevolent ruler over a vast country (*chakravartin*) the best guarantee of an undisturbed life for their sangha and its missionary activities. The Buddhist ideal of the chakravartin came nearest to realization in the third Mauryan emperor, Ashoka (who ruled c. 273–232 BC). After he had for several years continued the expansionist policy of his predecessors, the devastating consequences of one particular conquest changed his mind. He began to favour Buddhism and inaugurated an era of exemplary and caring rule: peace, education and social care became the main pillars of Ashoka's policy. Yet even Ashoka was obliged, at the insistence of his ministers, to honour the tradition which required him to observe the rules of royal behaviour (*rajadharma*). Apparently, the Indian *genius loci* was strong enough to withstand any pressure for too great a deviation from its traditional course.

Ashoka's role in the development of Buddhism has been compared to that of Constantine with respect to Christianity. Yet the record of their respective policies seems to indiate that Ashoka's religious conviction was more sincere and profound than Constantine's. This however may be due to structural differences between the Buddhist and Christian organizations. Whilst the Christian Church took on her shoulders a lot of charitable activities, the Buddhists had no comparable institution and their monastic community (sangha) was thrown upon the charity of the laymen. Thus a Buddhist ruler enjoyed a wider scope for showing concern for his fellow men than did his Christian counterpart.

Otherwise Ashoka, like Constantine, was concerned with order and discipline in his religious community. With this in mind he summoned a council (*samhiti*) of Buddhist monks to the capital, Pataliputra. The council succeeded in tightening monastic discipline and in fixing religious doctrine by agreeing an authorised version of the Buddhist writ. This is known as the Pali Canon, after the language in which it was written. It consists of 'Three Baskets': the *Vinaya*, which deals with the discipline of the monks and nuns; the *Sutta* (the Pali equivalent of the Sanskrit *Sutra*), containing the utterances ascribed to Buddha or his disciples; and the *Abhidhamma* (*dhamma* is the Pali equivalent of *dharma* in Sanskrit), which contains a symbolic interpretation of Buddha's psychological and ethical teaching. The second basket, the *Sutta*, includes among other things a collection of popular, phantastic legends about the previous incarnations of Buddha – the *Jatakas*; and a collection of no less popular rhythmic aphorisms – the *Dhammapada*. It shows clearly the extent to which the originally sophisticated doctrine has by this stage attracted a body of popular lore.

The forty years or so of Ashoka's rule were not only an epoch that saw the triumph of Buddhism and wide-ranging social change. The same era also brought a reorientation in the arts. Indians ceased to restrict their artistic creativity to audial media; prompted by Persian and above all Hellenic influences, they began to cultivate visual art, too. At first their products were naturalistic and rather naive, but soon after they had mastered the new techniques, they developed their own style in sculpture, architecture, reliefs and painting.

6.3.3 The Spread and Split of Buddhism

From about the third century BC to the third century AD Buddhism seems to have played the dominant role in India. During this epoch, in contrast to the preceding and subsequent periods, there is little evidence of donations or bequests to the benefit of brahmins and their cults.

But what is most significant is that in contrast to the Vedic religion, Buddhism became an exportable, proselytizing faith. It was especially in Bactria (nowadays north Pakistan and Afghanistan) that the rulers of foreign origin, Greek and later Kushan, were so impressed by the Buddhist teaching that they gave it their full support. In that social climate, Buddhists developed their first major school of visual art (the Hellenizing art of Gandhara).

Around 20 BC the Kushans, coming from the north, wrested north-west India from the Graeco-Bactrian princes and thus opened the door to Central Asia for Buddhist missionaries. After less than a century of their rule in what is now Pakistan, Punjab, Afghanistan and Soviet Central Asia, the Buddhist missionaries entered the Chinese world and began their long march for the spiritual conquest of the Far East.

But against all these tremendous successes must be counted the fact that Buddhism failed to gain the Indian countryside. In the villages the brahmins as a caste survived the worst crisis of their existence. Active in various professions, devoting most of their energies to maintaining their families and social status, albeit under changed circumstances, the brahmins revealed an extraordinary vitality and flexibility, which enabled them to gradually recapture the lost ground.

Around the beginning of our era the brahmins started their patient drive towards the renaissance of the Indo-Aryan heritage, which however, through their own endeavours, became enriched with elements of their main rival, Buddhism, and above all with the religious genius of a hitherto rather silent people – the Dravidians of Southern India.

Buddhism managed to remain the dominant religion only in some peripheral areas of India: Ceylon, Nepal, and above all Gandhara (approximately the present Punjab, both Indian and Pakistani). Exposed to foreign invasions and infiltrations, Gandhara became the testing ground for Buddhist missionary activity and, as has already been said, a stepping stone for its eastward expansion. But Gandhara was also the scene of the great split within Buddhism itself, the schism between what is known as the Greater Vehicle (Mahayana) and the Lesser Vehicle (Hinayana) or, as the followers of the latter prefer to say, the Theravada (i.e. the Way of the Elders).

The main issue in the split was whether Buddha was only a man or something more. In the Indian context it was not necessary to conceive him as God's messenger or the son of God. The generally accepted principle of metempsychosis, understood in the Buddhist tradition as a cycle of rebirths, provided a less tortuous basis for viewing Buddha's appearance as an extraordinary event. Guatama's enlightenment might have been due to the occurrence of a particular spiritual quality – the *bodhicitta* (Buddhahood). On the other hand for those who could understand religion only in its theistic form Buddha could be presented as *devatideva*, i.e. God above gods, an object of highly devotional worship.

And this is what happened in Mahayana. There, Buddha became a superhuman being capable of repeated reincarnations; of these the historical one (in the second half of the sixth century BC) was considered to be crucial in this particular epoch of the long-term cosmic cycles. Thus whilst Hinayana continued to be basically a philosophy of salvation by one's own effort, Mahayana became a religion where men could derive a considerable benefit from the grace of a superhuman being. Whereas in Hinayana the only transcendental element was the belief in the cycle of rebirths, in the Mahayana transcendence assumed wider proportions. Furthermore, in Gandhara, the door was open to foreign influences. Among the notions that crept into Buddhism this way was the belief in paradise, the abode of those souls whose spiritual virtue was such that they needed to take only one small step to enter nirvana.

Besides the different strength of the transcendental elements in the two brands of Buddhism, there is also a striking contrast in their respective concepts of sainthood. For the Theravada the ideal is the *arhat*, i.e. the person who attains nirvana. For Mahayana however this is not enough. One has to follow Buddha's practice rather than his theory: one has also to think of others. Therefore, in Mahayana, the ideal is the *bodhisattva*, i.e. a person who does not enter nirvana, despite being entitled to do so, but endures further rebirth in order to help others to attain the final goal. This may be done by word, by example or, and this is the most spectacular means, by bestowing on a deserving devotee a portion of the bodhisattva's accumulated spiritual merit. Thus as well as, and even instead of, effort, grace becomes the key element of salvation.

The accumulation and dispensation of divine merit, however, is not only the work of the bodhisattvas; the religious imagination was stimulated into creating a series of legendary, celestial Buddhas who then became a particularly rich source of grace. One of them, the Buddha-Amitabha, i.e. the Buddha of eternal light and life, is held to be the ruler of the Western Paradise, an abode of eternal blessedness. Some of these supernatural beings also appeared as feminine deities, such as the Prajnaparamita, the Mother of the Buddhas, or the female saviour named Tara, a convenient counterpoise to the ghost Mara, a personification of evil who tempted the historical Buddha during his search for enlightenment. The doctrine of the periodic appearance of Buddhas also included a redeemable Buddha who would appear in the future – the Buddha-Maitreya. Thus the personal eschaton, completing the wheel of rebirths by a lucky escape to nirvana, was matched by an eschatological soterology of the Buddhahood.

Whether this happened under Zoroastrian influence, thus bringing the common theme of the Western religions into the Eastern orbit, or whether this was simply the result of a logical projection or extrapolation of past events into the future, is of secondary importance for our quest. What matters is that the craving for a happy end found its way into the Buddhist world view both on the personal and on the cosmic level.

6.4   TOWARDS A PAN-INDIAN CIVILIZATION

6.4.1   The Renaissance and the Move Eastward

The first centuries of our era witnessed not only the far-reaching split of Indian Buddhism but also the remarkable renaissance of two essential features of the Vedic epoch. First, there was a renaissance and expansion of Sanskrit as the common literary language and lingua franca of the educated strata. Hand in hand with this came the re-emergence of topics which were traditionally dealt with in the Sanskrit language. Secondly, there was a revitalization and proliferation of the caste system.

As the above formulation of these two points indicates, it was by no means a return to the past, but a renaissance of features which could well be used for a further advance: *Reculer pour mieux sauter*, as it were.

Through the renaissance of Sanskrit the trend towards the linguistic differentiation of Indian society at the literary level was brought to a halt for almost a whole millennium. This happened at a time when Pali, the language of early Buddhism, was ceasing to be spoken, and the *prakrts,* i.e. vernaculars, had the chance to establish themselves as literary languages. However only Tamili (out of the Dravidian languages) and Maharashtri (out of the Aryan languages) succeeded in doing so at that time.

Sanskrit, both as a literary language and as a lingua franca, had several advantages over any competitor. It was the language of the commentaries to the Vedas, the Upanishads and all the normative literature of the pre-Buddhist era. Furthermore, it had continued to be used by the brahmin writers during the era of Buddhism's predominance. The most popular epics, such as the Mahabharata and Ramayana, were written in Sanskrit. Playwrights put it into the mouths of people of noble origin, letting only the common folk talk in one of the seven prakrts, which were deemed suitable for that purpose. Last but not least, Sanskrit became so attractive that, whoever wanted to keep abreast with the times, had willy-nilly to adopt it. Thus, the Buddhist Mahayana became Sanskritized: the Mahayanics abandoned the traditional Pali and turned to Sanskrit as their exclusive language. From then on, wherever the Indian civilization expanded, it was Sanskrit which became the language of the new converts. No wonder that the Indian scholar, Srinivas, called the process of absorption into the Indian culture 'Sanskritization'.

Let us now turn to the second item of the renaissance: the revitalization of the caste system, a manifest corollary of the decline of Buddhism. The proliferation of the castes was due especially to the division of labour, to the absorption of new ethnic groups into the Indian body social, and, last but not least, to the growth of religious sects.

The transformation of the professional guilds into hereditary groups with particular cultic and ritual obligations was apparently a quite natural process. The endogamous character of these groups came as an accessory element; it was particularly strengthened by the fact that many autonomous tribes were incorporated into the tissue of the nationwide social structure.

Whilst a caste as a whole represents an endogamous group, in its internal structure there are smaller groups, known as *gotras*, which abide by the principle of exogamy. It is difficult to say to what extent the combination of endogamous caste and exogamous gotras reflects a specific knowledge of genetics, but it has been suggested that this arrangement was devised for two reasons: the large-scale endogamy was intended to protect the group against external hybridization, while the small-scale exogamy was to prevent the emergence of new types within the group.

These two measures operating together are supposed to ensure an excess of males over females.[21] The Indian civilization, like so many others, indulged in the cult of masculinity, and as the main reason was religious rather than martial, the habit proved particularly tenacious.

Yet all this may be an *ex post* rationalization concocted by outsiders. In fact, the caste system as it is known to Europeans is the result of a long-term development, in which spontaneous forces played a more substantial role than deliberate planning. This however does not exclude the possibility that behind these social forces, there was some apprehension of ends and means. In general, it can be argued that in the early stages of its revitalization, the caste system was often an element of social change, of further differentiation or adaptation. In conjunction with the belief in reincarnation it represented an extremely efficient device for keeping a multiracial society together on the basis of an acceptable form of apartheid. Only after many centuries did the caste system acquire those rigid contours which eventually came to be loathed by those who came under the spell of values cherished by other civilizations.

The two-fold renaissance of the literary language and the caste system did not herald a return to the past. In the spiritual field, in art and in commerce, there was a great move forward. Indian society abounded with energy. Though a lot of it was absorbed by internecine warfare, intrigue and rivalry – that monotonous kaleidoscope of all political histories in the world – there was nevertheless a good deal left for positive ventures.

The most conspicuous of these was expansion overseas. Its original impulse was apparently commercial and was prompted by the incessant demand for spices and luxury goods from the Greek and Roman customers of Indian traders. Also the trade with China was looking for an overseas route. The discovery of the regularity of the monsoons combined with the navigational skill of the Dravidian peoples made it possible for the Indians to undertake large-scale maritime ventures. At the time when the Parthians were beginning to expel the Hellenic intruders from Iran, the Indians started to sail across the Ocean and settle on the shores of Burma, Malaya and Indochina, as well as in Indonesia.

It was a great venture, which in size and cultural impact can be compared with the Hellenic expansion to the Levant in the fourth century BC, but which in terms of duration, overshadows the record of Hellenism. Whilst the Hellenistic period in the Levant (Egypt and Western Asia) was only an interlude lasting four to five centuries, after which the native societies carried on developing their own civilizations, the offshoot of the Indian civilization in South-East Asia flourished for almost one thousand years.

6.4.2 The New Religious Spectrum

In the first centuries of our era Indian civilization was developing into a very complex and many-faceted entity. The unity of its literary language contrasted with the wide variety of its religious ideas, which, however, seem to have affected mainly the upper strata of society. The common folk lived with their exuberant and colourful folklore, undisturbed in their mythopoeic world-view by the sophisticated arguments and discussions which swayed the intellectuals.

The literati of that epoch were divided and subdivided into many schools. Indian historiography, had it existed, could have claimed with much more justification than could the Chinese of China, that there were a hundred schools of thought in India at that time. Their main concern – as in all Indian thought from the time of the

Upanishads – was the search for true happiness. But there was also a lot of searching for pure knowledge, and for new, expressionistic forms of art.

Buddhist philosophy was moving towards a greater and more daring abstraction. This process has been tellingly described by S. Radhakrishnan. According to him there was a logical movement in the development of Buddhist thought. In the summary by J. Nehru[22] the logic runs as follows:

> The Buddhist philosophy begins with a dualistic metaphysics looking upon knowledge as a direct awareness of objects. In the next stage ideas are made the media through which reality is apprehended, thus raising a screen between mind and things. These two stages represent the Hinayana schools. The Mahayana schools went further and abolished the things behind the images and reduced all experience to a series of ideas in their mind. The ideas of relativity and the sub-conscious self come in. In the last stage – this was Nagarjuna's Madhyamika philosophy or the middle way – mind itself is dissolved into mere ideas, leaving us with loose units of ideas and perceptions about which we can say nothing definite.
>
> Thus we arrive finally at airy nothing, or something that is so difficult to grasp for our finite minds that it cannot be described or defined. The most we can say is that it is some kind of consciousness – *vijyana* as it is called.

Yet this seemingly nonsensical obsession with nothingness had a very practical corollary which contributed to a breakthrough in mathematics, namely the discovery of the use of zero for the decimal system. It is not surprising that mathematics became one of the successful areas of Indian thought. By its nature, mathematics is well suited to the preference of the Indian mind for abstractions which can be based on a few axioms. The formal system of mathematics, independent of any empirical corroboration, contrasted favourably with the doctrines which had to cope with the everchanging phenomena perceived by our senses, phenomena which the Indian world-view considered to be illusion – *maya*.

The brahmins wanted to catch up with the euphoric philosophising of the Buddhists, but for a long time their efforts seemed like a pale, pedestrian echo of the Buddhists' sophistication. Of the six brahminic schools which crystallized at that time only two deserve special attention: the so-called *vedanta*, based on the identity of the cosmic principle – *brahman* – with the universal soul – *atman*; and yoga, which in fact was not so much a philosophy as a theory of contemplation and concentration, a theory of the path to liberation (moksha) – a state which the Brahmins also now began to call nirvana.

The revival of philosophical speculation and the new upsurge of scholarship were matched, on the popular level, by the proliferation of religious writings known as the *Puranas*. Some of this vast complex of literature was apparently put together by the brahmins, and it is assumed that this took place at the time of the Vedas. Yet the bulk of this literature seems to have been written by other people between approximately 300 BC and 600 AD, and up to 1000 AD; most of it was destined for the lowest caste, the shudras. Being excluded from the Vedic worship, the shudras could not be properly integrated into the Verdic version of the Indian civilization. Though their social status improved in the epoch of Buddhism's predominance, the renaissance of Vedic values could have robbed them of any gains they had made. Fortunately for the shudras, the brahmins showed enough political wisdom to recognize all the Puranas as legitimate sources of religious inspiration and experience, whilst at the same time trying to smuggle into them their own values and a respect for their particular status. As however, people felt free to make what changes they wanted in the texts of the Puranas, it is impossible to trace the development of individual components of Puranic thought.

According to the traditional definition each Purana had to contain a treatise on the world's creation by the supreme God, a chapter on later creation by other (lower) gods, the genealogy of gods and wise men (the rishis), a chapter on the cosmic cycles, and finally, a chronicle of royal dynasties. Furthermore individual Puranas contain numerous legends, comments on the duties of individual castes, on festive days and rites, hymns, etc., but also a good deal of philosphical speculation.

The cult of Vedic deities such as Indra, Varuna, etc., had receded into the background and, through the combined effects of the great national epics, Mahabharata and Ramayana, and of the Puranas, originally minor deities such as Shiva, Vishnu and Brahma became popular. Individual Puranas were often orientated towards one of the new dieties, as a rule either Shiva or Vishnu. This gave them a tremendous advantage over the Vedic ritual even amongst the three upper castes.

The difference between the Vedic and the Puranic cult has been characterized by Sir Charles Eliot, as follows:

Whereas the Vedic sacrificers propitiated all the gods impartially and regarded ritual as a sacred science giving power over nature, the worshipper of the later deities is generally sectarian and often emotional. He selects one for his adoration, and this selected deity becomes not merely a great god among others, but a gigantic cosmical figure in whom centre the philosophy, poetry and passion of his devotees. He is almost God in the European sense, but still Indian deities, though they may have a monopoly of adoration in their own sects, are never entirely similar to Jehovah or Allah. They are at once more mythical, more human and more philosophical, since they are conceived of not as creators and rulers external to the world, but as forces manifesting themselves in nature. An exuberant mythology bestows on them monstrous forms, celestial residences, wives and offspring: they make occasional appearances in this world as men and animals; they act under the influence of passions which if titanic, are but human feelings magnified. The philosopher accommodates them to his system by saying that Vishnu or Siva is the form which the Supreme Spirit assumes as Lord of the visible universe, a form which is real only in the same sense that the visible world itself is real.[23]

The three main deities, Shiva, Vishnu and Brahma, (a kind of Trinity, the *trimurti*), do not represent different principles, but various aspects of divine power. The god Brahma appears in this context as creative power personified, and no longer as an absolute principle, as Brahma was conceived in the Upanishads, or as a sacrificial formula, the meaning of brahman in the Vedas. Shiva represents destructive power, and Vishnu reconstructive power. Significantly, the latter two deities acquired more importance in Indian religious practice than Brahma. They became the most popular objects of worship; the mythopoeic imagination of their devotees spun a phantastic tissue of legends around them and linked other supernatural beings to them.

Shiva became endowed with a wide gamut of representations, from that of a self-denying ascetic on the one hand, to that of a merciless destroyer on the other. A similar range of manifestations characterized a powerful female deity Kali, or Durga, who was sometimes presented as Shiva's consort. A particularly strong attribute of both these deities is sexuality, whence Shiva's symbolic phallus and Durga's vulva. The procreative function, however, is the only aspect of this attribute, which in the context of Hinduism acquires a wider, ritual meaning.

In the case of Vishnu what are most important are his incarnations in other supernatural beings (*avatars*); these incarnations or rather transfigurations, the main ones nine in number, provide the worshippers with an ample choice of rites and symbols, each of which represents a particular route towards a higher level of religious insight.

The theory of incarnations allowed Indian theology to absorb alien deities or saints into its own structure. In this way the historical Buddha was proclaimed to be the ninth avatar of the Hindu god Vishnu. The tenth avatar – Kalki – has yet to come and this will be the last incarnation. Thus the concept of a final healer, a kind of Messiah, did not remain confined to Buddhism; it also appeared in the Hinduistic pantheon.

The new deities also found their honorific place in Indian art. The dancing Shiva, or his consort Kali, or Krishna playing the flute, symbolize the process of the creation and existence of one particular world within the rhythmic sequence of cosmic epochs. The god dances or plays for his or her own pleasure and with this activity keeps the world in motion. Once the deity stops dancing or playing the flute, the whole cosmos vanishes; one of Brahma's days comes to an end – and after his night, Brahma recreates the cosmos, which again is kept in being by the mystical dance or flute playing. What a fascinating subject for visual art: the statuettes of Shiva Nataraja (king of dance), with his several hands and legs arranged in different variations, were among the most characteristic artefacts of Hindu culture and also – as the statuettes found in the debris of the ancient sites of the Indus Valley indicate – constituted a probable link with the Proto–Indian past.

With these changes Indian religion moved towards what Eliot dubbed the 'religious parliament' and what is now generally known as Hinduism. Any religious tendency could participate in this complex, provided it recognised two basic principles: respect for the Vedas and respect for the brahmins. Thus only Jainism and Buddhism remained outside this 'parliament'. Though quite legitimate within the framework of the Indian world-view, both these religions proved to be 'alienated children' in the family tree of Indian religions.

Whereas the main stream of Indian religion followed a complex pattern of development without clearly demarcated contours, Buddhism created a specific organization with more or less clearly agreed common principles and articles of faith. Thus the Buddhists like the Jainists crossed over the narrow border between what could and what could not be accepted by the nascent Hinduism as one of its many aspects. Though the Buddhist Mahayana adopted many forms of emotional and esoteric worship which brought it closer to the main stream of Hinduism, because of its principles it nevertheless remained beyond the pale.

What emerged as the rallying-point of Hinduism, the crux of its vast and many-faceted Holy Writ, was a piece of poetic religious literature known as Bhagavad-Gita, often called simply Gita (in translation the Song of the Noble, or Blessed One).

The Bhagavad-Gita is a typical product of the Indian mind. Neither its author nor the time of its composition is known. It emerged as a reflective insertion in the great epic, the Mahabharata, a story of an internecine war between close kith and kin. In the Gita the various concepts of ethics in Indian religion meet in a head-on collision and an attempt is made to explain away the contrasts between them.

The backbone of the Bhagavad-Gita is the dialogue between a prince, Arjuna, who is the commander of one side in the war, and Krishna, the eighth avatar of Vishnu, who appears on the scene in disguise as Arjuna's charioteer. Arjuna turns to Krishna proclaiming his abhorrence of killing: first as a matter of principle (*ahimsa*), and then because of the fact that on the enemy side are Arjuna's grandfather and teacher, to whom he owes the utmost respect. Krishna however rejects Arjuna's arguments and instead stresses the notion of caste duty, which for a kshatriya means the duty to fight, the shame of not doing so being worse than death. Thus against the general ethics of ahimsa, a prinicple accepted by Jainists and Buddhists, Krishna re-emphasizes the socially differentiated ethics of an earlier tradition and of the caste system. In doing so Krishna supports his point by explaining the principle of metempsychosis. In the second book of the Gita he says:[24]

Thou sorrowest for men who do not need thy sorrow,
And speakest words that (in part) are wise.
Wise men know no sorrow
For the living or the dead. (§ 11)

Just as in this body the embodied soul
Must pass through childhood, youth and age,
So too (at death) will he take another body up:
In this a thoughtful man is not perplexed. (§ 13)

Indestructible (alone) is That, – know this –
By which this whole (universe) was spun.
No one at all can bring destruction
On this which passes not away. (§ 17)

Never can this embodied soul be slain
in the body of anyone (at all).
And so for no contingent being
Hast thou any cause for sorrow. (§ 30)

Likewise consider thine own (caste)-duty (dharma),
Then too hast thou no cause to quail;
For better than a fight prescribed by duty
Is nothing for a man of the princely class. (§ 31)

After taking up this stance Krishna continues his – frequently
rather tedious – briefing on the basic tenets of Hinduism.

Like any other Holy Book, the Bhagavad-Gita is not wholly
consistent. Indologists have discovered contradictions on the philosophical plane: between the monistic and dualistic bases of various
brahminic schools. But in real life, and thus also in the context of
our study, it is more important that the Gita acknowledges the three
main paths of Indian religiosity as equally legitimate, though not
equally valuable: the path of works and rites (*karma marga*); the
path of contemplation and cognition (*jnana marga*); and the path
of devotion (*bhakti marga*). It is also extremely tolerant towards
any kind of worship.

In this respect the Bhagavad-Gita represents the meeting point,
the coming together of various phases of the development of religion
in India. The dominant role of ritual in the Vedas, the crucial role
of contemplation in Buddhism, and the pre-eminence of devotion
in later Hinduism – all are accepted by this Indian Holy Writ. Yet
it has to be stressed – and this is apparently the sign of a coming
change – that the path of devotion is here accorded pride of place.
To borrow Zaehner's words:

From this point on, 'liberation' is no longer regarded as the ultimate goal. Total detachment from the world is still rigorously insisted on, for this brings one to the Nirvana of Brahman, but this is not enough; for the very first words of the next chapter are: 'Attach thy mind to Me.' God must not only be experienced in his timeless eternity, He must be actively loved and worshipped;[25]

Though probably not of brahminic origin, the Bhagavad-Gita was, like the Puranas, eventually recognized by the brahmins as a source of religious inspiration. Thus the brahmins made an alliance with popular religion that helped them to return to the forefront of religious life in India. A prosaic sign of this comeback: from the fourth century AD the donations and bequests to the Buddhist monasteries and establishments of education decline considerably, and it is the brahmins who become the main beneficiaries of this kind of charity.

6.4.3 The Maturation of the Pan-Indian Civilization

By the fourth century AD Indian society had entered a period of high artistic creativity, accompanied by political concentration under strong dynasties. Although the attempt at political unification undertaken by the Gupta dynasty was limited in extent (it embraced only the north), in the cultural sphere there was a prolonged blossoming of art, science and religion which extended all over India. There emerged not only new religious writings and myths but also new fables, plays and poems destined for the general public. There were also advances in systematic scholarship, e.g. in mathematics, astronomy, linguistics and medicine. The geographical areas of the reading public extended not only over the whole Indian subcontinent but also to the newly Indianized world in South-East Asia. Furthermore from the eighth century onward the Muslim Arabs began to draw heavily on Indian knowledge in the above-mentioned disciplines. On the other hand there are fair indications that some Greek ideas also found their way into Indian astronomy.[26]

The most immediately visible unifying feature of Indian culture was the new style of architecture and visual art known as the Gupta style, which for the next thousand years was to represent the standard aesthetic taste of the Indian civilization. It is difficult to say whether the longevity of the Gupta style was due more to its extraordinary merits or to a growing bent towards conservatism in

Indian culture. But the fact that the Gupta style provided the inspiration for the no less fascinating overseas variants in South-East Asia seems to indicate that it possessed a particular vigour.

On the political plane two particular events seem to have disturbed the social equilibrium beyond the level of the inter-dynastic warfare. Firstly, in the second half of the fifth century a new wave of invaders, the White Huns who, in India and Iran (cf. Chapter 4) are better known as the Ephtalites, occupied north-west India. Their rule, however, ceased completely by the middle of the sixth century AD and their remnants were absorbed by the caste system and the Hindu religion. Secondly, southern India became the scene of what seems to have been religious strife between rulers who supported Buddhism and perhaps also Jainism, and others who supported the brahmins.

It is widely believed that until the coming of Western monotheistic religions, such as Islam and Catholic Christianity, India had not known religious oppression. In general this appears to be true. Indeed, in comparison with the historical record of Latin and Orthodox Christianity India's record in this respect is very good indeed. But this does not mean that there was no religious persecution at all. There is enough literary evidence to prove otherwise. Writing on the history of the predominantly Dravidian south of India, Nilakanta Sastri mentions a period of more than three centuries, for which the records are particularly scarce; but later references to that period in brahminic sources are full of bitterness, in significant contrast to the much more favourable view from the Buddhist side. It seems that the ruling dynasty of that epoch, the Kalabhras, favoured the Buddhists and probably also the Jainists and discriminated heavily against the brahmins and their cults.[27] Later we shall come across discrimination and even persecution that worked the other way.

The second half of the first millennium AD is the epoch during which the Indian civilization reached its greatest geographical extent. From the mountains of the Hindu-kush in the north-west to Sri Lanka in the south, and to what is now southern Vietnam and the central islands of Indonesia, stretched a single widely-ramified culture, using one literary language, Sanskrit, presenting in its art a style that was a source of inspiration far and wide, and spreading everywhere the knowledge both of brahminic and of Buddhist schools of thought and religious cults, thus making possible both a choice of cults and a wide-ranging syncretism.

This was a truly Indian epoch in southern Asia. In the history of Indian civilization this phase could perhaps best be described as Pan-Indian. The renaissance of Sanskrit, the revitalization and proliferation of the castes, the split and the 'religionization' of the majority stream in Buddhism, the emergence of the Puranas, the reconstruction of brahminic thought and the continuous quest for new combinations within the spiritual heritage: all these were factors which impressed upon the face of India an image in which old and new were blended together.

There was a continuing reverence for the Vedas but the shudras, excluded from the Vedic ritual, made their own triumphant contribution to the developing Indian tradition; their Puranas extolling the cult of the Hindu trinity became the backbone of the coming age of Hinduism. The Bhagavad-Gita gave expression to this age, with all its philosophical, ethical and cultic nuances and contrasts. Though Sanskrit became the lingua franca, this did not prevent the cultivation of local languages on the periphery, especially Tamili in southern India and the national languages of Farther India. The all-pervasive Gupta art inspired in Sri Lanka, and above all in Java and amongst the Khmers, local variants of its classical style.

In the field of religion, there was a continuous flux, characterized by changing roles, shifts of emphasis and new forms of syncretism. The kshatriyas, who at the time of the Upanishads had entered into competition with the brahmins on their own, religious-philosophical, ground, returned to their time-honoured power game. Perhaps after one of them – Gautama – had attained the supreme enlightenment and become the Buddha, there was no further scope left for their spiritual venture. Though the brahmins made their peace with the popular religion, they nevertheless had to face a new kind of competition, from the religious self-made men known as *gurus*. The Buddhist monks were progressively losing their appeal. The upkeep and educational activity of their monasteries depended more and more on the support of local rulers, which was forthcoming in peripheral areas such as Sri Lanka, Bengal and Farther India, rather than in the heartland of the Pan-Indian civilization.

The case of Sri Lanka was the most spectacular. Here, in the middle of the fifth century AD, Buddhism experienced a remarkable revival. It was due to the missionary activity of a north Indian monk by the name of Buddhaghosa. He succeeded in re-establishing in Sri Lanka the authority of the Pali Canon. Thus after a prolonged period of syncretism, fostered by the Mahayana tradition that was popular in Sri Lanka in those years, Sinhalese Buddhism returned to the more traditional and orthodox version of the Theravada and has remained faithful to it to the present day.

In contrast to Sri Lanka, in other areas where Buddhism found powerful sponsors, it was the Mahayana tradition which was the main beneficiary of government policy.[28] Thus neither in Bengal nor in South-East Asia was a barrier erected against the syncretic tendencies. Whilst in Bengal Mahayana Buddhism succumbed to the spell of a new kind of popular religion, the *Tantras*, to which we shall return shortly, in South-East Asia there prevailed an outright syncretism blending Buddhism with the current Hinduistic cults. Buddha there was identified either with Shiva (hence Shivabuddha) or with the whole trinity, Shiva, Vishnu and Brahma, deities considered to be emanations of the Buddha. The only place where Buddhism survived uncontaminated by other cults was Lower Burma, inhabited at that time by an extremely talented and receptive ethnic group, the Mons.

6.4.4 The Pan-Indian Synthesis and a Look Backwards

In the spiritual life of India everything moved towards what may be called a nuanced synthesis. The principles of Mahayana and Hinduism continued to converge. Action was valued more than idleness but the action had to be disinterested. This was just as much the paradigm of the bodhisattvas as it was the message of Bhagavad-Gita. The Buddhist ethic also found its echo in the popular writings of Hinduism. According to the Mahabharata, people of all castes and ashramas (stages of life) have to avoid anger and enmity, cultivate gratefulness, charity, forgiveness, and chastity, and have children within the confines of marriage. The *Vamanapurana* summarizes the ethical precepts in ten points: the first ordains non-hurting (*ahimsa*), and the last one asceticism (*tapas*).

But the main act of synthesis at the turn of the eighth and ninth centuries AD came from a brahmin from Kerala in Southern India, whose name, Shankara, meant 'mixing'. Though the coincidence of the personal name with its generic meaning was abundantly exploited by all those who did not like Shankara's ideas, the synthesis achieved by his genius was so powerful that all ridicule had to cease.

Shankara succeeded in striking a viable balance between various schools of thought. On the philosophical plane he linked up with the brahminic school *Advaita* (non-dualism), developing a time-honoured idea of the Upanishads on the absolute. The extreme idealism of this school, which considered the world which men perceive with their senses as illusion (*maya*), was shared in principle by the numerically largest school of Mahayana Buddhism, known as *Madhyamika-prasangika*. On the cultic side Shankara found a formula for reconciling popular religion and its personal gods on the one hand, with the non-theistic philosophy of the absolute which considered these gods as maya on the other. According to Shankara, the belief in personal gods may be a provisional help, useful and even necessary in the search for correct knowledge. Concentrating one's mind on a personal god makes identification with him possible. There the semblance of the dualism (*dvaita*), of the difference between the devotee and the subject of his devotion, disappears and the god sheds all personal attributes – and to borrow Glasenapp's words, 'The wise one recognizes himself as the ever blessed non-dual Absolute'.[29]

Thus, as in the Bhagavad-Gita, devotional worship may lead to the same end as the path recommended by the philosophy of Yoga. In order to give weight to this acceptance Shankara composed a hymn in honour of a personal god in female form, *Shakti*.

In order to preserve his synthesis against distortions, Shankara evenhandedly rejected both the empty ritualism cultivated by the widely influential brahminic school, the *Mimamsa*, and the emotional excesses of the newly emerging popular religion of the *Tantras* (see below). Shankara also rejected the belief in the living Buddha and the bodhisattvas, thus clearly drawing the line between Hinduism and Buddhism.

Shankara's enormous impact on the subsequent development of Indian civilization would not have been possible without his missionary zeal and organizational talent and, last but not least, without his understanding of the contemporary social climate. Having recognized the existence of the castes as a self-evident condition of social life, he however maintained, in agreement with the Buddhists, that ultimate knowledge could be attained by everybody, irrespective of their castes. To check the Buddhist influence on people inclined to collective meditation, Shankara organized monastic communities for the *sannyasins* (brahmins devoted to meditation and ascesis). In order to show that he recognized the value of popular cults he himself took part in the worship of Shiva.

By his relentless activity Shankara produced a striking contrast to the ideal of the quiet recluse which dominated the religious climate of India for more than a thousand years. For the next three hundred years his philosophy was accepted as a kind of Hindu orthodoxy.

At the time when, through Shankara's efforts, the synthesis of Hinduism was reaching its culmination, a new wave of popular religious literature stirred the cultic life of India. This consisted of the so-called *Tantras* (literally books) or *Agamas*, writings – like many others – by unknown authors. They dealt with the same subject as the Puranas, but their orientation was more towards ritual, which they mingled, like the Vedic literature, with philosophy. Furthermore, their ritual was very much bound up with magic. The erstwhile significance of the holy sound returned in the form of the belief that there was an esoteric connection between the universe and the sacred phoneme of the Vedas, *aum*. The written symbols were also believed to have a magic power.

Furthermore, there was a widespread belief that the human organism was a miniature copy of the cosmos; and that in the lowest centre of the human organism there was a seat of power identical with that which created the universe. Those who managed to lift this power to the highest centre could liberate the soul from the bondage of matter. Thus yoga obtained a new importance and became a key concept of the Tantras. Otherwise there were strongly devotional cults connected with the Tantras. Shiva, Vishnu, but mainly Durga (Kali) became objects of devoted worship.

In the worship of the female deity (*shakti*) two paths were distinguished: one known as the path of the right hand, the other as the path of the left hand. The right-hand path followed the usual method of contemplation and yoga. The left-hand path was the method of the orgiastic cults; their aim was to reach an exhaustion of the senses such as to allow maximum religious concentration.

The cult of female deities had favourable repercussions on the position of women in the Tantric communities. Here the women enjoyed a particular esteem: they could be teachers; they could remarry; *sati* (literally 'faithful wife'), the custom of immolating a widow on her husband's funeral pyre, was forbidden; and the murder of a woman was considered to be a particularly grave crime. In this respect the Tantric communities differed favourably from the rest of Indian society. Can we perhaps see in this stance, together with the increased role of ritualism and magic, a partial return to pre-Aryan past?

The Tantric cults also highlighted the dual, contradictory character of Hindu deities, especially Shiva and his consort Kali (Durga). The goddess could be venerated both as a tender, loving mother and as a merciless, cruel destroyer. This contradiction was rationalized by the explanation that birth and death are twins, that grace and horror come from the same source, and that a joyful acceptance of both is a precondition of a higher spiritual life.

In taking this stance Hinduism was in a position to overcome the ubiquitous dualism of good and evil, a dualism which in all other great religions of the world has produced a problem difficult to resolve. The contrast is most striking when Hinduism is compared with orthodox Zoroastrianism, where the struggle between the Wise Lord of Truth (*Ohrmazd*) and the Evil Spirit of Lie (*Ahriman*) overshadowed the monistic principle; the latter had to be relegated to its eschatological dimension, to the victory of Ohrmazd at the end of time. In evaluating these contrasts we cannot deny that both these extreme positions possess a strong dose of realism. But for a Hindu the position is easier to cope with. Above his deities is the law of karma which regulates his reincarnations and eventually offers him the chance to escape. A Zoroastrian had to take comfort in the Last Judgement.

The Tantric influence was so strong that even Buddhism, as far as it survived, could not escape its impact. In fact in Bengal and Assam there developed a third, Tantric version of Buddhism, also known as *Vajrayana* (the Diamond vehicle) or *Mantrayana* (the vehicle of magic formulae). In the middle of the eleventh century Vajrayanic missionaries were able to complete the conversion of Tibet, where the first proselytizing attempt had failed three hundred years earlier.

Vajrayana (known also as esoteric Buddhism) accepted the philosophical role of polarity in interpreting reality and in the practical endeavours of the yogis to apprehend it. Its Buddha was not the historical figure; instead there was a hierarchy of cosmic Buddhas (each, theoretically, having his earthly incarnation during some world period) with their female counterparts, the *dakinis*. The so-called right-handed Vajrayana accomplished the integration of the two principles in the psyche by meditation (cf. Jung's equivalent, the integration of the *anima* and *animus*), while the left-handed Vajrayana maintained that a ritual enactment of the union on the physical plane enhanced the meditational realization of the unit of opposites.

In Tibet, however, Vajrayana was subjected to a considerable transformation; the Tibetan Buddhism of the lamas assumed quite distinct forms dictated by its own *genius loci*. In Bengal and in the neighbouring areas Vajrayana and the whole of Buddhism was wiped out with the destruction of the monasteries in the Muslim conquest in the thirteenth century.

In the meantime cultural life in the heartland of India began to stagnate. Ritualism and magic in religion, formalism and traditionalism in art and literature show the prevalence of routine over creative effort. The stress was on the external and conspicuous forms of life. An artificial style and sensual themes were the height of fashion. Scholarly works became scarce and Sanskrit was losing its prestige. The creative spirit moved to the periphery, to the Dravidian south, and above all, to South-East Asia.

6.5 THE THREE ORBITS: HINDUISM, THERAVADA AND ISLAM

6.5.1 The Challenge of Islam

With the coming of the second millennium AD India was subjected to a new foreign invasion, this time of people united not so much by blood as by their common creed – Islam. The Muslim invasion came, as had so many others in the past, from the north-west, and within three hundred years had conquered the whole Indian subcontinent; during the subsequent two centuries the insular part of Farther India was largely converted to Islam. In India proper the Islamic conquest was carried mainly by the sword of the Afghans, whereas in Indonesia it was mainly the work of Persian and Arabic merchants and missionaries.

The contact of Islam with Hinduism was in the first instance a confrontation of fundamentally different world views. Western monotheism clashed with Eastern pantheism in a polytheistic garb. In religious terms nothing could be more contradictory than on the one hand the belief in one exclusive and omnipotent God, creator of the universe and judge of all mankind, and on the other hand the belief in an unchangeable absolute principle which, as the only reality, is behind the world of essentially illusory phenomena. In addition the equality, at least in theory, of all human beings before their creator and judge in Islam contrasted with the hierarchy of existential positions at different distances from nirvana in Hinduism.

In real life however, the equality of all Muslims before God was not reflected in any equality before their commanders, be they caliphs, emirs, sultans or whatever. The socio-economic and also political stratification of Islamic society was no less marked than the stratification of Hindu society. Yet, the religious significance of the castes and the fact that a substantial proportion of the Indian population were outside, or rather below, the castes made the scope of stratification in Hindu society more extensive and the gaps between strata wider. If this was not necessarily reflected in the range of living standards it was certainly true with respect to the scales of social status and human dignity.

Bearing in mind the form taken by Hindu worship, we can hardly be surprised that at their first contact with the Hindus the Muslims saw in them the embodiment of devilish idolatry. The destruction of the Hindu temples was the natural result. The remaining Buddhists in Bengal and Bihar met the same fate; their Vajrayanic monasteries made an equally disturbing impression on the pious Muslims as the Hindu temples, and thus in the view of the conquerors the monks did not deserve anything better than to be put to the sword.

The brahmins were more fortunate; scattered throughout the countryside rather than concentrated around their temples, and being more numerous than the monks, they survived the first onslaught. After the Muslims had established their first sultanate on Indian soil (named the Delhi sultanate after its capital), their rulers found it more convenient to tolerate their idolatrous subjects just as they tolerated the *dhimmis* (the non-Muslim monotheists, people of the Book).

The Muslim conquerors did not behave like the Spanish conquistadores in Mexico and in Peru. They did not destroy the Hindu civilization. Attempts to convert people to Islam by force were undertaken sporadically and without much consistency. Only much later, towards the end of the Muslim domination over India did Aurangzeb (1658–1707) launch a conversion campaign using force on a major scale. But such a venture proved to be beyond anybody's capacity.

Not counting two small outposts (Sindh and Multan) which the Muslims managed to establish in the first major thrust of their expansion at the beginning of the eighth century, the Muslim conquest of India occurred in three great waves. The first, between the eleventh and twelfth centuries, brought under Muslim rule the area between the Indus river and the Ganges estuary, i.e. almost the whole area of the ancient Aryavarta, excluding what is now Rajasthan. In the second wave, between 1308 and 1315, the whole of the Indian subcontinent (India proper) was overrun. This, however, provoked a mighty reaction. Between 1329 and 1336 the Muslims were expelled from the Dravidian south, where a mighty state with a new capital – Vijayanagar (city of victory) – emerged. For two hundred years to come the state of Vijayanagar was to be the bulwark of Hinduism against Muslim domination.

By the time the third Muslim advance to the south came, new intruders, the Portuguese, had already become established on the west Indian coast. In the middle of the seventeenth century the Muslim empire of the Mughals annexed the greater part of the Hindu state of Vijayanagar, and soon after that the last chapter of the Hindu–Islamic confrontation began. Its main beneficiaries, however, were to be eighteenth-century invaders from Western Europe. Within another one hundred years the whole of India was united under the British Raj.

The pressure of Islam on India could not but make a deep impact on both sides of this relationship. The Muslims became acquainted with a quite different culture from their own; but its impact on Islam operated mainly through the Sufis, whose mystical bent and devotional cult made them less alien to the Indian mind. In principle Sufism was quite close to the practices of contemporary Hinduism. With their endeavor to identify with their God the Sufis did not particularly differ from the Hindu yogins, and the position of the Sufi shayks was not dissimilar to that of the Hindu gurus. Otherwise, however, the Muslims found it necessary to stick to their basic values, though the caste mentality occasionally penetrated their ranks.

Similarly the Hindus stressed their adherence to the tradition and to its underlying trend towards devotional worship on sectarian lines. Strangely enough, of the Islamic social arrangements it was not so much the non-existence of the castes as the habit of secluding women (*purdah*) which seems to have made more impact on Indian life.

Yet between the entrenched positions of orthodox Islam on the one hand and uncompromising Hinduism on the other, there was a wide scope for syncretism or attempts at a synthesis. Islam found a sympathetic echo because of its egalitarianism, whilst Hinduism was attractive because of its devotional worship and the idea of reincarnation.

As far as the structure of Indian society is concerned, the Muslim conquest did not change its basic pattern; with the exception of areas whose population converted to Islam, Indian society remained organized in castes. Nevertheless the Muslim domination strengthened the already existent elements of feudalism. The rulers always tended to keep their warlords, and often also the priests, happy by allocating them the revenues from greater or smaller areas as benefices. In fact, the allocation of income also implied control over the respective area. The Muslims already had a well-established institution for this purpose: the *iqta'*. Thus, this type of feudal holding spread all over Muslim-dominated India. Yet this affected only the top level of socio-economic relationships, where the central issue was the upper, dispositional, ownership. The lower, working, ownership or posssession remained in the hands of the village commune. In fact, there was no need to introduce any kind of serfdom: peasants were in any case bound to their castes and villages, and mobility followed religious rather than economic lines. Also the working population in the towns continued to live according to their traditional pattern.

On the whole, it can be said that in the Muslim-dominated areas it was the new fief holders – the *iqtadars* – who became the ruling class. Being the military branch of government they succeeded in strengthening their position both *vis-à-vis* the sultans and *vis-à-vis* the predominantly Hindu subjects. Some fiefs were also allocated to the pious foundations (waqf) of the Muslim 'ulema or dervishes. But the representatives of Hinduism were not totally deprived of their possessions. After the first wave of iconoclasm, booty-grabbing and confiscations was over, the Muslim rulers preferred to make a deal with the priestly caste of their subjects. The brahmins continued to be exempt from taxation and their temple communities continued to be the upper owners of their estates. The Muslim rulers were more apprehensive of the heterodox sects than of the established religions. Whether Hindu, such as the Tantrics, or Muslim, such as the Qarmats, heterodoxy was often a target of persecution by the sultans.

But under the Hindu rule too the social structure underwent some changes. It is difficult to say whether the shifts in ownership were moving towards a partial feudalization, or whether there was a cycle resulting from the successive tightening and loosening of the grip of central government.

According to Mahalingam's study of economic life in the state of

Vijayanagar, there were three basic types of holdings and income:
(a) possession or property divided between the upper (dispositional)
rights of the feudatories (*jagirs* or *nayaks*) on the one hand, and
the working possession of the peasants (*kudi*) on the other hand;
(b) tenancy which occurred mainly in the case of lands newly brought
to cultivation (*kuthagai*); and (c) direct husbandry by the owner, a
kind of exclusive ownership (*pannai*), with the help of hired labour.

Both the dispositional and the working ownership could be either
collective (*ganabhogam*) or individual (*ekabhogam*). A collective
type of working ownership prevailed in the villages, whilst the
collective type of dispositional ownership occurred mainly with the
temple communities of the brahmins. These temple communities
were not only big landlords but also functioned, in the absence of
a royal mint monopoly, as banking institutions.[30]

6.5.2 The Reconstruction of Hinduism and the Syncretic Religions

At the time of the first wave of the Muslim conquest, the Indian
civilization was already losing its vitality. As we saw in the preceding
chapter, Indian culture displayed a general trend towards formalism
and routine. There was no significant innnovation in scholarship.
The migration of Indians to Farther India petered out and the
societies there began to develop in new directions.

Furthermore a protracted and devastating war raged for many
decades between Dravidian Chola (on the tip of the Indian peninsula)
and the empire of Srivijaya centred on Sumatra and Java. Although
the circumstances of this conflict are not clear, it seems that both
commercial and religious motives played a role in the confrontation.
The commercial interest focused on the Straits of Malacca, and the
religious strife was between the militant Shaivism of Chola and the
syncretizing Buddhism of the rulers of Srivijaya. This conflict also
involved Sri Lanka which, as a result, was occupied for a greater
part of the eleventh century by the Cholan armies. This event,
preceded by similar inroads in the past, further contributed
to Sinhalo-Tamil rivalry and to the strengthening of Sinhalese
nationalism.

The Shaivite militancy seems not to have been the only reaction
against foreign competition. All over India the glorious past became
a source of inspiration. Broadly speaking, two main alternatives
were tried out. Some brahmins tried to revitalize the ancient tradition
of the Vedas. While adhering theoretically to Shankara's philosophy,

they began to cultivate the time-honoured ritualism of the brahminic school of Mimamsa, yet, as it seems, failed to make any particular appeal to the population. In some areas of western and central Deccan it was the Jainists who made spectacular headway. With the support of local rulers Jainism experienced the Indian Summer of its missionary activity. However, towards the end of the twelfth century the rulers turned against the Jainists and a fierce wave of persecution in Gujarat and in the south of India once again tarnished the record of tolerance which had prevailed during most periods of Indian history.

Despite the efforts of the traditionalists to bring about a renaissance of the ancient concepts and forms of worship, the main trend, as has been said already, favoured the *bhakti marga*. In this respect the Vaishnavites were at the forefront of developments. Their spiritual leader Ramanuja (a Tamil guru who according to tradition lived from 1027 to 1137) preached the idea of a loving and righteous God who, by bestowing his grace on human beings, could deliver them from the bondage of the karmanic law. This grace could be won by those who approached their God with the utmost dedication and love. In this respect Ramanuja's teaching deviated from that of Shankara, for whom worshipping a personal god was only a provisional step in the search for true religious insight, which consisted in grasping the abstract, monistic concept of the absolute. By contrast, for Ramanuja and his followers the personal god, Vishnu or any of his avatars, was the ultimate source of salvation. In adopting this stance Ramanuja highlighted more acutely than ever before the inherent dilemma of theistic religions, namely whether man's salvation depends more on good works or on God's grace.[31]

The new mood did not remain limited to the Vaishnavite stream of Hinduism. Various gurus up and down the country preached a similar gospel. But regarding other points there was a greater degree of differentiation. Some new sects attempted to ignore the caste barriers, some stood for equality for women, some extolled the symbols of the procreative force in worship. In the fifteenth century one of the most popular Vaishnavite gurus, Ramananda, turned against the impediment of the castes in religious life; a similar current also prevailed in some Shaivite sects.

In taking this path, Hinduism was converging to a certain extent with the theistic approach of Western religions. This tendency also made the social climate more propitious for Hindu-Islamic syncretism.

The possibility of reconciling such contrasting opposites as were represented by Islam on the one hand and Hinduism on the other would seem to be remote indeed. Yet, as history abundantly reveals, no contrast of ideas is stark enough to avoid attempts being made to resolve it. Mental constructions often follow their own specific logic. The Indian social climate was particularly favourable to such an undertaking.

The Hindu-Islamic encounter inspired not only the gurus but also the rulers. We may say that the traditional competition between the brahmins and the kshatriyas re-emerged in a new garb. Amongst the popular gurus, it was mainly Kabir (d. 1518) and Nanak (d. 1538), respectively forerunner and founder of the Sikh religion, and amongst the crowned heads, the Mughal Emperor Akbar (who ruled 1555–1605) whose syncretism amounted to a new religious venture. However as always in this kind of situation, only a popular guru and not an emperor could make his teaching a going concern.

Akbar's syncretic religion, the *Din ilahi*, i.e. God's teaching, of which Akbar himself became the high priest, was a noble attempt to find common ground for the two main religions of his subjects. The basis of the new religion was Islam, but without the theologians ('ulema) and without the dervishes, and supported by the philosophical speculation of Hinduism. Akbar's synthesis however was not intended as a substitute for other religions; his rule was marked by exemplary tolerance.

Akbar abolished all discrimination against non-Muslims; this had particularly tangible results in the area of tax policy and when it came to employing Hindus in government service. Akbar also built up friendly relations with the Rajput princes who were the main supporters of the powerful Hindu state of Vijayanagar. From the point of view of Indian civilization Akbar's policy of tolerance and co-operation with the Hindu majority was more important than his religious innovations. It generated a new social climate in which the arts, especially architecture, painting and music, attained new peaks of creativity. Mughal art with its Persian influences is one of the finest products of a culture which derives its inspiration from two distinct cultural traditions. So too the language of the imperial chancellery, Urdu, was a combination of Indian vernacular (Hindi) with Persian elements.

Unlike the imperial religion, the popular syncretism was better equipped to win genuine converts: Kabir's followers still survive as a small sect and Sikhism became a religion in its own right. Its founder, Nanak, believed in the unity of God and the brotherhood of man, but the Sikhs developed into a tightly-knit military organization fighting not only the Muslims but sometimes also the Hindus. This outcome was not of their own making; it was a transformation they were pushed into by a hostile environment. Being uncompromising monotheists like the Muslims and rejecting the castes and the Hindu worship with its asceticism, mendicancy, pilgrimages, bathing in sacred waters, etc., the Sikhs were frowned on by the Hindus. But by adhering to the doctrines of karma, metempsychosis and nirvana, they became unacceptable to the Muslims.

As long as the Sikhs were living under tolerant rulers such as Akbar everything went all right. Under Akbar the Sikhs were allowed to build their temple at Amritsar, on land granted by the emperor himself; at the instigation of their fifth guru, Arjun Dev, they compiled their Holy Writ – the *Adi Granth* (i.e. the first book), written in a special script of their own (an adaptation of the main Indian script, the *devanagari*).

But Arjun became involved in the internal intrigues of the Mughal court against Akbar's successor Jahangir (1605–27), who then decided to liquidate the syncretic religion. Arjun was asked to choose between Islam and Hinduism, but he refused, and was tortured and executed (1606). His son and successor Har Govind reacted by providing the Sikhs with a military organization. This happened at a time when armed clashes between the Hindu sannyasins and the Islamic dervishes were becoming a disturbing phenomenon in Indian society.

Yet the official policy of the Mughal court continued to be one of tolerance; only the Sikhs were discriminated against. The turning point, however, came with the Emperor Aurangzeb (1658–1707), who attacked the mainstays of Akbar's policy in several ways. He excluded the Hindus from the higher echelons of the government service, re-imposed higher taxes on the Hindus, removed the artists and musicians from the court and ordered the destruction of many Hindu temples.

Around 1660 Hinduism was at its lowest ebb. Yet Aurangzeb's policy evoked a violent response organized by a vigorous ethnic group in west India, the Marathas. Joined by the redoubtable Rajputs and adroitly exploiting the fissiparous tendencies amongst the Muslims, the Marathas waged a major war against the Mughals. The Sikhs could not but join in on the side of the Marathas. In

1675 their ninth guru, Teg Bahadur, was commanded to convert to Islam; Aurangzeb did not allow him the choice that Jahangir had given his forefather. But the outcome was the same: refusal and execution. Under Bahadur's son and successor, Govind Singh (Singh meaning the lion, from then on an honorific name given to all male Sikhs), the Sikhs were transformed into a martial community – the *khalsa*. They ceased to follow the charismatic authority of the living gurus and accepted the authority of their Holy Writ, the *Adi Granth*, which Govind completed with his own verses.

Despite being defeated many times by the Mughal armies the Sikhs remained unbroken. By their brave stand against the Mughal Raj the Sikhs won many converts from amongst the peasantry. But the military nature of their community did not allow them to operate everywhere in the country. Their activity remained limited to the Punjab, which they could hold by force of arms; thus they could no longer aspire to become a nationwide religion.

Despite the fact that after Aurangzeb's death (1707), the Mughal court returned to Akbar's policy, it was too late to save anything. Both Hinduism and Islam were challenged by a new foe, who proved to be more formidable than he had at first appeared. Though entering India merely as merchants and involved in constant strife with other Europeans, the British – adroitly exploiting the dissensions amongst the Indians – eventually came to rule over the whole of India and thus initiated a new chapter in the history of Indian civilization.

At this point we have to add a concluding remark. Before the civilization of the European West became her main challenge, India underwent not only religious differentiation. From the ethnic point of view India was always a complex of many nations. But the common religion, or rather religions, co-existing more or less peacefully all over the country, and the common literary language, Sanskrit, make it a clearly demarcated cultural unit, and in view of her caste system, also a special social formation. It was a civilization in which the extent of a given social structure matched the extent of the corresponding culture.

At the time when the first Europeans, the Portuguese, arrived on the shores of India, about 20 to 25 per cent of the Indian population were Muslims and Sanskrit was losing its position as the lingua franca. Most gurus preached and wrote in their respective mother tongues; the great poet and religious teacher Tulsi Das (d. 1623), often hailed as the greatest evangelist of Hinduism, wrote in the most widely spoken Indian vernacular – Hindi. His *chef d'oeuvre* Ramacharitnamas, a free paraphrase of the time-honoured Ramayana, became the popular piece of Indian literature. Though it sealed the fate of Sanskrit, it gave the Indians a book whose content was acceptable to all the sects within the fold of Hinduism.

Although from the seventeenth century various Indian vernaculars spoken by the common folk developed into literary languages and thus became a divisive factor in the upper strata as well, the main division continued to be a religious one. India entered the age of Europeanism split into a Hindu and an Islamic section, with the small community of the Sikhs in between. The fifteen or so ethnic groups with their own national languages became an issue only when India became independent and divided into two states along religious lines.

6.5.3 The Civilization of Theravada

Divided into three or four parts according to language group and/ or religion, South-East Asia does not constitute a cohesive unit. Only from about 500 AD until about the fourteenth century did the greater part of South-East Asia live under the strong influence of the Indian civilization, whose style and largely also values predominated amongst the upper strata, especially at the royal courts. A small part in the north-east (precursor of the present-day Vietnam) came into the orbit of the Chinese civilization.

As a *caveat* with respect to the extent of the Indianization of South-East Asia we may quote the authority in this field, John E. Cady:

> It is obvious, nevertheless, that Indianized court civilization never completely dominated centers where indigenous cultural vitality was strong, as in Java or Cambodia. Southeast Asian peoples appear to have oscillated between their appropriation of Indian forms and the resurgence of pre-Indian standards of civilization. Old customs were often preserved under a veneer of Indianization. Much was rejected in the absence of any affirmative response – caste, and subordination of women, for example . . . Always operative as selective factor was 'local genius', which determined preferences for congenial aspects of the new culture pattern. Hence came the preference for Shiva over Vishnu in the eastern zone (eastern Java, Cambodia, Champa), where fertility and ancestral rites, combined with deification of the life-giving power

of the soil, constituted compatible elements of indigenous culture.[32]

In the fourteenth century, however, the Indianized sector of South-East Asia parted company with the rest. Whilst the continental part remained faithful to its Indian tradition, albeit one substantially adapted to the local circumstances, the insular and peninsular part of South-East Asia, inhabited by the Malayan ethnie, came under the sway of the Islamic civilization. In the sixteenth century the north-eastern part of the Malayan islands (which thereafter were known as the Philippines) became part of the Spanish empire and began to be Christianized. Thus the whole area was divided into four different civilizational sectors. In this section we shall focus our attention on the continental part of South-East Asia. Oddly enough this subcontinent has not got its own name in the English language. The occasionally used label, Farther India, applies to the whole area. The French use for its continental part the term 'Indochine', a term whose English equivalent Indochina refers merely to its formerly French colonial part.

The lack of attention given to this continent in European writings (even Arnold Toynbee with his wide-ranging coverage gives it only a cursory glance) may be a reflection of the view that nothing remarkable happened in that area. It did not give birth to any specific religion. Its culture was a kind of mixture of native and foreign elements. There were neither great spiritual nor major political ventures which cut across the natural boundaries of the area. In fact it would seem to be in the realm of architecture and visual art that it lays the greatest claim to our attention. Cambodia's Angkor Vat, Java's Borobudur and the sculptures of Buddha's smiling face, belong to the highest achievements of world art. The literature on the other hand seems to have clung more closely to the Indian tradition.

Yet a complete neglect of Indochina (in the French sense of the term) in our account would impoverish our review of those particular instances and processes which only when taken together can give us a true picture of the various paths of civilization.

In contrast to Indian history, the history of Indochina is marked more by ethnic and political ventures than by religious creativity. In that sense it is more reminiscent of European history. Like Europe, Indochina received a higher religion imported from another civilizational area. In that respect India was for Indochina what the Levant was for Europe. There is yet another parallel worth noting here. In India, as in the Levant, most polities emerged as dynastic states. In Europe and in Indochina there was a tendency to create states on an ethnic basis, though not always with one ethnic group being united in a single state.

After the first Indianized (or Sanskritized) state of Funan (comprising present-day Cambodia, South Vietnam and maritime parts of Thailand) dissolved, the main axes of political development in Indochina can be characterized by the geopolitical dimension of its ethnic contests. One axis was the divide between the south and the north. There were on the one hand the native peoples of the south, such as the Pyus, the Mons (often divided into several states), the Khmers (with their successive states of Chenla and Cambodia), and the Chams (their country being known as Champa); and on the other hand the newcomers from the north, the Burmese, the Thais and the Annamites (Vietnamese, then called successively Dai-Viet and Nam-Viet). The other axis ran between the west and the east. The struggle went on both between natives, the Mons versus the Khmers and the Khmers versus the Chams, and also between newcomers, the Burmese versus the Thais.

The struggles between the Indianized nations were only occasionally given an ideological dimension, when a leaning towards a particular religious cult – usually Buddhist or Shaivite – intervened. The thousand-year-long contest between the Vietnamese and the Chams, however, always was a struggle between two cultures, a Sinicized and an Indianized one respectively. After the conquest and absorption of the Chams by the Vietnamese in the fifteenth century AD the struggle continued with a further advance of the Vietnamese against the Khmers, a process which was only temporarily interrupted by the French colonization and American intervention (1884–1974).

Turning to the Indianized nations of Indochina we may perhaps characterize their main achievements as follows. The Mons and the Khmers were most successful in the cultural sphere. The Mons played a crucial role in the renaissance and blossoming of Theravada Buddhism and the Khmers scored their most outstanding achievements with their architecture and visal art, done mainly for syncretic cults of Indian origin – Shaivite, Vaishnavite, and Mahayana Buddhism. The Thais succeeded in establishing a special social system remarkable for its long-lasting stability, whilst the Burmese attempted to make Theravada Buddhism the religion of a universal empire.

The Burmese settled *en masse* during the ninth and tenth centuries AD in what is nowadays Upper Burma. Coming from the north and being related to the Tibetans they were apparently not ignorant of Buddhism, which they largely adopted in its Vajrayanic version, though with a strong admixture of animistic features. The Mons on the other hand, with their capital Pegu, represented, together with the Sinhalese in Sri Lanka, the only remaining strongholds of Theravada Buddhism. In the middle of the eleventh century, however, Theravada began its victorious thrust into the other parts of Indianized Indochina, and supported by intermittent contact with Sri Lanka, has maintained its position there up to the modern era.

The historical turning point occurred in 1056 when, according to the chronicles, the Burmese ruler Anawrahta was converted to Theravada by Shin Arahan, a monk from the Mon kingdom of Thaton, and decided to impose this version of Buddhism on his subjects. Thirty thousand Mons were reported to have been forcibly settled in the Burmese capital Pagan, and the Vajrayanic/animistic priesthood retreated to the wilderness.

But this was not the end of the reform. In 1074, at the request of the Sinhalese king Vijaya Bahu, Theravada monks, books and relics were sent from Burma to Sri Lanka, where they helped to tighten the monastic discipline and impose a stricter ritual purity.

This event turned out to be the first in a series of rectifying interventions by the two Buddhist countries in each other's affairs. Next it was Burma's turn to ask for help. This proved to have broader consequences. The Burmese mission to Sri Lanka at the end of the twelfth century was accompanied by a Cambodian prince who paved the way for further missionary activity by the Theravadin monks amongst the Khmers.

The official religious cult in Cambodia was syncretic – a compound of Shaivism, Vishnuism and Mahayana – and its most important exponents were the brahmins; with its great temples and pompous rites the cult was very costly and formalistic. At a time when the struggle against the advancing Thais was an additional burden on top of the traditional contest with the neighbouring Chams, Cambodian resources were stretched to the limit. The Theravadin monks who came to the country as modest and kind teachers contrasted favourably with the demanding and often arrogant brahmins.

The Chinese traveller Chou-ta Kuan, who visited Cambodia in 1296 or so, noticed a significant contrast: the Buddhists ran schools whereas the brahmins did not. It was the reverse of the situation in India, where it was the Buddhists and not the brahmins who became isolated. Everywhere they went, the Theravadin monks began to provide for a rudimentary male education. Gradually Theravada gained ground until, by the mid-fourteenth century, it became the official religion amongst the Khmers, the Thais and the Laotians. The brahmins survived as astrologists and court ceremonialists. Champa, where Shaivism prevailed, remained the only residue of the Pan-Indian epoch until her absorption by Vietnam.

The civilization of Theravada attained its golden age in the second half of the fifteenth century. From around 1420 until 1530 or so the Burmese and the Mons experienced an exceptionally long period of peace. Literature and art flourished. The pilgrimages to Sri Lanka were renewed and the standards of knowledge and discipline in the monasteries were raised again. From 1472 to 1492 the Mon kingdom of Pegu was ruled by a pious and cultured monk, Dhammazedi, whose moral authority was respected far beyond the borders of his country. Just as we encounter in other civilizations representative figures who encompassed and expressed their civilization's essential spirit – Aturpat in the Zoroastrian, Shankara in the Hindu, al-Ghazzali in the Muslim civilization – so too did Theravada Buddhism produce such a figure in the person of this exemplary saint – a phenomenon which may perhaps be called a paradigmatic incarnation.

In Thailand during the same period there was a no less outstanding but less saintly king, Boromo Trailokanat (1448–88). His main achievement was the re-organization of the state and its social structure. As in other parts of Indochina inhabited by newcomers from the north, there was a mixture of tribal and quasi-feudal elements in the social structure. Yet Trailokanat re-activated and reformed the traditional system of the *Sakdi Na* grades (stratification of social status) which gave every subject of the king the right to a certain acreage of land according to his social status. The assignment for a family in the lowest class was 10 acres, for one in the highest class 4000 acres, i.e. the disparity between the two extremes was 1:400. The systems of penal fines and of the benefices for government officials were similarly graded. Thanks to this arrangement Thailand became the most stable of all the states in Indochina; the system survived as long as there was enough land to be allocated according to its rules, i.e. until the mid-nineteenth century.

As in many other parts of the world, such as the Islamic Levant and Latin Christian Europe, the sixteenth century in Indochina was a period of acute internal strife; there was almost a schism in the body social, though it did not assume an ideological form. The Burmese, who were hard pressed by the recent incursions of the Shan peoples, overreacted and embarked on imperial expansion. The first campaign was directed against the cultured Mons, who were soon defeated. Then came the struggle against the Shan principalities which assumed the guise of a crusade on behalf of the Theravada. Finally came the turn of Thailand, whose capital Ayuthia was conquered, the king being taken into captivity along with a great number of his subjects. The Burmese king, Bayinnaung (1551–81), became ruler of about three-quarters of the lands populated by the followers of the Theravada tradition. Considering himself a chakravartin (universal ruler of the faithful) he felt entitled to the highest honour in the Buddhist world.[33]

Bayinnaung's rule was a mixture of piety, good sense and cruelty. Though savage in his punishments, he abolished the human sacrifices at nobles' funerals, which took a high toll of his subjects; he attempted to unify the law, and standardize weights and measures; and he tried to stamp out the use of liquor. One highly significant aspect of his imperial successes, however, was the fact that they were largely due to the support of artillery provided and manned by Portuguese merchants and mercenaries respectively. From 1519, when the Portuguese found their first commercial post in Lower Burma, to 1641, when the Dutch took over their last possession in the Malayan peninsula, the Portuguese were an important power factor in the internal strife in Indochina.

The struggle with the Mons and the Thais continued, with intermittent periods of peace, until the last quarter of the eighteenth century, lasting altogether more than two hundred years. The outcome was on the one hand the total defeat of the Mons (due perhaps more to demographic factors than to Burmese prowess)[34] and, on the other hand, the full re-establishment of Thailand's independence. The Thais transferred their capital to the new coastal city of Bangkok and with some success began to learn the new power game of the European invaders. They were also able to give some help to the Khmers hard pressed by the continuous Vietnamese drive towards the Mekong Delta. On the other hand the Burmese rulers, while not giving up their claims to imperial grandeur, preferred to close their eyes to the changes which ensued from the

European presence in the area. In contrast to Thailand Burma eventually had to pay for her pride with the loss of her independence. Yet, even within the orbit of the Theravada tradition, Burma's prestige did not match her power aspirations. When in 1753 the Sinhalese king of Kandy felt that his *sangha* needed reinvigorating, he turned for help to Thailand and not to Burma. Led by the distinguished scholar Upali, the mission of 15 Thai monks became the nucleus of the strongest Theravada sect (known as Upaliwong or Sayamwong) in Sri Lanka. Not until 1802 were Burmese monks invited again to Sri Lanka for missionary work.

Unlike in Christianity or in Islam, the differences between individual *wongs* (sects or streams) within Theravada were not so much doctrinal as ritual and in some instances also social. Membership of a particular wong was symbolized in the manner of dress, such as whether the left shoulder was clad or not. Social circumstances were of particular importance in Sri Lanka where Indian customs became more deeply rooted than in Indochina: the Upaliwong did not admit people from lower castes to its ranks, whereas the wong based on Amarapura, founded with help from Burma, was not choosy with respect to social origin. The fact that Amarapura demanded more in the way of theological knowledge, however, made it less popular than its rival.

The periodic rectification of any lapses in monastic life was particularly important because the monasteries were centres of education. The young male laymen were required to spend some time (several weeks, months, or even years) there learning how to read and write and understand religion. The classical monastic curriculum for higher education was Pali, Sanskrit, Grammar and History.

Broadly speaking it is hard not to conclude that in the Theravada civilization the predominant attitude was one oriented towards conservation, or at best towards revival, rather than towards real reform or reconstruction.

6.5.4 The Encounter of Civilizations in the Malayan World

As has been said already, the Malayan archipelago and peninsula came under the influence of the Indian civilization from the beginning of our era, and by the fifth century most of the area had been drawn into the Indian orbit. According to the report of the outstanding Chinese scholar and traveller, Fa-Hsien, who visited

Indonesia in 413–15 AD, the religious affiliation of people in those areas was Hindu rather than Buddhist. Generally it can be said that the Indian culture mainly affected the royal courts, the aristocracy and the merchants. The brahmins were used by the local rulers as 'advisers in affairs of government and things sacral';[35] they seem also to have been helpful agents in adapting Hindu ideas and habits to the native social climate. Only later did the Buddhist influence make itself strongly felt; it was represented mainly by the Mahayana and Vajrayana versions, more prone to syncretism than their Theravada (Hinayana) rival.

In section 6.5.2 we mentioned a great power war with commercial and perhaps also religious overtones, the war which raged in the eleventh century between Hinduistic Chola in Southern India and the widely syncretic Srivijaya in Indonesia. The competition for the Straits of Malacca, however, also involved other states in South-East Asia, such as Cambodia which, from that time until the end of the thirteenth century, experienced a political, economic and cultural 'golden age'. A factor contributing to this blossoming was the trade with China which was an important source of wealth wherever people were able to engage in it.

In the thirteenth century the gravitational centre of power in the Malayan world shifted from eastern Sumatra, the base of Srivijaya, to eastern Java (the state of Singosari), and the period of the most intimate fusion of Mahayana and Shaivism set in. Though both these cults continued to co-exist as separate religions, on the practical level of popular worship they coalesced. After his death in 1268 King Vishnuvardhana was venerated both as an incarnation of Shiva and as bodhisattva. His ashes were divided between the shrines of the two cults. The last king of Singosari, Kertanagara (1268–93), based the Shiva-Buddhist cult on the Tantric principles known as the *bhairava* cult, and attempted to make it the state religion. It is however difficult to evaluate objectively the real nature of Kertanagara's religious policy – some literary sources of the epoch describe Kertanagara as a debauchee, others as an ascetic.[36]

But the end of the thirteenth century brought to the Malayan world a new religion – Islam. It established its first stronghold in the eastern part of Sumatra and from there spread to the Malayan peninsula and all over the archipelago.

Islam was not brought to the Malayan area by conquerors – as it was to other parts of the world – but by merchants and missionaries. Only when the Islamic states established themselves in the Malayan peninsula and in the adjacent islands was war used as a means of supporting the missionary activities. It seems that the syncretic religion of Indian origin, with its exotic and exuberant cults, was gradually losing its appeal. At the same time a more simple and rational religion, with a more explicit stress on practical morality, appeared increasingly attractive. In addition, the Muslims' higher propensity to work may well have played some part in the socio-cultural transformation of the Malayan world.

The fourteenth century is the last epoch of the Pan-Indian culture in Indonesia. Its main bearer was the Javanese state Majapahit, which emerged after the short Mongolian military intervention in Java in 1292. A new type of Shiva-Buddhist syncretism, but with overwhelmingly Shaivite features, flourished alongside the earlier *bhairava* cult. But neither the rulers' support for these cults, nor their military ventures, sufficed to give the Pan-Indian civilization in the Malayan world a new lease of life.

One personal story deserves a particular mention in this context. As Majapahit destroyed the remnants of Srivijaya in Sumatra, the ruler of the latter, Paramesvara, retreated to Malacca, where in 1403 he converted to Islam and took the name Iskander – Alexander in Arabic – a testimony to the cosmopolitan impact of the Macedonian's glory.

The sultanate of Malacca (styled as such from 1424), geopolitically and dynastically the heir of the Indianized Srivijaya, became from then on the main political and economic bulwark of the Islamic civilization in the Malayan world. In the middle of the fifteenth century, after a protracted war, Malacca stabilized her border with Thailand and embarked on her campaign of expansion against Majapahit. By 1520 the latter had fallen apart under the concerted attacks of its vassals, who in the meantime had converted to Islam.

The period of the most intensive spread of Islam in Indonesia coincides with the appearance of new intruders from overseas, this time from as far away as Western Europe. One year after they had captured Goa and thus won a foothold in India, the Portuguese captured Malacca (1511), and one year later they established their posts in the Moluccas, where the conversions to Islam were only just beginning.

For five hundred years to come the Muslims of Malaya were to live with the European intruders, who eventually became the rulers of all their lands. Nevertheless during the whole of this period Islam not only survived but increased its strength.

Of the Europeans only the Portuguese and the Spaniards were interested in converting all their subjects to their religion – Roman Catholicism. In that respect the Portuguese had the more difficult task. They had to compete with the Islamic missionaries. The Spaniards, who took the north-eastern Malayan islands which then became known as the Philippines, found most of the people there still pagan, and here the catholic proselytizing was successful.

The Dutch who penetrated into the area at the beginning of the seventeenth century and within a hundred years became masters of the greater part of it were basically not interested in proselytizing. Against their Portuguese foes they did not hesitate to support the native religions. This policy proved especially beneficial to the Theravada Buddhism in Sri Lanka.

By 1800 the Islamization of most parts of the Malayan world and the Catholicization of the Philippines were completed. Only Bali and some primitive tribes in the interior of Borneo remained outside the Islamic orbit. On the other hand the Muslims succeeded in converting the population of the most south-westerly Philippine islands.

The Dutch and the British (the latter became involved in a part of the area from the time of the French revolution) ruled the Malayan area outside the Philippines and the eastern part of Timor (a residue of the Portuguese colonial empire) until World War II. Though they did not attempt to convert their Islamic subjects to their religion, they nevertheless made a deep impact on the culture of the Malayan peoples. When the hour of political emancipation arrived, the Malayans had to look for a new type of syncretism to which they could accommodate their Islamic creed.

7 The Chinese Path: The Paradigm of Continuity

7.1 THE SPIRIT OF CHINA

Unlike the Indians the Chinese did not neglect history. They have always been concerned with their past, be it on a family or on a social level. Historical records and the tradition of drawing lessons from history, real or imaginary, have always been key factors in China's culture.

At first glance it may seem that the whole spirit of the Chinese civilization is closer to that of Western Europe than to that of India. In China there is more stress on practical social issues and on the organization of the state than on fathoming the depths of the human soul in a search for the supernatural.

Although in China this particular quest is not wholly absent, it reveals, to borrow Needham's terms, a bent towards organic naturalism[1] which gives it quite another flavour than that which characterizes India. This naturalism of China's, coupled with a pragmatic ethos, gave her a lead in the world's technological development until about the 16th century AD. Yet another aspect of the Chinese mind, namely the lack of feeling for generalizations and abstractions, prevented the Chinese from making full use of their inventive talent and developing it to the level of real science.

This handicap seems to be related to the peculiar character of the Chinese language. In principle it consists of inflexible monosyllabic words, each represented in writing by an ideograph (scriptural design). The tense of a verb or number of a noun has to be recognized from the context of the sentence. This understandably enough does little to foster precision. It may also be surmised that once the ideographs standing for the whole words were adopted, their use hampered changes in grammar and thus prevented the development of the language towards inflection.

Yet, on the other hand, the Chinese type of script was most

215

helpful in making written Chinese understandable to people using various dialects or variants from different epochs. Bodde compares the Chinese ideographs with Arabic numerals which, though differently read, always represent the same concepts.[2] Similarly, one and the same Chinese ideograph stands for a concept which can be read by people who, in the spoken language, do not understand each other; thus the ideographic script, independent of pronunciation, became the main unifying factor of the Chinese culture, both in its geographical and in its historical dimension.[3]

The Chinese vocabulary for concrete phenomena is of an enormous richness, but the words for abstract concepts are lacking. In modern Chinese this insufficiency is made good by composite words or compounds. This is a method which is necessary in any case for avoiding ambiguities arising from what in writing look like homonyms. Though these are, as a rule, differentiated by various accents (in the present official language these are four in number), even this is often not enough and composite words have to be used, thus making the originally monosyllabic language into a polysyllabic one.

In spite of ingenious adaptations, the Chinese way of expression retains its peculiar flavour, which can even be perceived in translations into European languages. According to Marcel Granet,[4] the expression of ideas is achieved mainly by transposition into symbols destined to arouse a certain impression, with the help of which the whole idea is then summarized. This is an obstacle to precision and to the conveyance of abstract ideas, which is compensated for by the piling up of synonyms and the use of commentaries, complementary images and standard sayings, reminiscent sometimes of scholastic argumentation.

On the other hand, what the Chinese language loses in precision, it gains in richness of colour and emotional appeal. This is most applicable in the case of poetry. On top of that, a Chinese poem is at the same time a musical and also a pictorial (calligraphic) piece of art and thus virtually untranslatable into any other language.

The view of music is another Chinese peculiarity. From time immemorial music was considered an efficacious instrument of harmonization between the human and the cosmic order. Music enjoyed a significance similar to that of the rites which in the Chinese civilization played an all-important role much longer than they did in other civilizations.

Belief in the efficacy of rites and music was matched by the conviction that the whole universe could be transposed into a system of visual signs whose correct manipulation could bring about effects in the real world. The relationship between the perceptible and the ideal world stood for a long while at the centre of Chinese metaphysics. All these views nourished the belief in magic which was a particularly tenacious element in the *genius loci* of China. It is amazing how this bent in Chinese culture vied with the widespread propensity to pragmatic reasoning, which in our understanding implies less credulity *vis-à-vis* purely stochastic processes. No wonder that some sinologists talk of superstitious pragmatism as a characteristic feature of the Chinese mind.

Yet, as with all similar generalizations, we have to bear in mind that they are applicable only to the bulk of the people concerned. The respectable number of technical innovations which the Chinese produced ahead of other civilizations bears witness to a rational empiricism that a mind wholly imbued with magical imagination would not be capable of.

Both these kinds of pragmatism, the empirical and the superstitious, meet in the key value of Chinese social life, the coherence of the family. A big family or possibly the whole clan, was and still largely seems to be the basic societal unit and also a factor of social security. The care for progeny, especially male, is a duty which has strong religious connotations. Only the male descendant was supposed to be able to perform correctly the rites for the deceased which were the necessary condition of their *post mortem* well-being.

In China there was a general belief in a duality of souls, one – the *po* – created at the time of conception, the other – the *hun* – at the time of birth. From birth both souls lived together, but in death they again became separated. The po remained with the body in the tomb, dependent on offerings, without which it would become a dangerous ghost (the *guei*). Fortunately the po was thought to cohabit with the corpse only until the latter's presumed disintegration (usually after a year); this also was the period of prescribed mourning. After that all pos descended to the underworld kingdom of the dead, whilst from the moment of death the huns continued their existence in the celestial kingdom.[5]

This dualism of souls, which the Taoists later developed into a more elaborate pluralism, is reminiscent of the ancient Egyptian view on this matter. Yet there is one striking contrast. In Egypt, the position in the netherworld depended on the verdict of the tribunal of Osiris, in which ethical considerations mingled in a strange way with magic. In the Chinese imagination, on the other hand, there was at least in the ancient times, no reversal of social roles in the *post-mortem* existence. In both the celestial kingdom and the nether world, the respective souls assumed the same social position as they had when the deceased was still alive. Thus there was no hope for anything better hereafter, but an incentive for assiduous self-improvement in this life; here we find a greater degree of affinity with the spirit of Sumer than with that of Egypt.[6]

Yet nothing in social life is simple and straightforward. Irrespective of what was to happen after death, the Chinese developed a strong sense of human virtues which were considered necessary conditions of an orderly and prosperous life in this world. The prevalent tendency was for a situational rather than a general scheme of ethics. Unlike in India, however, where ethics were caste-bound, in China ethics focused on mutual obligations in personal relationships. We shall say more on this issue when we discuss the positions of various schools with respect to it. In this context we need to point out that the crucial role of the rites, combined with the pragmatic bent of the Chinese, tended to make the situational ethics into an elaborate system of etiquette. In this respect the Chinese by far surpassed a similar tendency in the moral doctrines of ancient Egypt. In Granet's terms, 'The civil morale, oriented towards an ideal of regulated politeness, seemed to tend uniquely to organize among people a system of relationships according to a protocol with the gestures for each age, each sex, each social condition and actual situation.'[7]

A partial counter-weight to the formalism of officialdom appeared during the time when Buddhism penetrated into China and Taoism became a mass religion. In these two religions which began their missionary activity almost at the same time, in the first centuries AD, the Chinese found scope for a more emotional approach and for a transcendental quest. Yet after centuries even these sources of a deeper spirituality became tied up with ritual and formalism. There remained only the secret religious associations, which were able to give individuals a sense of exciting exclusiveness and, occasionally, to foster the spirit of revolt. This, however, as will be shown on the following pages, did not break out of the framework of the basic world-view.

7.2 THE ROOTS OF CHINESE CIVILIZATION

The Chinese historians looked upon the Chinese past as a fount of wisdom. Mythical rulers of the prehistoric epoch and their consorts were supposed to have invented or decreed everything that constituted civilized life: writing, the rules of marital life, the calendar, agriculture, melting of metals, the cultivation of the silk-worm, weaving, etc. Nothing was left to spontaneous forces acting from below. And this was a feature which left a deep imprint on the development of the Chinese civilization up to modern times.

From the earliest time for which evidence is available Chinese society was divided into two clearly demarcated classes or estates: the aristocracy (nobles) and the common folk. The differentiation not only permeated all walks of social life but was particularly conspicuous in religious matters. Only aristocrats, or, as Maspero translates the Chinese term *shi'* the patricians, enjoyed some individuality. They were entitled to have their own family cult, with a specific priest in charge of ceremonies mainly for the deceased which, *inter alia*, guaranteed for the nobles a corresponding position in the other worldly hierarchy.

On the other hand the commoner was tied not only to his family but also to his village. Religious rites were performed on behalf of the whole settlement, in which life was meticulously regulated to conform to the rhythm of the seasons. A greater part of the year was taken up by work in the fields, often far from the peasant's home. In the spring, by a sacral act, the village was opened, bringing the opportunity for new marital liaisons. In winter, by a similar religious act, the village was closed. Everybody had to stay at home, in hibernation as it were, waiting until the superiors advised by the priests would give the order to restart working and living at full gear. It seems that there was no spontaneity, no scope for autonomous decisions by elders of the village of the sort that occurred in the villages of ancient India.

Let us cite the authority in the field, Henri Maspero.

Each year special agents told the peasant what crops he was to plant, when he was to sow and when to harvest. Others ordered him to leave his winter home and go to work in the fields, or to leave the fields and shut himself up again in his house. Others again looked after his marriage. Others parcelled out the land and distributed any extra portions according to the number of his children. A whole ministry, that of the *ssu-t' u*, was charged with the task of looking after him and of regulating everything for him. . . . The year was divided into two seasons which were in a way opposed: the season of outdoor activity in spring and summer, that of seclusion in winter. This division, which was of no importance for the noble class as regards religious observances, governed the whole life of the peasantry and was the guiding principle of its existence. Everything changed from one of these periods to the other: place of abode, way of life, occupation, even morals.[8]

The nobles were not bound by similar limitations. They were hierarchically ranged into several tiers or degrees, of which only that at the top could enjoy a certain freedom of action. Yet the rules of protocol had to be preserved. This applied also to the king whose responsibility for the whole country required a proper behaviour which was regulated in minute detail:

'The master must neither play nor joke', says Marcel Granet, referring to the sovereign:

He is supposed to listen only to regular music; he has to keep upright; he must sit down only in a certain way, and on a pillow correctly laid out; he has to eat only meals prepared according to the rules and walk in a strictly measured way. . . While, in his presence, the faithful, animated by the greatness of their service, move hastily as if they were flying . . . the master . . . has to remain immobile, inactive and almost dumb.[9]

And what about those in between the king ensconced in his golden cage of etiquette and the peasant caught in the net of his superior's regulations? Most authors agree that the socio-economic arrangements which emerged at the dawn of history established a kind of feudal relationship. The Chinese historian Hu Hou-xuan found the first vestiges of feudal relationships already in the Shang period (*c.* sixteenth to eleventh century BC) when the monarchical government was fairly centralized at the top.

Certain Shang kings apparently made a practice of conferring territories upon their wives, sons and prominent ministers, as well as upon a number of unnamed individuals who are simply referred to in the inscriptions as *hou*, or (less frequently) as *po* or *nan*. These terms were later to become well-known titles of nobility in the Zhou feudal hierarchy. Other territorial holders included neighboring tribal leaders who, originally independent had, in the course of time, apparently been reduced to positions of political dependency. These various land holders . . . vassals of the Shang kings . . . were in general obligated to perform one or several of the following duties: (1) defence of the Shang frontiers; (2) conducting of punitive expeditions against rebels; (3) tribute payment of tortoise shell and other valuable localised products; (4) tax payment of millet and other grains; (5) supplying of corvée labor for cultivation of the king's lands.[10]

The elements of ancient Chinese feudalism seem to have been reinforced by the great ethnic and dynastic change which occurred in the mid-eleventh century BC, when newcomers from the upper part of the Yellow River basin, the Zhou, unseated the Shang dynasty and subdued its people.

By the eighth century BC the Chinese state, which in those days embraced only the northern part of present-day China, was divided into a royal domain and about 500 fiefs (*guo*), whose holders received their investiture directly from the king. There were many more subvassals and holders of benefices; the preservation of mutual rights and obligations between the nobles and the suzerein was considered the most important virtue.

Yet the feudal relationship in the upper tier of the society was combined with a tough, we might say totalitarian, domination over the commoners. Furthermore, everybody of standing derived his position, at least in theory, from the king (*wang*), whose supremacy was not only political but above all religious. This made him the pivot of the whole society, the Mandatee of Heaven. The idea was embedded in a rather mechanistic metaphysical theory known as the Great Principle (*hong fang*) which, probably in the eighth century BC, systematized various diffuse political and religious ideas.

As a matter of fact the Great Principle belongs to the category of revealed truth. The revealer was Heaven, in this instance already conceived of as an abstraction (although the personal god of ancient custom continued to survive in the popular imagination), the receiver of the revelation was the legendary sage-emperor, the Great Yu. The revelation was a congeries of statements on the physical and social aspects of life welded together by what can only in a very rudimentary sense be described as a theory. Following Maspero's account its gist can be summarized as follows:

The perceptible world is a product of Five Elements – water, fire, wood, metal and earth. The Five Elements correspond to the Five Activities – gesture, speech, sight, hearing, thought. Each of the elements and each of the activities has its properties which, when in the state of natural order, are constant. To develop the Five Activities in conformity with the regular order of the Five Elements is the duty of the ruler and to that end he has the Eight Methods of Government. Of these, three are the main occupations – agriculture, artisanship and sacrifices. Then there are three ministers – of Public Works, of Justice and of what may be described as all other affairs ranging from economic control to education. Finally there are two relations of the prince with his vassals: he may receive them as guests, which symbolizes peace, or he may discipline them by war.

The harmonious working of the Eight Methods of Government echoes the regular progress of the Five Regulators: the year, the month, the day, the constellation, the calendar. This agreement is made possible by the August Perfection or Noble Pinnacle, that is the royal power, which is the link between humanity and what is Around and Above it. In performing his all-important task, the ruler uses Three Manifestations of Activity: equity, severity and mildness. If he is uncertain which method to use, he has to resort to divination. Whether things are going well or not is ascertained by the examination of natural phenomena such as rain, sun, heat, cold, wind, which, depending upon whether they come in season or out of season, indicate whether the government is good or bad. 'If all goes well, the final result is the Five Happinesses: longevity, wealth, health, love of virtue, and a fitting end to one's life. If things go badly, there are Six Calamities: violent and premature death, illness, suffering, poverty, misfortune, weakness.'[11]

Nothing can better illustrate the spirit of the Chinese tradition than this theory, in which pragmatic observations and the wishful quest for harmony between men and nature are amalgamated in a peculiar kind of system. The success of the quest for harmony was to be guaranteed by good government, which in turn depended on wisdom, i.e. the ability to discern the will of Heaven. Heaven appears as the supreme lawgiver in both physical and human matters.

This is the basic framework of the world-view within which the Chinese philosopher looked for the most expedient ways to help the Mandatee of Heaven to perform his noble task. In this system there is no place for religious sentiments, no place for the emotional devotion which characterizes theistic religions. The relationship between man and the Beyond is, apart from the cult of ancestors, monopolized in the person of the ruler, though in the popular imagination the ancient pantheon of gods and demons remains alive as a focus of family worship.

The idea that the supreme ruler (earlier called king, known from 221 BC as emperor) is a Mandatee of Heaven seems to have been developed at the time when the Zhou took over from the Shang in about the mid-eleventh century BC. Probably at the same time the earlier concept of a personal god seated in Heaven gave way to a rather impersonal concept of Heaven as the supreme power.[12] But what is most important for our examination is how the relationship between Heaven and the worldly ruler was supposed to operate. Whether Heaven was happy with its Mandatee could be told by the regularity of the weather and the absence of natural disasters and social upheavals. Once however such disorders occurred, Heaven was supposed to reconsider its Mandate. But the fact that the Mandate had finally been withdrawn was only revealed when a new dynasty came to power and re-established order.

As will be shown later, this theory continued to function as a convenient explanation for any dynastic change until the beginning of the twentieth century AD. During all that time the Chinese considered their country to be the centre of the universe. The traditional name for China, Zhongguo, means the Middle Kingdom, or more precisely the kingdom in the middle of the four cardinal points, in relation to which she is the fifth. The present designation Zhonghua Renmin Gongheguo (the People's Republic of China) illustrates both the sense of continuity and the specificity of the Chinese language mentioned earlier.

7.3 THE CHINA OF A HUNDRED SCHOOLS

In view of what has been said in the preceding chapters, it is little wonder that the main concern of the Chinese thinkers was to look for means of ensuring the required harmony between nature and mankind. The weakening of the central government under the so-called Eastern Zhou (dating from the transfer of the capital eastward in 771 BC due to the incursion of barbarians from the north) and the growing power aspirations of the great feudatories, made the issue an even more urgent one. In the seventh century the Chinese state virtually disintegrated; its symbolic unity was preserved by occasional confederations of virtually independent states, amongst whom the strongest strived for hegemony over the weaker ones.

Towards the end of the sixth century China entered the iron age (the first mention of iron casting dates from 513 BC) and the great genius of Chinese culture, Confucius (551–479 according to tradition), began his pastoral mission. However, it took several centuries for the seeds sown by Confucius to germinate. The time-span 453–221 is described in Chinese historiography as the period of the Warring States (*Zhanguo*). It was an epoch of intense internal struggle during which the diminishing number of dominant powers strove to knock each other out of the ring.

However in the sphere of technology and culture it was a time of great advances. Large irrigation schemes and canal-building projects materialized and there was conspicuous progress in agriculture, astronomy and medicine. Like the Greeks of the same period, the Chinese embarked on their first philosophical ventures. Although these diversified into what Chinese hyperbole describes as a Hundred Schools, there is nevertheless a common nerve – the concern with the creation of an ideal society – and a mutual give and take which sometimes makes individual thinkers hard to allocate to a particular school.

If one focuses on essentials, the Hundred Schools may be reduced to four, or possibly six. Three of them were primarily concerned with social issues. Ranged in order from the most to the least influential they were: the Confucians (in Chinese *Ru Jia*, literally the school of the gentle), the Legalists (*Fa Jia*), and the Mohists (*Mo Jia*). The other three schools were less socially-minded and were concerned more with language, nature and the universe. Of these schools the most influential, in the long run, were the Taoists (*Dao Jia*), who eventually developed into a fully-fledged religion. The other two schools are better described in Chinese terms: the *Yin-Yang Jia*, translated by some (e.g. Maspero) as the Metaphysicians, and by others (e.g. Needham) as the Naturalists (Needham also includes here the theorists of the Five Elements – *Wu Xing siu*); and the *Ming Jia*, which can be literally translated as the Nominalists, or in view of the analogy with their Greek counterparts, the Sophists.

Confucius (his name in Chinese was Kong Fuzi, i.e. Master Kong), who linked up with the traditional occupations of scribes and annalists, did not consider himself as an innovator but as a preserver. This however should not confuse us. Even the most ardent revolutionaries often claimed nothing more than a desire to return to some pristine state of affairs. Yet Confucius would not have dreamed of using revolutionary means. Like Plato he looked for a prince who might listen to his advice. And like Plato he did not find one. but unlike Plato's ideas, those of Confucius and his disciples were to become for more than two thousand years the philosophy of the state.

Writings whose authorship was ascribed to Confucius are in fact collections of earlier authors that he cherished and developed further. These books are usually referred to as the Classics.

Confucius' main concern was human behaviour. People should cultivate good customs (*li*) and, as far as possible, become virtuous, superior men (*junzi*); this meant acquiring the cardinal virtue, *jen*. Some translate this as 'benevolence', others as 'human-heartedness', and still others as 'altruism'. Though for Confucius being a superior man was a matter not of noble birth, but of internal disposition and education, only junzi were supposed to be qualified for government service. Then, 'junzi has the virtue of wind, whilst the people have the virtue of grass'.[13]

Otherwise, as a general guiding principle, there was the well-known Golden Rule of Master Kong: 'What you do not want done to yourself, do not do to others.' A further elaboration of Confucian ethics was the principle of Filial Piety, closely related to the cult of the ancestors. After Confucius' death it was systematized into the precepts of the Five Relationships. Of these four concerned unequal partners, and one referred to equal partners: the first four relationships were those between father and son, husband and wife, older and younger, and ruler and subject: the fifth relationship was that between friends.

Once it had been accepted that virtue (*de*) could be fostered by learning, the door was wide open to those who wanted to learn. Yet not everybody believed in the power of education. The Legalists relied more on carefully measured rewards and punishments, which in the end left all virtue inherent in the laws themselves. Impersonal laws with an impersonal Heaven – this was one extreme of the spectrum within which the Chinese scholars attempted to resolve their key issue. At the other end of the range were the Taoists, who did not believe in anything except a spontaneous harmonization with the way of nature and the universe. But even amongst those who did believe in education – and they were all people who in one way or another followed Master Kong – opinions diverged over how much human nature could be trusted. Was it basically good, or evil?

This issue continued to be a bone of contention long after Confucius' death. Kong himself seems to have had a balanced view in this matter: for him every man was potentially educable and the teachers had to look around to find suitable pupils. Under a paternalistic government there was no difference between ethics and politics, and both had to be dominated by wisdom. When asked what constituted wisdom, Confucius said: 'To give one's self earnestly to securing righteousness and justice among the people, and while respecting the gods and demons, to keep aloof from them. . .'[14]

An optimistic view of man's disposition to good was taken by the disciple of Confucius most renowned in the West, Mencius (Meng Zi, who died *c*.289 BC). Believing that human nature is basically good, he put more trust in people than many others did. Developing a point already found in earlier writings, Mencius concluded with a noble precept, namely that 'the voice of the people was to have predominant weight over other advice, and they were to be considered the most important element in a State, the spirits of the land and grain coming next, and the prince last'.[15]

On the other hand, the most erudite Confucian of that epoch, Master Xun Zi, maintained that the nature of man was evil and that only by assiduous training could man acquire goodness. Paternalism was not to be abandoned. The issue continued to be discussed with various attempts at reconciliation, but in practice the pragmatic approach was adopted. Everybody was considered educable, and those who were not had to bear the consequences. The Legalists' view that rewards and punishments were the necessary means of rectifying man's behaviour was never abandoned in practice.

The Legalists, of whom the best known is Han Feizi (d. 234 BC), did not set much store by human virtue. They saw man as a mechanism responding to punishments and rewards, and above all to the former, which they thought should be meted out to culprits with the utmost severity; any other approach was looked upon with suspicion and distrust. The Legalists recommended a system in which rewards and punishments would operate automatically irrespective of the quality of the ruler. Therefore the regulative principle should be the positive law (*fa*), which would not make any distinctions of status with regard to trespassers. Such a law, being precise and equally applicable to all, would not allow for juridical deliberations with respect to any other principles, be they social or ethical. This was in sharp contrast to the Confucians, who preferred to follow good customs (li), which Needham translates as 'the sum of the folkways whose ethical sanction had risen into consciousness'. Confucius had said, Needham further explains, 'if the people were given laws and levelled by punishments, they would try to avoid the punishment but would have no sense of shame; while if they were "led by virtue" they would spontaneously avoid disputes and crimes'.[16]

Good customs, altruism and filial piety, however, were not enough for the Mohists, followers of Mo Zi (fourth century BC), who proclaimed the principle of universal love as the guideline for human behaviour. For Mo Zi the love that makes distinctions was no virtue. Unlike Confucius and Han Feizi, Mo Zi was a deeply religious person believing in a personal God (Lord on High) and also in ghosts. Amazingly, the proof of the existence of ghosts was that many people did see and/or hear them. Apparently, Mo Zi's empiricism was not matched by a critical mind. But their strong ethical convictions led the Mohists to become defenders of the weaker against the stronger. While rejecting offensive wars, the later Mohists began to learn the military arts, including the construction of fortifications, in order to help the small states defend themselves against aggressors. In doing so, they made a contribution to technical progress in China.

Another school which may have operated in a similar direction, but with a different philosophical outlook, were the Taoists. The Dao, meaning the Way, i.e. the Way of the Universe, or Order of Nature, was a concept used by all Chinese schools of thought, yet the Taoists made it the alpha and omega, as it were, of their philosophy. Their ideal was to fit in, to behave naturally in the expectation that then everything would be all right. In contrast to the Confucians, Legalists and Mohists, who in their strong social-mindedness were keen to participate in the administration of the state, the Taoists preferred to withdraw from public life into a direct experience of nature and its processes.

They did not differentiate between speculation, poetry, empiricism and magic, thus creating a peculiar mix from which any follower of their path could derive comfort as he pleased.

The founder of the school, Lao Zi, is now considered a legendary rather than a historical figure. The book *Dao De Jing,* meaning the Book of the Virtue of the Dao, which was attributed to him, was probably written at the turn of the fifth and fourth centuries BC. Its statements are sometimes very difficult to interpret. Gernet describes them as 'Sybilline sayings probably intended to serve as themes for meditation'.[17] In Needham's view the book 'may be regarded as without exception the most profound and beautiful work in Chinese history'.[18]

In *Dao De Jing* the concept of Dao is explained as follows:

There is a thing inherent and natural,
Which existed before heaven and earth.
Motionless and fathomless,
It stands alone and never changes;
It pervades everywhere and never becomes exhausted.
It may be regarded as the Mother of the Universe.
I do not know its name.
If I am forced to give it a name,
I call it Dao, and I name it as supreme.
Supreme means going on;
Going on means going far;
Going far means returning.
Therefore Dao is supreme; heaven is supreme; earth is supreme;
  and man is also supreme. There are in the universe four things
  supreme, and man is one of them.
Man follows the laws of earth;
Earth follows the laws of heaven;
Heaven follows the laws of Dao;
Dao follows the laws of its intrinsic nature.[19]

'The Sage carries on his business without action, and gives his teaching without words'.[20] concludes the second chapter of *Dao De Jing*. The book advocates that government should proceed in a similar way. Not only should it be effortless but it should also prevent people from succumbing to ambition, greed and vanity. Some chapters of *Dao De Jing* can be read as arguments with the Confucians, who seemed to the Taoists to be arrogant and hypocritical formalists.

The author who, in Maspero's view, best expounded the doctrines of the Taoists and was the finest writer of ancient China into the bargain, was Zhuang Zi, who lived in the second half of the fourth century BC. According to him, to borrow Maspero's words, one must not rely upon books: they are 'the drugs and refuse of the ancients. Reasoning must itself be abandoned, for it obscures the true knowledge which is intuitive. . . The mystical life alone allows of laying hold upon the Dao, after one has passed through those great stages which mystics have described in all times and all countries. . . detachment . . . renunciation . . . ecstasies . . . and finally the mystical union which is the Great Mystery'.[21]

Yet the metaphysical or mystical speculation was only one side of the coin, the other being a baser quest for longevity, preservation of youth and even immortality, using meditation and various breathing and sexual exercises; these experiments eventually resulted either in magical practices or technical discoveries.

The magical aspects of the Chinese world view were due above all to the metaphysics which developed from the practice of divination. One of the technical means of the ancient diviners was a series of figures of six lines, some of them broken and some unbroken. Their combination gave altogether sixty-four hexagrams, which were supposed to be the basic elements of the ideal world. The ideal world of divination was considered to be real in the sense that it corresponded exactly to the material world, consisting of 11,520 things, a figure obtained by a combination of numbers symbolizing figures and lines of the hexagrams. It was believed that the knowledge of the links between the two worlds (two planes of the universe) made it possible to transform the hexagrams in such a way that they could achieve results on the material plane.

The hexagrams had a corollary in the form of trigrams, which in combination with the theory of *yin* and *yang* provided a more sophisticated model of the universe. In terms of this theory the world could be explained, without any supernatural intervention, by the reciprocal interaction of the two primordial substances, yang, the active or masculine, and yin, the reactive or feminine, which in their sequence of transformations produced all things. This theory was adopted by virtually all schools of thought, and in the process it acquired a wide range of applications, some proto-scientific, some mythical and other magical.

The fact that the path of proto-scientific inquiry was not developed to the further stage of a fully-fledged science of the West European type, could be explained by various circumstances: the already mentioned fact that the language and writing were not suitable for precise and abstract reasoning, the lack of a conceptual criticism which would have made it possible to dissociate magic and superstition from genuine knowledge (we must not forget that in Europe this did not happen until the seventeenth century AD), and also the one-sided orientation of the Confucians (who were eventually victorious in the competition of the various schools) towards ethics and history. Thus the advances in technology were left to the practitioners. But Needham suggests, tentatively, one more reason, namely the failure to combine the Taoist naturalist perspective with the logic developed by the Mohists.[22]

Unfortunately the logic of the Nominalists (*Ming Jia*) was not particularly helpful. 'Hindered by having to use a language that could not distinguish between singular and plural, abstract and concrete', says Gernet, 'the Chinese Sophists scarcely had the leisure to push their analysis of language very far or to develop a logic of speech. . . Chinese logic . . . followed the path taken by the specialists of divination. . . The manipulation of numbers and the combination of signs suited to translate the correct values of space-time were to serve as the basis of philosophical theories and of the sciences.'[23]

7.4   FROM THE WARRING STATES TO THE EMPIRE

Of the six schools mentioned in the previous section three made a significant and far-reaching impact on Chinese society. Marx might have said that they became 'material forces'.

The first major and innovative impact on Chinese politics and social life in general was made by the Legalists. Under their ideological banner China received a short sharp shock which, modified and mitigated by the subsequent dominant school, the Confucians, had a lasting effect upon Chinese civilization. The 230-year period of the *Zhanguo* (the Warring States, 453–221 BC) was also the era of warring ideologies, and these two factors together brought about, at least temporarily, fundamental changes in the social system in China – changes comparable in magnitude with those of the twentieth century AD, when the Guomindang and the Communists set out to push China out of her millennial cycle.

The changes of the period of the Warring States were no less complex than those of modern China. The main impulse seems to have come from the increasingly acute struggle for wealth and power of the diminishing number of the great feudatories who transformed their fiefs into virtually independent kingdoms, symbolized by the royal title '*wang*'. But this type of struggle is a continually recurring theme of world history. What made it unique in the China of the fifth to third century BC were the mental ferment and the large-scale technological advances, above all the spread and refinement of iron metallurgy.

The backcloth to both these processes was a pragmatic mentality which managed to emancipate itself to a considerable extent from the constraints of superstition, but also from moral inhibitions. Kings and their ministers who knew how to exploit the malleability of their subjects and the natural resources of their country were at an advantage.

In this context the geopolitical situation also played a substantial role. The cradle of the Chinese civilization was the middle basin of the Yellow River (Huanghe). From there China expanded mainly to the east and south until she reached the sea. While the eastward push was completed fairly soon, the southern shores were not attained until the second century BC. At the time of the great transformation of China which is the subject-matter of this section, the southern Chinese kingdoms stretched merely over the middle and lower basin of the Yangtze.

As a corollary of the long-term southward push there was a still longer-lasting, but intermittent, pressure on China by the 'Barbarians of the Northern Steppes'. Against them the Chinese border states built protective walls, and from them they learned new methods of warfare, such as riding horses instead of horse-drawn chariots.

This was the scenario in which the Warring States operated. In the mid-fifth century BC about a dozen small states between the Yellow River and the Yangtze (Chang Jiang) were surrounded by half a dozen larger kingdoms. The smallest of these, the Qin, situated on the western fringe of the Chinese heartland in the valley of the River Wei, became the focus of the most determined effort to innovate and to win the all-out contest.

Between 361 and 339 Qin was transformed from a peripheral backwater riven with anarchy and brigandage into an efficient machine for work and war. First, law and order were established by drastic measures. These included the division of the population into groups of five or ten families jointly responsible for one another. The fiefs and the communal holdings were abolished and land became private property, from which taxes in kind proportionate to the size of the field were levied. The draining of the marshes and the construction of canals substantially increased the cultivated area, and refugees from other kingdoms, attracted by the good prospects for entrepreneurs, further improved the economic potential.[24] Efficiency in all walks of life was enhanced by the substitution of merit for privileges of birth. Instead of the old aristocracy a new system of honours was introduced to reward military achievements. Later, honorary posts could also be bought for money.

In their unceasing fighting with the neighbouring barbarians the Qin soldiers acquired both the practical skills and the endurance which, combined with the extensive use of iron weapons and cavalry, became their main assets in the struggle with other kingdoms less successful in terms of technical and organizational innovation.

The final round of internecine warfare was completed in 221, when the last rival of the Qin, the state Qi (in what is now the province of Shantung) was defeated. The victorious king assumed the imperial title, Qin Shi Huangdi; under the ideological guidance of the Legalists, the political and socio-economic system of the state was extended to cover the whole empire.

The unifying measures included: a single currency, common measures of length and capacity, a new simplified standard writing, standardization of the gauge of cart-wheels and large-scale construction of roads and canals. Protective walls around individual kingdoms were pulled down and the new Great Wall against the northern barbarians was built. The possession of arms was made illegal and the highest-ranking aristocracy of the conquered states had to settle without arms in the imperial capital.

Finally in 213 ideological pluralism was abolished. All writings, with the exception of those written by the Legalists and writings of a technical nature, on subjects such as agriculture, construction, military matters, medicine and divination, were ordered to be burnt. Further copying of the banned books became a capital offence and their possession was punished with forced labour. The revolutionary transformation of China was to be complete. Tradition was not to hamper the will to direct life towards a greater economic and military efficiency. Yet, and this was to become typical of ideological purges in China, the emperor retained a college of seventy representatives of the various schools, perhaps in case there might be something valuable in them. Superstition was not to disappear from the cultural climate. Divination continued to be an important element of political decision-making, which also kept alive an interest in the Taoist practices. Unfortunately, the unification of China did not mark the end of warring. The push to the south had to be continued and the struggle with the Barbarians of the Northern Steppes was to be carried on more vigorously.

Thus the new regime asked for too much at once. It estranged too many people whose influence still mattered. The growing tax burden and the growing claims on military service and various kinds of corvée were also disturbing. Last but not least, the second emperor who took over the rudder lacked the ability necessary for such a task. Within a year uprisings broke out. The revolting forces soon became divided into two blocks: one led by a nobleman, the other by a minor official of lowly birth, Liu Bang. In 202 Liu Bang won and founded a new dynasty which was to become one of the most glorious in Chinese history, the dynasty of Han.

There are many astonishing things about this revolution, which ousted the son of the emperor unifier but preserved the unity of the empire. The Mandate of Heaven was apparently withdrawn from Qin for reasons other than the enforced unification; it was bestowed for almost four centuries to come upon the Han because they knew better how to preserve the necessary harmony. Such would be the traditional Chinese explanation. In our view Liu Bang and his descendants were able to strike a more sensible balance between the innovations sponsored by the Legalists and the tradition for which the Confucians stood. Liu Bang, however, was not concerned with theories but had the common sense to ensure a firm power base for his victory; he bequeathed to his descendants a solid establishment.

Tax reductions, the emancipation of slaves and a less severe penal code were without doubt popular measures. The land tax was fixed at 1/15th of the yield while everybody between 15 and 56 was liable to the poll tax. Private ownership and saleability of land were preserved. A particular innovation was the right of villagers to elect from persons over 50 their own magistrates. From these the authorities then chose the district officials (one district containing about a hundred villages). It is difficult to say whether this measure marked a return to the ancient custom of communal autonomy which some authors of a Marxist inclination believe held sway in the pre-historical era, or whether it was a brand new innovation. Given the fact that the pre-historical era was about fifteen hundred years earlier, the innovation has anyhow to be considered an epochal event.

Enterprizing people had many opportunities to enrich themselves. The royal coinage was abolished and minting became a matter of private banking. Free trade of all sorts was supported by the government's care for the infrastructure, for roads and for river transport, which together facilitated the transfer of goods from areas with a surplus to areas suffering from inadequate supply. Thus at the turn of the third and second centuries China moved close to what may be described as a kind of proto-capitalism.

Yet this was only one element, though a substantial one, of her complex structure. The difficulty was what to do with the aristocracy, made jealous by the promotions to government office from the middle class. Liu Bang attempted to strike a balance between what may be called the capitalist and the feudal elements. To appease the nobles, the highest imperial offices were reserved for them; also some kinds of conspicuous consumption could be indulged in exclusively by that class. Furthermore, aristocratic titles involving land but not tenure of office were renewed, and the emperor himself did not hesitate to bestow fiefs upon his supporters and family members, although he often withdrew them again. Government officials and army officers were rewarded with personal benefices.

A compromise was also sought in cultural matters. The edict of 213 prohibiting books became obsolete and was formally revoked under Liu Bang's successor, in 191 BC. Actually the ban had been enforced for only two years, during which about 450 scholars were sentenced to death and many more to forced labour. This was surely not enough to destroy the 'Hundred Schools'. In Maspero's view, the studies of traditional literature were more affected by the simplification of the script, which was at the same time facilitated by the invention of the brush as a writing tool.[25]

Whichever cause was the more important, the results can be summarized as follows. The Confucians, being the most numerous and scattered all over the country, survived best. The Taoists in their position of withdrawal from public life, also did comparatively well. On the other hand, all the other schools fared badly. With the establishment of a new balance in the social structure, both the Legalists and the Mohists seem for different reasons to have lost their *raison d'être*. Many Legalist ideas, however, were – as a matter of common sense – incorporated into the standard knowledge and survived in various classic works. On the other hand, the Mohist ideas found it more difficult to be absorbed by other schools.

In Maspero's view,

the school of Mo-Zi perished because it had been devoted to dialectic, the taste for which was only a passing fashion, and this died with the society which had given rise to it. On the contrary, the teaching of the rites among the Confucians and that of the mystical practices among the Taoists responded, in varying degrees, to the deep needs which social and political upheavals did not change. That was the salvation of those two schools and, of course, of the doctrines to which they were connected.[26]

7.5 CHINA TURNS TO CONFUCIUS

During the first century or so of the Han rule the transformation of China was completed; this took place not under the Legalist but under the Confucian banner. At first, the bureaucracy continued to be manned mainly by the Legalists, and government policy tended towards appeasement of the nobles at home and of the barbarians beyond the border. At home there were successful attempts to exploit the merger of capitalist and feudal elements to the benefit of the great aristocracy; the land tax was reduced and the poll tax, affecting the poor more than the rich, was extended to children over 7. Almost two-thirds of the land was held as fiefs. The most powerful feudatories were awarded the honorary title of wang, i.e. king. At the same time the pressure from the Hsiung-nu, Barbarians of the Northern Steppes, intensified and some wangs did not hesitate to make common cause with them against the emperor. This collusion culminated in the rising of seven wangs in 154 BC, the suppression of which required the utmost effort. But from then on the tide turned against the feudal residues and foreign encroachments.

The turning-point came with the long reign of emperor Wu (Wu Di, 141–87), who inaugurated a new era in the history of Chinese civilization. His policy was marked not so much by novelty but by its consistency. First of all the government offices became increasingly manned by the graduates of the schools which began to be organized throughout the empire. From 124 BC the highest education for the government service – the mandarinate – was provided by the Great School (*Tai Xue*) in the capital. The curriculum of this – as it were – State University consisted of teaching the Classics attributed to Confucius (these were in fact much earlier writings, which Confucius edited and completed).

There were altogether five Classics attributed to Confucius; to these was added the sixth, the Filial Piety Classics probably composed in the third century BC, which was the only one concerned with the common man. The five Classics contained first, the old divination forms, hexagrams, trigrams and their respective commentaries (Book of Changes); second, ancient ballads and songs (Book of Odes); third, moralizing stories, descriptions of sacrificial rituals and dances, including the treatise on the already mentioned Great Principle (Book of Annals); fourth, a chronicle of the state Lu (Spring and Autumn Annals); and fifth, a recital of all kinds of aristocratic rites and ceremonies, including the archery competition (Book of Rites).

At the Great School various interpretations of the Classics were taught and the number of lectureships depended on the number of interpretations. Each Classic was studied for at least a year. Philosophical reflections linked with various themes in the Classics were often derived from schools other than the Confucian *Ru Jia*, but the ethics remained Confucian and gave the whole mix its dominant tone. The Great School contributed much to the fixing of doctrine and to the standardization of education. Together with the provincial schools it became the main factor in the ideational integration of China.

The spread of Confucian teaching, however, was matched by a decline in its quality. Superstition worked its way into the ranks of the literati, who more and more began to abandon the purity of their Master's rationality. In the words of the most competent authority in the field, the modern Chinese philosopher Hu Shi, the situation developed as follows:

this New Confucianism should be a great synthetic religion into which were fused all the elements of popular superstition and state worship, rationalized somewhat in order to eliminate a few of the most untenable elements, and thinly covered up under the guise of Confucian and pre-Confucian classics in order to make them appear respectable and authoritative. In this sense the New Confucianism of the Han Empire was truly the national religion of China. It was a great conglomeration of popular beliefs and practices of the time through a thin and feeble process of rationalization. . . It frankly discarded the naturalistic philosophy of a previous age which had been accepted by such prominent Confucian thinkers as Xun Zi. It frankly rejected the agnosticism of Confucius himself and openly took a theistic position similar to that of the school of Mo Zi, whom the earlier Confucian philosophers had condemned. These New Confucianists of Han believed that they knew the will of God and were capable of interpreting the hidden meaning of all its manifestations in Heaven and on Earth. They believed in magic and practised alchemy.

They borrowed their methodology from the astrologers and spent their lives in trying to interpret the significance of physical catastrophes and anomalies by means of historical and scriptural analogies.[27]

This debasement helped the creation of a syncretic state religion, with the cult of Confucius as the central symbol and the emperor as the high priest. Spectacular rites and magical practices including some elements taken over from the barbarians, made the whole mix more appealing not only to the traditional Chinese but also to the populations of newly conquered areas, which were gradually integrated into what may be described as the Chinese Confucian Civilization.

To give the reader some idea of what this meant, in tangible terms, we have to say a few words on the main socio-economic arrangements; they give us a picture of something that can hardly be squeezed into the standard sociological categories.

Under Wu Di the high nobility was deprived of all governmental power; this was transferred to the appointed bureaucrats – the mandarins. The new law awarded equal rights of inheritance to all male descendants, thus preventing the creation of dangerously large estates. On the other hand, the gentry whose sons were largely recruited for the government service improved their social status. Furthermore there was a boost for the propertied middle class, titles of nobility could be bought and there was no barrier between the bourgeoisie and the aristocracy. But free enterprise had to cope with government competition in industrial undertakings (especially in ceramics and textiles). In 113 the imperial monopoly of coinage was renewed and further imperial monopolies, affecting iron, salt and wine, were established. The Chinese economy became a mixed economy in the modern sense, combined with the understanding that the government was responsible for its good running.

In order to prevent sharp fluctuations in food prices and the resulting speculation, the government established a wholesale agency intended to equalize supply and demand. It was to purchase food in years and in areas that yielded a bumper crop, and sell when and where there was a shortage. Yet as so often with good intentions in economic matters, nature frustrated the plan. The scheme began to operate at a time of widespread drought which spelled its failure. The opponents of the regulated economy, the 'Friedmanites', as it were, enforced the abolition of this policy. Tradition has it that the initiator of the scheme was severely punished: he was cooked alive.[28]

Greater success attended the government's efforts to control the accumulation of wealth. In 119 BC a prosecution resulted in large-scale confiscations and in the sentencing of one million convicts to forced labour. Otherwise however penal codes from the Qin era were significantly moderated. Furthermore, as a matter of social policy, large numbers of people were transferred from regions affected by floods or devastation to sparsely populated areas. The Legalists' heritage remained alive in the concern with accuracy, which on the one hand encouraged quantitative measurement and the use of statistics, but on the other hand often degenerated into red tape.

From what has been said so far, we cannot classify the Chinese society of the Han epoch in simple terms. Needham calls the society of imperial China bureaucratic feudalism. Orthodox Marxists both in the USSR and in China talk about the slave-holding formation. Yet on the basis of imperial censuses the French sinologists, such as Maspero[29] and Gernet,[30] estimate the number of slaves in Han China at about 1 per cent of the total population. The Soviet historian Stepuginova[31] infers a developed slave-holding in the Han epoch on the strength of the many titles of enslavement (captivity, conviction, insolvency, and various kinds of purchase) and on the strength of numerous documents concerning the transfer of slaves. On the other hand the East German Marxist Erkes[32] concludes that slaves were never particularly numerous in China, being employed mainly in domestic service. According to Mark Elvin, 'plausible estimates for the former Han Dynasty (202 BC–8 AD) ranged from one to ten per cent.[33]

The majority, according to Maspero probably 70–80 per cent, of the Chinese population consisted at that time of rural folk, who either owned or rented family plots or were hired workers. It seems that, as time went on, many small owners were converted into tenants. In Gernet's words:

One of the social peculiarities of the Han period as a whole was in fact the existence of very rich families who combined agricultural enterprises (cereal or rice production, cattle raising, fish farming) with industrial undertakings (cloth mills, foundries, lacquer factories) and commercial businesses, and who had at their disposal a very large labour force. In the areas where agriculture was the principal resource the rich families confined themselves to exerting pressure on poor peasants by making loans at exorbitant rates of interest and inducing their debtors to let or sell their land.[34]

Another great burden which fell upon the commoners was the great power policy of expansion towards the southern coasts, to Manchuria, Korea and Central Asia. Whilst the southward and eastward drive meant primarily a territorial expansion of Chinese power and the Chinese civilization, the thrust to the west followed mainly strategic and economic considerations, being a bid to outflank the nomads and get hold of the rich oases on the main trade routes between eastern and western Asia. Access to the excellent breed of stallion in Ferghana also played an important role.

Yet the expansion brought gains mainly to the treasury and to the big merchants, whereas the common folk had to foot the bill with increases in military service, corvée and taxation; the poll tax for instance was extended to anybody from 3 to 80 years of age and additional indirect taxes were introduced.

The new inventions of that epoch, such as the heavy plough for a twin yoke and the plough with a seat and sowing device, do not seem to have been used widely enough to offset the increased tax by gains in productivity. Attempts to check the continuing concentration of landed and industrial ownership and its corollary, the pauperization of the peasantry, were ineffective. By the end of the BC era, weak and vicious emperors dominated by the families of their wives and by the eunuchs on the one hand, and riots amongst the hard-pressed peasantry on the other, heralded the decline of the dynasty.

Thus a cycle was approaching its end, a cycle which was to repeat itself many times in the course of Chinese history. The new dynasty's improvements in administration and justice brought about improvements in social relations and a strengthening of the economy. This in its turn gave the emperor more scope for military ventures, which eventually outgrew their economic base. In the meantime, intergenerational dynastic decay, a phenomenon detected by Ibn Khaldun in the Islamic civilization, set in. New extortions and new mismanagement aroused discontent and riots, which pointed to the withdrawal of the celestial mandate from the dynasty in question.

The Han dynasty was saved from the worst by a short interruption caused by a usurper, Wang Mang (6–23 AD), who attempted to resolve the crisis by radical reforms: the redistribution of land, prices and interest policies, renewed and new government monopolies (including fishing and slave-holding), government intervention in the food and silk trades, etc. The running of a regulated economy required extended policing and harsher penalties. Yet Wang Mang, like so many before and after him, in China and elsewhere, was shown that economic life cannot be streamlined by administrative means alone, especially when the situation is turbulent.

The abrupt changes in the reform policy and the drastic means used to enforce it, combined with increased taxation, led to a series of uprisings. From these there eventually emerged as victor a scion of the House of Han who, after a protracted civil war, was able as emperor Guang Wu (Guang Wu Di 25–57 AD) to re-establish law and order. The reimposition of Chinese domination over the countries conquered by the Former Han, however, took rather more time. Nevertheless the Han dynasty[35] obtained a new lease of life of one hundred and fifty years or so, before a new great crisis bore witness to the fact that yet another cycle had run its full course.

In the meantime the Confucians managed to settle their doctrine. As early as 25–22 BC a special committee had worked out a list of controversial passages in the Five Classics and put it to the emperor for arbitration. But the turbulent times did not favour a quick decision. The issue was only tackled much later, at the emperor's command, in 79 AD. All the texts attributed to Master Kong were engraved in stone tablets. Yet this did not prevent the copyists, who at that time began to use a newly invented and more convenient writing material, paper, from making errors.

The imperial university swarmed with students (in 130 AD more than 30,000 of them) and the incoherence of the doctrine was a serious obstacle to proper learning. Only towards the middle of the second century AD did an outstanding scholar, Ma Jong, succeed in elaborating a coherent commentary to all the Classics. In his quest for a unified philosophical interpretation, however, he could not resist the influence of Taoism; from then on, its cosmology remained firmly anchored in Confucian thought.

Another remarkable scholar, Cheng Xian (*fl.* 160–201), completed Ma Jong's work by summarizing the whole doctrine; it may be worthwhile to restate briefly in shorthand, as it were, the gist of its normative message. The physical and the moral world are subject to the same laws; a continuous circulation of the five elements dominates the moral qualities of individual dynasties just as it does the sequence of the seasons. Therefore, a superior man (gentleman, *junzi*) has continuously to strive for perfection; in performing correctly his public functions he contributes to the orderly course of the universe, whose way is also the way of mankind.

The summary of the core of the doctrine was followed by another, technically more perfect setting down of the basic texts. Between 175 and 183 they were, again at the emperor's command, engraved in stone tablets, but this time in such a way that whenever required a copy could be taken. Thus everything was done to avoid the possibility of misunderstanding and controversy. The supreme wisdom was to be fixed for ever.

Yet neither nature nor history allows for a definitive solution. At the very time when its fixing and summation were taking place, Confucianism failed on two counts, one socio-economic, the other psychologico-religious.

In the socio-economic realm the main trouble was that the noble principle of justice (*I*) could never be properly implemented in practice. The equitable distribution of land, for which the paradigm was sought in the nine-field system (eight private plots around a common one in the centre with a well) of idealized antiquity, remained a dream, despite occasional attempts to introduce it. Free trade in land led to the concentration of ownership in fewer and fewer hands, and taxation and other public burdens continued to be biased heavily to the detriment of the poorer classes. The technical innovations of that epoch, such as the blast engine, the water mill, the water engine, etc., were not used enough for productivity to be increased to the necessary extent. Nor did the great and ingenious waterworks, such as the canals, always benefit the small peasantry. The gap between the elite and the poor was so enormous that it made a mockery of all noble ideas of harmony.

Thus it was little wonder that people looked to religion for consolation. The old recipes of contact with the supernatural, various kinds of magic or witchcraft, were always available, but for the time of distress a deeper religiosity was needed. Towards the end of the second century AD this kind of demand began to be met by an ample supply, from two sources simultaneously: one native, Taoism, which turned into a church-like religion, and the other imported, the message of Buddha, which came to China via trade routes protected by her westward expansion. And it was these two spiritual forces which opened up a new chapter in the history of the Chinese civilization.

7.6 CHINA DIVIDED

7.6.1 The Emergence of the Taoist Church

At the time when the Confucians were summarizing and fixing their doctrine, the undercurrent that was to issue in another, religious China, was already well advanced. Domestic need and foreign influence proceeded hand in hand. Though Taoism was a time-honoured, native philosophical doctrine, its mutation into a church-like religion may have been conditioned by foreign influences, especially from Central Asia.[36]

The promoter of Taoism as a popular religion was a Sichuan mystic, Zhang Ling, who under the name of Zhang Dao Ling became the founder of what may be called the Taoist church. He demanded of his followers the confession of sins and penitence, and prayer to the three highest deities (Heaven, Earth and Water); with the help of these deities and of the angels the believers were supposed to attain health, and paradise after death. Zhang Dao Ling preached chastity and forbearance. His priests were required to take only a modest reward for their services: five pecks of rice or corn per year (*wu dou mi dao*). This modesty was to become a paradigm for Taoist reform and revolutionary movements in the future. Zhang Dao Ling's authority, though not institutionally formalized, was supposed to be inherited by his male descendants.

The Taoists recognised only two strata: the lower one, attending collective services, where, among other rituals, sins were washed away by the sprinkling of water; and the upper stratum, a kind of religious virtuosi (to borrow Max Weber's term), who by means of complicated practices, both physical and spiritual, sought immortality. The apparent snag, however, was that the Taoist concept of immortality required that the body and the spiritual substance (which was imagined as a twofold entity and transcended the traditional Chinese concept of soul) be kept together, a belief which any actual death must have revealed as illusion. In contrast to the ancient Egyptians, who attempted to overcome this disturbing fact in their world-view by mummification and similar practices, the Taoists took refuge in an explanatory quibble, maintaining that the dead body is not the real body of the person, who did attain immortality and consequently left the world and joined that of the immortals, but merely a substitute object which had been supplied in order not to disturb the society where death is a normal phenomenon.[37] A pious fraud in which metaphysics was intertwined with a kind of sorcery. But Taoist religiosity was not wholly otherworldly. The Taoists were too imbued with the Chinese tradition to believe in the necessity of harmony between nature and men, and could not resist occasionally trying to help in this respect. In 174 AD the Taoist high priest Zhang Qiao had a dream of a forthcoming period of great peace (*tai ping*) which was to be manifested in the change of the azure Heaven into a yellow Heaven, an event due to happen, according to our reckoning, in 184.

There is an interesting, revolutionary, point in this proposition. Whilst up to then, and also ever since, Heaven was not supposed to change but only to withdraw its mandate from the decaying dynasty, now Heaven itself was to undergo a thorough transformation. Surely something more than a dynastic change was expected, but there is no evidence of any concrete ideas of what actually should have happened. Apparently, so much faith was put in this heavenly transformation that all men had to do was help the change to materialize. This was taken up by a movement which, apart from religious practices such as communal feasting, participation in ceremonial assemblies and fasts of purification, organized themselves on military lines, wearing yellow turbans as a sign of allegiance.

But before the Yellow Turbans could strike, the power elite in the Chinese empire fell apart. There were in all three groupings vying for supremacy – the Confucian scholars, the military, and (a symbol of dynastic decay) the eunuchs, who occasionally happened to be supported by the powerful aristocratic clans, jealous over the dominant role of the literati. The first round of the struggle was won by the eunuchs.

Yet at that point in time the Yellow Turbans began to appear dangerous, and the government decided to strike first; this happened in 183 before the expected arrival of the Yellow Heaven. The Yellow Turbans, apparently not yet ready for the showdown, were completely defeated within two years; but their splinter groups continued for many more years to cause disturbances in some outlying provinces. As the victory was won by the army, the generals became more self-confident, and it was now their turn to take on the eunuchs; in 189 those of them who were at the court were massacred wholesale. The machiocracy and the aristocracy dominated the stage. Yet individual warlords could not agree upon a common ruler; so, supported by mutually jealous aristocrats, they began to fight each other. After a thirty years war, in 220 the Han dynasty disappeared completely from the stage of history. Within two years China was divided into three independent kingdoms; Wei in the north, Shu in the west, and Wu in the south-east.

Religious Taoism, however, was only one new force whose spread throughout China gave her a new spiritual climate. The other was Buddhism, the first great foreign doctrine to make a deep impact on the socio-cultural development of China.

7.6.2 The Coming of Buddhism and its Subsequent Development

Buddhism entered China by the gate the Chinese themselves had opened. When the second emperor of the Late (Eastern) Han succeeded in recapturing the oases in Central Asia (in the mid-seventies of the first century AD), it was not only traders but also prisoners of war and hostages who came from there to China. And among these were Buddhists, since at that time Buddhism in both its versions was widely spread throughout the Kushan empire, and all over Central Asia.

For those who had eyes only for the cultic forms, Buddhism looked similar to Taoism. Indeed it was the emotional aspect of worship which in both religions made the initial appeal to the Chinese mind.

The first Chinese Buddhist texts were notes taken from the commentaries of the foreign missionaries, dealing with morality and meditation, breathing exercises, hell and paradise, Buddha's life, etc. It took a long time before the doctrinal tenets of Buddhism could be tackled in the Chinese language, and even then there was wide scope for misunderstandings. But most of these seem to have been overcome after two hundred years or so of thorough study.

Bearing in mind what has already been said concerning the Chinese language, translation from Sanskrit or Pali must have been a formidable task. Buddhist historiography in China divides this enterprise into three stages: first, the ancient translations (of the second to the fourth century AD), when too many concessions were made to Chinese thought and style; secondly, the old translations (of the fifth to the sixth century), marked by a substantial progress in accuracy; and thirdly, the new translations (of the seventh to the ninth century), attaining a uniform terminology and technical exactitude, but, as Gernet puts it, lacking the literary interest provided by the works of the previous epoch.[38]

This timetable may serve as an illustration of the conceptual distance between the two civilizations, the Indian and the Chinese. On the emotional level, the distance seems to have been much smaller. Yet, it may be maintained, it was the timing rather than the general disposition which mattered.

In the first centuries AD the civilized zone of the Old World (A.L. Kroeber's Ancient *Oikoumene*) was strongly permeated by an emotional religiosity, coupled with a conspicuous bent towards mysticism and gnosis. In this study, we have already had the opportunity to touch upon this phenomenon with respect to Iran (section 4.4) and India (section 6.4), and we have to add that a similar development took place in the Hellenized world.

It was apparently a reaction against the arid mix of rationalism and superstition which had prevailed among the sophisticated elite of the most advanced societies, such as Greece, Iran, India and China, for the previous half millennium or so. The reason for this reaction may be seen in the failure of the respective societies to live up to their own moral principles, and further in the fact that the traditional popular religions could no longer provide a satisfactory consolation for the frustrated populace.

As this spiritual turning-point occurred in so many places at the same time, it seems reasonable to suggest that the concept of 'axial time' (*Achsenzeit*) coined by the German philosopher Karl Jaspers could be used as a generic term: not only for the epoch of the great prophets and philosophers who began the struggle for a rational instead of a mythical approach to transcendence (this, according to Jaspers' reckoning, occurred in the civilized world, between 800 and 200 BC), but also for the first centuries AD, when the overpowering wave of gnosis and religious devotion opened the door to the mystical quest for transcendence, which thus became the legitimate layer of religious thought and experience.

In China, the failure of the Mandatees of Heaven to preserve harmony became evident towards the close of the Late Han dynasty. By that time China had already been opened wide to the 'Western Wind' blowing from the great melting pot of ideas and civilizations in Central Asia.[39] Buddhism was apparently the most dynamic element in that arena. Buddhists coming to China met there with a keen demand for a more emotional response to religious needs than the ancient primitive cults could provide. Buddhism was also the kind of religion which could speak and offer consolation to people on various intellectual and ethical levels. It was thus a religion capable of having a nationwide impact.

Though Taoism moved in a similar direction and from the third to the fifth century made a stronger impact, from then until the end of the millennium it was Buddhism whose influence on the shaping of the Chinese civilization was the more pronounced. It was the Buddhist philosophical concepts and forms of organization and worship which influenced Taoism and even Confucianism, rather than the other way round.

Furthermore, Taoism remained a nation-bound religion, whereas Buddhism succeeded in establishing itself throughout the whole of southern, central and eastern Asia, thus setting up a common conceptual and emotional framework for a lively cultural interchange. For a while, that part of Asia was offered a vision of a common, albeit doctrinally and ethnically variegated, pan-Buddhist civilization.

Yet the vision was of a potential rather than a real event. At the time when Buddhism was capturing the minds of millions of Chinese, it was already on the wane in its country of origin, India; and in the area of its first great advance, south-eastern Asia, it was in the process of getting lost in the high tide of syncretism. In Central Asia, Buddhism fought, so to speak, a rearguard battle with the expanding Nestorian Christianity and the new, synthetic messsage of Mani. To complete the picture of the unpropitious synchronization we may add that the resurgence of Theravada in Burma, Thailand and Cambodia, and the blossoming of Japanese Buddhism, occurred only when in China Buddhism had already passed its zenith and was destined to give way to the Confucian renaissance.

The chances of a pan-Buddhist civilization, however, were not only frustrated by adverse timing. It seems that by its very nature, Buddhism lacked the capacity to become a viable backbone of a supranational civilization. A religion which is to become a socially integrative force has to show a more determined effort in this direction. Buddhism scored integrative successes only on a more or less national basis, such as in Tibet and South-East Asia in particular, and to some extent in Japan. Based as it was mainly on the monasteries for monks and nuns (and, unlike other great religions, lacking a local clergy with pastoral concern for the laity), and being too dependent on the support of the secular authorities, Buddhism was particularly vulnerable to the effects of persecution. On the other hand its readiness to accept symbiosis with other cults was favourable to its survival wherever religious pluralism was accepted as a way of life.

It would go beyond the limits of this book to give an account of the various Buddhist schools and denominations which emerged in medieval China. We have to restrict ourselves to a few highlights which will be mentioned in the course of our subsequent discussion. However, we do want to say some more about the political and socio-economic conditions within which Buddhism was to operate.

7.6.3 The Social Face of Divided China

Politically, the most important factor was that China ceased to be united. Though attempts at reunification were not lacking, their success was historically ephemeral and also geographically limited. Most of China became united, under a dynasty known as the Western Jin, in 280–316. Then for a long while (until 589) China again became divided between what Chinese historiography describes as the Northern and Southern dynasties (*Nan bei chao*). North China, fragmented for most of that time, was ruled by foreign dynasties, of Turkic, Mongolian, Tungus and Tibetan origin. South China, strengthened by the mass exodus of population from the north, was ruled by several successive dynasties with their seat in Nanjing (the Southern Capital). Heaven apparently was not lucky with its choices of Mandatees.

In these circumstances, it was extremely difficult to organize strong and orderly government. The peasantry was exposed to more than the usual exactions by unscrupulous authorities, and on top of that to acts of extortion and destruction on the part of the warring factions. Law and order became a scarce commodity, and people were ready to trade off for it whatever things of value still attached to their status as imperial subjects. The situation was ripe for commendations, a phenomenon known from the history of almost every civilization.

In the China of that epoch, commendations took the form of adscription to the patrons, owners of fortified residences commanding a sizeable armed retinue, rather than of an adscription to the soil. The commendants, or clients, were of two categories, one called the guests, for board and lodging, apparently used for various services, the other named the guest-cultivators. The decline of the market economy brought with it the fading away of the merchant class and of industrial manufactures. Craftsmen tended to look for the same kind of protection as peasants, thus becoming 'clients' of powerful families. According to Maspero, at the beginning of the third century AD about five-sixths of the Chinese were in some kind of dependent relationship to the remaining one-sixth.[40]

This process was matched by the disappearance of the mandarinate as a profession based on the scholarly exams. There prevailed a tendency to divide the population into nine categories, allegedly according to moral and intellectual standards (the system was called 'rectification') but in fact with respect to degrees of noble birth. And the appointments to the government service followed these 'rectified' criteria. Furthermore, the rulers took up the old habit of allocating fiefs (*guo*) to their favourites. Occasional attempts to limit the tenure of fiefs to the period during which the office was held and to allocate a fixed acreage of land to peasant households were not particularly successful. Nevertheless these attempts, which cropped up more in the north than in the south, bear witness, in that long epoch of disunity, to a strong awareness of traditional Chinese values amongst individual rulers, whether native or foreign.

In terms of cultural orientation, however, the Confucian tradition could hardly compete with the high tide of religious sentiment, for which Buddhism and Taoism offered a wide range of outlets. Secular authorities were quite keen to give the religious organizations their support. In the less populated and less sinicized south, where the nobility – immigrants from the north – owned large estates and exercised a good deal of autonomous power, religious communities were primarily dependent on these nobles for support. In the north, where the sinicized dynasties of foreign origin had a firmer grip on their subjects, religious policy was so to speak more centralized.

In both instances support was given to both religions, but on the whole the Buddhists, who were better organized, fared better. More often than not the monks and nuns were granted exemptions from all public duties, such as military and work service, and, last but not least, taxes; monasteries were endowed with land, which tended to increase through the commendations of peasants keen to escape government taxation and other duties. People also forged themselves registrations as monks. No wonder that eventually the Taoists, in an attempt to bolster their position, also began to organize monasteries of their own.

The monastics were linked to the Buddhist laity by (among other things) associations founded to give financial support to religious activities and also, to some extent, to provide charity. As a further step in that direction the monasteries began to function as pawnshops, auctioneers, money lenders, and productive users of capital put into a common stock, thus echoing the practice established earlier in India.

The Buddhists, like the Christians in the Roman Empire, managed to create their own institutions within the state, which in granting the above-mentioned exemptions from government duties deprived itself of a good deal of revenue and a sizeable labour force. The Confucians could not but resent this practice and occasionally succeeded in persuading the ruler to put a stop to it, but without any lasting effect. Buddhist historiography refers to 'four persecutions' within five hundred years, all of them short-lived. Three of them affected only the north and had as their main aim the secularization of the monasteries: the first in 438–446 AD, the second, directed also against the Taoists, in 574, and the last, much later, when China was again briefly divided, in 955. The whole of China was affected by the persecution under the declining Tang dynasty in 842–5. This, however, was directed against all foreign religions, such as (apart from Buddhism) Manichaeism and Nestorian Christianity; only Buddhism was strong enough to survive this ordeal.

In the meantime Buddhism exerted a considerable influence on all ethnic segments of Chinese society. Sinicized barbarians such as the Toba (or Northern Wei), from whose dynasty only one ruler succumbed to the lures of the Confucian scholars, became the most dedicated sponsors of Buddhist culture. Under their rule the penal code was significantly humanized (mutilation as a punishment was abolished) and Buddhist art in China attained its peak. The Wei sculptures are among the world's greatest achievements in this art-form.

China's learning from India was part of a two-way traffic. Indian monks and scholars came to China, and the Chinese adepts travelled extensively throughout India and other Buddhist countries. As has already been mentioned in Chapter 6, the accounts of these travellers are the most valuable documents on what was going on in the countries they visited.

It took some time though before the Chinese themselves began to create their own schools of Buddhist thought. Ultimately the most successful of these was the *Tientai* school, named after the mountain where its first monastery was founded in 575 by the monk Chi Yi. Tientai was a bold attempt at a synthesis of the two main versions of Buddhism, Mahayana and Hinayana, enriched with elements of the Chinese philosophical tradition.

7.7   TOWARDS AN ELUSIVE SYNTHESIS

Towards the end of the sixth century, the many repeated attempts to reunify China were eventually successful. In 581 a warlord, Yang Qian, assumed power in the north by a *coup d'état*, and in 589, as the first emperor of the Sui dynasty ousted the last ephemeral dynasty of the south from their capital, Nanjing. Thus the unity of imperial China was re-established and a vigorous campaign began to restore the country's imperial greatness. Yet this happened at too fast a pace and thus, because of the usual overstretching of resources, the second ruler of the Sui dynasty forfeited the Heavenly Mandate. In 618 he was murdered by his rebellious generals.

History almost followed the pattern of the first unification and period of imperial greatness, under Qin and Han. With the unifier's son and heir the dynasty which had done the most difficult job was out, and after a civil war a new, glorious and long-lasting dynasty, the dynasty of the Tang, took over. And like the Han, the Tang dynasty was also to rule as it were in instalments (618–755 and 763–902), of which the second, however, was far from glorious.

Yet in comparison to the epoch of the Han, the Tang era was from the cultural point of view more differentiated. In the Han empire the Confucian interpretation of the Classics was the dominant ideology, albeit diluted by many elements from other schools, especially the Legalists and Taoists, and also by elements from popular cults and superstitions. Under the Tangs China's culture was fed by three independent but interacting spiritual sources: Buddhism, Taoism and Confucianism. And the Chinese emperors, in degrees that varied according to their personal tastes, sought inspiration in all of them.

The founder of the Sui dynasty shifted his imperial favours from Confucianism to Buddhism. Considering himself a *chakravartin* (universal monarch in the Buddhist tradition) and ostentatiously sponsoring the Buddhist cult, in 601 he ordered all Confucian schools to be closed with the exception of one, in the capital, with a quota of seventy students.[41]

The Tangs continued to bestow their favours on both religions; some emperors worshipped Buddha, some were practising Taoists (even to the point of drinking an elixir which brought them quickly to the other world). But in their practical policy they tended to follow the advice of the scholarly bureaucrats, who thus re-emerged alongside the aristocracy and machiocracy as an influential segment of the elite. The qualification for government service again began to depend on passing an examination. The rectification system of nine categories already abrogated in the south was now abolished in the whole of China.[42]

A new official edition of the Classics, compiled by Confucius' descendent, Kong Yinda (d. 648), marked the first step in what may be called a Confucian renaissance. The greater stress on normative than on divinational aspects pointed to the new trend in the development of the doctrine, the spread of which was later greatly helped by a new invention, the woodcut printing of whole pages.

The official sponsorship of Confucianism, however, did not adversely affect the other schools of thought and worship. Both Taoism and Buddhism enjoyed extensive support, and the Zoroastrians, the Nestorian Christians and the Manichees, who were amongst the people newly arrived from Central Asia, were allowed to build temples and gain converts. It was also in this epoch that various previously unknown nuances of Indian Buddhism became accessible to the Chinese public; later between 713 and 741, the Taoists compiled their canon, the Splendid Doctrine of Three Mysteries, in 3744 scrolls.[43]

Traditional statesmanship, and also common sense, required a more straightforward relationship between the emperor and his administration on the one hand and the subjects on the other. Thus measures were taken against the feudal elements in the socio-economic structure. First the clientships (commendations) of peasant farmers were abolished and the large estates were allowed to employ only hired labourers, on whose behalf they had to pay the poll tax.

Secondly, the government, as the supreme owner of the land, began, this time with a considerable measure of success, to allocate it equally to the peasants. According to the law of 624 each peasant over 18 years of age was to obtain 80 *mu* (*c.* 4 hectares), and the head of each family 20 mu (*c.* one hectare) on top of that as a hereditary plot. Mulberry and other useful trees were considered as perpetual property. All plots were inalienable and illegal buyers not only forfeited the price but were punished with ten strokes of the stick for each mu. The actual allocations, however, depended on the population density. In the south, there seems to have been no particular problem, but in the north the allocations hardly attained a half of the norm.[44]

The first decades of the Tang rule saw not only a re-invigoration of the peasantry but also a new upsurge of industrial and commercial activity. There was also a conspicuous cultural blossoming. It was the golden age of Chinese sculpture and Chinese poetry. The French sinologists called the first half of the eighth century, when artistic creativity, technical progress, economic prosperity and also imperial expansion and cultural radiation attained their zenith, the *grand siècle*. During that time not only Korea and Vietnam, which had already been under the political and cultural influence of China, but also Japan came powerfully under the sway of the Chinese civilization.

At the same time, China was itself receptive to foreign influences. Apart from Buddhism, already mentioned, there were various motifs from the steppe nations which enriched Chinese art. Something of a cosmopolitan mentality coloured the first half of the Tang rule in China.

Yet as on previous occasions, ambitions of imperial grandeur eventually outstripped the human and economic resources available. Rivalries between aristocracy and machiocracy exacerbated the tension. Ominous signs of the withdrawal of the Heavenly Mandate began to appear.

The trouble first became evident in Central Asia, where China was challenged by the new forces of an expanding Islam. In the first confrontation in 715–18 the Chinese advanced as far as Kashmir and Afghanistan: but then the arrogant treatment of local dignitaries by the Chinese governor made the native, mainly Turkic population side with the Arabs. The outcome was the total defeat of the Chinese in 751 and the permanent loss of their dominion over what is now the greater part of Soviet Central Asia. In the same year the Chinese armies also suffered defeats by the 'barbarians' in the north-east and south-west.

For the next two hundred years things mostly went wrong in the Middle Kingdom. An internal war (755–63), unleashed by a frustrated general, and finished only with the help of a foreign nation, the Uygurs, who settled in the Tarim basin, put an end to the enlightened agrarian policy of the Tang. Further problems such as the Tibetan invasion, and plundering by itinerant gangs, were accompanied by a weakening of the administration, increased taxation, the re-appearance of commendations and a decline in the population.[45]

During that period of decay attempted rallies were not totally lacking, but they could not reverse the trend. The emperors did not look so frequently to the Confucian scholars for advice, and oscillated in their sympathies between the Buddhist and the Taoist religions. In 819 one of them, to the great dismay of the literati, installed Buddha's relics in state; but he ended his life a year later, most likely by drinking the Taoist elixir of immortality. His son and successor was an ardent Taoist who decided to finish with all foreign religions. In 842 he proscribed the Manichees and in 845 he took on the Buddhists; their monasteries were disbanded, their land confiscated, and monks and nuns were ordered to work as laymen. A similar measure was taken against the small communities of Nestorians and Zoroastrians.

These measures were the culmination of a xenophobic wave which came in response to the interference of foreign warlords in China from 755, and which manifested itself in occasional massacres of foreigners. Even government policy became affected: in 836, the Chinese were forbidden any relations with 'people of colour', i.e. foreigners from beyond the Pamirs and from South-East Asia.[46]

The rationale of the measures against Buddhism was that monasteries and people working for them enjoyed exemption from state duties, and also that Buddhist institutions were withdrawing copper from monetary use, using it to produce bells, statues, etc. Yet, and this is characteristic of Chinese proscriptions (cf. the abolition of the Confucian schools in 601), a few Buddhist temples and monks were authorized to stay.

The proscription of Buddhism, however, did not last long and was not given enough time for it to be applied throughout the whole country. In 847 the emperor passed away after taking the Taoist elixir. His son and successor substantially mitigated the ban and allowed monastic life to be restored to some extent; he too finished his life in a Taoist way.

But whether the emperor followed the Taoist or the Buddhist path, the Mandatee of Heaven could not stop the progressive decay. From the sixties of the ninth century China was ruled by the eunuchs and internal disorder grew apace. In 902–9 the empire split into several independent kingdoms.

7.8 THE CONFUCIAN RENAISSANCE AND THE TECHNO-ECONOMICAL LEAP FORWARD

After half a century of disunity, disorder and mounting interference by Turko-Mongolian tribes, in 960 the officers of the north Chinese army proclaimed their general, Zhao Kuangyin, emperor, with the name of Tai Zu, i.e. the great founder. And indeed he was the founder of the remarkable dynasty of the Song.

Yet the Song did not succeed in reuniting all the territories which had belonged to China under the Tang. The frontier areas in the north-east remained under the rule of the Khitans, the already largely sinicized people of Turkic origin; in the north-west, the Himalayan people of the Tanguts carved out a kingdom for themselves; and in the south, which was only re-absorbed into the Song empire after nineteen years of fighting, Vietnam regained its independence.

With the Song, imperial policy came closest to the Confucian ideal. Tai Zu (960–76) succeeded in transforming his top officers into civil administrators and, together with his brother and succcessor, Tai Zong (976–97), re-established the mandarinate, i.e. the bureaucracy educated in the Confucian interpretation of the Classics. Buddhism and Taoism lived on in a transfigured form. On the one hand they passed some of their philosophical heritage over to the Confucians, who were thus able to replace the traditional elements of superstition in their doctrine with a more sophisticated metaphysics. On the other hand, both Buddhism and Taoism increasingly became part of the religious folklore, a role they have continued to play up to the present day.

There were two circumstances which seem to have contributed to the revitalization of Confucian teaching: the need to cope with the socio-economic problems, and the quest for a more sophisticated approach to the philosophical basis of the doctrine.

The socio-economic problems were of a complex nature. On the one hand there was the perennial problem of inequalities in the distribution of land, and of unequal taxation. Around 1000 AD only about 30 per cent of the cultivated area was liable to tax; this was the land held by small farmers, and the tax was assessed according to the extent of the holding. The other 70 per cent, which was either owned by great landowners or held as fiefs by members of the imperial family or as benefices by government officials, was exempt from the land tax. They paid only the poll tax to which everybody was liable except the clergy. Not only the peasant farmers but also small craftsmen were at a disadvantage *vis-à-vis* the rich merchants who dominated the guilds of artisans and traders.

The unequal tax burden and unequal imposition of corvées, accentuated by the high interest on loans of seeds, etc., caused widespread discontent which in times of poor harvest exploded into riots. Understandably, this situation had bad consequences for defence, which was yet another reason for reform.

In the middle of the eleventh century the internal political development of China became dominated by the struggle between two factions of the mandarinate – on the one hand, the reformers led by Wang Anshi, and on the other, the conservatives led by Sima Guang, a historian. In brief, the reformers stood for government regulation, the conservatives for the free market.

In 1068 Wang Anshi got the opportunity to try out his ideas in practice. First, he tried a policy (already attempted several times before, but without success) of regulating the supply and thus also the prices of corn and rice by means of government purchases and stock-keeping. The government granaries were also intended to grant cheap loans of seed, etc., charging 20 per cent interest instead of the 50 per cent required by the private lenders. Furthermore, tax exemptions were abolished, land-registers reassessed and some corvées commuted into taxes payable in money. The number of mercenaries was reduced by half and a militia was introduced instead.

As the new policy required positive knowledge and a pragmatic approach rather than an acquaintance with the Classics and a literary style, Wang Anshi tried to reform the education of the mandarins accordingly. But a change in this respect required more time and energy than he had at his disposal. The lack of adequately trained and honest officials was one of the main stumbling blocks in the way of reform.

The other and even more serious obstacle lay in the fact that individual emperors had different views: one favoured the reformers, the other the conservatives. From 1068 to 1125 there was a seesaw situation. One emperor even changed sides twice during his reign. Thus, reforms could not take root properly. Eventually, the reformers' energy petered out and the two parties turned into factions characterized merely by personal rivalries. The only lasting effects of the reforms were the considerable extension of the cultivated area due to the new irrigation network, and the substantial increase in productivity in agriculture.

The situation, however, was eased by the great expansion of industrial and above all commercial activity. The disgruntled peasants found all sorts of employment in crafts, commerce, entertainment and in other services in the growing cities, which were quickly losing their erstwhile identities as aristocratic and bureaucratic settlements. The growing market economy required a more plentiful money supply than the traditional copper currency could provide. Earlier, in a similar situation, lead, iron and even clay tokens had been put into circulation, but this practice did not make much headway. This time, under the Song, a not totally unsuccessful experiment was made with paper money.

Yet the commercialization and monetarization of the economy were only two of the outstanding features of the epoch. Another important factor was the shift of population from the corn-growing north to the rice-producing south. The migration from the north to the south was a prolonged process; after each foreign invasion or troubled period in the north there was an exodus of people, who settled in the much less populated south. Around 1000, however, the south caught up with and even overtook the north in population density and also became more important in the economic sphere.

The technical improvements in the cultivation of rice substantially increased the yields. With more food available, the population, which from the end of the Han period had apparently been more or less stationary (though subject to fluctuations), almost doubled. According to the census in 1083 China, though smaller in extent than in the Tang era, had a population of almost 90 million. The growth was especially rapid in towns and cities.[47]

But Chinese society was not only larger. It was also more mobile, both in geographical and in occupational terms. The flight of the peasants to the towns produced some problems for the large estates, and the government attempted to stem this trend by requiring the authorization of the landlord for such moves. Thus, oddly enough, an element of bondage reappeared in the increasingly mobile, free market society.

Another salient aspect of the changes in China was the growing importance of shipping, both on the inland waterways, rivers and canals, and on the sea. The maritime trade on the sailing ships reached beyond the Malayan islands into the Indian Ocean and to the shores of India and Africa. Whereas in the Han and Tang eras the main contact was with the west via the Tarim basin and on horseback, under the Song, China was open by sea to the south. While in the earlier epoch, the horse was a key factor in transport and in military operations, during the Song epoch ships became the dominant factor in transport, and instead of cavalry China had to rely on her new arms. The horse-breeding regions were lost to the

Tanguts and Khitans. But the martial spirit was also no longer to be found in the elite, where the mandarinate replaced the aristocracy; mercenaries rather than conscripted levies formed the core of the army.

China's main asset in those days was technical progress. The magnetic compass for navigation, gunpowder for firearms, wider use of coal as fuel, and wood-blocks, and later even moveable letters, for printing books: these are only a few of the key inventions which began to play a socially relevant role in the Song era.

Whilst Taoist geomancy is supposed to be behind the experiments with magnetism, the invention of wood-block printing is attributed to the Buddhists; their writings were also amongst the first known to have been printed in this way. But Buddhism was no longer in a position to profit from the new technique. The spirit of the times was moving in another direction. Also inspiration was no longer forthcoming from India; the contact via Central Asia was interrupted by the Muslims and in India proper Buddhism was losing momentum. The renaissance of Theravada in Burma and Thailand did not radiate beyond the Sino-Indian civilizational border in Indochina.

The main beneficiary of modernized book-printing was the Chinese renaissance, that rediscovery and reinterpretation of the Classics known in the West as neo-Confucianism. Taoism, the native counterpart of Buddhism, was no match for the neo-Confucian competition in intellectual circles.

In the middle of the eleventh century, a school of literati in Luoyang began to open up again the time-honoured problems of human nature and its relationship with the cosmos, adopting a serious metaphysical and cosmological approach.[48] They called their interpretation *daoxue*, i.e. the correct interpretation of the doctrine. Later their school was labelled *xing li*, which refers to its two main concepts, *xing* (nature) and *li* (internal regularity).

Of the six prominent neo-Confucians, the most distinguished was Zhu Xi (1130–1200), who accomplished an ingenious summary and synthesis of the Chinese philosophical tradition – a summary which in 1241 was given official recognition by the emperor. Zhu Xi's philosophy has often been described as naturalist. Its dualism is based on the concepts *zhi*, meaning roughly matter, or energy matter, and *li*, often translated as form, but also as reason (*ratio*), or as Needham suggests, organization.[49] As with other Chinese concepts, here too the choice of translation depends greatly on the philosophical orientation of the translator. The main point at issue is whether the term *li* should be understood as a transcendental concept, or whether it expresses the dynamic aspect of a basically materialistic thought. Wherever the truth may lie, it seems clear that the theory did not involve any theistic principle. The creation of the world was explained by the reunion of the two principles li and zhi, constituting the Great Unity, which then, in a perpetual rhythm alternating between yang and yin produced the Five Elements (wood, fire, earth, metal, water) and eventually everything in the universe.[50]

While leaving open the question of how the word li should be interpreted, we have to bear in mind that any philosophy, in order to become sociologically relevant, eventually has to come to terms with popular needs and dispositions. In the China of the Song epoch this took the form of a 'pragmatic syncretism' which made possible a kind of symbiosis between, on the one hand, a rationalistic philosophy, bolstered by the state cult of its time-honoured founder (Confucius), and on the other hand the Taoist and Buddhist religious practices, the link being the situational ethics developed from the principle of Filial Piety.[51]

This framework provided ample scope both for art and for technological progress. The spiritual climate was less favourable to military ventures, though there were good reasons for a bolder imperial policy. From 1004 peace with the foreign kingdoms on Chinese soil was bought by paying a regular tribute to the Khitans (whose dynasty took on the Chinese name Liao), and from 1044 to the Tanguts (in Chinese Xi Xia). Yet by themselves the Chinese had little chance of getting rid of these obligations and recovering lost ground, even in the eventuality of the Khitan (Liao) kingdom experiencing an internal crisis. Therefore the imperial government made a deal with another barbarian nation, ancestors of the later Manchus, the Jürchen. With their help the Khitan kingdom was overrun, but the victorious allies fell out as they could not agree on how to divide the conquered land between them. The ensuing war ended with the total defeat of the Chinese, who had to abandon the whole of north China to the Jürchen, whose dynasty having entered the orbit of the Chinese civilization adopted the Chinese name Jin. The Song from this time on are known as the Southern Song. After a great deal of uninterrupted fighting, during which the Jürchen advanced beyond the River Yangtze, in 1142 a peace was concluded which fixed the border between the two empires on the River Huai and obliged the Song to pay an annual tribute. Thus the Song were thoroughly humiliated, and lost half their empire for good.

Yet they did not learn from bitter experience. When another dynamic barbarian nation, this time the Mongols, appeared on the horizon, the Song did not hesitate to help them against the Jürchen, who had meanwhile become largely sinicized. In 1234, the Jürchen empire was wiped out by the Mongols. But the Song did not obtain any recompense for their assistance. On the contrary: the Mongols, quickly acquiring the superior military technology of the Chinese, turned on the south; after outflanking the Song from the west, in the campaign of 1272–9, they took the rest of China and put an end to the Song empire.

7.9 THE MONGOLIAN INTERLUDE

The Mongols were the first foreigners to conquer the whole of China. They were unique in several ways. Beginning with the founder of their empire, Genghis Khan, their rulers were much more ambitious and more successful in their ambitions than were other nomads, as long that is as 'natural decay through a higher culture', a phenomenon elaborated into a general principle by Ibn Khaldun, did not begin to take effect.

The Mongolian rulers were well aware of the corrosive effects of acculturation to a more comfortable living standard. In China, they tried harder than the Khitan and Jürchen rulers had done to keep their people and garrisons throughout the country separate from the subject population. Yet even so, their rule did not survive five generations, and the last of them were already under a heavy strain.

Like other conquerors, the Mongols superimposed their own social structure upon those of the conquered nations. Thus in the Mongolian domains there were two scales of stratification: one was based on political criteria and encompassed the whole nation; the other was based on social status within one's own ethnic group.

When after the death of Genghis Khan the Mongol empire was partitioned amongst his sons in 1227, the situation began to develop differently in individual appanages. The grand khan elected by the assembly of the higher nobility could co-ordinate the common military strategy and, to some extent, preserve the unity of the law (*yasa*), but otherwise in each appanage (*ulus*) a different process of assimilation with the *genius loci* set in.

In China, whose conquest proceeded at the slowest pace, the acculturation was the fastest. Both these circumstances point to the particular position of China with respect both to her military strength and to her powers of assimilation.

In China, as elsewhere, the first reaction of the Mongolian conquerors to the settled life was to destroy villages and turn the fields into pastures. Yet unlike elsewhere, it was already the first generation, Genghis Khan himself, who followed the advice of his Khitan adviser Yelü Chuchai (d. 1244) to tax rather than to destroy the peasants. The wise men of Iran had to wait almost half a century, and those of Central Asia twice as long, before they could persuade the Mongolian rulers to adopt a similar policy.

China, extended by the Mongolian conquest in the south and in Korea, became united with the native Mongolian territory into one ulus, which was by far the most important in the whole Mongolian world. The rulers of this ulus were also concurrently elected as grand khans.

The whole population of the grand khans' ulus was divided into four basic groups: (1) Mongols; (2) various races, i.e. those who were neither Mongols nor Chinese and were not sinicized; (3) Northern Chinese and sinicized peoples of north China such as the Khitans and Jürchen; (4) new subjects, i.e. Southern Chinese, whose social status was the lowest in the whole empire.

The social system of the Mongols has been described by Vladimirtsov as nomadic feudalism. The word feudalism, however, conjures up various images, and one epithet by itself hardly suffices to clarify it adequately. In the case of the Mongols of the thirteenth to fourteenth century we would prefer to talk of a militarized hierarchy of bondage. The bondage was not to the land (*adscriptio glebae*) but to one's superior in the military hierarchy of commanders; from the bottom up they commanded ten, one hundred, one thousand and ten thousand soldiers respectively. All commanders were appointed to their respective posts by the khan from the ranks of the nobility (*noyon*), who on that occasion gave the khan their vow of allegiance. Unlike in European feudalism, this did not imply any contractual obligation on the part of the sovereign.

The rank-and-file soldiers, the commoners (*nökör*), were subject to their commanders not only in military but also in civilian matters, especially the allocation of pastures. The legal assumption was that the supreme right to dispose of land belonged to the khan, who distributed it amongst his military commanders, who then allocated it further down the hierarchical line. On the other hand, horses, cattle, etc., were fully at the disposition of their possessors, who had to pay a tax in kind from their flock.

Heavy menial work was largely performed by slaves, recruited mainly from prisoners of war. In areas inhabited by the sedentary population, all the commoners were obliged to perform additional corvées such as the postal services and work for the Mongolian garrisons.

Like many other conquerors, the Mongols looked for some kind of accommodation with the upper classes, who in exchange for the recognition of their privileged position amongst the natives were ready to collaborate with the foreign masters. To facilitate their domination the Mongolian rulers did not hesitate to adopt some techniques and symbols of the traditional Chinese administration. Confucianism became a favoured doctrine and from 1315 the state examinations were reintroduced; however equal quotas were reserved for the four ethno-political groups into which the whole population of the empire had been divided. It was a good example of 'positive discrimination' in favour of those who were unable to stand free competition.

Otherwise the Chinese classical tradition could hardly be of particular interest to the Mongols. They appreciated mainly two kinds of knowledge: practical technology and religious magic, both of which they regarded as means of achieving more wealth and power. From their homelands the Mongols brought a particular appreciation of people who were wise men (*shamans*), magicians and healers in one person. They were superstitious but not prejudiced and were ready to give sorcerers other than their own the chance to prove their efficacy. They also seem to have been interested in the ideas behind the various practices. So they allowed all sorts of religions to display their charms. They were also occasionally interested in listening to religious disputations, and thus provided an arena in which all the great religions of the world could meet for peaceful discussions. However, these were only occasional discussions by individual representatives, not that kind of widespread give and take which had for instance characterized Central Asia between 300 and 700.

The struggle for the succession which, after the death of the Grand Khan Mongke in 1259, broke out between his brothers Arik-boga and Kublai, was not merely a matter of personal rivalry; Arik-boga stood for the preservation of the Mongolian tradition and apartheid *vis-à-vis* the subject peoples. Kublai on the other hand was strongly attracted by the Chinese civilization. The struggle was decided, by force of arms, in Kublai's favour. In 1264 his position as the grand khan was recognized by the khans of the other appanages (ulus).

With these events, the Mongols' empire-building took another turn. The internal struggle allowed the Egyptian Mamluks in 1260 to inflict a crushing defeat on the Mongolian armies and thus to stop their advance beyond the Euphrates. The idea of a further advance in Europe and India was abandoned. The empire-building dynamic remained limited to the Far East, where the conservatives had in vain attempted, with the help of the Central Asian khans, to put a stop to the sinophile orientation. This latter was manifested by Kublai's adopting the imperial title and thus founding a new dynasty of China, the Yuan dynasty, with its seat in Beijing (i.e. the Northern capital).

Without withdrawing his favours from the Buddhists and without ceasing to be tolerant towards all other religions, Kublai did his best to obtain the support of the literati; his imperial policy could not succeed without the help of China's economy and military know-how. Korea, which had been subdued in a devastating 27-year war (1231–58), was also enlisted, having been cajoled by Kublai with a dynastic marriage. But not all subsequent campaigns were successful. The two great attacks on Japan, in 1274 and 1281, failed. In the meantime, in 1279, the conquest of south China was completed. Vietnam and Champa were subdued only for a short time and the expeditions to Java (1292–3) and Burma (1300) failed to achieve their objectives. What, however, remained a permanent asset for China was the conquest of the kingdom of Nan Chao, inhabited by a people related to the Thais – an area which from then on became the Chinese province Yunnan.

In many ways the Mongolian bid to create the great Asian-European empire can be compared with the great venture of the Muslim Arabs. Both attempted to unify under their dominion peoples of quite different civilizations, in vast areas of the world which until then had never experienced any kind of unity. The range of the Muslim Arabs was from Christian Spain to the ethno-religious melting pot in Central Asia and to the shores of the Indian Ocean. The Mongolian range was wider: from the Pacific Ocean and Sea of Japan in the east to Asia Minor and Romania in the west and from Siberia in the north to Indochina in the south.

Both attempts were carried by peoples on the threshold of civilization, with a more (in the case of the Mongols) or less (in the case of the Arabs) nomadic way of life. Both were marginally touched by the neighbouring cultures, the Arabs more than the Mongols. However these quantitative differences were less important than the basic difference in quality. What in our opinion mattered most was that the Arabs were united under the banner of a new, to borrow Toynbee's term, 'higher', religion with a strong proselytizing potential and with a capacity to adapt to changing circumstances. The Mongols on the other hand could not advance their superstitious pragmatism past the stage of eclecticism, and did not develop anything exportable on the spiritual plane; instead of carrying their own faith with them and attempting to build up their own civilization, within three or four generations they succumbed everywhere to the civilization of the country they had conquered.

In China, after a short period during which Taoism became their most favoured religion (1223–42), the Mongolian rulers turned their sympathies to Buddhism: first to the school known by the name of Chan (descended from the Indian Dhyana and an ancestor of the Japanese Zen), then to the Lamaist version of Buddhism with which they became acquainted during the conquest of Tibet in the 1250s. In 1260 the Tibetan Lama 'Phangs-pa was entrusted with the general superintendance of all the religions in the Yuan empire. After the final defeat of the Song, the supervisory power of the lamas was extended to southern China as well.

The favours bestowed upon Lamaist Buddhism, however, did not serve to recommend it to the Chinese. Their Buddhism was of another brand; the contrast was so striking that it was the Buddhist secret societies such as the White Lotus, Red Turbans, etc., who eventually became the rallying points of dissent and of the armed liberation struggle. Nor was Lamaist Buddhism particularly helpful in bolstering the spirit of the Mongols. After the death of Kublai's grandson and successor Temur in 1307, the Yuan dynasty lost its vigour. Weaklings displaying little but viciousness and Lamaist bigotry were unable to stem the growing dissent, which was exacerbated by the corrupt and exploitative administrative apparatus to which many foreigners were appointed, not only from the sinicized nations but also from the Muslim ones.

Also at that time many Muslim craftsmen and merchants settled in China, and Islam won many converts in some areas, such as the not yet fully sinicized Yunnan and the north-western provinces, where the Turkic and other immigrants mixed with the Chinese population. That period also saw the beginning of the mass conversions of Mongols to Islam in Iran and Central Asia.

In 1351 the discontent with the Mongolian rule in China erupted in a series of revolts. In 1359, one of their military leaders, Zhu Yuanzhang, son of an agricultural worker and disciple of a Buddhist monastery, managed to organize an orderly government in Nanjing. After eliminating all rival claimants to the Celestial Mandate, in 1368 Zhu chased the Mongolian armies out of northern China and in Nanjing declared himself emperor under the name Hong Wu. Thus was founded the last long-lived native dynasty of China, the Ming dynasty.

Backed by a nationalistic upsurge, Hong Wu was able to reassert his power in the deep south-west, which only became a part of China under the Mongols, and eventually to launch attacks on the Mongols in their native land. There, in 1388, their army was utterly routed. In 1392 Korea used this opportunity to substitute a pro-Chinese for a pro-Mongolian dynasty. Thus within two hundred years the great Mongolian venture was over. But, as will be shown later, this was not yet the end of the role of the 'Barbarians of the Northern Steppes' in Chinese history.

In conclusion we have to say a few words on the Mongolian legacy to the internal life of China. As has already been said, the Mongolian rulers, the Yuan, were primarily interested in practical know-how, both military and civilian. In building roads and ships, in extending canals and in regulating rivers they substantially improved the transport facilities, to the great benefit of long-distance trade. The trade, passing through all the Mongolian domains and bringing merchants of many nations in contact with each other, was undoubtedly an asset for the countries under Mongolian rule. Kublai also returned to the Song experiment with paper money and made it a generally valid currency. But only his first finance minister (a Muslim from Central Asia) eschewed the temptation of easy money and avoided inflation.

With respect to agriculture Kublai attempted the time-honoured but rarely fully successful strategy of price regulation by means of government purchases and sales and the maintenance of public granaries. On the whole, it seems that by the end of the thirteenth century China had recovered from the devastation of the Mongolian conquest. In the 1290 census 13.2 million families were counted; this means a population of almost 59 million, with possibly a higher proportion of urban dwellers than ever before.

The Yuan administration was polyglot. Mongolian, Uygur, Turkic and Persian texts mingled with the mandarin Chinese, which, as a result of a less rigorous examination system, absorbed many elements of the common Chinese language. Side by side with this development, the vernacular (*bai hua*) was used for literary purposes. It became the language of the new genres of literature, until then unknown in China, namely the drama and the novel. As the anthropologist A.L. Kroeber pointed out, mandarin Chinese enjoyed such a dominant position *vis-à-vis* the spoken language that it needed a period of foreign domination to break the grip of officialdom with respect both to the language and to literature.[52] A further advance of bai hua, however, was stopped by the subsequent renaissance of Chinese traditionalism under the Ming.

The visual arts were enriched by new motifs, but on the whole continued in the Song tradition, with painting as the most successful genre. In science it was mainly astronomy and mathematics which experienced a brilliant, but rather brief efflorescence. The Classics in Zhu Xi's interpretation enjoyed canonical authority throughout the whole empire, but in the life of the Chinese people it was Buddhism which dominated the folk culture.

Buddhist secret societies, first legalized, but then banned again, played an essential role in the nationalistic upsurge of the fourteenth century. The leader of the Red Turbans society was regarded as the reincarnation of Maitreya, the Buddha of the Future. After the chiliastic movement of the Taoist Yellow Turbans who expected the change of Heaven at the end of the third century, there came, in the fourteenth century, the Buddhist Red Turbans who believed that their Messiah had come to lead them to victory. In another five hundred years it would again be the Taoist turn to take up arms in order to bring about the millennial dream of Taiping (the Great Peace of Harmony).

7.10   A FRUSTRATED MOMENTUM

Unlike what happened in the lands dominated by Islam, the Mongols in China did not merge with the native population. Eventually they were expelled as an alien element. China experienced a new bout of xenophobic feeling, a wave of nationalism, a rallying around traditional values, stressing the time-honoured concept of the Middle

Kingdom as the pivot of the world.

The founder of the Ming dynasty, the Emperor Hong Wu (1368–98), was, as any winner in a many-cornered war has to be, an extremely able but also ruthless man. Once he had won he sincerely wanted to make his empire wealthy and powerful; under his auspices, a lot was done for the rehabilitation of agriculture, for re-afforestation[53] and the stimulation of industrial activity, but the glory of his imperial majesty was his primary concern. A parvenu, deeply mistrusting everybody, even his closest and most well-tried associates, he inaugurated a regime which out of all the regimes China experienced through the ages, was the one that most closely fitted the European label of oriental despotism.

In the previous regimes, though despotic features were far from being completely absent, there were strong elements of either bureaucracy or aristocracy or even meritocracy which to some extent put a brake on the emperor's arbitrary rule. Under Hong Wu all these pillars of a limited pluralism were indeed re-established, but a kind of centralized imperial administration was superimposed upon the traditional structure. The contrast with the regime of the Song was particularly striking. J. Gernet describes it in the following words:

> Right from the start the Ming empire carried in embryo the absolutist tendencies which were to assert themselves in the fifteenth and sixteenth centuries. Whereas the political system of the Song was based on the co-existence of independent organisms which checked each other and of various different sources of information, and whereas political decisions in that empire were the subject of discussions in which contradictory opinions could be freely expressed, the Ming government was characterized, as early as the end of the fourteenth century, by a tendency to the complete centralization of all powers in the hands of the emperor, to government by means of restricted, secret councils, by the isolation of the imperial authority, and by the development of secret police forces entrusted with the task of supervising the administration at its various different levels. The 'Guards with Brocade Uniforms' (*Qin-yi-wei*), a sort of political police for spying on high officials, were created in 1382 by Hong Wu, who thus set his successors a hateful example.[54]

In many respects Hong Wu behaved in a way which calls Stalin to mind. Two fabricated trials each involving about fifteen thousand persons, with his closest associates set up as ring-leaders who had allegedly plotted with the Mongols and the Japanese against the emperor, led to numerous executions and confiscations of property. A form of high treason was even seen in the use of certain written characters which were supposed to contain a veiled criticism of Hong Wu's person and origins.

Yet the whole system was far removed from the Stalinist type. Unlike Stalin, Hong Wu was happy with having personal control of the commanding heights and was not interested in overhauling the whole elite; he was satisfied with a narrow circle of sycophants. Hong Wu's policy was in many respects conservative. He tried to re-establish viable peasant holdings; many large estates and monastic lands were parcelled. Yet his policy was not consistent. There was a widespread tenancy of farms belonging to the large owners and waged work became more frequent. On the other hand fief and benefice holdings did not disappear; the emperor himself created new ones for his favourites.

There was also an attempt to freeze the bulk of the social structure. Peasantry, artisanship and soldiery were to become hereditary, each under the supervision of a special ministry. Soldiers were to create self-supporting farming communities, scattered throughout the border areas and possible trouble spots. Only the aristocracy and merchants were allowed to enjoy social mobility. Eunuchs, an important social group in the palace service, were forbidden to learn to read and, under penalty of death, to interfere in politics.

But neither of these measures was effective, least of all the last one. Within half a century the eunuchs became the main recruiting group for the top government service. Though the literati were still considered. to be the backbone of the empire and Zhu Xi's interpretation of the Classics enjoyed a privileged position, the real wielders of power were these mutilated creatures who strove for power and wealth as a form of overcompensation. Though the literati organized themselves in self-defence and were occasionally able to win imperial favour and thus influence, by and large they were on the losing side. Fortunately the struggle between the literati and the eunuchs did not assume the acute form which marked the close of the Han period.

The society now was more complex and both the eunuchs and the literati had other areas in which they could assert themselves, including trade and industrial monopolies and extensive landed property; furthermore the literati had strong links with the country gentry and especially with the growing middle class of the cities, a kind of bourgeoisie.

The sustained economic growth of the preceding three centuries or so, supported by technological improvements in agriculture, crafts and transport, gave the state the opportunity to embark on an expansionist policy. It was a two-pronged one, involving as it did both traditional territorial expansion, and an overseas venture aimed at establishing not only trading contacts but also supremacy over the lands of the southern seas.

The initiator of the overseas expansion was the Emperor Yong Le (1403–24), but the drive did not outlive him for long. Nevertheless the range of undertakings was remarkable. At a time when the most daring European seafarers, the Portuguese, were not sailing further than 1400 km from their shores (to Azores), the Chinese navy, armed with the magnetic compass and able to carry 20,000 men on a single expedition, managed to cover 9000 km. In several expeditions, between 1405 and 1433, the Chinese ships reached the Persian Gulf, the Red Sea and the east coast of Africa.

During these campaigns Vietnam was temporarily annexed (1407–27), and the Chinese emperor's sovereignty was formally recognized by Champa, Java, Malacca, Sri Lanka, Calicut and Cochin in south India. All these expeditions enormously enhanced the geographical knowledge of the Chinese, whose cartography had as early as the Song epoch reached a level far superior to anything achieved in Europe in the same era. Among the other gains from the overseas expeditions, it is worth mentioning in particular the growth in the variety of traded commodities and the virtual disappearance of piracy from the Chinese coasts.

Yet the whole great maritime venture of the Chinese was a mere episode. It was an exclusively government matter, involving two successive emperors, Yong Le and Xuan De, and one eunuch-admiral Zheng He; in order to prevent illicit trading everybody else was strictly forbidden to navigate overseas. The whole enterprise lacked that broad, popular base of spontaneous effort that was later to characterize the maritime ventures of the European nations. Thus, though being the first and succeeding in nautical undertakings undreamed of by the Europeans of that epoch, the Chinese were prevented by the paradoxical policy of their despotic emperors from achieving an epochal take-off in maritime expansion. After Zheng He's return from the last expedition (in 1433), the edicts against sailing abroad were enforced still more vigorously. Overseas trade was left to foreign navigators who, bound as they were to come to suitable harbours, were easier to control and tax, this apparently being the main reason for the isolationist policy.[55]

China's turning her back upon her overseas venture, in which she had scored such a significant advantage *vis-à-vis* other nations, was the beginning of the process which was to lead to the Chinese civilization losing its advanced position on the world scale. But because of the extent of her advantage, as well as her size and geographical position, China was well able to survive four more centuries in her splendid isolation without realizing the consequences of the blunder of her great Ming emperors.

In the meantime the main danger for China was still coming from the northern steppes. Consequently the centre of gravity of imperial policy was located in the north. As early as 1421, when the maritime venture was still in full swing, Beijing was made capital city instead of Nanjing. All the military might was to be marshalled against the barbarians on the northern and north-western front. But to no avail; in 1449 the forces of the Oirats, a Mongolian tribe newly emerging on the stage of history, defeated the Ming Emperor Cheng Tong, took him prisoner and released him only after eight years for a ransom. The Chinese were humiliated and had to give up some territory.

Fortunately the Middle Kingdom was strong enough to absorb the shock. It had many assets that were still intact. The Ming despotism, though weighing heavily on Chinese society, did not permeate it to such an extent that all strata and walks of life were profoundly affected. As has been said already, the oriental despotism of the Ming was not of a totalitarian brand. Though they often indulged in arbitrary rule, bestowing favours on people of dubious moral and intellectual quality who were the very opposite of the Confucian ideal of junzi, trying to squeeze revenue from the booming trade by extending the scope of government monopolies, and squandering economic resources, there existed at the same time a vigorous civil society with a pulsating and colourful life of its own.

The Ming did not impose upon their subjects such an extensive ban on creative spontaneity as was the case with the ideological despotism of the Safavids in Iran (cf. section 5.10), or with the totalitarian rule in Soviet Eurasia. The eunuchs were neither *mujtahids* nor party cadres; they were merely ordinary, unprincipled profiteers. Their main opponents, the literati, were simply excluded from influencing government decisions, and only occasionally persecuted; in their own circles they could write and say whatever they believed right. If not all ideas were tolerated, it was a matter of self-imposed restraint, of reverence for tradition and for its most cherished interpreter, the great scholar of the Song epoch, Zhu Xi.

But despite the strong traditionalist bias of the literati, there were enough scholars who either suggested new interpretations of the classical tradition or were keen on expanding practical knowledge. A vast range of scholarly disciplines was cultivated and further improvements in technology were made. These encouraging tendencies were manifested especially in the fields of art and scholarship. Though progress was mainly in quantity rather than quality, it was nevertheless a period that saw achievements of a high standard in the novel, in poetry and drama, in painting and sculpture, in architecture and ceramics. Foreigners who did not understand the language and could therefore not appreciate the written and spoken art were nevertheless full of admiration for what China produced during that epoch in stone, earth (caolin), wood and colour in addition to the long established glory of the Chinese silk. The printing of books using moveable letters produced enormous amounts of printed matter. To give only one example, 1609 saw the completion of an illustrated encyclopaedia in 22,000 volumes, a work which had about 2000 authors.

Amongst the classical scholars several remarkable men were able to step beyond the limits set by the Zhu Xian orthodoxy. One of them, Wang Yang-ming (1472–1528), believing in innate moral knowledge and in the spark of goodness inherent in man's heart, transposed the arid classicism to a level where feelings and sentiments found their voice. Another one, Wang Gen (1483–1541), dreamt of a society of equals ruled by the principles of universal love. Yet another, Li Zhi (1527–1602), even went so far as not to recognize tradition as the criterion of truth. Apart from these thinkers there were many other nonconformist ways of thought some of which became highly appreciated by posterity. Needham discovered in that epoch a re-affirmation of materialism and a new experimental philosophy.[56]

Yet the impact of these thinkers on the society at large was marginal. How could it be otherwise, when the literati were not admitted to the government and lingered on the periphery of political life? Their rallying point was the academy of Tonglin in the province of Jiangsu, founded in the twelfth century. From the beginning of the seventeenth century it became the centre of intellectual opposition against the oppressive and exploitative regime of the eunuchs, whose ability to manipulate the emperor continued to grow as the vigour of the dynasty progressively decayed.

The common folk understood the classical tradition through the growing amount of literature in the vernacular: novels, drama and poetry. People found it easiest to understand the various personal stories, which acquainted them with the virtue of filial piety and the situational ethics of the Five Relationships. Confucius and other prominent classical and neo-Confucian writers were worshipped as national heroes, an extension of the cult of family ancestors.

The Buddhist monks and Taoist adepts catered for more emotional religious needs. The former were popular as intercessors with deities for a better deal in the life hereafter, the latter were renowned as exorcists and healers. Various Buddhas, *bodhisattvas* (amongst whom the female one, Guanyin, 'the goddess of mercy' was the most popular) and *arhats* (in Chinese *luohans*), together with various Taoist saints, were endowed with miraculous powers, far beyond those of the deceased ancestors and the official heroes.

There was an ample choice of worship for everybody. Neither Buddhists nor Taoists developed a centrally organized priesthood or organized congregations. Most Chinese were not exclusively Confucian, Taoist or Buddhist. Their ethical standards, belief in the gods and the life to come, and their world-view in general were moulded by all three systems. But as Latourette put it,

> the religion of the masses was not just a composite of these three faiths. The additional elements had in them a great deal of animism. . . The religion of the majority also contained much of the polytheism – a polytheism augmented by the state cult and by Buddhism and Taoism, but which in its list of deities was much larger than the sum of all three of the other pantheons. There was much of divination and of the observance of lucky and unlucky days.[57]

Thus the three very different schools of thought and worship plus the vast hot-bed of animism constituted a compound, from the elements of which the ordinary Chinese drew their world-view and chose their kind of worship. The logical contradictions between the individual elements of this compound either did not matter or were nicely speculated away. Thus for instance, as Maspero demonstrated,[58] the contradiction between, on the one hand, the eternal life of the soul in various kinds of existence after death, which was the traditional belief in China, and on the other hand, the Buddhist concept of reincarnation, was overcome with the help of the Taoist concept of the plurality of souls: some were deemed to stay with the corpse, others were believed to be re-incarnated. The re-incarnation was imagined as taking place after complicated court proceedings, in which various deities and mythical beings intervened both as judges and as witnesses – a reminder of the tribunal of Osiris in Pharaonic Egypt mentioned in section 2.2. In conclusion let us quote C.K. Yang's assessment of the interplay between Confucianism and religions in China:

> It should be recognized that the dominance of a largely rationalistic thought such as Confucianism, and the organizational weaknesses of religions, have not made the traditional Chinese social order a 'rational' one. Religious influence remains pervasive and strong, and powerful religious movements have risen from time to time in Chinese history to challenge the supremacy of Confucianism. Such religious movements did not arise suddenly from a 'rationalistic' social foundation but, rather, stemmed from religious roots already deep in Chinese society.[59]

7.11 CHINA UNDER TUTELAGE

In the sixteenth century the Chinese became acquainted with a new kind of foreigner: the Portuguese merchants and the Catholic missionaries. At the same time, the already familiar Japanese began to step up their piratical activities, which especially around the middle of that century attained disastrous proportions. Between 1592 and 1598 China had to intervene twice to help to repulse Japanese attacks on Korea.

In contrast to their situation in India, South-East Asia and America, the Catholic missionaries in China could not rely on the armed support of their fellow-countrymen. They were completely on their own and had to establish their influence against the heavy counter-pressure of a cultured and sophisticated elite. Faithful to their pragmatic approach, albeit one often peppered with elements of superstition, the Chinese judged the missionaries according to their practical know-how rather than according to their beliefs and metaphysics. Astronomy and mathematics, architecture and the production of firearms were the main avenues through which the missionaries were able to win the emperor's favour and make a breakthrough to the Chinese elite. Though distrusted by most literati, the Catholics were nevertheless allowed to proselytize; around 1610 there were reported to be about 300 churches scattered throughout the country with its *c*. 100 million population.

Another, perhaps more penetrating, influence came from the trade with the Spanish possessions in the Pacific. New crops from America, maize, peanuts, sweet and white potatoes, and tobacco, came to be widely grown in China. Silver imported from Peru and Mexico bolstered the supply of this metal to such an extent that silver became legal tender in China. In the last third of the sixteenth century international trade spanned all the oceans and, for the first time in history, assumed truly world-wide proportions. But contrary to the hopeful expectations of a century earlier, it was not the Chinese, but the 'Barbarians of the Southern Seas', the Europeans, who achieved this.

But for two centuries to come the main menace for China was still lurking amongst the 'Barbarians of the Northern Steppes'. At the beginning of the seventeenth century it was the turn of the Manchus (the descendants of the Jürchen who in the twelfth century had ruled over vast stretches of northern China before they were supplanted by the Mongols). The Manchus, who like their ancestors the Jürchen were strongly under the sway of Chinese culture, gained strength by absorbing some east Mongolian tribes, and while China was wracked with internal troubles, they began to expand into her territories to the north of the Gulf of Chihli (Bo Hai).

From the start of the seventeenth century the Ming dynasty experienced events which clearly marked the withdrawal of the Celestial Mandate. Disorderly administration, embezzlement on a large scale, arbitrary increases of taxes, widespread usury and concentration of land ownership as a result of the indebtedness of small farmers, led in 1627 to a great peasant uprising which eventually brought about the fall of the Ming dynasty. The insurgents conquered most of north China, redistributed the land amongst the smallholders and, in 1644, took Beijing, where the emperor committed suicide. But the Heavens did not bestow their Mandate upon the leader of the victorious hosts. A Chinese general decided to avenge the emperor, made an alliance with the Manchus and with their help reconquered Beijing. Yet, once the Manchus were in, their leader decided to take up the vacant Mandate for himself and proclaimed himself emperor. The new dynasty assumed the name Daqing, meaning 'the Great Qing'. The conquest of the south of China was, however, a hard nut to crack and was not completed until 1659; even after then, occasional uprisings had to be quelled.

The role of the Manchu dynasty in Chinese history was, in several respects, a paradoxical one. On the one hand, they remained alien to Chinese society, on the other hand they became extremely effective upholders of Chinese traditions and values.

During the two and a half centuries of the Manchu rule China experienced various kinds of fortune; prosperity and growth contrasted with oppression and decay. The oppression occurred in two waves. The first was at the time of conquest and immediately after, when revolts of the supporters of the defeated Ming flared up and were suppressed with the utmost cruelty. The decline in the size of the population points to the grimness of that epoch. The second took place a century later, at the height of the Qing power, when the neo-Confucian orthodoxy seemed to be menaced by the free thinkers. On the other hand, economic prosperity and imperial growth were the hallmarks of the period between c. 1685 and 1775. At that time, to borrow Gernet's terms, the crafts were practised on an 'industrial' scale and the country enjoyed an 'unprecedented commercial expansion'.[60] From then on, however, as will be shown shortly, the troubles began to accumulate. After seventy years or so the troubles developed into an overt crisis, which after yet another seventy years of revolution and foreign wars brought about the fall of the Qing dynasty.

The Manchus, like their predecessors, the Jürchen and the Mongols, but with more consistency, pursued a policy of segregation vis-à-vis their Chinese subjects. As a visible sign of their submission, the Chinese had to wear pigtails; they were forced to evacuate the southern Manchurian provinces, where they had settled under the Ming, and a part of the capital city, Beijing, was also reserved exclusively for the Manchus. Similarly, the Manchu garrisons, situated in strategic places all over the country, had to live their segregated life as farmer-soldiers.

Yet, amazingly, despite all the oppression and discrimination, the Qing managed to be a great Chinese dynasty which was for almost two centuries readily accepted by their Chinese subjects. The success of the Qing was rooted in two strategies. First, they helped to revitalize agriculture; they recognized the parcellation of large estates undertaken during the revolution against the Ming in 1627–44 and kept the taxation of the peasants at a comparatively low level. Secondly, the Qing succeeded in winning the co-operation of most literati. The cult of Confucius and Zhu Xi's interpretation of the Classics were acknowledged as the exclusive doctrine of the state. Filial piety was extolled as the cardinal virtue, as the basis of personal ethics and of loyalty to the emperor. Education was intensified by creating new schools for broader strata of the population.

However, only orthodox views were allowed an airing. The promising crop of new ideas which had marked the later Ming epoch was looked upon with suspicion. In 1687 an index of proscribed books was compiled and gradually the censorship was tightened up. It affected not only the heterodox scholarship but also the popular literature in the vernacular which was deemed to offend the puritanical attitudes of the eighteenth-century Qing. The policy culminated in a straightforward inquisition in 1774–89. At that time, of the 10,237 works on the index, 2320 were completely destroyed; exile, forced labour, confiscation of property and even execution were the penalties for those who defied this policy. It has to be pointed out that this persecution lasted much longer and also had more infelicitous consequences than that ordered by Qin Shi Huangdi in 213 BC. Even if some great independent thinkers such as the polymath Tai Jian (1723–77) or the philosopher of history Zhang Xuecheng (1736–96) were not silenced, their voices remained without the resonance which would have made of these trickles a mightier stream.

Nor did West European knowledge, in which especially the Emperor Kang Xi (1661–1722) showed a great interest, make a deeper impact on the Chinese mind. Mediated mainly by the Jesuits, the spread of European know-how was linked to ulterior motives, i.e. conversion to Catholicism. The Jesuits were also quick to realize that only by recognizing some elements of the Chinese tradition compatible with Catholic Christianity would they be able to succeed in their missionary work. Yet in 1704 and again in 1715, the Pope, influenced by arguments earlier put forward by the Franciscans and Dominicans, forbade the missionaries in China to tolerate any ceremonies in honour of the dead, whether they be ancestors, Confucius or other sages of antiquity. Also in the Chinese translation of the Bible no concessions were to be made to the non-personal conception of God. As a retaliatory measure against what the emperor understood as an affront, Catholic missionaries were forbidden to proselytize; in 1724 they were banned from China, while only a few technical experts were allowed to stay at the court in Beijing.

In their religious policy, the Qing continued to favour Buddhism, especially in its Lamaist form. From 1652, when the Dalai Lama had been received with great pomp, Beijing became the centre of Lamaist publishing and missionary activity amongst the Mongols and the Manchus. In 1732 the imperial palace was converted into a Lamaist temple. Tibet herself, incorporated in 1751 into the Qing empire, was treated with utmost respect and enjoyed a large measure of autonomy.

At the time when the Qing were in the process of building up their power in China, the Turkic tribe of the Dzungars established themselves on her western border in Central Asia. By the end of the seventeenth century they had built up their own nomad empire and were becoming a serious menace to the Qing. The ensuing struggle lasted until the late 1750s, when the internal dissensions amongst the Dzungars enabled the Manchu and Chinese armies to crush the last formidable people of the steppes who were in a position to challenge the sedentary societies. New provinces in Central Asia, extending as far as Balkash (at present in the USSR), were incorporated into the Chinese empire.

Before this happened, the border with the Russians, who in their long march to the east had penetrated as far as the Okhotsk Sea, was negotiated by the treaties of 1689 and 1727.

In the last third of the eighteenth century, however, omens of worse times to come began to accumulate. The population explosion, the rate of which is reflected in the census figures – 1741: 142 million; 1762: 200 million; 1775: 264 million; 1812: 360 million – could no longer be matched by a commensurate exploitation of economic resources. The extension of cultivable land reached the limits imposed by the current technology, and the most obvious outlet for the excess population, the interior of Manchuria, was not open to Chinese immigration until the third quarter of the nineteenth century.[61] Meanwhile the growing peasant distress and indebtedness, combined with the free trade in land, resulted in a concentration of landed property. A new kind of landlord, absentee rather than living in the manor, emerged, and the corollary was a new type of tenant farmer who, in contrast to the manorial bondsmen of the Ming epoch, was directly exposed to the vagaries of the market and usury. An increasing number of peasants were at the mercy of unscrupulous landlords and money-lenders. Peasant uprisings, often led by the Buddhist and Taoist associations, occurred all over the country.

In the stagnant social climate neither economy nor culture moved forward. And this was the time when the new kind of foreigner appeared on the horizon and, in the 1840s, forced China to open her doors to Western trade and influence. A new dramatic chapter of Chinese history began to unfold. In several successive stages, together lasting one and a half centuries, China was set on a new civilizational course.

8 The Rhythm of the Far East: Reception and Adaptation

8.1 GENERAL OUTLINE

An interesting and significant feature of the Chinese and Indian civilizations was that, unlike the Levantine civilizations (especially Islam) they expanded only eastward, not westward. Though individual ideas and practices of Indian and Chinese origin found their way to the west both in the early Zoroastrian and Hellenic eras and in the later Islamic and Christian periods, it was only the nations of the Far East that adopted the religious and philosophical systems of the two great Asian civilizations as a whole and made them essential co-determinants of their domestic culture.

Looking first at India, we realize that her main 'exportable' cultural product was Buddhism. It travelled first south, to Sri Lanka, and north beyond the Pamir to the heart of Central Asia. Then, in the first centuries of the Christian era, it turned eastward; in the south to Indonesia and Indochina, in the north via the Tarim basin to China. In the eleventh century, after three or four centuries of hesitation, the last great enclave between China and India, Tibet, opted definitively for Buddhism and began to develop its own Lamaist variant.

As has been shown in section 7.6., the reception of Buddhism in China was a lengthy process. Buddhism had to accommodate many local peculiarities and, above all, lived in symbiosis with the parallel domestic religion, Taoism, and with the domestic philosophy of the state, Confucianism. In contrast to Tibet, where Lamaist Buddhism became an exclusive cultural orientation, Chinese Buddhism, differentiated into many schools, created only one of China's three basic cultural determinants. With its differentiation, Buddhism in China recalls the position of Buddhism in India; it has to be stressed, however, that the various schools of Chinese Buddhism were not simply a reflection of the Indian spectrum.

From China Buddhism undertook a further journey eastward, to Korea and Japan, and southward, to Vietnam. Buddhism began to penetrate to Korea towards the end of the fourth century AD; the main thrust to Japan occurred in the middle of the seventh, and to Vietnam towards the end of the tenth century. In the thirteen century, the Lamaist Buddhism of Tibet expanded to the north-east, and became the national creed of the Mongols.

The radiation of Chinese Buddhism was either preceded (in Korea and Vietnam) or accompanied (in Japan) by the spread of Confucianism. Eventually it was not so much Buddhism or Confucianism in their own right but the Chinese mix of them which mattered. It was above all the imperial prestige and glory which invited imitation. Thus it was the reception of the Chinese civilization rather than of a particular religion or philosophy which brought the originally Indian ideas to the shores of the northern Pacific.

There was nothing peculiar about that. The original, Indian, Buddhism also travelled to South-East Asia in conjunction with all the other Indian religious beliefs and cults. As has been shown in section 6.4., all the main streams of the 'religious parliament' of India were brought to Farther India, which by the middle of the first millennium AD had become a thriving part of the Pan-Indian civilization.

Furthermore, whether the particular civilization spread from China or from India, its domestication never implied a total assimilation, as was generally the case with the spread of Christianity up to the seventeenth century. Nor was there any parallel with the Islamic community which, as has been shown in Chapter 5, was superimposed as the dominant layer upon people of non-Islamic religions who were to be tolerated as the subject communities. The Indian and Chinese paradigm allowed for a considerable degree of selective reception, for new combinations of adopted elements and, above all, for a blending of these with the domestic ideas and traditions to form a specific type of civilization.

Thus, as has been shown in sections 6.4 and 6.5, various combinations of Buddhism and Hinduism flourished in Farther India and, from the eleventh to twelfth century AD, the continental part of this subcontinent had the Theravada version of Indian Buddhism as its socio-cultural backbone.

8.2 THE 'LITTLE CHINA' OF KOREA AND HER SPLENDID ISOLATION

Of the Far Eastern countries Korea was the first to come into the orbit of Chinese influence. During the period of Warring States (453–221 BC) many Chinese refugees settled in Korea and the policy of the Han dynasty was aimed at exacting tribute from Korea as a token of Chinese suzerainty. Then, after the empire collapsed and disintegrated, it was mainly Buddhism which shaped the development of civilization in Korea, which was for most of the time divided into three kingdoms. The trend continued during China's renewed striving for hegemony under the early Tang, but with the ninth century AD Buddhism began to lose its vital momentum in both China and Korea.

In 1258, after a war lasting 27 years, Korea submitted to the sovereignty of the Mongolian dynasty in China. The Mongols' official support of Buddhism in general and of its Lamaist version in particular produced a strong anti-Buddhist reaction. Although after the expulsion of the Mongols in the thirteenth century a pro-Buddhist faction continued to be strongly represented amongst the Korean nobility, the rulers of the dynasty installed in Korea in 1392 decided, after a vain attempt at reform, to secularize the monasteries and pagodas and thus to deprive Buddhism of its institutional basis and influence in the country. Neo-Confucianism became the official doctrine and Confucian scholars exercised such a degree of control over the education of the people that Korea became, in Chinese eyes, a little China.[1]

The Ri dynasty (1392–1910) also followed the socio-economic pattern of the Chinese dynasties – conspicuous improvements to begin with and widespread decay towards the end. The confiscation of monasterial and aristocratic property brought about a more equitable distribution of land, but the new power elite of the literati-mandarins gradually acquired the lion's share of the landed property and largely substituted material interests for the ethico-political guidance of the people. Nevertheless the fifteenth century AD seems to have been a peak period in the development of Korean culture. Having devised their own phonetic script (*enmun*, inaugurated in 1446)[2] which suited their language much better than the Chinese script used up to then, and knowing how to print books using moveable type, the Koreans found themselves at the forefront of publishing activity in the Far East.

Unfortunately the social climate did not favour new literary ventures and the mandarinate squandered its energies in mutual bickering. In the sixteenth century Korean society experienced increasing discontent and a number of peasant uprisings, the result of widespread corruption in the government service.

In such a situation Korea became an easy prey for foreign powers. Fortunately the Japanese attacks of 1592 and 1597 were fended off – the first with Chinese help, the second because the Japanese themselves withdrew as a result of the death of their leader. But then both Korea and China were exposed to one and the same formidable foe – the Manchus, who in two campaigns (1627 and 1637) made Korea their satellite, before establishing their own dynasty in China in 1644.

In the general malaise generated by these mishaps Korea closed her doors to foreigners. Contact with the Japanese was restricted to a single harbour (Fusan), and contact with the Manchus and Chinese was confined to government officials who had only one place where they could meet their foreign partners. It is worth emphasizing that the policy of strict isolation was by no means a Japanese speciality. Of all the Far Eastern countries Korea was in this respect the most consistent and persistent. But to be fair we have to point out that the first to adopt this policy were the Chinese, who as early as the fifteenth century had established on the Korean border a sixty-mile wide zone from which all the population was removed; all contacts with Korea were concentrated in a single town.[3]

Understandably, the Korean policy of isolation also applied to contacts with Europeans. Yet in this respect Korea was better protected by her geographical position. She was sheltered from the land to the west by China and from the sea by the Japanese islands. Nevertheless from the 1830s onwards Catholic missionaries (mainly of French origin) managed to penetrate secretly to Korea and gain converts. As an antidote to their 'Western Teaching', the young intellectuals began to build up a syncretic 'Eastern Teaching' from elements of Confucianism, Buddhism and Taoism. But the government was afraid of any innovation and decided to suppress both Western and Eastern teaching alike. A half-hearted French intervention was easily repulsed. No other attempt was made by Western powers. Korea was to be opened up to the worldwide challenge of Europeanism by another Far Eastern nation – Japan.

8.3   THE LONG MARCH OF VIETNAM

Vietnam is the modern name of a nation which, under various names, has a history reaching back more than 2000 years. The main outward mark of this history is the persistent, though periodically interrupted, move southwards. From their original homes in south-east China the forefathers of the present-day Vietnamese were pushed to the far south of China and the Red River basin, where from 111 BC they were subject to Chinese rule, which continued until 939 AD.

This was a sufficiently long period to make the Vietnamese a member nation of the Chinese civilization. As their adoption of this civilization took place at a time when Confucianism was its dominant ideology, it is no wonder that the Vietnamese culture and institutions were also framed by the Confucian world-view. And as so often happened with peripheral nations, Confucianism remained the backbone of Vietnamese culture even at the time when in China Buddhism and Taoism were stealing much of its prestige and popularity.

Only towards the end of the tenth century, when Vietnam was already independent, did Buddhism and Taoism join the traditional Confucianism as official doctrines. It was in particular Buddhism which enjoyed government support. The new religious orientation brought the Vietnamese closer to the neighbouring nations of South East Asia, the Thais and Laotians who, from the twelfth century onwards, looked to Buddhism as their main source of religious inspiration.

On the other hand, the relationship with the Chams, who inhabited what is now central Vietnam and who adhered to the brahmanic version of Indian civilization, became increasingly hostile. Whereas in the previous epoch Champa occasionally went on the offensive and Vietnam had to be protected by her Chinese masters, from the beginning of the second millennium AD Vietnam resumed her march towards the south. A 500-year struggle with the Chams set in. Though often interrupted by conciliatory policies on both sides, especially at the time of the Mongolian invasion (1257–88) and after, when a dynastic marriage took place which was meant to seal the friendship of Champa with Vietnam, it eventually became a life and death struggle. During the years 1370–90 the Chams were on the advance and successfully raided the Vietnamese capital, but the fifteenth century saw their demise. The final solution was however delayed by the Chinese occupation (1407–28), resulting from a call for help by an unsuccessful pretender to the throne in Hanoi. Twenty-one years of Chinese rule acquainted Vietnam with superior administrative and military techniques, a welcome contribution to the final phase of the struggle with Champa (1446–71), during which the latter lost most of her territory. The decimated Chams lingered on for another 250 years on a substantially reduced territory, until, under renewed pressure from Vietnam, they seceded to Cambodia.

As in Korea, the fifteenth century in Vietnam was a period of cultural blossoming and probably also of comparative economic prosperity; the sixteenth century was marked by internal strife, which in the 1620s culminated in the division of the country between north and south, each ruled by its own mandarin dynasty.

Yet this division by no means brought about an end to the Vietnamese southward drive. A large-scale infiltration of Vietnamese settlers into Cambodia set in, accompanied by repeated interventions and annexations of territory. Thus the Vietnamese divided Cambodia into two parts, one of which, later called Cochin-China (the area round the Mekong estuary), was entrusted in 1698 to a Vietnamese governor. During the eighteenth century it was settled by the Vietnamese to such an extent that the Khmers virtually disapeared in the flood of the new population.

That the remaining sparsely-populated part of Cambodia (present-day Campuchea) was saved from a similar fate was the result of the international constellation, which confronted Vietnam with a new challenge. As in Korea, so too in Vietnam the Japanese acted in a way as instruments for the impact of the European West. Catholic missionaries expelled in 1614 from Japan found refuge in southern Vietnam, which at that time was culturally and administratively not yet as well integrated as the north, and won many converts there. The script, known as *quoc-ngu*, constructed by these missionaries for the Vietnamese language on the basis of the Latin script, gradually became generally accepted.

The re-unification of Vietnam in 1802 was the outcome of a struggle lasting 25 years; the internal war started with the insurrection against the southern dynasty and culminated in the conquest of the north by the insurgents. But then, with the help of artillery and instructors supplied by the French King Louis XVI, the last surviving member of the southern dynasty won the day and became emperor of reunited Vietnam.

Understandably, the rule of the first emperor was favourable to the Catholic faith; his successors however preferred the neo-Confucian orientation, and began to suppress Christian activities. This was a signal for France, then protector of the Catholic faith, to intervene. Between 1858 and 1893 Vietnam, Cambodia and Laos were all transformed into parts of French Indochina, consisting of one colony (Cochin China) and protectorates for the other territories. Of all the Far Eastern countries Vietnam alone became directly subject to a European power.

8.4 CREATIVE RECEPTION IN THE LAND OF THE RISING SUN

8.4.1 The Japanese Predicament

Of all the recipients of foreign civilizations in the Far East the most independent was Japan. The whole of Japanese history can be characterized as a continuous interplay of a vigorous *genius loci* with the irresistible influence of a particular foreign civilization, an interplay which, in the course of time, produced various combinations of the two elements, both on the cultural and on the economico-political plane.

The combination of domestic with foreign elements is nothing exceptional in the history of individual civilizations. But usually, one part of the combination creates the axis and the other part constitutes the admixture to the compound. This means that either the domestic tradition continues to prevail and the civilization in question preserves its identity, or the key elements of a foreign civilization, i.e. the new world-view, values and institutions, are accepted as dominant, downgrading the domestic tradition to a kind of local colour.

Japan had to resolve this dilemma twice in her history: firstly in the seventh century AD when her rulers decided to follow the Chinese example; secondly in the nineteenth century, with the turn towards the Western, Euro-American, civilization. The second case is a recent phenomenon and the assessment of its long-term implications requires a certain degree of caution. At the time of writing it seems that it might be a similar kind of reception to the one witnessed in the case of the Islamization of Iran and Indonesia. But the historical experience of Japan twelve centuries earlier should warn us against drawing any hasty conclusions.

While embracing the Chinese civilization Japan did not go as far as Korea or Vietnam. The Japanese preserved several salient features of their own tradition, which subsequently grew beyond being mere admixtures and became ingredients of a particular socio-cultural and economico-political identity of the Japanese civilization.

As elsewhere, the Chinese paradigm became attractive to Japan because of the combination of the high prestige of its culture and the efficiency of the imperial administration. At that time (the turn of the sixth and seventh centuries AD) Chinese culture was deeply imbued with Buddhism, with its gentle and sophisticated attitude to life, but at the same time Confucian values of filial piety constituted a key factor in the ideological integration of Chinese society. In China the emperor did not face the kind of problem which confronted the Japanese ruler who, though deemed to be of godly origin (i.e. in theory more than a Mandatee of Heaven) merely occupied the position of chief of an unruly tribal confederation. Last but not least, the material superiority of China in all walks of life – a superiority which became more evident as trade developed – was another major spur to attempts at emulation.

But the Japanese were not ready to give up their key views and values without trying to make them constitutive elements of the foreign civilization which framed their outlook. We can distinguish three main areas in which the Japanese *genius loci* followed its own path while accommodating a foreign paradigm. First, as the *tennō* (the title, meaning heavenly sovereign, was adopted in emulation of the Chinese example) was believed to be a descendent of the sun-goddess Amaterasu, there was no question of a withdrawal of the Celestial Mandate as in China. The only alteration was to deprive the tennō of real power, without however taking away his status and sacerdotal functions. Thus instead of a Chinese-style imperial bureaucracy Japan developed the ingenious dualism of emperor and shogun, positions which in particular circumstances underwent further duplications.

Secondly, the Japanese could not abandon their own religious tradition, the Shintō. Their deities, the *kami*, were, in essence, awe-inspiring natural phenomena whose worship, to paraphrase E.O. Reischauer, was not an organized religion with a clear teaching or moral code but a loose conglomeration of cults with a deep sense of ritual and bodily purity.[4] Though the foreign religion which the Japanese took over was Buddhism, i.e. a religion which unlike its Christian or Islamic counterparts was not against a more or less intimate coexistence with the primitive local cults, in the Japanese case this kind of *convivium* went much farther than for instance in South-East Asia. In Japan the Buddhists themselves suggested the identification of the Shintō deities with the Buddhas and bodhisattvas, a straightforward syncretism which later became known as *Ryōbu Shintō*.

Thirdly, the martial men in the Japanese power elite could not be easily replaced by or combined on an equal footing with the scholar-bureaucrats or eunuch officials, as was the case with China. There was a period in Japanese history when even the Buddhist monks became warriors. Eventually the warlords, whether laymen or clerical, had to be harnessed in an original way, with the lay warriors remaining, at least in theory, the top stratum of society. The Chinese social system could be transplanted to Japan neither in its ideal (theoretical) form, nor in the real form in which it operated in China. Japan was to develop her own social system in which naked pragmatism tended to overrule ideological consider-ations.

8.4.2   Japan under the Spell of the Chinese Civilization

The interplay of the three salient elements of the *genius loci* with the propensity to emulate a foreign example lies at the root of the cultural and structural changes in Japanese history.

The seventh century AD was characterized by the growing predominance of the receptionist tendency. From the Prince Regent Shōtoku declaration of intent in 604 (in the so-called Seventeen Article Constitution), via the *Taika* (i.e. great change) reform decreed by Emperor Tenchi in 646, to the *Taihō* (great treasure) Code of 701, the emperors tried hard to transplant Chinese institutions, laws and habits into Japanese soil.

However all these attempts soon revealed that it is easier to transplant the form than the content of government institutions, and to imitate material rather than spiritual aspects of a civilization. Thus it is no wonder that the most successful imitation was the new capital, Nara, which functioned in that capacity from 710 to 784, and for which the model was the Chinese capital of the day, Changan. This was also the case with Heian (later known as Kyōto), which became the capital in 795.

On the other hand, it proved impossible to establish a scholarly trained, Confucian-type government service. Native sentiment con-tinued to consider birth a more important qualification for ministerial appointments.[5] As most land was possessed by 'big houses' (aristocratic clans) it was also extremely difficult to transfer to Japan the equal-field system which was then becoming a widespread fact of life in China, perhaps for the first time in her imperial history. Problems also arose with the reception of the Buddhist institutions. In the 8th century Buddhist monks, looked upon as the 'guardians of the state', acquired considerable influence at the court. In 769 the Empress Shōtoku (a namesake of the earlier Prince Regent) promoted a faith healing monk of humble origins to the chancellorship. This episode, however, had fatal consequences both for women's power and for the power of the monks. Shōtoku (d. 770) was the last woman on the Japanese throne, and the aristocracy headed by the powerful clan of the Fujiwaras closed their ranks in order not to admit parvenus to government positions.

The six Buddhist sects which established themselves in eighth-century Japan were not particularly popular. No wonder that the sensible monks, like Gyōki, realized the necessity of assimilating substantial elements of the native religion, the Shintō, into the Buddhist tenets. At the beginning of the ninth century new Buddhist sects from China were introduced to Japan by prominent monks, such as *Tientai* (*Tendai*), brought in by Saichō, and Tantric *Chen jen* (*Shingon*), imported by Kūkai. Yet the greatest impact was made by the latter's teaching that Buddhas and bodhisattvas revealed themselves in part in Japan as the Shintoist deities (*kami*), a teaching which removed worries about divided loyalties from the minds of the devotees.

Another problem which had to be resolved was the adaptation of the Chinese script, suited to a basically monosyllabic language lacking inflections but using various tones, to the Japanese language, which is polysyllabic, inflected, without tones and without clusters of consonants. It took several centuries before the two forms of the adaptation, the more complex *hiragana* (85 Chinese characters written cursively, each representing a syllable or vowel) and the more simple *katakana* (abbreviated Chinese characters standing for 48 syllables virtually sufficient for the Japanese language) became widely used. Amazingly, there eventually prevailed the tendency to combine both these types of writing with the original Chinese script in the same piece of written work. Though there are now established rules for this kind of combination, it is, from the rational point of view, an unnecessary complication for a language ideally suited to a simple syllabic alphabet.

There is here a striking paradox: the culturally more sinicized Koreans, who however speak a language related to the Japanese, developed their own phonetic script (enmun); likewise, the Vietnamese, with a language structure similar to that of the Chinese, eventually accepted the phonetic quoc-ngun designed for their language by the Catholic missionaries. On the other hand the – in other respects – most independent Japanese remained, in their writing, the most attached to the Chinese example.[6]

8.4.3   Towards Japan's Own Social System: The Kamakura Shogunate

As the transplant of Chinese statesmanship failed and the traditional system of clans (*uji*) could no longer function as its substitute, the further development of the Japanese polity involved a new adaptation. A new system crystallized from the residues of the traditional one and from the impact of the fragments of the Chinese system which the receptionist policy succeeded in implanting on Japanese soil.

The consequences of the Chinese implant relevant for this further development were twofold. First, there was the court aristocracy, which ousted the educated bureaucracy from all the functions of government administration in the capital, leaving the posts in the provinces in the hands of the local warrior-type aristocracy. Secondly, there were the disgruntled peasants who instead of receiving secure holdings and a tolerable burden of taxation, were exposed to all sorts of extortion, resulting from the insufficient supply of land for allocation and from the unscrupulous behaviour of government agents. It also has to be stressed that the imperial government abolished the traditional autonomy of the villages.

Because of the fact that the central government could not enforce its measures concerning the land held by the aristocracy, only peasants on imperial land were subjected to regular tax in kind, the labour tax (corvée), and military service. Each soldier had to fit himself out from his own means, and in his absence his dependants were not relieved by a proportional reduction of their duties. Government attempts to alleviate the burden of the peasantry by loans went wide of the mark; the provincial governors exacted exorbitant rates of interest and often made these loans compulsory in order to enrich themselves.[7] For many peasants the situation became desperate and they either turned to brigandage or looked to powerful people for protection. The latter option was available mainly in outlying provinces, which at that time were inhabited by the aboriginal, non-Japanese population.

The main island, Honshū, was only settled in one half by the Japanese whilst the other, the northern part, was inhabited by aboriginal tribes whom the Japanese continually fought and pushed further to the north. Medieval Japan, like seventeenth to nineteenth-century North America, had her frontier, the Emishi and the Ainu being the counterparts of the Red Indians. The northern tip of Honshū was not wrested from the Ainu until the sixteenth century.

The new land taken from those peoples was, as a rule, given in vast stretches either to the court nobles or to religious institutions, i.e. Buddhist monasteries or Shintō shrines, ownership being perpetual and tax-free. The fugitive peasants found employment there under more favourable conditions than on the state-owned land. Also the small-holders in the adjacent areas were keen to trade off the title to their holdings for the advantages resulting from the fewer duties required by the landlord than by the state.

This was the beginning of large estates or manors (*shō*) with commended peasants, hired labourers, and military staff. Each of them, including the manorial lord, had a certain right to the income (*shiki*) which itself was alienable and further divisible. This manorial system also spread to the interior of the country, where both the great landlords (who were often at the same time provincial governors) and the small-holders were interested in commendations. The attempts of several emperors to stem this tide were of little avail.

Thus there gradually developed what A. Gonthier called the 'feudality outside the state'. It was a social structure very different from that which had been postulated by the Taika-Taihō edicts and which survived, as a separate entity, mainly in the imperial capital Heian, in the small number of towns, and in the shrinking area that still remained at the disposition of the central government.[8] But the official, civil, administration and manorial systems had their acute problems of sovereignty, discipline and efficiency.

From 967 until 1068 the central government was totally in the hands of the Fujiwara clan, who derived their power from the help they gave to the emperor at the time of the Taika reform, and from marrying their daughters off to members of the imperial house. By dint of skilful manipulation the Fujiwara succeeded in depriving the throne of all real power. When eventually Emperor Gosanjō

(1068–72), exceptionally not the son of a Fujiwara mother, attempted to reverse the trend, he found his hands so tied by ceremonial duties that he used an unprecedented stratagem: in 1072 he formally abdicated in favour of his son, a minor, and retired to a monastery, from where he could then better pursue his desired policy than from the throne. A strange position, but one which was perpetuated for about 70 years. From 1086 until 1156, the Fujiwara power was matched by the power and even supremacy of cloistered emperors. Thus, within the official structure of the state, there were three seats of authority: the nominal emperor (*tennō*), the office of the cloistered emperor (*inchō*), and the ramified Fujiwara clan, with between them an interplay rife with manipulation and intrigue, and exacting a tax of blood that was paid, as a rule, by lesser people.

In contrast to the tug-of-war in the official sphere, the unofficial, manorial structure developed into an open battlefield. As military conscription had long been abolished (in 792), the local governors organized their own companies of warriors (*bushidan*), the nucleus of what was later to develop into the military estate (almost a military caste). The weaker leaders of such warrior bands commended themselves to the protection and leadership of the mightier ones. Thus the bushidan gradually developed a hierarchical structure with a bilateral lord-vassal (*shujū*) relationship. Alongside the manorial system, this contributed the second pillar of what may be described as Japanese feudalism.[9]

The almost continuous warfare in the provinces affected all walks of civilian life. Whilst art found refuge at the court in Heian, where it flourished with an amazing vigour and against the background of a refined sense of formal beauty, religious life had to contend against heavy odds in the countryside. The Buddhists reacted in two contrasting ways. On the one hand, they sought consolation in an emotional piety relying on divine grace and salvation by faith rather than by good works. On the other hand, monks began to play the war game: first hiring their own *bushidan*, then arming themselves and learning the military arts. In the eleventh century fortified monasteries and monkish warbands (*sōhei*) became an additional element of the Japanese power structure.

The emergence of 'feudality outside the state' was an opportunity to test the strength of arms, bonds of loyalty and skill at deception. But in order to become an overlord, a leader of a faction in these circumstances, some sort of legitimation was also needed. Thus, the main contending clans, Taira and Minamoto, were both distant branches of the imperial family. Their rivalry issued in an all-out war, in which Taira won the first round but eventually, in 1185, Yoritomo Minamoto utterly destroyed his rivals and became the undisputed apex of the feudal pyramid. To secure his position, he imposed on each vassal estate (shō) his steward (*jitō*), and on each province or group of provinces, a constable (*shugo*) from his leading vassals.

In 1192 the emperor acknowledged the *fait accompli* and bestowed upon Yoritomo the title of *Seii-tai-shogun* ('Barbarian-Quelling Generalissimo') with his seat in Kamakura. There Yoritomo established his own administration, known as the *bakufu* (i.e. tent government), a name which characterized the military nature of this institution in contrast to the civil imperial government in Kyoto.

Thus the most salient peculiarity of the Japanese political system i.e. the dualism of the imperial court and the shogunate, the latter more powerful than the former, was formally established. When in 1221 the cloistered emperor of the day attempted with the help of a few military and monastic supporters to shake off the shogun's power and failed, large-scale confiscations and the imposition of control officers at the imperial court further extended the shogun's power.

The strength of the new institution was demonstrated when Yoritomo's sons failed as leaders (and the most talented of his clan was eliminated by Yoritomo himself) and real power passed to the Hōjō family of Yoritomo's widow; only figureheads from a noble family were elevated to the post of shogun and the Hōjō ruled as their regents (*shikken*). Thus a strange situation emerged, whereby neither the emperor nor the shogun, but the latter's deputy, was the real ruler. In 1232 the new situation was formally codified (The Jōei Code), this putting it beyond any doubt that the Taika reform and Taihō Code were in many respects dead letters.

8.4.4 The Domestication of Buddhism in Japan

The Hōjō regency, which lasted from 1219 to 1333 and thus coincided with the greater part of the duration of the Kamakura shogunate, happened to mark a fortunate period in Japanese history. Comparative calm and order allowed the peasants, working as free (i.e. not serf) tenants or commended small-holders on the estates, as well as other commoners, to enjoy the fruits of their labour more than previously. The village self-government (*mura*) abolished at the time of the reception of the Chinese model, was re-introduced and became the basic unit of local administration. More people were in a position to participate in cultural life, which both in the arts and in religion witnessed the supreme achievements of what may be called the Shintō-Buddhist civilization.

As we mentioned above, the Japanese Buddhists reacted in two ways to the widespread and incessant warfare; militarization on the one hand and pietization (to coin a term) on the other. Whilst the former response was a blind alley, the latter completed the domestication of Buddhism in Japan.

The Japanization of Buddhism was closely connected with the idea of reform, with the need for more sincerity and ardour in religious life, which had been damaged by an excessive devotion to worldly interests and a lack of discipline among the monks. Against this background, the turbulent end of the twelfth century gave birth to two outstanding schools of Japanese Buddhism, the Pure Land (*Jōdo*), founded by the extraordinarily gentle monk Hōnen Shōnin, and the True Pure Land (*Jōdo Shin*), founded by Hōnen's disciple, Shinran.

To borrow Sir C. Eliot's words, Hōnen, 'in disturbed and comfortless times preached a simple creed which offered salvation to those who could justify themselves neither by learning nor by good works and gave a decisive impetus to one of the greatest religious movements which Japan has witnessed'.[10]

Shinran developed his ideas while his teacher was still alive, and believed that they incorporated Hōnen's true intentions. In abolishing celibacy, Shinran brought Buddhism closer to the Japanese – and indeed to the broader Far Eastern – ethos, in which the family constituted the basic social and religious unit and thus the firmest bond of loyalty. Like Hōnen, Shinran stressed the way of devotion (*bhakti marga*, to use the terms of Indian Buddhism) in religious practice. As their main, in fact exclusive, object of devotion was Amida Buddha, they can be said to have introduced into Buddhism an element of monotheism.

But the way of faith and devotion alone (*tariki*), relying more on divine grace than anything else, was not palatable to all seekers after religious truth. At that time the monk Ensai popularized in Japan the Chinese adaptation of the Indian school *dhyana* (in Chinese *chan*); shorn of the neo-Confucian and aestheticizing elements which this school acquired in China, in Japan it absorbed the rough spirit of the Kamakura machiocracy. Thus a typically

Japanese school of Buddhism, Zen, took shape. Seeking salvation in a concentrated mind and self-discipline (*jiriki*) instead of relying on divine grace, Zen became a religion tailored to the military caste, which from the end of the twelfth century to the nineteenth century constituted the backbone of the Japanese polity.

The second half of the thirteenth century brought yet another element into the Japanese search for a religious orientation. In all civilizations there have always been people who do not find religious pluralism comfortable; so also in Japan, an attempt was launched at a unified approach. But as usual, the attempt ended by creating an additional division in Japanese Buddhism, the Lotus sect. Its initiator was the monk Nichiren (1222–82), who sought to achieve unification by reviving an older Buddhist school, the Tendai, which had been introduced to Japan from China at the beginning of the ninth century by one of the patriarchs of Buddhism in Japan, Saichō, posthumously known as Dengyō Daishi.

Nichiren preached the unification not only of Buddhism but also of the Japanese nation; realizing the enormity of his task, he did not eschew force as a means of achieving his aims. His self-righteousness and intolerance twice landed him in exile and his followers became known for their fanaticism rather than for any genuinely religious qualities.

On the other hand, the religious virtues of Buddhism spread beyond Buddhism itself. Shintō, the native religion, lost a good deal of its original simple nature-worship and, apparently under Buddhist influence, developed its magico-ritual and ethico-philosophical dimensions as well. There appeared a tendency for the lesser deities to be absorbed by the greater ones, and the magico-ritual symbols began to be interpreted in terms of ethical values; the idea of pantheism also emerged.[11]

8.4.5 The Time of Troubles and the Restructuring of the Society

The Mongolian eruption which in the thirteenth century affected most of Asia touched Japan only marginally. Two attacks, one in 1274 and the other in 1281, were launched on Japan from Korea. In both instances bad weather turned against the Mongols, who had to withdraw with a decimated navy and heavy losses. The storms were viewed as the divine winds of destruction (*kamikaze*), which strengthened the Japanese belief in their divine origin. Thus by the end of the thirteenth century Japan was triumphant. The prestige of the warriors in the south-west who had to bear the brunt of the Mongolian attacks increased to such an extent that it could not be matched by an comensurate material reward.

At the same time however, the country as a whole began to suffer from the growing disproportion between the needs of the military administration and the actual revenues. Since in addition the practice of divided inheritance caused the parcelling out of family claims on income (*shiki*), the shogunal personnel were faced with a decline in living standards, which they tended to avoid by borrowing. By the end of the thirteenth century the indebtedness of the warrior caste became a widespread phenomenon. The occasional cancellation of debts undertaken by the shogunate could provide only individual and temporary help, and in general made borrowing conditions still more difficult.

The latter part of the thirteenth century also saw a further weakening of imperial power. When in 1272 the cloistered Emperor Gosaga died without making clear the order of succession, and two lines of his sons claimed the heritage for themselves and for their descendants, the shogunate arranged for an alternation of both lines in the succession. Yet in 1318 Emperor Godaigo of the junior line attempted to change the arrangement in favour of his line exclusively, and also to use the opportunity to get rid of the shogunal tutelage, by instigating plots against the Kamakura regime. Though exiled by the shogun's forces, he managed to escape, and with the help of the clans hostile to the Hōjō regency, restored the imperial power in 1333 for three years (the so-called *Kemmu* Restoration). But such a solution was not to the taste of the military, who easily matched this move by declaring their support for the other, senior, branch of the imperial house. From a prolonged and complicated struggle (1336–68), in which prominent warrior houses took part on both sides, a new shogunal dynasty emerged victorious: that of Ashikaga. In 1392, they eventually managed to end the existence of the two contending courts.

In contrast to the Kamakura shogunate under the Hōjō regency, the Ashikaga held the position of the shogun themselves, but their administration was much less comprehensive and efficient than that of the Hōjō. This is the more striking inasmuch as the Ashikaga transferred their seat to the imperial capital Kyōto and did their best to integrate their regime with that of the imperial court. This led A. Gonthier to describe the time of the Ashikaga shogunate (1338–1573) as the period of 'feudalism within the state'.

Yet the Ashikaga shogunate has also been characterized as a period of anarchy and at the same time as the epoch of a new adaptation. The anarchic conditions led to a new wave of hierarchization within the power elite and to the concentration of property. This process was facilitated by the development of more costly military equipment and fortifications, and above all by the coming into effect of an older law of inheritance, which abolished the practice of divided heritage and gave the father the right to decide which of his sons would inherit the whole estate.

The competition between religious institutions also played a substantial role. The great Buddhist monasteries, with adjacent Shintō shrines and with smaller vassal monasteries throughout the country, and with large warrior bands at their command, became formidable centres of autonomous power. Paradoxically it was the Pure Land sect rather than Zen which took a prominent part in this new wave of monastic militarization. It seems that in the case of Japan devotion and reliance on divine grace were ethically less edifying than the path of self-reliance and discipline.

The process of concentration of property and hierarchization of the elite which began in the middle of the fourteenth century and gathered momentum in the 1470s continued until the end of the sixteenth century. The Japanese, imitating the Chinese terminology, called the period between 1477 and 1568 the Period of Warring States (*Sengoku jidai*). It has to be stressed, however, that the war raged only in the provinces; the capital Kyōto was spared the troubles and enjoyed a cultural blossoming in which, for the first time in Japanese history, broad masses of the population participated. The cultural radiation from the capital reached both the rising merchant class in the towns and the peasantry in the villages. Amazingly, as before in the ninth to tenth centuries (known as the Heian period), so too during this period (named after the seat of the Ashikaga shoguns in Kyōto, Muromachi) war did not prevent the arts from flourishing. The credit for this belongs in particular to the Zen Buddhists, whose keen interest in foreign culture meant that new ideas and styles were brought to Japan. The Zen temples were also instrumental in reviving the trade with China and Korea, which in the previous period had almost come to a standstill.

8.4.6 The New Structure and the Struggle for a New Type of Polity

As a result of the drastic shake-up of loyalties and ownership arrangements the whole of Japan was by the middle of the sixteenth century redivided into several hundred new, more or less independent, domains whose owners bore the title *daimyō* (meaning the great name), or in the case of a religious institution, *hon* (i.e. principal). Owners of smaller, vassal estates, the *shomyō* (i.e. little name), also enjoyed a considerable degree of independence. All the rest of the military caste served as vassals or sub-vassals of the above-mentioned owners and partly also as direct vassals of the shogun. The traditional estate or manor (*shō*) ceased to be an administrative unit and the associated rights to revenue (*shiki*) were, in the case of upper grades of vassalage, replaced by beneficial holdings (*shoryō*); these holdings brought with them not only administrative and financial, but also judicial jurisdiction. All this brought about a considerable differentiation amongst the military nobility.

On the other hand the position of the peasantry tended to become more uniform. The difference between the tenants and the commended farmers virtually disappeared. As time went on, the villages became more autonomous. By taking over the collective responsibility for paying taxes, which on average amounted to *c*.40 per cent of the crop, they increased their administrative power, and it was up to them, not up to the fief holders, to decide whether people could leave the land or not.

The towns, which until then had mainly been administrative centres, more and more became home to craftsmen and merchants. This development was due mainly to the revival of international trade, preceded by a long period of piratical attacks on foreign shipping.[12] New towns emerged mainly in the south-west and under the auspices of monasteries which by a contract with the merchant guild fixed their mutual rights and duties. Many of these towns had already in the course of the fifteenth century become strong enough to defend their freedoms, or rather privileges (administrative and judicial autonomy and liberation from the labour tax), without monastic protection. Within the towns, however, the guilds (*za*) pursued a policy of economic regulation and restrictions on the number of businesses.

People in the countryside also became more economy-minded.

The daimyō, though military men par excellence, began to devote some effort to the amelioration of their estates; new irrigation and land reclamation schemes were helped by the co-operative labours of the villagers.[13]

The growing urban society also provided an extended market for cultural values. New art-forms such as lyrical drama and farce, painting emancipated from the Chinese fashion, garden architecture, and the tea ceremonies, became typical of the Japanese culture of that epoch, known in Japanese history as the Muromachi era.

The restructuring of loyalties and ownership arrangements gave birth to a structure that was virtually a hierarchy minus an effective apex. At the same time a new factor appeared on the shores of Japan: Portuguese ships with soldiers and firearms, merchants and missionaries on board.[14] The Japanese merchants were keen on commerce with the newcomers and often regarded their religion as a bargaining counter. But in the south-western island of Kyūshu the dedicated missionaries from the Society of Jesus were able to notch up many sincere conversions. At that time Japanese Buddhism was suffering from a certain malaise and the most successful rival of Catholic Christianity was neo-Confucianism, which became the fashion amongst educated people.

The main contest, however, did not break out between the two foreign world-views, but between two domestic socio-economic orientations: one predominantly urban, favouring free trade and based in the south-west of the country, the other predominantly rural, favouring regulation and based in the eastern part of the main island, Honshū.

The contest was fought in three stages which are known by the names of the three condottieri who were successively masters of Japan: Oda Nobunaga, Toyotomi Hideyoshi and Tokugawa Ieyasu. Only when the struggle was over could its socio-economic parameters be clearly identified.

Oda Nobunaga, a squire from the lower nobility, who as the vice-shogun ruled Japan from 1568 to 1582, managed to compel most daimyōs to obey him, destroyed the military power of the leading monasteries, and sequestrated their property. As a promoter of economic growth Nobunaga supported the new type of guilds (*rakusa*) which stood for free trade; he built new ships, new harbours and roads, unified the currency, abolished internal customs-duties and waged an effective war against piracy, a constant menace to foreign trade. Nobunaga's benevolence towards the Christians was the obverse side of his dislike of the power aspirations of the Buddhist monasteries. In 1580 the Portuguese Jesuits were given the harbour town of Nagasaki for their trade and missionary activities.

Nobunaga's vassal and successor, the first non-aristocratic ruler of Japan, Toyotomi Hideyoshi, gave further support to the urban economy and free trade, but tightened his grip on the rural sector, both in a political and in an economic sense. A tight discipline was introduced into the hierarchical structure of vassalage and the taxes from agriculture, forestry and mining were substantially increased. Hideyoshi also became suspicious of the ulterior motives of the Catholic missions; he took Nagasaki from the Jesuits in 1587, and occasionally embarked on the persecution of missionaries.

But the most ambitious project which Hideyoshi undertook was the attempt to conquer Korea. The campaign started in 1592. Whether Hideyoshi wanted to drain his daimyō and samurai of their fighting energy, whether his project was the imperial dream of a parvenu, or whether both these motives were in his mind, must remain an unanswered question. The fact is that after their initial success, the Japanese were stalled by the Chinese coming to the help of the Koreans, and when Hideyoshi died in 1598, they gave up the campaign and retreated.

The imperial disaster was a signal for the forces based in the predominantly agrarian east and north to take over the lead. This happened under the leadership of the wealthy Ieyasu from the Tokugawa clan. After defeating his rivals in a decisive battle in 1600, he had himself nominated shogun by the emperor in 1603 and began to build up a new type of shogunate with its seat in Edo (later Tōkyō).

8.4.7 The Tokugawa Solution

The epoch of the Tokugawa shogunate has been the most intensively studied aspect of 'pre-modern' Japan. The focus has mainly been on the prospects for an economic take-off similar to that which in Europe was connected with the rise of capitalism. In the broader context of Japanese history, however, these prospects appear to have been much brighter in the preceding epoch of Nobunaga and Hideyoshi, who were more interested in experiments and innovations. The Tokugawa policy aimed at a petrification of the social structure at home and at the isolation of Japan from all foreign influences.

In a way it was a *tour de force* which had both a pragmatic and an ideological component.

Pragmatic considerations played the decisive role in political matters. Here the Tokugawa had few prejudices; their distrust of spontaneity was dictated by the experience of past ages. In the first instance Ieyasu undertook a large-scale redistribution of property in favour of his faithful vassals and also of himself (about 20 per cent of all cultivated land was his property). Hideyoshi's decree that vassals must not change their masters without their consent was upheld but his policy of free trade was abandoned. There was no place for the new guilds; the crafts became hereditary again and the guilds saw to their regulation.

The main dangers were seen to lie in foreign influences and in an institutionalized focus of domestic opposition. Christianity was deemed dangerous on both counts and therefore banned from Japan in 1614. In 1635 each citizen was required to register his religious affiliation and all religious sects were forced to co-operate with the shogunal government (*bakufu*) through the commissioner of shrines and temples. (Significantly the decree of 1614 also affected the extreme branch of the Buddhist Lotus sect known as *Fujufuze*, whose exclusive self-righteousness was resented.) The subsequent persecution virtually eradicated Christianity from Japan for more than two centuries.

In the 1630s the shoguns passed a series of edicts prohibiting foreign contacts. Not only were formal bans proclaimed but the possibility of bypassing them also had to be eliminated. In 1635 the Japanese were forbidden to build ships capable of navigation overseas and in 1636 all foreigners were concentrated on Deshima, a small island off Nagasaki. Foreign trade was limited to a trickle. Only a small number of Dutch merchants were allowed, subject to humiliating conditions, to trade from that island with Japan. Before the end of the seventeenth century all other foreign contacts were made impossible.

Potential domestic causes of trouble were checked with equal single-mindedness. The socio-economic position of the daimyō and their vassals was left intact; but the daimyō were forced to spend a certain time each year in the capital, where they had to keep a costly residence and house some of their family in it, virtually as hostages. The vassals had a similar duty towards their daimyōs. The system was known as the rotation of services, *sankin kōtai*. Furthermore, the building of fortresses, the nomination of daimyōs' heirs and mutual contact between daimyōs all required the shogun's approval. Understandably, the enforcement of these provisions called for a widely-ramified and efficient apparatus of control, and secret police. In general, the bakufu became highly bureaucratic.

Strict paternalism permeated the whole society. There was even a decree of 1649 which attempted to regulate the peasants' behaviour, enjoining them to get up early in the morning and to eat cereals other than rice (considered to be the staple diet of the higher estate), proclaiming bans on smoking and drinking liquor, and recommending them to repudiate lazy wives. The position of women in general deteriorated not only in fact but also in law.

In their economic policy the Tokugawa took positive measures for land improvement (extension of irrigation, marsh drainage, a halt to the division of farms below a certain size and yield, etc.). Agricultural experts of the time recommended all sorts of yield-increasing measures including a reduction in consumption by the producers. Yet the general level of taxation, which had been substantially increased by Hideyoshi, was reduced once more to the previous level of 40 per cent of the yield.

A clear dividing line was drawn between the peasantry and the warrior estate (the samurai); only the latter were entitled to arm themselves and wear swords. The general tendency was towards a caste-type demarcation of the basic professional groups.

In theory, following the neo-Confucian paradigm, there were four estates, ranged in diminishing order of prestige as follows: firstly, the warriors; secondly, the peasants, encompassing 80–85 per cent of the population; thirdly, the craftsmen; and in the lowest position the merchants. Outside and below these estates there were people engaged in 'unclean' professions such as butchers, tanners, sewage workers, executioners, etc., and also professional beggars.

In practice the merchants were becoming the most thriving and prosperous group. Though socially heavily discriminated against, they enjoyed the benefit of lower taxation. This is a particularly interesting aspect of Tokugawa policy, one of the few items where they were subject to an ideological bias. Like the European Physiocrats of a later epoch, the Tokugawa, inspired by Confucian theories, did not consider the merchants' profession a productive one and believed that by taxing it, they would only raise the level of prices. As pragmatic people, however, the Tokugawa could not allow the merchants' profits to escape government participation altogether; they imposed upon commercial activities various kinds of licences and fees which could not be as efficient as a regular form of taxation.

In striking contrast to the growing wealth of the merchants, a part of the warrior estate suffered a conspicuous economic decline. As a result of the extensive confiscations and transfers of property in the struggle for unification many samurai remained landless and had to earn their livelihood in menial administrative jobs or rural crafts. In the Tokugawa peace imposed upon them they had hardly any opportunity to exercize their real martial virtues; thus they turned them into a ritual. As time went on and dire necessity began to break down estate barriers, marriage to a daughter from the despised merchant estate came as a welcome solution to the samurai's economic plight.

The choice of neo-Confucianism as the philosophy of the state was also dictated in part by pragmatic considerations. As E.O. Reischauer put it, 'a stable, peaceful Japan needed a detailed book of rules . . . Confucianism, heavy with the wisdom and prestige of China, fitted the need admirably, providing a perhaps overly emotional people with the external controls they required to form a well-regulated, peaceful society. Confucianism emphasized etiquette and ceremony. It exploited the sound psychological principle that one learns proper attitudes by starting out with proper conduct.'[15]

The key Confucian virtue was that of filial piety, which provided the most effective pillar of loyalty in a clearly hierarchical structure of authoritarianism. In the Tokugawa era the whole population had to be imbued with this virtue. The control of education was entrusted to the neo-Confucian scholar Hayashi Razan (d. 1657); his descendants administered this department until 1868.

In this respect Confucian education found a most helpful counterpart in Zen Buddhism, which contributed remarkably to the development of the ethical code of honour (*bushidō*) for the warrior estate. In Gonthier's view, this code embodied ideas from all three basic schools of thought in Japan. The Shintō provided the sense of unconditional loyalty, Confucianism gave it its doctrine of filial piety, and Buddhism contributed the readiness to submit quietly to the inevitable. The imperatives of the bushidō imposed themselves without any prospect of compensation but for the inward satisfaction of a duty well performed.[16]

One might suggest that the epoch of the Tokugawa completed the creation of the Japanese character as it is known to us today.

The self-restraint imposed on an emotional nature created a personality structure admirably fitted for life in densely populated conurbations with little space for privacy.

But the warrior elite was not the pace-setter in all walks of life; in culture, i.e. in art and literature, it was on the one hand the court in Kyōto and on the other hand, and to a greater extent, the commoners, especially the merchants of Edo and of other cities, who set the tone. Though the ethics of the urban merchants in many respects matched those of the samurai and peasants, they developed by way of compensation for their inferior status a particular penchant for luxuries, elaborate ceremonies and sophisticated outings to the 'red-light quarters'.

8.4.8   The Twilight of the Old and the Eve of the New Reception

In a way, the Tokugawa policy can be viewed as the second wave of the Japanese reception of the Chinese civilization. Whilst in the meantime Buddhism had become thoroughly Japanized, its militaristic bent curbed and its sects reduced to helpful agencies of the regime, the society needed an integrative world-view which would cater not only for the transcendental but also for the immanent needs of the human psyche.

Confucianism fulfilled this function admirably well. Stressing obligations and not rights, it helped to overcome the tension between those who possessed prestige but no wealth and those who were in the converse position, a tension which is widely believed to have been one of the causes of the French revolution. In the Japanese context, it was not the estate or class struggle, but the conflict of loyalties that became the main issue. The dualism of shogun and emperor provided the institutional basis for such a confrontation. But the Tokugawa shogunate had more than two and a half centuries to run before the confrontation broke out.

Tensions multiplied with the economic difficulties which began to crop up with the coming of the eighteenth century; though the area under cultivation increased substantially and urban production increased as well, the samurai were getting ever deeper into debt and the treasury suffered from a lack of metal for the coinage. Repeated monetary reforms, devaluations and revaluations and abrupt price fluctuations fostered discontent.

But given the commanding position of Confucianism, there was no alternative social or economic theory available. The occasional criticism of Zhu Xi's interpretation of the Confucian traditions did not provide a sufficient foundation for new ideas. The only alternative sources of inspiration lay in the distant past or abroad. Thus, in the course of the eighteenth century, Japan experienced a revival in three areas of scholarly interest: first, Japanese history; secondly, the Japanese language (in the Tokugawa era Japanese became heavily permeated by Chinese elements); and thirdly, foreign culture.

With respect to this last, material became available from 1720, when the government allowed the importation of books written by the Jesuits in China. Towards the end of the eighteenth century contact with the Dutch was made easier, and translations of their writings became available; thus Western knowledge became known as 'Dutch Learning'.

All three areas of interest fostered a new mental outlook which, though turning backwards and outwards, prepared the ground for fundamental changes to come. Loyalty to the emperor and his family became the key factor in the teaching of the nationalistic literati, the *vagakusha*, who in the last quarter of the eighteenth century began to engage in sharp polemics with the Confucian literati, the *kangakusha*. The Russian penetration via the Kurile Islands to the proximity of the Japanese island of Hokkaidō, was a further reminder of the outside world which could not be ignored. But the Napoleonic wars turned the attention of Russia westward and the Tokugawa regime considered the danger from the north averted.

With the beginning of the nineteenth century criticism became more widespread and the government began to vacillate in its policy. In 1808 the Dutch were allowed to settle in the city of Nagasaki. Medicine was the most sought-after thing their culture had to offer. In 1824 a German doctor of medicine, Siebold, was allowed to lecture in Edo. His teaching was so successful that in 1830 the government charged him with spying and banned him from the country. Most of his pupils were compelled to commit suicide. The Dutch were again confined to the small island of Deshima and subject to tight controls.

In 1839 the enlightened minister Mizuno Tadakuni embarked on a series of economic reforms (the *Tenpo* reform) aimed at the liberalization of business activities and increasing social mobility, but in 1843 the opposition of influential daimyō forced him to resign. In 1851 the regulated economy of guilds and government monopolies was reinstated. The suggestions of European powers, that commercial contacts or ports should be opened up, were rejected. The shogunate took a hard line and showed beyond any doubt that change could only be brought about by the combined pressure of internal and external forces.

Although there was no conquest, foreign gunboats had to appear in Japanese ports several times (beginning in 1853) in order to convince the shogun and his government that they could not isolate their country any longer and that Japan, however painful it might seem, had to take some lessons from overseas. The military superiority of the foreigners was the most convincing argument.

After a period of vacillation, intrigues and in-fighting, the shogun surrendered supreme power to the emperor. This was the first step towards the imperial 'restoration' (*ōsei-fukko*) formally inaugurated in January 1868. Clans supporting the shogun, however, opposed that change and had to be defeated in a civil war which lasted until mid-1869. Meanwhile, in October 1868, a period of far-reaching reforms, the Period of the Enlightened Government (*Meiji*) was inaugurated. Force still had to be used, however, against those who wanted to reverse the trend. The last revolt of the counter-reformers (the Satsuma revolt in Kyushu) was defeated in 1877.

Then the issue was no longer whether a thorough transformation had to take place, but how far the reception of the foreign civilization had to go.

Notes and References

2 The Rise of the Levant: The Cuneiscript and Pharaonic Civilizations

1. K.A. Wittfogel, *Oriental Despotism, A Comparative Study of Total Power* (New Haven and London: Yale University Press, 1976), p.193.
2. Actually Wittfogel himself qualified his system to this effect in 'Ideas and Power Structure' in *Approaches to Asian Civilizations*, eds. W.M. Theodore de Bary and A.T. Embree (New York and London: Columbia University Press, 1964).
3. F. Lexa, *Výbor ze starší literatury egyptské* [Anthology of ancient Egyptian literature] (Prague, 1947), pp.20–2.
4. H. Frankfort, *Ancient Egyptian Religion* (New York: Harper and Row 1962), p.18.
5. Ibid., pp.91 and 96–102.
6. Quotations from the translation by John A. Wilson in J.B. Pritchard (ed.) *Ancient Near Eastern Texts*, 3rd. ed., (New Jersey: Princeton University Press, 1969), pp.412–14.
7. Ibid. pp.422–3.
8. Frankfort, *Ancient Egyptian Religion*, p.65.
9. G. Roux, *Ancient Iraq* (Harmondsworth: Penguin, 1980), p.93.
10. S.N. Kramer, *The Sumerians* (University of Chicago Press, 1963), p.123.
11. Ibid.
12. Ibid., p.125.
13. There exists a simplified, cursive version of the Egyptian hieroglyphs, but this is believed to be a much later invention.
14. H. Frankfort, *The Birth of Civilization in the Near East* (London: Benn; and New York: Barnes and Noble, 1968), p.77.
15. Translation by Robert H. Pfeiffer in J.B. Pritchard (ed.) *Ancient Near Eastern Texts*, p.424.
16. The Babylonian celebration of the New Year, lasting 12 days, is vividly described by J. Hawkes, *The First Great Civilizations: Life in Mesopotamia, The Indus Valley and Egypt* (New York: Knopf, 1977), pp.197–200.
17. Although the evidence for city-type settlements in pre-unification Egypt is rather thin, it would be over-hasty to rule out this possibility. Cf. A.L. Oppenheim, *Ancient Mesopotamia* (University of Chicago Press, 1964), pp.126–7.

18. J. Černý, Starý Egypt (Ancient Egypt) in *Dějiny lidstva* (*History of Mankind*), vol. I (Prague: Melantrich, 1940), p.216.
19. As the main guide on this point I am following the classical work of H. Breasted, *A History of Egypt* (2nd. ed., London, 1946). I do not think that the main lines of his presentation have been significantly altered by the more recent research.
20. F. Petrie, *Religion and Conscience in Ancient Egypt* (London: Methuen, 1898), pp.130–31.
21. E. Meyer, *Geschichte des Altertums* (3rd. ed., vol. I, Stuttgart, Berlin, 1925), pp.27 ff.
22. This is for instance the view of H. Breasted, *A History of Egypt*, and of V.I. Avdiev, *Istoria drevnego vostoka* (Moscow, 1948).
23. E.g. P. Calvert, *Revolution* (Pall Mall, London, 1970), pp.24 ff.
24. W.W. Halls and W.K. Simpson, *The Ancient Near East* (New York: Harcourt Brace Jovanovich, 1971), p.246.
25. Hawkes, *The First Great Civilizations*, p.391.
26. A.J. Toynbee, *A Study of History*, Vol. IV (London: Oxford University Press, 1939), p.412.
27. Hawkes, *The First Great Civilizations*, p.386.
28. A collection of contradictory opinions of Akhenaten's religion and policy has been edited by Donald Kagan in *Problems in Ancient History*, vol. I: *The Ancient Near East and Greece* (New York: Macmillan; London: Collier-Macmillan, 1966), pp.36–68. F.G. Bratton's view is taken from *The First Heretic: The Life and Times of Ikhnaton the King* (Boston: Beacon Press, 1961), pp.178–86; John A. Wilson's from *The Burden of Egypt* (University of Chicago Press, 1951). For a further evaluation of arguments for and against, see F.J. Giles, *Ikhnaton, Legend and History* (London: Hutchinson, 1970).
29. The Libyan and Nubian rule in Egypt after the breakdown of the New Kingdom can be compared to a certain extent with Germanic rule in Western Europe after the collapse of the Roman Empire. In both cases, ecclesiastical organization formed the backbone of the civilizational framework and its continuity. Even so, the priestly organization in Egypt at that time bore more resemblance to a professional guild than to the Roman Catholic Church when the whole of the latter's history is taken into account. Both claimed to provide exclusive fulfilment of the transcendental needs of the population in their respective countries. In both cases the invaders took over and respected the established organization, their only imposition on it being the elevation of their own favourites to its important posts. In both cases the main stronghold of conservation, the main support of tradition rested in a country beyond the radius of the superimposed rule. Thus, in the first few centuries after the fall of Rome, Christianity flourished in the Byzantine East, and while Egypt declined, a para-Pharaonic Egyptian civilization was thriving in the Nubian south. But here the parallel ends. Whereas Rome became the centre of a new spiritual drive and the force behind the successful civilizational reconstruction of Western Europe, no such potential existed at Thebes. Amon's church was not capable of playing the role of 'chrysalis', in Toynbee's sense of the word (A.J. Toynbee,

A Study of History, vol. VII, pp.392 et seqq.). The Libyans and Nubians had mastered a world whose spirituality was dying out, and their own creative efforts were not equal to its successful revival. All the Nubians were able to achieve was a transplant of the Pharaonic civilization, in the form of its last hierocratic stage, to their own native land, where the whole cycle of a Pharaonic civilization was then lived through once more.

30. As the composition of these bodies and the scope and manner of their functioning are matters of conjecture, it is difficult to draw a sensible comparison with the collective bodies (of elders and plebians) in Graeco-Roman antiquity. T. Jacobsen's suggestion of a primitive democracy in ancient Mesopotamia must be taken with some caution (T. Jacobsen, *Journal of Near Eastern Studies*, 2, 1943, pp.159–72).

31. I.M. Dyakonov, *Obshchestvennyi stroi drevnego Dvurechiya* (Moscow, 1959).

32. Remnants of 'primitive democracy' might have survived in the organization of the judiciary. This, at least, is the view put forward by T. Jacobsen in 'Primitive Democracy in Ancient Mesopotamia' (cf. n. 30). Although the evidence of popular assemblies acting as courts of law comes from a later period (the Old Babylonian), it is difficult to judge whether this type of judiciary was an Amorite innovation or a survival from Sumerian times.

33. Dyakonov, *Obshchestvennyi*, p.251.

34. B. Hrozný, 'Kultura hethitských a subarejských národů' (The Culture of the Hittite and Subaraean Nations), *Dějiny lidstva* (*History of Mankind*), vol. I (Prague: Melantrich 1940), p.374.

35. For a careful assessment of the 'feudal' elements in Kassite Mesopotamia see e.g. Burr C. Brundage, 'Feudalism in Ancient Mesopotamia and Iran' in R. Coulborn (ed.) *Feudalism in History* (Hamden, Conn.; Archon Books, 1965), pp.97–9.

36. This point has been particularly stressed by A. Götze, *Hethiter, Churriter und Assyrer* (Oslo, 1936), pp.72–3.

37. When discussing the Hittites we are resorting for brevity's sake to a simplification. We are leaving aside the variety of the ethnic groups for which the collective name Hittites is (not quite correctly) being used. The reader keen on penetrating further in this matter is advised to look into O.R. Gurney, *The Hittites* (London: Allen Lane, 1975), esp. pp.121–3.

38. The Hurrian state of Mitanni is another ethnically complex phenomenon. The affinity of the Hurrians with the other nations in the area has not yet been firmly established; the Hurrians might have been the descendants of the ancient Subaraeans, already known to the Sumerians in the first millennium BC, or immigrants from the Caucasus area. More intriguing however is the fact that the state of Mitanni, in which they constituted the bulk of the population, was created and ruled not by them but by a military aristocracy, most probably of Indo-European origin, whom the Hurrians called *mariyanni*. This political domination, however, does not seem to have particularly influenced the Hurrian culture, which was able to absorb various foreign elements and

developed in close association with the Hittite culture. To borrow Sir Leonard Woolley's words:

> The relations between the Hurrians and the Hittites prove to be unusually intimate, a fact which is abundantly reflected in virtually every phase of the Hittite civilisation. Indeed, we are justified in speaking of Hurro-Hittite symbiosis which for closeness and effect is second only to that blend of Sumerian and Akkadian elements which constitutes the composite culture of Mesopotamia.

J. Hawkes and Sir L. Woolley, *History of Mankind*, vol. I: *Prehistory and the Beginnings of Civilization* (London: Allen and Unwin, 1963), p.729.

39. V. Groh, 'Babel, Aššur a Israel: Dějinný vrchol semitského živlu' (The Historical Apogee of Semitic People') in *Dějiny lidstva* (*History of Mankind*), vol. I (Prague: Melantrich, 1940), p.425.
40. I am combining the accounts of I.M. Dyakonov, *Obshchestvennyi stroi drevnego Dvurechiya* (Moscow, 1959), and N.S. Kramer, *The Sumerians* (University of Chicago Press, 1963). For a well-rounded and balanced account of social life in the valleys of the Twin rivers and of the Nile see esp. Hawkes, *The First Great Civilizations* pp.144–85 and 375–405.
41. Hawkes and Woolley, *History of Mankind*, vol. I., p.508.
42. Until then only three Babylonian cities enjoyed that status: Babylon, Nippur and Sippar. Now seven more were added to that list.
43. I.M. Dyakonov, *Razvitie zemel'nykh otnoshenii v Assirii* (Leningrad, 1945).
44. F. Lexa, 'Veřejný život ve starém Egyptě' (Public Life in Ancient Egypt), ČSAV, Prague, 1955, vol. I., pp.186–7.
45. Hawkes, *The First Great Civilizations*, p.394.
46. J. Pirenne, *Histoire de la civilisation de l'Egypte ancienne*, vols. I–III (A. Michel, Neuchâtel; Baconnière, Paris, 1961–3); the documentation of this theory is contained in J. Pirenne's *Histoire des institutions et du droit privé de l'ancienne Egypte* (Brussels, 1934), but the material collected there is too patchy to permit such a far-reaching conclusion.

3 The Contrasts of Syria: Peoples of the Script and People of the Book

1. For more detail on these notions see for instance: K.M. Kenyon, *Amorites and Canaanites* (London: Oxford University Press, 1966), D.J. Wiseman (ed.) *Peoples of the Old Testament Times* (Oxford: Clarendon Press, 1973); and S. Moscati, *Ancient Semitic Civilisations* (London: Elek Books, 1957).
2. Gerhard Herm, *The Phoenicians* (London: Gollancz, 1975) p.200.
3. Donald Harden, *The Phoenicians* (Harmondsworth: Penguin 1971), p.77.
4. O. Eissfeldt, *Tautos und Sanchunjaton* (Berlin, 1952), p.28. The texts discovered in Ugarit confirm this rendering of Sanchuniathon's ideas.

S. Moscati, *Ancient Semitic Civilisations* (London: Elek Books, 1957), p.106.

5. A.J. Toynbee, *A Study of History* I (London: Oxford University Press, 1934), p.102.

6. A.T. Olmstead, *History of Palestine and Syria* (New York, London, Chicago University Press, 1931), p.66.

7. I am following the account by S. Moscati, *Ancient Semitic Civilisations*, pp.183–94, and P.K. Hitti, *History of the Arabs*, 10th ed. (London, New York: Macmillan, 1973) pp.49–66.

8. D.M. Dunlop, *Arab Civilization to A.D. 1500* (London: Longman, 1971) p.8.

9. But, as C.D. Darlington, a biologist turned to social science, points out, the Arabian camel, the dromedary, also 'contributed on the debit side to the erosion of Arabia, the expansion of the desert and the decay of the Hadramaut basin'. (C.D. Darlington, *The Evolution of Man and Society* (London: Allen and Unwin, 1969) p.328.)

10. M.M. Kaplan, *Judaism as a Civilization* (Philadelphia and New York: Jewish Publication Society of America, 1981) pp.186–208 (1st ed. 1934).

11. Ibid, p.194.

12. I am indebted especially to the following authors: A. Lods, *The Prophets and the Rise of Judaism* (London: Kegan Paul, Trench, Trubner, 1936); M. Bič, *Zrod a zvěst Starého zákona* (*The Origin and Message of the Old Testament*) (Prague: Kalich, 1951); M.A. Beek, *Geschichte Israels von Abraham bis Bar Kochba* (transl. from Dutch) (Stuttgart, 1961).

13. H.H. Rowley, *From Joseph to Joshua, Biblical Traditions in the Light of Archaeology* (London: British Academy, Oxford University Press, 1950). For further detail see for instance R. de Vaux, *The Early History of Israel*, 2 vols. (London: Darton, Longman and Todd, 1978).

14. H.H. Rowley puts the date of Exodus at *c*. 1230 BC. For his chronology, see *From Joseph to Joshua*, p.194.

15. 1 Samuel 15, 1–34; the explicit command to destroy one's enemies can also be read in Deuteronomy 20, 16–18.

16. Nevertheless even in much later writings (Esther 9, 16; Psalms 137, 8–9) we find outburst of what within the historical and literary context appears to be a powerless longing for vengeance rather than a commandment supposed to come from Yahwe.

17. All quotations from the Bible and the Apocrypha are from The New Oxford Annotated Bible with the Apocrypha, expanded edition, revised standard version (New York: Oxford University Press, 1977).

18. P.K. Hitti, *History of the Arabs*, pp.196–7.

19. A.T. Olmstead, *History of Palestine and Syria*, p.504.

20. M. Rostovtzeff, *The Social and Economic History of the Hellenistic World*, II (Oxford: Clarendon Press, 1953), pp.704–5.

21. Mircea Eliade, *A History of Religious Ideas* (London: Collins, 1979), vol. I, pp.346 and 355.

22. The story is told in minute detail in E. Mary Smallwood, *The Jews under Roman Rule* (Leiden: Brill, 1981).

23. Except for one day in each year, when the Jews were allowed to lament

the fate of their holy city at the Wailing Wall (E.M. Smallwood, *The Jews under Roman Rule*) p.460.
24. Ibid., pp. 348 ff.
25. A.J. Toynbee, *A Study of History*, vol. XII (London: Oxford University Press, 1964) p.505.

4   The Great Iranian Ventures: The Peripeties of Ahura Mazdah

1. Quoted according to R.C. Zaehner, *The Dawn and Twilight of Zoroastrianism* (London: Weidenfeld and Nicolson, 1961) p.40.
2. M. Boyce, *Zoroastrians, Their Religion, Beliefs and Practices* (London: Routledge and Kegan Paul, 1979) p.19.
3. Zaehner, *Dawn* p.45; Boyce, *Zoroastrians*, p.22.
4. Zaehner, pp.61 and 63; I.M. Dyakonov (*Ocherk istorii drevnego Irana*, Moscow, 1961) translates the old Persian *Haurvatat* as wealth or happiness.
5. The argument in favour of the older date is based on the affinity of the language of the Gathas to the language of the Rig-Veda. However, even if this is taken into consideration, the estimates of the period when Zarathushtra lived range from 1700 BC (Boyce, *Zoroastrians*, p.18) and 1100 BC (T. Burrow, 'The Proto-Indoaryans', in *Journal of the Royal Asiatic Society*, 1973, p.139). The date *c.* 600 BC is based on the Zoroastrian tradition. A more recent study by Gherardo Gnoli concludes, after much searching, that Zarathushtra lived towards the end of the second or the beginning of the first millennium BC (G. Gnoli, *Zoroaster's Time and Homeland* (Naples: Instituto Univer *i*tario Orientale, 1980) p.227).
6. Zaehner, *Dawn*, p.82.
7. R. Ghirshman, *L'Iran des origines à l'islam* (Paris, 1951) pp.161 and 165.
8. M. Rostovtzeff, *Social and Economic History of the Hellenistic World*, vol. I, (Oxford: Clarendon Press, 1953) pp.129–30.
9. Zaehner, *Dawn*, p.182.
10. The Pahlavi language was written in a new type of script, also called Pahlavi, which was developed from the Aramaean script but was not fully emancipated from it; the Pahlavi texts are dotted with Aramaeic ideogramms which, however, have to be read in the Iranian, Pahlavi, language.
11. These events are given particular attention in N. Pigulevskaya, *Goroda Irana v rannem srednevekove* (Moscow, 1965), pp. 105–6. In her opinion the insurrection was due to the unwillingness of the common folk to condone the exclusion of the general assembly from the decision-making process in Seleucia; but two competing pretenders to the Iranian throne were also involved.
12. Unfortunately, Tansar's edition of the Avesta has not been preserved. However, it can be assumed that the whole ancient Iranian text was accompanied by a translation and interpretation in Pahlavi (the Zand). Both the Avesta and the Zand were conceived in three parts: Yasna

(liturgy), Vispered (little liturgy, more or less repeating what is in Yasna) and Videvdat (Law against the demons, concerned mainly with ritual purity). Apart from this there were two further documents, the Yasht (the book of panegyrics on different deities) and the Little Avesta containing ancillary texts, documents which were both so incomprehensible to the magi of the Sassanid epoch that they were not translated at all.

13. Zaehner, *Dawn*, p.176.
14. Boyce described this policy as iconoclasm. (M. Boyce, *Zoroastrians*, pp. 106–8).
15. Zaehner, *Dawn*, p.27.
16. O. Klíma, *Manis Zeit und Leben* (Prague: Tschechoslowakische Akademie der Wissenschaften, 1962) pp.232 ff.
17. Zaehner, *Dawn*, p.185.
18. Ibid., p.186.
19. Ibid., p.243.
20. Ibid., p.268.
21. Here we can mention especially the many-faceted myth of the defection of woman from Ohrmazd to Ahriman; the consanguineous marriages of the magi; the sacral nature of fire, earth and water, requiring the exposure of corpses to the effects of the weather or scavengers so that the cleaned bones could be buried (also, because water was sacred, public baths were not allowed); and the magi's practice of killing animals of the species supposedly created by Ahriman.
22. Zaehner, *Dawn*, p.301.
23. Peroz also rightly appreciated the political advantage of supporting the Christian dissidents against the official church of Rome and Constantinople. Under Peroz Nestorians and Monophysites were free to organize their churches in Iran. (A. Christensen, *L'Iran sous les Sassanides* (Copenhagen: Levin and Munksgaard, 1936) pp.286–7.)
24. Unfortunately, sources on Mazdak and his movement are at many points incomplete and even contradictory. Nothing written in Pahlavi (whether sympathetic or hostile to Mazdak) has been preserved. The Arabic writings of a much later period apparently used some Pahlavi texts, but their authors were interested in telling an attractive story rather than in reporting what had really happened. The Byzantine writers too had their stories at second hand and neither they nor the Arabic authors had a full grasp of the issue involved in a foreign religion. Thus, the Iranologists had to build, ingeniously, on conjecture. I am following above all Christensen, Klíma and Pigulevskaya (see quotations further on), and am trying to fit their respective findings and comments into the context of what I consider to be the pattern of development of the Zoroastrian civilization.

   Recently, an attempt to cast doubt on what had become the established body of knowledge on the subject was made by Heinz Gaube in 'Mazdak: Historical Reality or Invention?' (*Studia Iranica*, XI, 1982, pp.111–22). Although Gaube bases his argument on contradictions in the sources, he uses only a very partial selection of these for his documentation, and thus considerably weakens his case. The authors quoted in this chapter have made a much more serious effort to make sense of the conflicting information.

25. Arthur Christensen, *L'Iran*, p.316.
26. N. Pigulevskaya, *Les villes de l'état Iranien aux époques Parthe et Sassanide* (Paris: Mouton, 1963) pp.195–230.
27. O. Klíma, *Mazdak, Geschichte einer sozialen Bewegung im Sassanidischen Persien* (Prague: ČSAV, 1957), p.250.
28. Klíma, *Mazdak*, pp.240–4.
29. Zaehner, *Dawn*, p.297.
30. Christensen, *L'Iran*, pp.324–5.
31. F. Altheim and R. Stiehl, however, understand the Mazdakite programme as a kind of religious communism aiming at abolition of individualism (*Abtötung der Individualität*). The individualistic attitude, a corollary of hatred and combativeness, is supposed to be of Evil Spirit. Thus in order to come nearer to God, men should consider the cultivable land and women common goods like water, fire and pastures. (Franz Altheim and Ruth Stiehl, *Ein Asiatischer Staat, Feudalismus unter den Sasaniden und ihren Nachbarn* (Limes Verlag, Wiesbaden, 1954) pp.304–5.)
32. Klíma, *Mazdak*, p.138.
33. Thus, for instance, the whole population of the Syrian city of Antioch was transferred to the newly built city on the Euphrates near the Sassanid capital Ctesiphon.
34. Pigulevskaya, *Les Villes*, p.218.
35. Klíma, *Mazdak*, p.292.
36. Zaehner, *Dawn*, p.301.
37. Klíma, *Mazdak*, p.286.
38. R.N. Frye, *The Heritage of Persia* (London: Weidenfeld and Nicolson, 1962) p.235.
39. T.W. Arnold, *The Preaching of Islam* (Lahore: Sh. Ashraf, repr. 1966) p.211.
40. Ibid.
41. An attempt has even been made to quantify the rate of Islamization of Iran. On the basis of the number of Muslim names in the biographical dictionaries of the epoch and on the basis of reported religious conversions in two Iranian cities, Isfahan and Nishapur, R.W. Bulliet constructed a logistic (S-shaped) curve of the rate of conversion between 622 and 1010 AD. This exercise shows that between 770 and 865 possibly 40 per cent and around 1000 about 80 per cent of the population of Iran were Muslims. (R.W. Bulliet, 'Conversion to Islam and the Emergence of a Muslim Society in Iran' in N. Levtzion (ed.) *Conversion to Islam* (New York, London: Holmes and Meier, 1979) pp.30–51.)

5 The Ways of Islam: Integration and Disintegration

1. H.A.R. Gibb, *Mohammedanism*, 2nd ed. (London, New York: Oxford University Press, 1969) p.26, quoting Koran.

2. M.W. Watt, *Islam and the Integration of Society* (London: Routledge and Kegan Paul, 1961) p.42.
3. Ibid., p.56.
4. P.K. Hitti, *Makers of Arab History* (London: Macmillan, 1969), p.3.
5. P.K. Hitti, *History of the Arabs*, 10th ed. (London: Macmillan, 1973) p.353.
6. R. Levy, *The Social Structure of Islam* (London, New York: Cambridge University Press, 1957) p.195.
7. Ibid., p.194.
8. Ibid., pp.91–2.
9. Gibb, *Mohammedanism*, p.25.
10. For the meaning of this term in Arabic tradition see W.M. Watt, *Islamic Political Thought* (Edinburgh University Press, 1968) pp.32–3.
11. Watt, *Islamic Political Thought*, p.84.
12. C.A. Julien, *History of North Africa*, transl. from French by J. Petrie. (London: Routledge and Kegan Paul, 1970) p.33.
13. Jamil M. Abun-Nasr, *A History of the Maghrib*, 2nd ed. (London and New York: Cambridge University Press, 1975). p. 75.
14. Julien, *History of North Africa*, p.31.
15. P.K. Hitti, *History of the Arabs*, 10th ed. (London, New York: Macmillan, 1973) p.441.
16. Ibid., p.429.
17. F.Rahman, *Islam* 2nd ed. (University of Chicago Press, 1979) p.91.
18. Ibid., p.92.
19. Ibid., p.128.
20. Watt, *Islam and the Integration of Society*, p.247.
21. Gibb, *Mohammedanism*, pp. 95–6.
22. M.G.S. Hodgson, *The Venture of Islam*, vol. II (University of Chicago Press, 1974) p.219.
23. Rahman, *Islam*, pp.156–7.
24. In his best renowned work, *The Muqaddimah* (*An Introduction to History*), Ibn Khaldun develops this theory at length. His empirical basis is the history of the Islamic states, most of them ruled by dynasties of nomad origin. But the thesis is applicable to any other upstart family development. The following quotation from Ibn Khaldun shows the relevance of his thesis to the rise of the Mamlukdom:

People, meanwhile, continue to adopt ever newer forms of luxury and sedentary culture and of quiet, tranquility, and softness in all their conditions, and to sink ever deeper into them. They thus become estranged from desert life and desert toughness. Gradually, they lose more and more of (the old virtues). They forget the quality of bravery that was their protection and defence. Eventually, they come to depend upon some other militia, if they have one . . . This is what happened to the Turkish dynasty in the East. Most members of its army were Turkish clients. The (Turkish) rulers then chose horsemen and soldiers from among the white slaves (Mamelukes) who were brought to them. They were more eager to fight and better able to suffer privations than the children of the earlier white slaves

(Mamelukes) who had grown up in easy circumstances as a ruling class in the shadow of the government. Ibn Khaldun, *The Muqaddimah, An Introduction to History*, transl. F. Rosenthal, vol. I (New Jersey: Princeton University Press, 1967) p.342.

25. To illustrate the point we may quote a few verses with which the already mentioned Seljuk vizier Nizam al-Mulk concluded the chapter on the decline of the Samanid dynasty in his Book of Government: 'One obedient slave is better than a hundred sons: for the latter desire their father's death, the former long life for his master.' Quoted from D. Ayalon, *The Mamluk Military Society* (London: Variorum Reprints, 1979) p.216.

26. Abdallah Laroui, *The History of the Maghreb*, transl. R. Manheim, (New Jersey: Princeton University Press, 1977) p.158.

27. The epic of the Maghreb is tellingly reported in Charles-André Julien, *History of North Africa*.

28. The extent to which the Christian churchmen asked the Mongolian rulers for help against their rivals within their own churches is astonishing, as is the amount of privileges which they were granted by the Ilkhans. However the latter were not consistent in their sympathies and antipathies. This can also be seen from their shifts in bestowing favours now upon the Sunnites, now upon the Shi'ites, while often being ill-disposed towards Islam in general. For more detail see B. Spuler, *Die Mongolen in Iran* (Berlin: Akademie Verlag, 1968) pp.198–244.

29. F. Tauer, *Svět Islámu (The World of Islam)* (Prague, Vyšehrad, 1984) pp.66–7.

30. D.C. Dennett, *Conversion and the Poll Tax in Early Islam* (Harvard and Oxford University Press, 1950) pp.116–18.

31. Ann Lambton, *Landlord and Peasant in Persia* (London, New York: Oxford University Press, 1969) pp.29–30, 52.

32. C. Cahen, *L'évolution de l'iqta du IX au XIII siècle, (Annales, Économies, Sociétés, Civilisations)* t.8, no.1, Paris, 1953, pp.27–54.

33. In Ann Lambton's view, the element of mutual obligation is notably absent from Islamic feudalism. A. Lambton, *Landlord and Peasant* pp.53–4.

34. B. Vladimirtsov, *Le régime social des Mongols, le féodalisme nomade*, transl. from Russian by M. Carsov (Adrien-Maisonneuve, Paris, 1948) pp.134–5.

35. I.P. Petrushevskiy, *Zemledelie i agrarnye otnosheniya v Irane XIII–XIV vekov* (Moscow-Leningrad: Izdatel'stovo Akademii nauk SSSR, 1960)

36. A.N. Poliak, *Feudalism in Egypt, Syria, Palestine and the Lebanon*, 1250–1900, (Philadelphia: Porcupine Press, 1977) p.64 and Appendices; and L.A. Semenova, *Salah ad-Din i mamljuki v Egipte* (Moscow: Izdatel'stvo vostochnoi literatury, 1960), p. 51 ff.

37. Hassanein Rabie, *The Financial System of Egypt, A.H. 564–741/A.D. 1169–1341* (London, New York: Oxford University Press, 1972) pp.30–1.

38. Rabie, *Financial System of Egypt*, pp.63–72.

39. Tauer, *Svět Islámu*, p.160.

40. Petrushevskiy, *Zemledelie*, pp.394–6.

41. Ibid., pp.310–11; the term *avamili panjganeh* points to the counting of the tools and the animals as one unit (Lambton, *Landlord and Peasant*) p.423.
42. Lambton, *Landlord and Peasant*, p.83.
43. A sympathetic account of the Sarbadar venture, stressing the progressive role and class-conscious policy of the Sufi shayks, by Petrushevskiy (*Zemledelie*, pp.424–66), contrasts with a more recent and sober analysis of the sources by J.M. Smith, Jr, *The History of the Sarbadar Dynasty 1336–1381 A.D. and its Sources* (The Hague, Paris: Mouton, 1970).
44. Grousset, *Histoire de la Chine*, p.164.
45. C.D. Darlington, *The Evolution of Man and Society* (London: Allen and Unwin, 1969) p.347.
46. Hitti, *History of the Arabs*, p.375.
47. J. Poncet, '*Le mythe de la 'catastrophe hilalienne*' (*Annales, Economies, Sociétés, Civilisations*, Paris, 1967), p.1118.
48. Julien, *History of North Africa*, pp.138–9.
49. Al-Hakim ordered the demolition of many churches, including that of the Holy Sepulchre in Jerusalem (1009 AD), a deed which 86 years later, after the church had been rebuilt by his son and successor, was invoked as one of the reasons for the Crusades; he subjected Christians and Jews to petty discrimination, forcing them to wear black robes, to ride only on donkeys, and while bathing to display visible signs of their religious affiliation. In that respect he surpassed by far the vexatious measures introduced by the exceptionally pious Umayyad Caliph Umar II, who was however prevented by the shortness of his rule (717–20) from doing more serious damage.
50. Franz Babinger, *Mehmed the Conqueror and His Time* (New Jersey: Princeton University Press, 1978), p.112.
51. Levy, *Social Structure of Islam*, p.267.
52. Klaus Röhrborn, *Untersuchungen zur osmanischen Verwaltungsgeschichte* (W. de Gruyter, Berlin, New York, 1973) esp. pp.54–5.
53. Mehmed Fuad Köprülü, *Les origines de l'Empire ottoman* (Philadelphia: Porcupine Press, 1978) p.123.
54. Franz Babinger, *Mehmed*, p.413.
55. R. Savory, *Iran under the Safavids* (London, New York: Cambridge University Press, 1980) p.23.
56. Ibid., p.43.
57. Lambton, *Landlord and Peasant*, p.105.
58. Ibid.
59. Toynbee, *A Study of History*, vol. I, p. 401.
60. Savory, *Iran under the Safavids*, p.80.
61. Ibid., p.184.

6 From Indus to Mekong: Between Brahma and Buddha

1. K. Werner, *Yoga and Indian Philosophy* (Delhi: Motilal Banarsidass, 1977), p.17.
2. This is a view conveyed especially by the Upanishads (cf. R.C. Zaehner,

Hindu Scriptures (London: Dent, 1972) pp.10–11.
3. D.H. Gordon, *The Pre-Historic Background of Indian Culture* (Bombay, 1958), p.57–8.
4. Bridget and Raymond Allchin, *The Rise of Civilization in India and Pakistan* (London, New York: Cambridge University Press, 1982) pp.213–16.
5. Some archaeological evidence points to there having been still other ethnic elements who took part in what may be described as the *Völkerwanderung* in the Indus Valley, but their appearance was short-lived and left behind no notable traces.
6. S. Radhakrishnan, *The Principal Upanishads* (London, 1953), p.45.
7. Ibid., pp.23–4.
8. It is difficult to imagine any possible link between Vedic India and the much older Pharaonic civilization of Egypt. Should, for instance, the Proto-Indians have taken anything from the Levant, it would have not been from the Egyptians but from the Mesopotamians, with whom they traded. Yet in the Cuneiscript civilization it was not the cosmic principle but the gods who, acting as a collegiate organ, decreed in their *me* the principles of human behaviour. And after the Pharaonic civilization passed away, Egypt, too, like the whole of the Levant, became incorporated into decidedly theistic civilizations, first Christianity and then Islam.
9. At the Indian census of 1901, 2378 castes and subcastes were recorded. J.H. Hutton, *Caste in India, Its Nature, Function, and Origin* (Cambridge University Press, 1946) p.128.
10. I am following here, at least in principle, the version that I consider to be the most accessible to Western understanding, namely the school known as Samkhya-Yoga. Zaehner, *Hindu Scriptures*, p. xiii.

Terminological note

For the sake of clarity the derivations from the word-root *brahm* are here used as follows:
1. Brahman (neuter) – meaning impersonal principle of Absolute or Universal Spirit or, in the early Vedic period, the creative power of a duly performed sacrifice.
2. Brahma (masculine) – theoretically (but not from the point of view of worship) the key god of the Hinduistic trinity: Brahma, Shiva and Vishnu.
3. Brahmana – the second main division of the Vedic writings.
4. Brahmins, also Brahmans – the first of the four castes. In order to ease differentiation, I use the first alternative: Brahmins.
5. Brahminism or Brahmanism – the ancient religion propounded by the Brahmins, one of the main roots of Hinduism, the other being the popular cults of the Puranas and later also the Tantras, and above all the teaching of the Bhagavad-Gita.
6. Brahmi – the earliest Indian script known to us.
7. Brachmacharya (literally, divine faring) – in this context, the first *ashrama* (stage of life) of men in the brahmin caste.

11. Hutton, *Caste in India*, p.136.
12. J. Nehru, *The Discovery of India* (Bombay, New York: Asia Publishing House, 1969).
13. A.K. Narain (ed.) *Studies in the History of Buddhism* (Delhi: B.R. Publishing Corp., 1980) p.xxiv ff.
14. In this context, it has to be said that musical notes as such most probably have their origin in India; by the fourth century BC they had attained a high level of completeness.
15. It should also be pointed out that writing in India was subject to many changes, and that often individual ethnic groups developed their own types of script. Thus in contrast to the tendency towards a unified literary language in India, a tendency which prevailed until the beginning of the second millennium AD, there is a conspicuous differentiation in the forms of the writing. At the end of the nineteenth century, the Dutch scholar, K.F. Holle, identified in the whole area of Indian culture, i.e. including South-East Asia, 198 different types of script. K.F. Holle, *Tabel van oud en nieuw indische alphabeten* (Batavia, 1882).
16. Amongst followers of the Buddha still other honorifics are bestowed on Gautama, such as the Shakyamuni (the Sage of the Shakyas), the Bhagavat (the Blessed or Noble One), the Tathagata (the Accomplished One), etc.
17. N. Smart, *The Religious Experience of Mankind* 2nd ed. (Scribner, New York, 1976), p.99.
18. Padmasiri de Silva, *An Introduction to Buddhist Psychology* (London, New York: Macmillan Press, 1979) p.ix (foreword by John Hick) and p.16.
19. The Buddhist literature (the Jatakas) and the Hindu Literature (the Puranas) both present a picture of considerable social mobility which did not respect caste barriers and hierarchies. Cf. R.C. Harza, *Studies in the Puranic Records* (Delhi: Motilal Banarsidass, 1975) p.210 ff.
20. Unfortunately Kautilya's book the 'Arthashastra' has only been preserved in copies from much later periods.
21. For a more detailed discussion of this issue see, for instance, Hutton, *Caste in India*, pp.114–15.
22. Nehru, *The Discovery of India*, p.174.
23. Sir Charles Eliot, *Hinduism and Buddhism, An Historical Sketch*, vol.II,(London, 1921; repr. Barnes and Noble, New York, 1971) pp.136–7.
24. Quoted from Zaehner's translation in *Hindu Scriptures*, pp.255 and 257.
25. Zaehner, *Hindu Scriptures*, p. xviii.
26. For more detail on these issues see W.E. Clark, 'Science', in *The Legacy of India*, ed. G.T. Garratt (Oxford: Clarendon Press, 1967) pp.335–69.
27. K.A. Nilakanta Sastri, *A History of South India* (3rd ed., London: Oxford University Press, 1966) p.144.
28. Regarding the condition of Indian Buddhism in the seventh and eighth centuries AD, our best information comes from the writings of Chinese

Buddhist travellers to India. Coming from a pragmatically oriented background, they were more concerned with reporting matters of fact than were Indian writers.

29. In German: 'der Weise weiss sich selbst als das ewig-selige zweitheitlose Absolute.' Helmuth v. Glasenapp, *Der Hinduismus* (München, 1922) p.173–4.

30. T.V. Mahalingam, *Economic Life in the Vijayanagar Empire* (Madras, 1951).

31. Ramanuja's teaching also left unresolved the dilemma between the monism of the absolute and the dualism of devotee and object of devotion. An attempt to cope with both these dilemmas was undertaken by another Tamili Vaishnavite, Madhva, who died in 1276 AD. Madhva abandoned the traditional concept of the absolute and taught that each soul is distinct from every other and from God, who is eternally distinct from the natural world which he sustains and recreates at the beginning of each time-cycle. Smart, *Religious Experience of Mankind*, p.148.

This pluralism of existence was matched in Madhva's philosophy by a plurality of salvations, graded from eternal bliss in the presence of God, through the eternal cycle of transmigration, to eternal damnation. The idea of predestination, or foreknowing, was a brand new phenomenon which seems to reflect the influence of Christianity on Hinduism. As Christian communities did exist on the south-west coast of India, probably from the fourth century AD (according to tradition they were founded by the apostle St Thomas but critical historians tend to the view that they were planted by refugees from the occasional bouts of persecution in Sassanid Iran) the possibility of a Christian influence on religious thinkers of southern India cannot be excluded.

32. J.F. Cady, *Southeast Asia: Its Historical Developmen* (McGraw-Hill, New York, Toronto, London, 1964) p.45.

33. This highest honour took the form of receiving the most precious relic – Buddha's tooth – from its shrine in Kandy in Sri Lanka. The fate of this relic deserves to be mentioned in this context, because it illustrates a symbolic point in the contact between two civilizations. Unlike the Dutch and the British later, the Portuguese built their colonial empire under the ideological banner of their religion, which was Roman Catholicism; they considered it their duty to proselytize and to convert whole nations to their creed. 'First pepper, then souls' seemed to be the principle. In their zeal, the missionaries seized what they believed to be the Buddha's tooth and, in spite of attractive offers of ransom and of commercial advantages in the Theravada countries, they destroyed it. Yet the Sinhalese Buddhists maintained that what the Portuguese had destroyed was only a replica, while the precious original was safely hidden.

34. The ranks of the Mons were depleted by emigration from the devastated areas into Thailand, whilst the numerical strength of the Burmese profited from the assimilation of the Shan tribes.

35. W.F. Wertheim, *Indonesian Society in Transition: A Study of Social Change*, pt I (New York and The Hague, 1956), p.274.

36. For more detail see D.G.E. Hall, *A History of South-East Asia* (London: Macmillan, 1964) pp.70–1.

7 The Chinese Path: The Paradigm of Continuity

1. Joseph Needham, *Science and Civilisation in China*, vol.2 (Cambridge University Press, 1962) p.xxiv.
2. D. Bodde, *Essays on Chinese Civilization* (New Jersey: Princeton University Press, 1981) p.43.
3. This advantage of the Chinese script was already appreciated by the Iranian scholar, Rashid ad-Din (*c*.1247–1318), who maintained that this script, being independent of pronunciation, was superior to Arabic writing. J. Gernet, *A History of Chinese Civilization* transl. from French by J.R. Foster (London and New York: Cambridge University Press, 1982) p.524.
4. M. Granet, *Etudes sociologiques sur la Chine* (Paris: Presses Universitaires de France, 1953) p.154.
5. I am following Henri Maspero, *China in Antiquity*, transl. from French by F.A. Kierman and J.R. Dawson (University of Massachusetts Press, 1978) pp.104–6.
6. Later, as will be shown in section 7.9, the Buddhist concept of reincarnation led to a substantial modification of this stance.
7. M. Granet, *La civilisation chinoise* (Paris, 1929), p.501.
8. Maspero, *China in Antiquity*, pp.69–70.
9. Granet, *La civilisation chinoise*, p.305.
10. Hu Hou-hsüan, *Collected Essays on Shang History Based on the Bone Inscriptions* (Chengtu, 1944) (quoted in D. Bodde, *Essays on Chinese Civilization*) (Princeton University Press, New Jersey, 1981) p.87.
11. Maspero, *China in Antiquity*, pp.278–80.
12. Ch'en Meng Chia, 'The Greatness of Chou', in H.F. MacNair (ed.) *China* (Berkeley and Los Angeles, 1946) pp.63–4.
13. Needham, *Science and Civilisation in China*, p.10.
14. Ibid., p.13.
15. Ibid., p.16.
16. Ibid., vol.2., p.544.
17. Gernet, *A History of Chinese Civilization*, p.93.
18. Needham, *Science and Civilisation in China*, p.35.
19. *Tao Te Ching*, transl. by Ch'u Ta-kao (London: Unwin, 1972) p.37.
20. Ibid., p.13.
21. Maspero, *China in Antiquity*, pp.306–7.
22. Needham, *Science and Civilisation in China*, p.182.
23. Gernet, *A History of Chinese Civilization*, p.98.
24. It may be tempting to relate the despotic regime in Qin to the 'hydraulic agriculture' in terms of Wittfogel's theory. But we prefer to heed D. Bodde's caveat in this matter and assume merely a marginal importance of hydraulic works for the political development of ancient China. (Bodde, *Essays on Chinese Civilization*) p.115–18.
25. H. Maspero and J. Escarra, *Les institutions de la Chine* (Paris: Presses

Universitaires de France, 1952) p.56.
26. Maspero, *China in Antiquity*, p.356.
27. Hu Shi, 'The Establishment of Confucianism as a State Religion During the Han Dynasty', *Journal of the North China Branch of the Royal Asiatic Society*, vol. IX (1929) pp.22,34,35,39,40; quoted in Toynbee, *A Study of History*, vol. V (1939) pp.555–6.
28. Granet, *La civilisation chinoise*, pp.135–8.
29. Maspero and Escarra, *Les institutions de la Chine*.
30. Gernet, *A History of Chinese Civilization*.
31. I. Stepuginova in *Istoriya mira*, vol. II (Moscow, 1956–9), pp.497–500.
32. E. Erkes, *Das Problem der Sklaverei in China* (Berlin: Sächsische Akademie, 1952.)
33. M. Elvin, *The Pattern of the Chinese Past* (London: Methuen, 1973) p.32.
34. Gernet, *A History of Chinese Civilization*, p.143.
35. In Chinese historiography the two periods are distinguished with respect to the location of their respective capital cities: the Earlier being known as the Western, and the Later as the Eastern Han. The capitals are Changan and Luoyang respectively.
36. This at least is the suggestion made by H.D. Dubs in an essay on 'Taoism', in *China*, ed. MacNair, p.286. Here Dubs mentions in particular Zoroastrianism as a possible source of inspiration.
37. This account of the Taoist concept of immortality is based on H. Maspero, 'Les religions chinoises' in *Mélanges posthumes sur les religions et l'histoire de la Chine*, vol. I, ed. P. Demieville (Paris: Musée Guimet, 1950) pp.201–4.
38. Gernet, *A History of Chinese Civilization*, p.225.
39. D.A. Scott, 'Bactria 250 BC–750 AD', a doctoral dissertation at the University of Lancaster, 1983.
40. Maspero and J. Escarra, *Les institutions de la Chine*, p.74.
41. A.F. Wright, 'The Formation of Sui Ideology, 581–604', in *Chinese Thought and Institutions*, ed. J.K. Fairbank (University of Chicago Press, 1973) pp.100 and 362.
42. Only the sons of some mandarins were granted the privilege of access to the government services without examination.
43. O. Franke, *Geschichte des Chinesischen Reiches*, vol.IV (Berlin, 1948), p.415.
44. Maspero and J. Escarra, *Les institutions de la Chine*, pp.95–6.
45. Although the Chinese censuses have to be taken with a certain caution (which by no means diminishes our appreciation of the immense task mastered by the Chinese administration), they nevertheless reveal the basic changes in the social structure of the country.
46. Gernet, *A History of Chinese Civilization*, p.294.
47. On the basis of scattered data available for several prefectures and counties in 1100 AD, Mark Elvin estimated the proportion of the urban population in China as a whole at 20 per cent (M. Elvin, *The Pattern of the Chinese Past*) p.176.
48. According to Needham, as early as the Tang era, the Confucians began to feel their lack of cosmology in competition with the Taoists, and

their lack of metaphysics in competion with the Buddhists. (Needham *Science and Civilization in China*, vol. 2) p.453.
49. Ibid., p.472 ff.
50. Maspero and J. Escarra, *Les institutions de la Chine*, p.109.
51. In C.K. Yang's view it is no accident that the Confucian ethical system came to dominate Chinese social institutions; Confucianism possessed a far more comprehensive, consistent, and practical system of ethical values for secular life than any traditional religion in China. (C.K. Yang, 'The Functional Relationship between Confucian Thought and Chinese Religion' in *Chinese Thought and Institutions*, ed. Fairbank) p.280.
52. A.L. Kroeber, *Configurations of Culture Growth* (Berkeley and Los Angeles, 1944), p.191.
53. This was especially needed in the north where forests had virtually disappeared and erosion had exposed the river valleys to devastating floods.
54. Gernet, *A History of Chinese Civilization*, p.396.
55. According to Elvin, the decline of the government's interest in the navy was also caused by the reconstruction of the Grand Canal to Beijing, which around 1415 made possible a large-scale shift from risky and high-cost sea transport to a safer and low-cost transport by inland water. (Elvin, *The Pattern of the Chinese Past*) p.220.
56. Needham, *Science and Civilisation in China*, vol.2, pp.511–2 and 516–17.
57. K.S. Latourette, *The Chinese, Their History and Culture* (New York: Macmillan, 1964) p.550–1.
58. Maspero, *Les religions chinoises*, p.138.
59. C.K. Yang, 'The Functional Relationship Between Confucian Thought and Chinese Religion', p.290.
60. Gernet, *A History of Chinese Civilization*, p.482 ff.
61. Southern Manchuria (the province of Liaoning) was open to Chinese emigration from as early as 1776.

8 The Rhythm of the Far East: Reception and Adaptation

1. M.F. Nelson, *Korea and the Old Orders in Eastern Asia*, (Baton Rouge: Louisiana State University Press, 1946) p.85
2. H. Jensen, *Die Schrift in Vergangenheit and Gegenwart* (VEB Deutscher Verlag der Wissenschaften, Berlin, 1958) pp.197 ff.
3. Nelson, *Korea and the Old Orders*, pp.84–5.
4. E.O. Reischauer and A.M. Craig, *Japan, Tradition and Transformation* (London and Boston, Allen and Unwin, 1979) p.10.
5. The Japanese looked on education as a condition of government service in a similar way as did individual Chinese states during the long period of disunity from the third to the sixth century AD, when the appointment system was 'rectified' by the nine categories of nobility.
6. My sources on various types of writing in the Far East: H. Jensen, *Die Schrift in Vergangenheit und Gegenwart*, pp.170–1, and C. Loukotka,

Vývoj písma (*The Development of Script*) (Prague: Orbis, 1946), pp. 157, 178–83.

7. I am following the explanation given by H.P. Varley in A.E. Tiedemann (ed.) *An Introduction to Japanese Civilization* (New York and London: Columbia University Press, 1974) pp.42–3.

8. In 914 AD it was estimated that only one third of the population was subject to the central government and paid taxes. (A. Gonthier, *Histoire des institutions japonaises* (Bruxelles, 1956), p.63.

9. For a summary account of Japanese feudalism see esp. E.O. Reischauer, 'Japanese Feudalism' in R. Coulborn (ed.) *Feudalism in History* (Hamden, Conn: Archon Books, 1965) pp.29–48.

10. Sir C. Eliot, *Japanese Buddhism* (London, 1935) pp.226–7.

11. D.C. Holton, 'Shintoism' in *The Great Religions of the Modern World* ed. E. Jurji (New Jersey: Princeton University Press, 1946), pp.153 ff.

12. It may seem strange that the Japanese did not make a more wide-ranging use of sea navigation than they did. Though living on an island, they did not become a sea-faring nation until modern times. Much more enterprising in this respect were the inhabitants of the small island of Okinawa in the Ryukyu archipelago. After the Chinese had given up their maritime venture in the middle of the fifteenth century, the Okinawans became the main sea-trading nation in the Far East, and were to retain this position for the whole century to come, until the arrival of the Portuguese.

13. Takeo Yazaki, *Social Change and the City in Japan* (Tokyo, 1968), p.87.

14. It is amazing that though firearms were in use in China from the thirteenth century, the Japanese only learnt their use from the Portuguese three centuries later.

15. E.O. Reischauer, *The United States and Japan* (Cambridge, Mass., 1957) pp.135–6.

16. A. Gonthier, *Histoire des institutions japonaises* (Bruxelles, 1956) p.211.

Bibliography

Books

Abun-Nasr, J.M., *A History of the Maghrib* (London and New York: Cambridge University Press, 1975).

Albright, W.F., *Archeology and the Religion of Israel* (Baltimore: John Hopkins Press; London: Oxford University Press, 1953).

Allchin, Bridget and Raymond, *The Rise of Civilization in India and Pakistan* (London and New York: Cambridge University Press, 1982).

Alt, A., *Essays on Old Testament History and Religion*, transl. R.A. Wilson (Oxford: Blackwell, 1966).

Altheim, F. and Stiehl, R., *Ein Asiatischer Staat, Feudalismus unter den Sasaniden und ihren Nachbarn* (Wiesbaden: Limes Verlag, 1954).

Archer, J.C., 'Hinduism' in E. Jurji (ed.) *The Great Religions of the World* (New Jersey: Princeton University Press, 1946).

Arnold, T.W., *The Preaching of Islam* (Lahore: Sh. Ashraf, 1966).

Ashrafyan, K.Z., *Deliskii sultanat* (Moscow: Izdatel'stvo vostochnoi literatury, 1960).

Avdiev, V.I., *Istoriya drevnego vostoka* (Moscow, 1948).

Ayalon, D., *The Mamluk Military Society* (London: Variorum Reprints, 1979).

Babinger, F., *Mehmed the Conqueror and his Time*, transl. R. Manheim (New Jersey: Princeton University Press 1978).

de Bary, T. and Embree, A.T. (eds) *Approaches to Asian Civilizations* (London and New York: Columbia University Press, 1964).

Beasley, W.G., *The Meiji Restoration* (Stanford: Stanford University Press and London: Oxford University Press, 1973).

Beek, M.A., *Geschichte Israels von Abraham bis Bar Kochba* (Stuttgart, 1961).

Bellah, R.N., *Tokugawa Religion* (London: Collier-Macmillan; New York: The Free Press, 1969).

Bermant, C. and Weitzman, M., *Ebla – An Archeological Enigma* (London: Weidenfeld and Nicolson, 1979).

Bič, M., *Zrod a zvěst Starého zákona* (*The Origin and Message of the Old Testament*) (Prague: Kalich, 1951).

Bodde, D., *Essays on Chinese Civilization* (New Jersey: Princeton University Press, 1981).

Böttger, W., *Kultura ve Staré Číně* (*Culture in Ancient China*), transl. Z. Černá (Praha: Panorama, 1984).

Boyce, M., *Zoroastrians, Their Religious Beliefs and Practices* (London and Boston: Routledge and Kegan Paul, 1979).

Boyce, M., *A Persian Stronghold of Zoroastrianism* (Oxford: Clarendon Press, 1977).

323

Bratton, F.G., *The First Heretic: The Life and Times of Ikhnaton the King* (Boston: Beacon Press, 1961).

Breasted, J.H., *A History of Egypt*, 2nd ed. (London, 1946).

Brockington, J., *The Sacred Thread, Hinduism in its Continuity and Diversity* (Edinburgh University Press, 1982).

Brundage, B.C., 'Feudalism in Ancient Mesopotamia and Iran', in *Feudalism in History*, ed. R. Coulbourn (Connecticut: Archon Books, 1965).

Bulliet, R.W., *Conversion to Islam in the Medieval Period* (Cambridge, Mass. and London: Harvard University Press, 1979).

Bulliet, R.W., *The Camel and the Wheel* (Cambridge, Mass.: Harvard University Press, 1975).

Cady, J.F., *Southeast Asia: Its Historical Development* (London and New York: McGraw-Hill, 1964).

Calvert, P., *Revolution* (London: Pall Mall, 1970).

Černý, J., 'Starý Egypt' ('Ancient Egypt') in *Dějiny lidstva* (*History of Mankind*) vol. I (Prague: Melantrich, 1940).

Ch'en Meng Chia, 'The Greatness of Chou' in *China*, ed. H.F. MacNair (Berkeley and Los Angeles, 1946).

Cheng Tien-Hsi, *China Moulded by Confucius* (London: Stevens, 1946).

Christensen, A., *L'Iran sous les Sassanides* (Copenhague: Levin and Munksgaard, 1936).

Clark, W.E., 'Science' in *The Legacy of India*, ed. G.T. Garratt (Oxford: Clarendon Press, 1967).

Conze, E., *Further Buddhist Studies* (Oxford: Cassirer, 1975).

Cook, M.A., *Population Pressure in Rural Anatolia 1450–1600* (London and New York: Oxford University Press, 1972).

Cook, J.M., *The Persian Empire* (London and Toronto: Dent, 1983).

Creel, H.G., *Chinese Thought from Confucius to Mao Tse-tung* (University of Chicago Press, 1975).

Darlington, C.D., *The Evolution of Man and Society* (London: Allen and Unwin, 1969).

Dennett, D.C., *Conversion and the Poll Tax in Early Islam* (Harvard and Oxford University Press, 1950).

Die Reden Gotamo Buddhos, transl. K.E. Neumann (München, 1922).

Diffie, B.W. and Winius, G.D. *Foundations of the Portuguese Empire, 1415–1580* (Minneapolis: University of Minnesota Press, 1977).

Dubs, H.D., 'Taoism' in *China*, ed. H.F. MacNair (Berkeley and Los Angeles, 1946).

Dunlop, D.M., *Arab Civilization to A.D. 1500* (London: Longman; Beirut: Librarie du Liban, 1971).

D'yakonov, I.M., *Razvitie zemel'nykh otnoshenii v Assirii* (Leningrad, 1949).

D'yakonov, I.M., *Istoriya Midii* (Leningrad, 1956).

D'yakanov, I.M., *Ocherk istorii drevnego Irana* (Moscow, 1961).

D'yakonov, I.M., *Obshchestvennyi stroi drevnego Dvurechiya* (Moscow, 1959).

Eissfeldt, O., *Tautos und Sanchunjaton* (Berlin, 1952).

Eliade, M., *A History of Religious Ideas* (London: Collins, 1979).

Eliot, C., Sir, *Hinduism and Buddhism; An Historical Sketch*, 3 vols. (New York: Barnes and Noble, 1971).

Eliot, C., Sir, *Japanese Buddhism* (London: Routledge, 1935).

Elvin, M., *The Pattern of the Chinese Past* (London: Methuen, 1973).

Erkes, E., *Das Problem der Sklaverei in China* (Berlin: Sächsische Akademie, 1952).

Fairbank, J.K. (ed.), *Chinese Thought and Institutions* (University of Chicago Press, 1973).

Fasā'i's, H., *History of Persia under Qājár Rule*, transl. H. Busse (London and New York: Columbia University Press, 1972).

Franke, H., *Geld und Wirtschaft in China unter der Mongolen-Herrschaft* (Leipzig: Harrasowitz, 1949).

Franke, O., *Geschichte des Chinesischen Reiches*, vol. IV (Berlin, 1948).

Frankfort, H., *Ancient Egyptian Religion* (New York: Harper and Row, 1961).

Frankfort, H., *The Birth of Civilization in the Near East* (London: Benn; New York: Barnes and Noble, 1968).

Frauwallner, E., *Die Philosophie des Buddhismus* (Berlin: Akademischer Verlag, 1958).

Freyne, S., *Galilee from Alexander the Great to Hadrian 323 B.C.E. to 135 C.E.* (Wilmington, Del.: M. Glazier and University of Notre Dame Press; Indiana: Notre Dame, 1980).

Frye, R.N., *The Heritage of Persia* (London: Weidenfeld and Nicolson, 1962).

Fukutake, T., *The Japanese Social Structure*, transl. R.P. Dore (University of Tokyo Press, 1982).

Garratt, G.T. (ed.) *The Legacy of India* (London: Oxford University Press, 1967).

Gellner, E., *Muslim Society* (London, New York: Cambridge University Press, 1981).

Gernet, J., *A History of Chinese Civilization*, transl. J.R. Foster (London, New York: Cambridge University Press, 1982).

Ghirshman, R., *L'Iran des origines à l'islam* (Paris, 1951).

Ghirshman, R., *Iran from the Earliest Times to the Islamic Conquest* (Harmondsworth: Penguin Books, 1978).

Gibb, H.A.R., *Mohammedanism* (London, New York: Oxford University Press, 1969).

Giles, F.J., *Ikhnaton, Legend and History* (London: Hutchinson, 1970).

Glasenapp, H. von, *Der Hinduismus* (München, 1922).

Glasenapp, H. von, *Die Philosophie der Inder*, 2 Aufl. (Stuttgart: Kröner, 1958).

Glasenapp, H. von, *Buddhism, a non-theistic religion* (London: Allen and Unwin, 1970).

Glassenapp, H. von, *Buddha: sein Leben, seine Lehre, seine Gemeinde*, 13. Aufl. (Stuttgart: Cotta, 1959).

Glasenapp, H. von, *Image of India* (New Delhi: Indian Council for Cultural Relations, 1973).

Gnoli, G., *Zoroaster's Time and Homeland* (Naples: Instituto Universitario Orientale, 1980).

Gokhale, B.G., *Ancient India, History and Culture* (Bombay, Calcutta, 1956).
Gonthier, A., *Histoire des institutions japonaises* (Bruxelles, 1956).
Gordon, G.H., *The Pre-Historic Background of Indian Culture* (Bombay, 1958).
Götze, A., *Hethiter, Churriter und Assyrer* (Oslo, 1936).
Granet, M., *La pensée chinoise* (Paris: A. Michel, 1968).
Granet, M., *La civilisation chinoise* (Paris: La Renaissance du Livre, 1929).
Granet, M., *Études sociologiques sur la Chine* (Paris: Presses Universitaires de France, 1953).
Gray, J., *The Canaanites* (London: Thames and Hudson, 1964).
Groh, V., 'Babel, Aššur a Israel' in *Dějiny lidstva* (*History of Mankind*), vol. I (Prague: Melantrich, 1940).
Grousset, R., *Histoire de la Chine* (Paris, 1942).
Gryaznevich, P.A., Prozorov, S.M. (eds) *Islam, religiya, obshchestvo, gosudarstvo* (Moscow: Nauka, 1984).
Gurney, O.R., *The Hittites* (London: Allen Lane, 1975).
Hall, D.G.E., *A History of South-East Asia* (London: Macmillan, 1981).
Hall, J.W. and Jansen, M.B. (eds) *Studies in the Institutional History of Early Modern Japan* (New Jersey: Princeton University Press, 1968).
Hall, J.W., Keiji, N. and Yamamura, K., *Japan Before Tokugawa* (New Jersey: Princeton University Press, 1981).
Halls, W.W. and Simpson, W.K., *The Ancient Near East, A History* (New York: Harcourt Brace Jovanovich, 1971).
Harden, D., *The Phoenicians* (Harmondsworth: Penguin, 1971).
Hazra, R.C., *Studies in the Puranic Records on Hindu Rites and Customs* (Delhi: Motilal Banarsidass, 1975).
Hawkes, J., *The First Great Civilizations* (New York: Knopf, 1977).
Hawkes, J. and Sir Wooley, L, *History of Mankind*, vol. I. *Prehistory and the Beginnings of Civilization* (London: Allen and Unwin, 1963).
Hempel, R., *The Heian Civilization of Japan* (Oxford: Phaidon, 1983).
Herm, G., *The Phoenicians* (London: Gollancz, 1975).
Hitti, P.K., *History of Syria including Lebanon and Palestine* (London: Macmillan, 1951).
Hitti, P.K., *History of the Arabs from the Earliest Times to the Present*, 10th ed. (London, New York: Macmillan, 1973).
Hitti, P.K., *The Arabs – A Short History*, 5th ed. (London and Toronto: Macmillan, 1968).
Hitti, P.K., *Makers of Arab History* (London and Toronto: Macmillan, 1968).
Hodgson, M.G.S., *The Venture of Islam*, 3 vols (London and Chicago: University of Chicago Press, 1974).
Holle, K.F., *Tabel van oud en nieuw indische alphabeten* (Batavia, 1882).
Holton, D.C., 'Shintoism' in E. Jurji (ed.) *The Great Religions of the Modern World* (New Jersey: Princeton University Press, 1946).
Hourani, A., *Europe and the Middle East* (London: Macmillan, 1980).
Hourani, A., *The Emergence of the Modern Middle East* (London: Macmillan, 1985).
Hrozný, B., 'Kultura hethitských a subarejských národů' (The Culture of

the Hittite and Subaraean Nations) in *Dějiny lidstva* (*History of Mankind*), vol. I (Prague: Melantrich, 1940).

Hughes, E.R. (ed. and transl.), *Chinese Philosophy in Classical Times* (London: Dent; New York: Dutton, 1944).

Hu Hou-hsüan, *Collected Essays on Shang History Based on the Bone Inscriptions* (Chengtu, 1944).

Hutton, J.H., *Caste in India* (London: Cambridge University Press, 1946).

Iriye, A., (ed.) *The Chinese and the Japanese Essays in Political and Cultural Interactions* (New Jersey: Princeton University Press, 1980).

Jacobsen, T., *The Treasures of Darkness – A History of Mesopotamian Religion* (London and New Haven: Yale University Press, 1976).

Jensen, H., *Die Schrift in Vergangenheit und Gegenwart* (Berlin: VEB Deutscher Verlag der Wissenschaften, 1958).

Johnson, P., *A History of the Jews* (London: Weidenfeld and Nicolson, 1987).

Julien, C.A., *History of North Africa*, transl. J. Petrie (London: Routledge and Kegan Paul, 1970).

Kagan, D., *Problems in Ancient History, The Ancient Near East and Greece*, vol. I (London: Macmillan and New York: Collier-Macmillan, 1966).

Kane Pandurang Vaman, *History of Dharmasastra*, vols I–V (Poona: Bhandarkar Oriental Research Inst., 1973–5).

Kaplan, M.M., *Judaism as a Civilization* (Philadelphia and New York: The Jewish Publication Society of America, 1981).

Kato, H., (ed.), *Japan and Western Civilization, The Collected Essays of Takeo Kuwabara* (Tokyo: University of Tokyo Press, 1983).

Kenyon, K.M., *Amorites and Canaanites* (London: The British Academy, Oxford University Press, 1966).

Khaldun Ibn, *The Muqaddimah, An Introduction to History*, 3 vols, transl. F. Rosenthal (New Jersey: Princeton University Press, 1967).

Kitagawa, J.M., *Religion in Japanese History* (New York and London: Columbia University Press, 1966).

Kitchen, K.A., *Ancient Orient and Old Testament* (London: The Tyndale Press, 1966).

Klíma, O., *Manis Zeit und Leben* (Prague, Tschechoslowakische Akademie der Wissenschaften, 1962).

Klíma, O., *Mazdak, Geschichte einer sozialen Bewegung im sassanidischen Persien* (Prague: Tschechoslowakische Akademie der Wissenschaften, 1957).

Klíma, O., *Beiträge zur Geschichte des Mazdakismus* (Prague: Tschechoslowakische Akademie der Wissenschaften, 1977).

König, F., *Zarathustras Jenseitsvorstellungen und das Alte Testament* (Wien and Basel: Herder, 1964).

Köprülü, M.F., *Les origines de l'empire ottoman* (Philadelphia: Porcupine Press, 1978).

Kramer, S.N., *The Sumerians, their History, Culture and Character* (London and Chicago: University of Chicago Press, 1963).

Kroeber, A.L., *Configurations of Culture Growth* (Berkeley and Los Angeles, 1944).

Kulke, H. and Rothermund, D., *A History of India* (London and Sydney: Croom Helm, 1986).

Kung-chuan Hsiao, *A History of Chinese Political Thought*, transl. F.W. Mote (New Jersey, Princeton University Press, 1979).

Lambton, A.K.S., *Landlord and Peasant in Persia* (New York and London: Oxford University Press 1969).

Langlois, J.D., Jr (ed.) *China under Mongol Rule* (New Jersey: Princeton University Press, 1981).

Laroui, A., *The History of the Maghrib*, transl. R. Manheim (New Jersey: Princeton University Press, 1977).

Latourette, K.S., *The Chinese – Their History and Culture* (London and New York: Macmillan, 1964).

Legge, C.D., *Indonesia* (New Jersey: Prentice-Hall, 1964).

Lehmann, J.P., *The Roots of Modern Japan* (London: Macmillan, 1982).

Lévêque, P., *Les Premières Civilisations* (Paris: Presses Universitaires de France, 1987).

Levy, R., *The Social Structure of Islam* (London: Cambridge University Press, 1957).

Lexa, F., *Výbor nejstarší literatury egyptské* (*Anthology of Early Egyptian Literature*) (Prague: Šolc and Šimáček, 1947).

Lexa, F., *Veřejný život ve starověkém Egyptě* (*Public Life in Ancient Egypt*) (Prague: ČSAV, 1955).

Ling, T., *A History of Religion East and West* (London: Macmillan; New York: St Martin's Press, 1968).

Lods, A., *The Prophets and the Rise of Judaism* (London: Kegan Paul, Trench, Trubner, 1936).

Loewe, M., *Chinese Ideas of Life and Death* (London: Allen and Unwin, 1982).

Loukotka, Č., *Vývoj písma* (*The Development of the Script*) (Prague: Orbis, 1946).

Mahalingam, T.V., *Economic Life in the Vijayanagar Empire* (Madras, 1951).

Maspero, H., *China in Antiquity*, transl. F.A. Kierman, Jr (University of Massachusetts Press, 1978).

Maspero, H., 'Les réligions chinoises' in P. Demiéville (ed.) *Mélanges posthumes sur les réligions et l'histoire de la Chine*, vol. I (Paris: Musée Guimet, 1950).

Maspero, H. and Escarra, J., *Les Institutions de la Chine* (Paris: Presses Universitaires de France, 1952).

May, H.G. and Metzger, B.M., *The New Oxford Annotated Bible with Apocrypha* (New York: Oxford University Press, 1977).

McAleavy, H., *The Modern History of China* (London: Weidenfeld and Nicolson, 1968).

Meyer, E., *Geschichte des Altertums*, vol. I, 3rd ed. (Berlin and Stuttgart, 1925).

Moorhead, F.J., *A History of Malaya and Her Neighbours*, vol. I (Kuala Lumpur: Longman of Malaysia, 1965).

Morgan, K.W., (ed.), *The Path of the Buddha* (New York: The Ronald Press, 1956).

Moscati, S., *Ancient Semitic Civilizations* (London: Elek Books; Toronto: The Ryerson Press, 1957).
Naipaul, V.S., *India: A Wounded Civilization* (London: André Deutsch, 1977).
Narain, A.K., (ed.) *Studies in the History of Buddhism* (Delhi: B.R. Publishing Corporation, 1980).
Needham, J., *Science and Civilisation in China*, vol. II (London and New York: Cambridge University Press, 1962).
Nehru, J., *The Discovery of India* (Bombay, New York, London: Asia Publishing House, 1969).
Nelson, M.F., *Korea and the Old Orders in Eastern Asia* (Baton Rouge: Louisiana State University Press, 1946).
Neuman, A.A., 'Judaism' in E. Jurji (ed.) *The Great Religions of the Modern World* (New Jersey: Princeton University Press, 1946).
Nivison, D.S. and Wright, A.E. (eds) *Confucianism in Action* (California: Stanford University Press, 1966).
Nosco, P., (ed.) *Confucianism and Tokugawa Culture* (New Jersey: Princeton University Press, 1984).
Olmstead, A.T., *History of Palestine and Syria to the Macedonian Conquest* (New York and London: Chicago University Press, 1931).
Oppenheim, A.L., *Ancient Mesopotamia, Portrait of a Dead Civilization* (London and Chicago: University of Chicago Press, 1964).
Petrie, W.M.F., *Religion and Conscience in Ancient Egypt* (London: Methuen, 1898).
Petrushevskiy, I.P., *Zemledelie i agrarnye otnosheniya v Irane XIII–XV vekov* (Moscow: Izdatel'stvo Akademii nauk SSSR, 1960).
Pieris, R., *Sinhalese Social Organization* (Colombo: Ceylon University Press, 1956).
Pigulevskaya, N., *Les villes de l'état iranien aux époques parthe et sassanide* (Paris and La Haye: Mouton, 1963).
Pigulevskaya, N., *Goroda Irana v rannem srednevekove* (Moscow and Leningrad, 1956).
Pigulevskaya, N., *Araby u granic Vizantii i Irana v IV–VI vv.* (Moscow: Izdatel'stvo Akademii nauk SSSR, 1960).
Pirazzoli-t'Serstevens, *The Han Dynasty*, transl. J. Seligman (New York: Rizzoli, 1982).
Pirenne, J., *Histoire des institutions et du droit privé de l'ancienne Egypte* (Bruxelles, 1934).
Pirenne, J., *Histoire de la civilisation de l'Egypte ancienne*, 3 vols (Paris: A. Michel and Neuchâtel: Bacconièree, 1961–3).
Poliak, A.N., *Feudalism in Egypt, Syria, Palestine, and the Lebanon, 1250–1900* (Philadelphia: Porcupine Press, 1977).
Pritchard, J.B., (ed.) *Ancient Near Eastern Texts*, 3rd ed. (New Jersey: Princeton University Press, 1969).
Rabie, H., *The Financial System of Egypt A.H. 564–741/ A.D. 1169–1341* (London and New York: Oxford University Press, 1972).
Radhakrishnan, S., *The Principal Upanishads* (London, 1953).
Rahman, F., *Islam*, 2nd ed. (London and Chicago: University of Chicago Press, 1979).

Rawson, P., *The Art of Tantra* (London: Thames and Hudson, 1973).

Reischauer, A.K., 'Buddhism' in E. Jurji (ed.) *The Great Religions of the Modern World* (New Jersey: Princeton University Press, 1946).

Reischauer, E.O., *The United States and Japan* (Cambridge, Massachusetts, 1957).

Reischauer, E.O., 'Japanese Feudalism' in R. Coulborn (ed.) *Feudalism in History* (Hamden, Conn.: Archon Books, 1965).

Reischauer, E.O. and Craig, A.M., *Japan, Tradition and Transformation* (London, Boston and Sydney: Allen and Unwin, 1979).

Rhoads, D.M., *Israel in Revolution: 6–74 C.E.* (Philadelphia: Fortress Press, 1976).

Röhrborn, K., *Untersuchungen zur osmanischen Verwaltungsgeschichte* (Berlin and New York: de Gruyter, 1973).

Ronan, C.A., *The Shorter Science and Civilisation in China, An Abridgement of J. Needham's Original Text* (London and New York: Cambridge University Press, 1978).

Rosenthal, E.I.J., *Islam in the Modern National State* (London: Cambridge University Press, 1965).

Rostovtzeff, M., *The Social and Economic History of the Hellenistic World*, 3 vols (Oxford: Clarendon Press, 1953).

Roux, G., *Ancient Iraq*, 2nd ed. (Harmondsworth: Penguin, 1980).

Rowley, H.H., *From Joseph to Joshua, Biblical Traditions in the Light of Archeology* (London: The British Academy, Oxford University Press, 1950).

Ruben, W., *Beginn der Philosophie in Indien* (Berlin: Akademischer Verlag, 1955).

Ruthven, M., *Islam in the World* (Harmondsworth: Pelican, 1984).

Sadar, Z., *The Future of Muslim Civilisation* (London: Croom Helm, 1979).

Saddhatissa, H., *Buddhist Ethics, Essence of Buddhism* (London: Allen and Unwin, 1970).

Sanders, E.P., Baumgarten, A.I. and Mendelson A. (eds) *Jewish and Christian Self-Definition* (London: SCM Press, 1981).

Sanson, G.B., *Japan, A Short Cultural History* (London: The Crescent Library, 1987).

Saran, K.M., *Labour in Ancient India* (Bombay, 1957).

Sastri Nilakanta, K.A., *A History of South India*, 3rd ed. (London: Oxford University Press, 1966).

Savory, R., *Iran under the Safavids* (London and New York: Cambridge University Press, 1980).

Scott, D.A., *Bactria 250 B.C. – 750 A.D., Dynamics of Religious Interactions* (PhD thesis, University of Lancaster, May 1983).

Semenova, L.A., *Salah ad-din i mamlyuki v Egipte* (Moscow: Izdatel'stvo vostochnoi literatury, 1966).

Semenova, L.A., *Iz istorii fatimidskogo Egipta* (Moscow: Izdatel'stvo Nauka, 1974).

Semenova, N.I., *Gosudarstvo sikchov* (Moscow: Izdatel'stvo Akademii nauk SSSR, 1958).

Sen Bhowani, *Indian Land System and Land Reform* (Delhi, 1955).

Sharpe, E.J., *The Universal Gita* (London: Duckworth, 1985).

Silva de Padmasiri, *An Introduction to Buddhist Psychology* (London and New York: Macmillan Press, 1979).

Simon, H., *Ibn Khalduns Wissenschaft von der menschlichen Kultur* (Leipzig: Harrasowitz, 1959).

Singhal, D.P., *A History of the Indian People* (London: Methuen, 1983).

Smallwood, E.M., *The Jews under Roman Rule* (Leiden, The Netherlands: Brill, 1981).

Smart, N., *Doctrine and Argument in Indian Philosophy* (London: Allen and Unwin, 1964).

Smart, N., *The Religious Experience of Mankind*, 2nd ed. (New York: Scribner, 1976).

Smith, J.M., Jr *The History of Sarbadar Dynasty 1336–1381 A.D. and its Sources* (The Hague and Paris: Mouton, 1970).

Smith, B.L. (ed.) *Essays on Gupta Culture* (Delhi: Motilal Banarsidass, 1983).

Smith, V.A., *The Oxford History of India*, 3rd ed. (London: Oxford University Press, 1970).

Spear, P., *A History of India*, vol. II (Harmondsworth: Penguin, 1965).

Spuler, B., *Die Mongolen in Iran – Politik, Verwaltung und Kultur der Ilchanzeit 1220–1350* (Berlin: Akademie Verlag, 1968).

Spuler, B., *History of the Mongols* (London: Routledge and Kegan Paul, 1972).

Stcherbatsky, T., *The Conception of Buddhist Nirvana* (Leningrad: Izda-tel'stvo Akademii nauk SSSR, 1927).

Stepuginova, I., in *Istoriya mira*, vol. II (Moscow, 1956–9).

Tao Te Ching, transl. Ch'u Ta-Kao (London: Unwin, 1972).

Tauer, F., *Svět Islámu* (*The World of Islam*) (Prague: Vyšehrad, 1984).

Thapar, R., *A History of India*, vol. I (Harmondsworth: Penguin, 1966).

Tiedemann, A.E. (ed.) *An Introduction to Japanese Civilization* (London and New York: Columbia University, 1974).

Toynbee, A.J., *A Study of History*, 12 vols (London: Oxford University Press, 1934–64).

Udovitch, A.L. (ed.) *The Islamic Middle East, 700–1900: Studies in Economic and Social History* (New Jersey, Princeton: The Darwin Press, 1981).

Varley, H.P., 'The Age of the Court Nobles' in *An Introduction to Japanese Civilization*, ed. A.E. Tiedemann (London and New York: Columbia University Press, 1974).

de Vaux, R., *The Early History of Israel to the Period of the Judges*, transl. D. Smith (London: Darton, Longman and Todd, 1978).

de Vaux, R., *Ancient Israel, Its Life and Institutions*, transl. J. McHugh (London: Darton, Longman and Todd; New York: McGraw-Hill, 1961).

Vladimirtsov, B., *Le régime social des Mongols; le féodalisme nomade*, transl. M. Carsov (Paris: Adrien-Maisonneuve, 1948).

Vladimirtsov, B.Y., *Obshchestvennyi stroi Mongolov* (Leningrad, 1934).

Watt, W.M., *Islam and the Interpretation of Society* (London: Routledge and Kegan Paul, 1961).

Watt, W.M., *Islamic Political Thought* (Edinburgh University Press; Chicago: Aldine Press, 1968).

Wayman, A., *Buddhist Insight* (Delhi: Motilal Banarsidass, 1977).
Weber, M., *Ancient Judaism*, transl. H.H. Gerth and D. Martindale (London: Collier-Macmillan, New York: The Free Press, 1967).
Weber, M., *Gesammelte Aufsätze zur Religionssoziologie*, 3 vols (Tübingen: Mohr, 1921).
Weber, M., *Gesammelte Aufsätze zur Sozial- und Wirtschaftsgeschichte* (Tübingen: Mohr, 1924).
Werner, K., *Yoga and Indian Philosophy* (Delhi: Motilal Banarsidass, 1977).
Wertheim, W.F., *Indonesian Society in Transition: A Society of Social Change* (New York and The Hague, 1956).
Widengren, G., *Mani and Manichaeism*, transl. C. Kessler (London: Weidenfeld and Nicolson, 1965).
Wilber, D.N., *Iran, Past and Present*, 9th ed. (New Jersey, Princeton University Press, 1984).
Williams, L.E., *Southeast Asia: A History* (New York: Oxford University Press, 1977).
Wilson, J.A., *The Burden of Egypt* (Chicago: University of Chicago Press, 1951).
Wiseman, D.J. (ed.) *Peoples of Old Testament Times* (Oxford: Clarendon Press, 1973).
Wittfogel, K.A., *Oriental Despotism, A Comparative Study of Total Power* (New Haven and London: Yale University Press, 1976).
Wittfogel, K.A., 'Ideas and Power' in T. de Bary and A.T. Embree (eds) *Approaches to Asian Civilizations* (London and New York: Columbia University Press, 1964).
Wright, A.F. (ed.) *Confucianism and Chinese Civilization* (California: Stanford University Press, 1964).
Wright, A.F., 'The Formation of Sui Ideology' in J.K. Fairbank, (ed.) *Chinese Thought and Institutions* (Chicago: University of Chicago Press, 1973).
Yazaki, T., *Social Change and the City in Japan* (Japan Publications Inc., 1968).
Yang, C.K., 'The Functional Relationship Between Confucian Thought and Chinese Religion' in J.K. Fairbank (ed.) *Chinese Thought and Institutions* (Chicago: University of Chicago Press, 1973).
Zaehner, R.C., *The Dawn and Twilight of Zoroastrianism* (London: Weidenfeld and Nicolson, 1961).
Zaehner, R.C. (ed.) *Hindu Scriptures* (London: Dent, 1972).

ARTICLES

Briggs, L.P., 'The Ancient Khmer Empire', *The American Philosophical Society* (1951).
Burrow, J., 'The Proto-Indoaryans', *The Journal of the Royal Asiatic Society* (1973) 123–40.
Cahen, C., 'L'évolution de l'iqta du IX au XIII siècle', *Annales, Économies, Société, Civilisation* (1953) t.8, no.1.

Gaube, H., 'Mazdak: Historical Reality or Invention?', *Studia Iranica* (1982) XI.

Hu Shi, 'The Establishment of Confucianism as a State Religion During the Han Dynasty', *Journal of the North China Branch of the Royal Asiatic Society* (1929) vol.IX.

Jacobsen, T., 'Primitive Democracy in Ancient Mesopotamia', *Journal of Near Eastern Studies* (1943) 2, 159–72.

Klíma, O., 'The Date of Zoroaster', *Archiv Orientální* (1959) vol.27.

Krejčí, J., 'Civilization and Religion', *Religion* (1982) 12, 29–47.

Krejčí, J., 'Civilisation and Social Formation: A Dichotomy in the Quest for Social Systems', *History of European Ideas* (1987) 8, 349–60.

Krejčí, J., 'Religion and Civilization: Iran and China as Two Test Cases of Mutual Inter-Dependence and Development', *Ching Feng* (1976) Hong Kong.

MacFarland, H.N., 'Religion and Social Change in Japan', *Revue France – Asie* (1962) 254 ff.

Poncet, J., 'Le mythe de la "catastrophe" hilalienne', *Annales, Économies, Sociétiés, Civilisations* (1967) 1099–1120.

Scott, D.A., 'Ashokan Missionary Expansion of Buddhism Among the Greeks', *Religion* (1985) 15, 131–41.

Author Index

Subject Index

Subject Index 343

Minamoto Yoritomo (the first
shogun), 290–1
Ming (Chinese dynasty), 265–73
passim
Ming Jia (Nominalists), 224, 230
Missionaries, 275, 283, 288
Mitanni (state in Mesopotamia),
22, 38, 307
Mizuno Tadakuni (Japanese
reformer), 303
Mohenjo-Daro (Proto-Indian city),
161
Mohists (followers of Mo Zi), 224,
227, 234
Mo Jia, see Mohists
Moksha (liberation of the spirit),
159, 166, 172–3
Mon(s) (nation in Burma), 192,
207–8, 318
Möngke (Mongolian ruler), 126,
261
Mongols, Mongolian, 73, 123–7,
151, 259–65, 293
Monophysites (Christian
denomination), 126
Morocco, 112
Moses, 6, 55, 104
Mo Zi (Chinese scholar), 227, 234
Muawiyah (Caliph), 107
Mughal (Indian dynasty), 155, 169,
198, 202–4
Muhammad, 97, 100–6, 118
Mujtahids (scholastics), 154–5, 269
Mura (village self-government),
291
Murji'a, Murji'ites (Islamic
denomination), 114
Muromachi (place and epoch,
Japan), 295, 297
Muqta' (fief holder), 130, 133
Mu'tazila, Mu'tazilites (Islamic
denomination), 114–15, 142
Muzari'a (crop-sharing), 134

Nabukadnezar (Babylonian King),
59
Nagarjuna (Buddhist philosopher),
183
Nagasaki, 298–9, 303

Nagasena (Buddhist monk), 159
Nanak (founder of the Sikh
religion), 202–3
Nanjing, 247, 250, 264
Napata, Napatan (city and state in
Nubia), 30
Nara (city and epoch, Japan), 286
Nehemiah (Judaic law-giver), 61
Neo-Confucians, 257, 292, 297
Nestorians (Christian
denomination), 126, 136, 246,
249, 251
New Kingdom (Egypt), 26, 43
Nichiren (Buddhist monk and
denomination), 293
Nirvana, 159, 166, 173, 189
Nizam al-Mulk (Islamic statesman),
120, 130, 314
Nobunaga, see Oda Nobunaga
Normative literature, 12
Nubia, Nubians, 26, 30, 117, 306

Oda Nobunaga (vice-shogun), 297
Ohrmazd (Ahura Mazdah), 81, 87,
98, 195, 311
Oirats (nomadic tribe), 269
Okinawa, 322
Old Kingdom (Egypt), 26
Osei-fukko (restoration), 304
Osiris, Osirian myth, 13, 24, 272
Ottoman Empire, 146–55

Pagan (city in Burma), 208
Pahlavi (Iranian language), 87–9,
310–11
Pali Canon (Buddhist), 174
Pali language, 174, 211, 244
Paper (technique of making),
139–40
Para-Pharaonic civilization, 20, 306
Parsees (modern Zoroastrians), 73
Parthia, Parthians (Iranian nation),
71, 80
Pataliputra (modern Patna), 175–6
Pegu (city in Burma), 209
Pentateuch (books of Moses), 53,
61
Peroz (Iranian Shah), 90